THE ECONOMY OF IRELAND

The Economy of Ireland

Policy and Performance
of a Small European Country

Edited by

J. W. O'Hagan

GILL & MACMILLAN

Gill & Macmillan Ltd
Goldenbridge
Dublin 8
with associated companies throughout the world
© J. W. O'Hagan 1995

0 7171 2403 7

Origination Photo Images Ltd. Dublin

Printed and bound in Great Britain by
Antony Rowe Ltd
Chippenham, Wiltshire

10   9   8   7   6   5   4   3
04   03   02   01   00   99   98   97

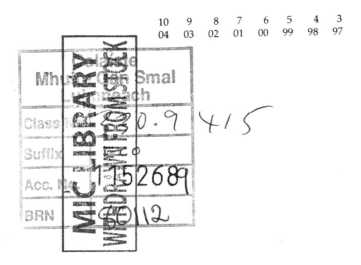

Contents

Preface   ix

Contributors   xiv

List of Tables and Figures   xvii

Chapter 1   **The Historical Background**   1
                  Jonathan Haughton
          1   Why Economic History?   1
          2   Growth and Early Industrialisation: 1690-1815   3
          3   Rural Crisis: 1815-1850   10
          4   Fewer but Richer: 1850-1921   19
          5   From Independence to 1973   26
          6   Into Europe: the Economy since 1973   37
          7   Concluding Observations   44

Part I
POLICY OBJECTIVES

Chapter 2   **Primary Policy Objectives**   50
                  Andrew John
          1   Introduction   50
          2   Economic Efficiency, Economic Policy,
                    and the Market Mechanism   51
          3   Distribution   61
          4   Evaluating Public Policy   71
          5   Conclusions   83

Chapter 3		**Secondary Policy Objectives**	86
		Dermot McAleese	
	1	Inflation	87
	2	The Balance of Payments	94
	3	Conclusion	98

Part II
POLICY IMPLEMENTATION

Chapter 4		**Government Intervention**	104
		Philip R. Lane	
	1	The Role of Government Intervention	104
	2	Public Expenditure	106
	3	Other Methods of Intervention	118
	4	Conclusion	125
Chapter 5		**Taxation Measures and Policy**	127
		Frances Ruane and Francis O'Toole	
	1	Introduction	127
	2	Principles of Taxation	128
	3	Structure of Irish Taxation	131
	4	Aspects of Income and Consumption Taxes in Ireland	141
	5	Tax Policy and Reform	150
	6	Further Issues in Taxation	155
Chapter 6		**Fiscal, Monetary and Exchange Rate Policy**	159
		Anthony Leddin and Jim O'Leary	
	1	Introduction	159
	2	Fiscal Policy	159
	3	The Central Bank of Ireland: Origins and Development	174
	4	Monetary Policy	176
	5	Exchange Rate Policy and the Decision to join the European Monetary System	180
	6	European Monetary Union	188
	7	Conclusion	194

Part III
PERFORMANCE AND POLICY ISSUES AT A NATIONAL LEVEL

Chapter 7   **Economic Growth: Performance and Explanations** 198
Cormac Ó Gráda and Kevin O'Rourke
1   Introduction   198
2   The Sources of Economic Growth   198
3   Irish Performance since 1950   210
4   Analysing Irish Performance   215
5   Conclusion   225

Chapter 8   **Employment and Unemployment**   228
John O'Hagan
1   Introduction   228
2   Labour Supply   230
3   Employment: Growth and Composition   233
4   Unemployment: Extent and Features   237
5   Causes of Unemployment: Global Factors   244
6   Structural Rigidities in Labour Market   250
7   Long-Term Unemployment   257
8   Conclusion   261

Chapter 9   **European Integration, the Balance of**
                  Payments and Inflation   265
Dermot McAleese and Fiona Hayes
1   International Trade   266
2   Balance of Payments   271
3   Integration with the European Economy   278
4   Inflation, the Exchange Rate and EMU   285
5   Conclusion   291

Part IV
POLICY ISSUES AT A SECTORAL LEVEL

Chapter 10   **Competition and Efficiency in the Services Sector** 296
John Fingleton
1   Introduction   296
2   The Nature and Diversity of Services   299
3   The Services Sector in Ireland   304
4   Competition and Efficiency   310
5   Competition Policy   314
6   Application to the Irish Economy   319
7   Conclusion   324

Chapter 11   **Agricultural Competitiveness and**
                 Rural Development   328
                 Alan Matthews
       1   Introduction   328
       2   Characteristics of the Agricultural Sector   330
       3   Structural Change in Irish Agriculture   334
       4   The Policy Environment   337
       5   Policies to Maintain and Improve Competitiveness   345
       6   Rural Development   350
       7   Consumer and Environmental Concerns   355
       8   Conclusion   359

Chapter 12   **Manufacturing and Global Competition**   363
                 Mary O'Sullivan
       1   Introduction   363
       2   Industrial Policy and Trends in Industrial Output
                 1950-1995   364
       3   Theoretical Approaches to Industrial Development
                 and Implications for Industrial Policy   372
       4   The Organisation of Manufacturing   380
       5   An Assessment of Policy towards Industry in Ireland 389
       6   Future Prospects and Challenges   393

Selected Bibliography   397

Subject Index   399

Preface

Ireland is a small country, an island to the west of Britain, which in turn is a somewhat larger and much more densely populated island to the west of mainland Europe. These are inescapable geographical facts which are important, as shall be seen in this book, to an understanding of the Irish economy. The island of Ireland consists of two political units, the larger portion of which forms the Republic of Ireland and the smaller portion of which forms Northern Ireland, which is part of the UK. This book is about the Republic of Ireland economy, and henceforth the terms economy of Ireland and the Irish economy refer to this economy, unless otherwise stated.

The division of the island into two political units, and hence two economies, dates from 1922. Chapter 1 of the book, in providing the broad historical background to the economy from the late seventeenth century to the present day, will clearly throw light on the reasons for this division. It also highlights the fact that the Irish economy always depended on trade for its survival, a dependence which has become particularly marked in the last twenty years. The chapter also draws attention to the importance of emigration as a feature of the Irish economy, beginning in the early part of the nineteenth century and continuing to the present day. Most important perhaps it dispels some of the more facile explanations for certain aspects of Ireland's historical development, drawing attention to the complexity of the explanatory factors and indicating the importance of often chance factors to an explanation of this development.

The rest of the book concentrates on the modern-day economy and is divided into four main sections, corresponding to the following themes: policy objectives, policy implementation, policy performance and issues at a national level, and policy issues at a sectoral level respectively. Part I of the book looks at policy objective in terms of definition, measurement and desirability. This section is general in nature and could in fact be applied to any small economy. Chapter 2 examines the objectives of economic growth, full employment, and a 'fair' distribution of income in a rather novel and specifically Irish-oriented way. Chapter 3 looks at the 'secondary' policy objectives of price stability and balance in a country's foreign payments position. These objectives are secondary in the sense that their importance derives solely from the fact that they affect the achievement of the primary objectives of growth, full employment and an acceptable distribution of income and wealth. Some might argue that it is self-evident what the various objectives are, how progress towards their achievement is measured, and why they are desirable. It is argued strongly in these chapters that this is not so; in the Irish case, for example, the incorporation or otherwise of emigration into the discussion of full employment, the use of GNP or GDP to measure national well-being, the consequences of increased equality, and the desireable rate of inflation are all matters upon which there is little clarity or consensus.

Part II of the book is concerned with policy implementation, and particularly the role that the government must play in this regard. Chapter 4 examines this issue in a general sense, highlighting not only the role of public expenditure, but also the other mechanisms by which the state influences the economy such as regulation, social partnership, and cooperation with other sovereign governments. The latter is in fact a theme running throughout the book, namely that the autonomy of a government overseeing a small open economy such as that of the Irish economy is severely constrained. The only way perhaps the Irish government can have any significant say over the global factors that now affect its labour, financial and other markets is through pooling its sovereignty with that of other governments, particularly those of the European Union (EU). This is also increasingly the case in relation to the provision of public goods such as national defence, macroeconomic stability, and a clean environment. It is for these reasons that the Irish government is such an enthusiastic supporter of the move to closer economic union in Europe, in marked contrast to its nearest neighbour the UK. What happens in the UK however continues to have a marked bearing on the Irish economy, for the geographical and political reasons mentioned earlier, because of the increasing cultural integration of the two countries, brought about by past and continuing high levels of two-way migration, and because the UK economy is many times larger than that of Ireland and the latter still depends so heavily on the former for trade.

Chapter 5 contains a detailed description and discussion of the main tax measures and issues that arise in the Irish economy in the late 1990s. Once again the international dimension to Irish economic policy is evident, with a declining freedom of manoeuvre in relation to tax matters for the Irish government becoming increasingly evident. None the less there are still some significant aspects of tax policy which are almost wholly within the remit of the Irish government, a fact to which the chapter draws due attention. The theme of a small open economy and its interdependence with the international economy crops up in an extreme form in the discussion of fiscal and monetary policy in Chapter 6. Until 1979 there was an effective monetary union between Ireland and the UK, and since then there has been an increasing tendency towards monetary integration with the rest of Europe. This is why the issue of a single currency in Europe and possible monetary union within the next decade is given such prominence in this chapter. The implication of these developments is that effectively Irish interest rates, inflation rates and money supply are determined outside the country, and hence the attractions of participation in a single currency and a European central bank where Ireland will have at least some say over the external events which so influence its economy.

Part III as mentioned is concerned with policy performance and issues at a national level. Chapter 7 looks at economic growth in this regard and takes a rather critical stance on the failure of successive policy initiatives to bring living standards in Ireland more into line with those in the rest of the EU. Despite this, the growth of output and living standards in Ireland in the last ten years has been remarkable: besides, living standards in Ireland in the 1990s are several times higher than they were thirty years ago, and many times greater than those pertaining in large parts of the globe. Chapter 8 examines perhaps the greatest failure of Irish economic policy in the last twenty years, namely the failure to create enough jobs to stem the continuing high level of emigration and to reduce the persistently very high levels of unemployment. Some of the explanation for this can be attributed to factors that apply at the European level, but clearly there are domestic factors that set Ireland apart in terms of its almost unique failure to provide nearly sufficient jobs for those who want them. A feature of past failure in this regard is that a very high proportion of unemployment in Ireland is now long-term in nature, a problem that poses a very serious economic, political and social challenge for the country. Chapter 9 examines performance in terms of the country's foreign payments position and rates of inflation, with a rather more successful picture emerging here. It also documents in some detail the growth and extent of the country's involvement in the international economy, particularly at a European level. The enthusiastic embracing of an outward-looking and pro-European trading and investment stance by the country in the last few decades is evident from the discussion here.

Part IV looks at policy issues at a sectoral level, the division into chapters corresponding to the traditional sectoral divide of services, agriculture and industry. Chapter 10 looks at the services sector and argues strongly that the lack of policy emphasis on that sector in the past has been fundamentally misguided. It examines in detail the issues of competition and competition policy and highlights their importance to all sectors of the economy, particularly the services sector. With decreasing autonomy in macroeconomic policy, measures of a microeconomic nature such as those relating to competition are assuming fundamental importance to a small economy such as that of Ireland. Chapter 11 looks at the issues of competitiveness in the agricultural sector and rural development. The chapter outlines clearly the major changes that have occurred, and are occurring, in relation to agriculture both at a European and world level and how these will impact on Irish agriculture. These include not just the reduced level of protection that is likely to apply to the sector, but also the increasing emphasis both on the safety/quality of the produce and on environmentally-friendly production methods. The agricultural sector is clearly of much less importance to the Irish economy in the late 1990s than was the case some decades ago and this is why in recent years the policy emphasis has been on preserving rural communities rather than the agricultural population *per se* and the chapter examines this changing emphasis. Chapter 12 concludes the book with a critical but challenging appraisal of policy towards the manufacturing sector in Ireland in the last thirty years. Drawing on experience in Germany, Japan and the Scandinavian countries it attempts to explain the failure of indigenous Irish industry to expand and the failure of the large number of multinational companies in the country to provide linkages with the rest of the economy. It is these failures and those identified in Chapters 10 and 11 that lie at the root perhaps of any solution to the employment failure identified in Chapter 8.

This book has grown out of an earlier book, first published in 1975 with the sixth and last edition appearing in 1991. I would like to thank the Irish Management Institute for publishing these editions and for being so accommodating in agreeing to the publication of this new book. I would like to thank Giovanna Davitti of Macmillan Press for taking the initiative in this publication and for seeing it to its conclusion so satisfactorily. Photo Images Ltd. in Dublin prepared the camera-ready copy and did so with considerable expertise and efficiency, and more important perhaps with a graciousness which made our task all the more enjoyable: for this I thank sincerely Mary Mullally and Seamas Daly. I would like to acknowledge the valuable finance that the Trinity College Arts and BESS Benefactions Fund contributed towards the administrative costs associated with the preparation of the book. There are many others who contributed in various ways towards the production of this book, particularly my wife and family, and I gratefully acknowledge their assistance and/or encouragement. My main debt however is to Fiona Hayes. She prepared the index and the contents and bibliography pages. She also assiduously and painstakingly read and checked the whole manuscript and was responsible for the overall copy-editing of the book. On top of this she is a joint-author of one of the chapters.

The book, of course, would not exist without the contributed chapters. It is difficult to thank enough the different authors for devoting so much time, effort and enthusiasm to the writing of their chapters, especially when the contributors are such distinguished and highly-qualified researchers. I very much appreciate their input and greatly enjoyed working with them in preparing this book.

Finally, I would like to devote this book to my mother. It is she who instilled in me the interest and perseverance that is required to start and finish a book of this length. She also insisted on buying, and not receiving a complimentary copy, of my previous books. There will be one less sale this time around.

John W. O'Hagan
Trinity College Dublin
August 1995

Contributors

Chapter 1

Jonathan Haughton has a B.A.(Mod.) from the University of Dublin (Trinity College), and a Ph.D. from Harvard University. His current position is Assistant Professor of Economics, Northeastern University.

Chapter 2

Andrew John has a B.A.(Mod.) from the University of Dublin (Trinity College), and an M.A., M. Phil and Ph.D. from Yale University. His current position is Assistant Professor of Economics, University of Virginia.

Chapter 3

Dermot McAleese has a B.Comm. and M.Econ.Sc. from the National University of Ireland (University College Dublin), and an M.A. and Ph.D. from Johns Hopkins University. His current position is Whately Professor of Political Economy, University of Dublin (Trinity College).

Chapter 4

Philip Lane has a B.A.(Mod.) from the University of Dublin (Trinity College), and an M.A. and Ph.D. from Harvard University. His current position is Assistant Professor of Economics, Columbia University.

Chapter 5

Francis O'Toole has a B.A.(Mod.) from the University of Dublin (Trinity College), an M.Mangt.Sc. from the National University of Ireland (University College Dublin), and an M.A. and Ph.D. from Georgetown University. His current position is Lecturer in Economics, University of Dublin (Trinity College).

Frances Ruane has a B.A. and M.A. from the National University of Ireland (University College Dublin), and a B.Phil and D.Phil from the University of Oxford (Nuffield College). Her current position is Associate Professor of Economics, University of Dublin (Trinity College).

Chapter 6

Jim O'Leary has a B.A. and M.A. from the National University of Ireland (University College Dublin). His current position is Chief Economist, Davy Stockbrokers, Dublin.

Anthony Leddin has a B.A. and M.A. from Essex University and a Ph.D. from the National University of Ireland (University College Dublin). His current position is Senior Lecturer in Economics, University of Limerick.

Chapter 7

Kevin O'Rourke has a B.A.(Mod.) from the University of Dublin (Trinity College), and a Ph.D. from Harvard University. His current position is Lecturer in Economics, National University of Ireland (University College Dublin).

Cormac Ó Gráda has a B.A. and M.A. from the National University of Ireland (University College Dublin), and a Ph.D. from Columbia University. His current position is Associate Professor of Economics, National University of Ireland (University College Dublin).

Chapter 8

John O'Hagan has a B.A., B.E. and M.A. from the National University of Ireland (University College Dublin), and a Ph.D. from the University of Dublin (Trinity College). His current position is Associate Professor of Economics, University of Dublin (Trinity College).

Chapter 9

Dermot McAleese (see Chapter 3)

Fiona Hayes has a B.A.(Mod.) from the University of Dublin (Trinity College). Her current position is postgraduate student in economics, London School of Economics.

Chapter 10

John Fingleton has a B.A.(Mod.) from the University of Dublin (Trinity College), and a B.Phil and D.Phil from the University of Oxford (Nuffield College). His current position is Lecturer in Economics, University of Dublin (Trinity College).

Chapter 11

Alan Matthews has a B.A.(Mod.) from the University of Dublin (Trinity College), and an M.S. from Cornell University. His current position is Associate Professor of Economics, University of Dublin (Trinity College).

Chapter 12

Mary O'Sullivan has a B.Comm. from the National University of Ireland (University College Dublin), and an M.B.A. from Harvard University. Her current position is Ph.D. student in business economics, and Lecturer, Harvard University.

List of Tables and Figures

Tables
1.1 Value of Irish Exports and Imports (£000) ... 5
1.2 The Pattern of Irish Agricultural Exports ... 6
1.3 Annual Percentage Rate of Population Growth ... 11
1.4 Real Product Per Capita (UK=100) ... 12
1.5 Ratio of Dublin to London Wage Rates ... 20
1.6 Measures of Recent Performance ... 39
4.1 General Government Expenditure as a Percentage of GDP, 1960-93 ... 106
4.2 Composition of General Government Expenditure (Major Items) ... 107
4.3 General Government Tax Revenue, 1960-93 ... 115
4.4 General Government Gross Public Debt as a Percentage of GDP, 1980-96 ... 116
5.1 Major Sources of Tax Revenue in Ireland and the European Union, 1992 ... 133
5.2 Marginal Percentage Rates of Income Tax for Irish Employees ... 143
5.3 Average Percentage Rates of Income Tax for Irish Employees ... 144
5.4 Distribution of Replacement Ratios for Unemployment Claimants in Dublin, 1989 ... 147
5.5 Standard Percentage Rate of VAT in EU Member States, 1986 and 1993 ... 148
5.6 Effects of Taxes and Benefits on Households by Income Level in the UK (IR£ per year) ... 149
5.7 Major Discretionary Tax Expenditures (IR£m) in Ireland, 1980/81 and 1991/92 ... 154
6.1 The Public Sector Borrowing Requirement (PSBR) and its Components as a Percentage of GNP, 1977-95 ... 167
6.2 Government Current Spending and Revenue as a Percentage of GNP, 1980-95 ... 168
6.3 The National Debt and Interest Payments, 1977-95 ... 169
6.4 Factors Governing Sustainability of Public Finances ... 171
6.5 General Government Deficits and Debt as a Percentage of GNP ... 173
7.1 Average Annual Growth Rates, GDP per capita, 1950-94 ... 212
7.2 Gross Investment (Per Cent of GDP), 1960-90 ... 215
7.3 Gross Investment (Per Cent of GDP), 1950-88, Relative to European Norm ... 216

7.4 Investment by Use (Per Cent), 1953-90   217
8.1 Age Composition of Population (000s) in Ireland, 1991-2005   231
8.2 Labour Force Participation Rates and Labour Force Growth in
        Selected OECD Countries   232
8.3 Employment and Employment Growth in Selected OECD Countries   234
8.4 Sectoral Composition of Employment (000s)   236
8.5 Unemployment and Unemployment Rates in Selected OECD
        Countries   237
8.6 Discouraged Workers and Involuntary Part-time Workers as a
        Per Cent of the Labour Force in Selected OECD Countries, 1991   241
8.7 Standardised Unemployment Rates, by Duration, in Selected
        OECD Countries, 1993   242
8.8 Educational Qualifications of Those at Work and Unemployed, 1993   243
8.9 Occupational Background of Those at Work and Unemployed, 1993   243
8.10 Trade Union Density (%) in Selected OECD Countries   252
9.1 Comparative Figures of Trade Dependence   266
9.2 Composition of Merchandise Trade by Commodity Group,
        1961 and 1995   267
9.3 Percentage Composition of Merchandise Trade by Geographical
        Area, 1960 and 1995   269
9.4 Terms of Trade (Goods and Services): 1968-95 (1980 = 100)   270
9.5 Balance of International Payments (IR£million), 1985-95   272
9.6 Ireland's Net Receipts (IR£m) from the European Union   281
10.1 Percentage Share of the Sectors in National Output and Employment   305
10.2 Percentage Shares of Sectors in Gross Value Added (market prices)
        in EU Member States, 1992   306
10.3 Share of Service Sub-Sectors in National Output   307
10.4 Barriers to Entry in Services Markets   321
11.1 Total EU and National Spending on Agriculture (in current terms)   329
11.2 Composition of Agricultural Output and Inputs, Selected Years
        (per cent of gross agricultural output by value)   331
11.3 Comparison of Farm and Non-farm Incomes   333
11.4 Index Changes in Family Farm Income Per Farm, 1955-83 (full-time
        farms except for 1955-58 and 1966-67)   335
11.5 Classification of Farm Households by Household Income (derived
        from the 1987 Household Budget Survey)   336
11.6 Viability Status of Irish Family Farms, 1993   336
11.7 The Competitive Advantage of Irish Dairying in the Late 1980s   346
12.1 Growth Rates of Manufacturing Output, Employment and Output
        per Head, 1950-92   366
12.2 Changes in Industrial Employment, 1973-94   369
12.3 Industrial Employment by Nationality of Ownership of Project, 1973-94   369
12.4 Industrial Employment by Sector, 1973-94   370
12.5 Total State Aids in the European Union   383

Figures
6.1 Real Exchange Rates, 1979-95   184
7.1 The Solow Growth Model   201
11.1 Agricultural Output, 1971-95 (1990=100)   332

CHAPTER 1

The Historical Background

Jonathan Haughton

1 WHY ECONOMIC HISTORY?

Why take the trouble to study history, and particularly the economic history of a minor European island? Five good reasons spring to mind.

History tests theory. The propositions of economics are often best tested by exposing them to historical evidence. Was Malthus right when he argued that population growth would inevitably outstrip food supply? Irish experience, even during the Great Famine, suggests not. Do farmers respond to changes in the prices they face? Evidence from late nineteenth-century Ireland confirms that they do. Does emigration serve to equalise wages between Ireland and Britain? Data for this century indicate that, broadly speaking, it does.

History gives perspective. Standard economics textbooks typically provide a short-run and partial approach to economic problems. While this may be appropriate for tracing the immediate effects of a shift in demand, or a monetary expansion, it provides fewer insights on the fundamental determinants of economic growth or of income distribution, since these may only be observed over long periods of time. The historian Joe Lee has made the point forcibly, writing that 'while contemporary Irish economics can be impressive in accounting for short-term movements, it has contributed relatively little to understanding the long-term development of the Irish economy'. He argues that most economists are 'blind to either long-term perspective or lateral linkage' and that 'with the exception of a handful of superior intelligences, Irish economists are far more impressive as technicians than as thinkers'.

An important lesson from economic history is that it provides a sense of the fragility of economic growth, and of its intermittent nature. For instance, we are inclined to look back to the 1960s as the golden era of Irish economic growth. Yet Kennedy, Giblin and McHugh, in their interesting study of Irish economic development in the twentieth century, argue that 'a sense of historical perspective would have encouraged greater modesty about the achievements of the 1960s by recognising that they depended heavily on a combination of uniquely favourable external and internal circumstances'.

History fascinates. While the study of any subject may be justified on the grounds of its intrinsic worth, economic history is particularly interesting. The visible remains of the past are everywhere – ports, houses, crooked streets, abandoned fields, ruined cottages. It is natural to wonder about their origins. Less visibly, our view of history informs our view of who we are, and what our culture stands for. These roots merit exploration. History also has its share of intellectual puzzles. Why was economic growth in the 1950s so anaemic? How did per capita incomes rise faster in Ireland between 1850 and 1920 than anywhere else in Europe? Was the tariff regime of the 1930s a failure?

History debunks. Ideologues of all stripes invoke history to bolster their claims. When John Mitchel argued that 'the Almighty indeed sent the potato blight, but the English created the Famine' he was revisiting history to support his nationalist position. Marxists turn to the land question as evidence of class conflict. An appreciation of history is essential if one is to make an informed judgement about the solidity of such ideas. Once again, Lee states it well, arguing that 'the modern Irish, contrary to popular impression, have little sense of history. What they have is a sense of grievance, which they choose to dignify by christening it history'. He concludes that 'it is central to my argument that the Irish of the late twentieth century have still to learn how to learn from their recent history'.

History instructs policy. Ireland has tried *laissez faire* (1815-1845); import substitution (1930-1958); export promotion with foreign direct investment (1958-1980). It has had budgetary discipline and chronic deficits, fixed exchange rates and floating, price controls, incomes policies, free trade zones, and public and private enterprise. Out of this varied experience there are lessons. While, in Santayana's famous words, 'those who ignore history are condemned to repeat it', the study of history is not merely to avoid making mistakes, but also to learn what works well and merits copying. The Irish experience is of particular interest to most less developed countries, which are typically small open economies with a colonial past. While Ireland was not a late developer, it has been a tardy bloomer, and a major theme of this chapter, indeed of this book, is to try to understand why, and what might be done about it.

The main focus of this chapter is on how Ireland has developed economically. Crotty defines such development as 'a situation where (a) more people are better off than formerly and (b) fewer people are as badly off'. By this yardstick it is necessary to look at population growth, since an economy whose development is accompanied by massive emigration has in some sense failed. This parallels the suggestion of the 1948 Emigration Commission, which proposed that 'a steadily increasing population should occupy a high place among the criteria by which the success of national policy should be judged'.

Economic development also requires that incomes rise (growth), including, or especially, those of the least well-off (equality), and this is presumably facilitated by an efficient use of resources (notably full employment).

The starting point, arbitrarily chosen, is 1690, with the consolidation of the Protestant ascendancy. The subsequent years are divided into sub-periods – growth and early industrialisation during 1690 and 1815, rural crisis between 1815 and 1850, the population decline which accompanied increasing prosperity from 1850 to 1921, the intermittent economic development between Independence and 1973, and the rapid changes since joining the European Union.

Some suggestions for further reading are given at the end of the chapter. A fully footnoted version of the chapter is available from the author. Naturally it is hoped that the reader will savour the chapter twice – once before launching into the rest of this book, and then to put it in perspective again afterwards.

2   GROWTH AND EARLY INDUSTRIALISATION: 1690-1815

The Economy in 1690
At the time of the Battle of the Boyne the Irish economy was predominantly rural, although it was no longer a 'woodland' society. Population stood at a little under two million, roughly double the level of a century before, and was growing at an historically high rate of at least half a per cent per year. With the spread of population the forest cover was rapidly disappearing, giving way to both grazing and tillage. The largest town, Dublin, had about 60,000 inhabitants.

The country was an important exporter, especially of grain, beef, butter, wool and, to a lesser extent, linen. Presaging the situation of three centuries later, almost half of all exports went to continental Europe, notably to France. Earnings from these exports were spent on items such as coal and tobacco, and a surplus on current account amounting to perhaps 10 per cent of exports allowed for the remittance of rents to absentee landlords. Between 1665 and 1686 tobacco imports almost doubled, and Cullen interprets this as evidence of rising prosperity over this period. Petty, visiting the country in 1672, commented on the large number of people who rode horses, and the high standard of clothing relative to France and most of Europe. He also noted the shabbiness of the houses, of which he reckoned only a fifth had chimneys. The implication was that Ireland was not significantly poorer, and was possibly better off, than most of continental Europe at that time, although less affluent than most of England.

Income was distributed unevenly. Land was owned by perhaps 10,000 landlords, and six-sevenths of the land was held by Protestants. Much of this was let out to farmers, who in turn frequently sublet small plots to cottiers, or hired casual labour. By one estimate a little over half of the population constituted a rural proletariat, with minimal access to land and close to the margin of subsistence. The potato had been introduced early in the seventeenth century, but was only an important part of the diet of the poor. Potatoes did not keep well, and were typically used from August to March in conjunction with oats (consumed as porridge), milk and butter. Bread was rare. In a few areas peas and beans were still cultivated extensively, a throw-back to earlier dietary patterns.

Population, 1690-1815
Ireland's population grew dramatically from a little more than a million people in 1600 to over eight million in 1841. Two turning points are of interest, notably the slowdown from 1725 to about 1750, and the particularly rapid growth from 1750 onwards, although the precise magnitudes of these changes have been much debated.

Until recently most effort has been put into explaining the acceleration in population growth after 1750. The now conventional explanation, first offered by Connell, is that the marriage age fell. This, he suggested, was because it had become easier for young couples to find land on which to grow potatoes, so they could set up a separate family at an early age. High marital fertility, coupled with earlier marriage, would together explain the rapid growth of population after 1750.

Drake argues that the evidence that the marriage age fell noticeably in the mid-eighteenth century is flimsy at best. An alternative explanation is that death rates fell; there does indeed appear to be some evidence that the number of child burials fell at this time. Lower death rates may be attributed to an increased use of the potato, which was both nutritious and reasonably reliable. However a potato-based explanation is not entirely satisfactory, since at the same time the populations of England and Finland were growing even faster, but largely without the potato. This would suggest a role for public health measures, such as a secular reduction (for unknown reasons) in the incidence of typhus or dysentery or, after about 1770, inoculation against smallpox.

An alternative approach, due to Cullen, sees a steady increase in population growth stretching back as far as 1600, in part due to the improvements in the diet of the poor, interrupted by famines in 1727-30 and 1740-41. The latter famine was extremely severe; the immediate cause was a long cold summer, 'Europe's worst on record'. The price of wheat doubled. By some estimates, a quarter of a million people died; as is true of nearly all famines, most of the deaths were not directly due to starvation, but rather to the ravages of dysentery, relapsing fever and typhus, which proved fatal to people deprived of adequate nourishment. Early in the century emigration from the North-East became standard and self-sustaining; in the difficult years of the 1770s the flow may have been as high as 12,000 annually .

Growth and Structural Change

The essential features of economic growth during the period 1690-1815 were a rapid recovery from the war, a period of relative stagnation (1700-20), twenty-five years of crisis which included two famines (1720-45), and a long wave of sustained and relatively rapid economic growth (1745-1815). The evidence for these is indirect, since few economic statistics were collected at the time. Possibly the best source of information is trade statistics, recorded because trade was taxed, although data on other tax receipts have also proved to be useful. Some interesting trade figures are shown in Table 1.1. The figures for exports and imports are in nominal prices, but no price deflator is available; except for the inflationary period of the Napoleonic wars (1793-1815), prices were as likely to fall as to rise, so the nominal figures are of some use.

Table 1.1

Value of Irish Exports and Imports (£000)

Year to March 25[1]	Exports	Imports	Imports/Exports %
1665	402	n.a.	n.a.
1700	815	792	97
1720	1,038	892	86
1740	1,260	850	67
1760	2,139	1,648	77
1780	3,012	2,128	71
1801	3,715	5,585	150[2]
1816	7,076	6,107	86

Source: L. Cullen, *An Economic History of Ireland Since 1660,* Batsford, London 1972, p.54.

[1] 1700 figures for year ending 25 December. From 1801 figures are for year ending 5 January.

[2] Exports are probably undervalued; Cullen believes exports exceeded imports here too.

A growing economy might be expected to trade more, especially so as to import luxury items such as tobacco which could not be produced locally. The value of imports showed little increase until the 1740s, after which it rose fairly rapidly. We may thus surmise that during the first four decades of the century per capita incomes did not rise. Since rents did rise during this period, it follows that those who rented land became poorer. It is conceivable that rent increases reflected some population pressure on land. On the other hand, after 1742 the country did not suffer a serious famine for a full century.

The seventeenth century saw dramatic changes in the structure of the Irish agricultural economy. These are mirrored in the export data presented in Table 1.2. Cattle exports gave way to beef; sheep exports fell and never recovered; butter and pig production soared; and the country turned from being a net importer, to an important exporter, of grain. At the same time Ireland became a major producer of textiles, notably linen. What caused these changes?

The first explanation focuses on English laws. In 1667 the Cattle Act excluded Irish cattle, sheep, beef and pork from England. The country responded by exporting wool rather than sheep, and by searching for new markets for meat, notably the important provision trade, serving transatlantic ships and the West Indies, and the extensive French market. It also shifted resources from dry cattle to dairying, and butter exports grew rapidly. This process was speeded by the Woollen Acts, passed in 1699, which prohibited the export of wool from Ireland or England to other countries, and imposed a stiff duty on Irish wool entering England. More positively, the granting of duty-free access to England for linen helped that industry. In the course of the century most of the restrictions on Irish trade were removed or eased; the Navigation Acts were relaxed in 1731 and abolished in 1780, and the Cattle Acts ended in 1759.

Table 1.2

The Pattern of Irish Agricultural Exports

Exports	1665	25/3/1758	25/3/1798	5/1/1818
		Mean of 5 years to		
Oxen (number)	57,545	22	12,143	35,634
Beef (cattle-equivalent)	14,632	81,724	60,065	52,137
Butter (cwt.)	26,413	197,552	300,160	422,189
Pigs (number)	1,446	–	4,273	59,107
Pig-meat (pig-equivalent)	3,134	60,004	321,758	563,240
Sheep (number)	99,564	–	–	21,990
Grain, net (tons)		-17,900	36,738	111,527
Of which Oats		6,193	34,138	71,070
Flour and meal (tons)		-3,631	3,106	6,627

Source: R.C. Crotty, *Irish Agricultural Production,* Cork University Press, Cork 1966.

The significance of English laws for Irish economic growth is a matter of controversy. Writers in the nationalist vein have stressed the ways in which English law handicapped Irish growth. For instance the Woollen Acts are viewed as the key reason why Ireland, unlike Yorkshire, did not develop a thriving woollen industry (although it is odd that the large domestic market did not support a more important woollen industry). The Navigation Acts, limiting the extent of direct trade with British colonies, were another source of grievance. Nationalist writers also point to instances where the Irish Parliament took a lead in promoting economic development, as in the case of Foster's Corn Law of 1784, which paid bounties for tillage and is credited with increasing the acreage under the plough (although the economic cost of this has not been calculated).

In an important piece of historical revisionism, Cullen has called into question the negative impact of such laws on the Irish economy. He argues that in response to the Cattle Acts the country successfully developed other outlets for cattle, and switched to other activities. Indeed by forcing the country to turn from ranching, which allegedly required few labour inputs, and orienting it towards tillage and dairying, the Acts may have provoked the economy to provide more jobs than would otherwise have been the case. The Woollen Acts were not, he claims, initially regarded as unduly detrimental by contemporaries, although by the 1720s opinion had changed, and Molyneaux and others vehemently criticised them; in any event they were passed against the wishes of the British government of the day, and responded to vested interests. As for the Navigation Acts, Cullen views them as 'a grievance to the Irish merchant rather than to the consumer'. Cullen's attacks on the nationalist view are now widely accepted, although in his zeal he may have underrated the harm done by these laws.

The second explanation for the structural change in agriculture rests on the response to an increase in the relative price of agricultural commodities, especially grain. In part this reflected the increasing urbanisation of Britain, and the resultant growing demand for food. The most dramatic price increases were during the Napoleonic wars, when Britain needed a secure source of food. The most important effect of this improvement in Ireland's terms of trade (i.e. price of exports relative to imports) was to raise the incomes of farmers. Ireland continued to export grain until the late 1860s, when the falling costs of shipping, coupled with the opening up of the American Mid-West, brought cheaper grain to Europe.

Agricultural structure was also influenced by the diffusion of the potato. By 1800 potato yields were close to 6 tons per acre, or enough to feed six adults for a year (eating six pounds of potatoes per day!). An acre of potatoes could support twice as many people as an acre of grain. Moreover potato cultivation does not reduce soil fertility, and potatoes contain substantial amounts of protein and essential minerals. Potatoes themselves are expensive to transport, but perhaps a third of the crop was fed to animals, especially pigs, and exported in this form.

There is a vigorous debate about the role played by the potato. The traditional view is that rapid population growth, coupled with the subdivision of (rented) land, forced relatively more and more people to depend on it as their main source of food. Others argue that causality runs the other way, with an abundant and nutritious potato fostering population growth. Cullen proposes a third view; cottiers increasingly ate potatoes instead of butter or oats, and sold these instead, using their earnings to buy other goods; thus the shift towards the potato is seen as 'related to commercialisation and the urge to increase cash incomes ... for luxuries'.

Industrial change was dominated by the rise of the linen industry which Cullen calls 'perhaps the most remarkable instance in Europe of an export-based advance in the eighteenth century'. From a low base in the 1690s linen exports rose rapidly, accounting for a quarter of all exports by 1731. The first linen weavers were mainly skilled immigrants, who were first attracted to the

North-East where land was more readily available; some of them were Huguenots who fled France after 1685. Duty-free access to the English market helped. In 1711 the Irish Parliament set up the Linen Board to regulate the industry, spread information and subsidise projects. As the industry grew in volume it also expanded geographically, and by the end of the eighteenth century flax was grown and linen spun throughout Ulster, in most of Connaught and even as far south as Kerry. Based solidly in the rural areas – in contrast with wool spinning and weaving, which was urban-based – the basic activities of flax growing, spinning and weaving could be undertaken at the household level. An elaborate network of merchants bought the raw linen and undertook the more capital-intensive activities of bleaching and finishing. By the early nineteenth century linen was increasingly spun and woven under the 'putting-out' system; cottiers would be provided with raw materials, and paid in cash for the amount they spun or wove.

Even as late as 1841 an astonishing one person in five stated their occupation as being in textiles, and most of these lived in rural areas. Fully a third of the counties reported in 1821 that more individuals were occupied in 'manufacture, trade and handicrafts' than in agriculture. It has been argued that this type of 'proto-industrialisation' is usually a prelude to full (i.e. factory-based) industrialisation, fostering as it does entrepreneurial skills, monetisation of the economy, and commercial links. In the Irish case no such evolution occurred, although it is not clear why.

Other industries also expanded and modernised, notably those based on the processing of agricultural products, such as brewing, flour milling, and distilling. After 1800 the cotton industry flourished, albeit relatively briefly.

It is important to realise that the industrial revolution did in fact come to Ireland, initially. The organisation of many industries was radically changed, with the establishment of breweries, textile factories, and glass works large enough to reap economies of scale. At first these factories were located where water power was available, but steam power was introduced early too. In the eighteenth century the road network was greatly improved and expanded, at first by private turnpikes and later by local government (the 'Grand Juries'). The first canals were built.

By 1785 Ireland was perceived as a viable competitor to English industry. When Pitt introduced his commercial propositions, which would have allowed Irish goods to enter England at low or zero tariffs, he was faced with a storm of protest from English industrialists, and the measures were quietly dropped. Irish industry was seen as having many of the same characteristics as British industry, but with the advantage of cheaper labour. Even in 1800 many, including Pitt, believed that Ireland stood to benefit from access to British markets, and would be a strong industrial competitor. By then this was not the view in Ireland, and it is ironic that the areas which most favoured union were Cork and the South, with their strong agricultural base; opposition was strongest in Dublin and the North.

Eighteenth-century Ireland experienced occasional recessions. The trigger was typically a poor harvest, which led to reduced exports without a similarly large reduction in imports. The resulting balance of payments deficit was financed by an outflow of money (gold and coin), reducing the money supply and leading to tighter credit. In the short run this tended to depress economic activity, although in the long run domestic prices simply fell, stimulating exports and restraining imports until the balance of payments deficit was erased.

Distribution of Income and Wealth

The benefits of economic growth in the late eighteenth century were not spread equally. The most evident rift was that between landowners and the large rural proletariat. Under the penal laws Catholic tenants were supposed to pay rent equal to two-thirds of the 'annual value of the land'. Although disregarded in practice, rents of a third of the gross output were probably normal. Thus a relatively few landlords, and the middlemen and farmers to whom they rented, and who in turn rented subplots to cottiers, extracted a large surplus from the poor majority. In 1687 Petty estimated rent payments at £1.2 million, of which £0.1 million was remitted to absentee landlords abroad. Rents thus came to approximately double the level of exports, or almost as much as a quarter of national income. It was this surplus, and tithes paid to the Church of Ireland, that financed the magnificent country houses, churches, Dublin squares, university buildings, paintings and follies that stand as monuments to the eighteenth century.

The burden of rents fluctuated, depending in large measure on how high agricultural prices were at the time the rents were due for renewal. Since agricultural prices were rising, on balance, during most of the eighteenth century, renters reaped a windfall between the time the price of their produce rose and when rents were adjusted upwards. This windfall gave rise to the interesting economic phenomenon of 'tenant right', whereby an outgoing tenant could extract a side-payment from the incoming tenant, presumably as compensation for access to a profitable asset. It is still a puzzle why landlords did not try to appropriate more of this windfall for themselves; perhaps they needed tenant goodwill, or wished to provide an incentive for tenants to invest in land improvement, or were too remote to be able to fine-tune the rent level (and could not set it too high or tenants would default in bad years), or felt rent levels were high enough given the risk faced by tenants.

Most farmers were tenants of large landlords, and in turn rented land out to cottiers. Frequently such plots were confined to conacre (potato land), whose quality improved as they were planted in potatoes. Cottiers also performed work for the farmers to which they were attached. Labourers did not have even the security implied by access to a plot of land. The position of these groups did not improve in the fifty years prior to 1745. There then appears to have been a period of rising real wages, which probably stopped in the 1770s, and may never have resumed.

A second divide was between Catholic and Protestant. The Penal Laws placed restrictions on the right of Catholics to purchase land, to worship, to run schools, to vote, to take public office, to enter the professions, to take long leases, and to bequeath property. Barred from the professions and politics, able Catholics often turned their energies towards commerce, and the expansion of trade helped create a significant Catholic middle class. By 1800 the wealthiest Dubliner was Edward Byrne, a Catholic businessman. Presbyterians and Quakers, faced with similar restrictions, also turned to commerce and industry, with some success. Over time most of the restrictions were removed or fell into disuse, and by 1793 Catholics could vote and attend Trinity College, but could not stand for office or fill certain government positions. At times the friction boiled over, as reflected in the strong sectarian component of the insurrection of 1798.

The third divide was between town and country. Dublin grew to be the second town of the UK by 1800, with a population of about 200,000. Cork, basing its role on the profitable provision trade, had 80,000 inhabitants, or approximately the same population as a century later. Third came Limerick, with a population of 20,000; Belfast was still a minor town. That the country was able to support such a significant urban population, and to export increasing quantities of food, reflected a growing agricultural surplus and rising agricultural productivity.

3 RURAL CRISIS: 1815-1850

The period 1815 to 1850 was one of rural crisis, culminating in the disaster of the Famine. The crisis was reflected in rising emigration. This was also the period when Ireland most clearly failed to participate in the industrial revolution which was then in full spate in Great Britain. After outlining the elements of the rural crisis and documenting the failure of the country to industrialise, there follows a discussion of why this was so.

Population
The census of 1841 enumerated 8.2 million people in Ireland, a higher level than any measured before or since, and over half the level of Great Britain. The central facts of Irish population growth are set out in comparative perspective in Table 1.3. Since 1750 the population had risen at an average rate of 1.3 per cent per year, which was well above the rates recorded in England, France or even Finland.

Table 1.3

Annual Percentage Rate of Population Growth

	1700-1845	1750-1845	1830-1845
Ireland	0.8	1.3	0.6
England	0.8	1.0	
France	0.8	0.4	
Scotland		0.8	
Denmark		0.7[1]	
Finland		1.0	

Source: C. Ó Gráda, *The Great Irish Famine*, Macmillan, London 1989, p.13.
[1] 1769-1845.

Yet by the 1830s the growth rate had fallen to 0.6 per cent, due almost entirely to massive emigration, which probably absorbed about half a per cent of the population annually after 1830. A majority of emigrants went to North America, and they accounted for a third of the free transatlantic migration of the period. Most of the rest went to Britain, which absorbed perhaps half a million Irish between 1815 and 1841. Once the flow of emigration became established it created a momentum of its own, as early migrants sent back money to pay the way for other family members, and helped to get new migrants established in America.

Without emigration, the pre-Famine population would have grown at a rapid 1.7 per cent per annum. Such an elevated rate of natural increase was largely due to high marital fertility, i.e. to married women bearing many children, once married. The age at which women married, and the proportion of women who married, were in line with contemporary European experience. There is no entirely satisfactory explanation for the high marital fertility, but it is possible that it was due to a good diet, a weak tradition of birth control (despite a reference to it in Merriman's Midnight Court), or a desire to have children, whether for the pleasure they might bring or because in the absence of children and a Poor Law it would be difficult otherwise to face old age. The death rate was not especially high. Infant mortality, while well above the levels of England or France, was lower than in Austria or Germany. Life expectancy at birth was 37-38 years, lower than in Britain or Scandinavia, but higher than in most of the rest of Europe. After 1770 significant progress had been made in reducing deaths due to smallpox, particularly in Dublin.

Growth and Incomes

On the eve of the Great Famine, Ireland was one of the poorest countries in Europe, as the comparative figures in Table 1.4 show. Per capita income was about 40 per cent of the British level, and half of it was generated in agriculture. Contemporary visitors judged the country to be very poor, and were particularly struck by the shabbiness of clothing and the poor state of rural houses. It has been calculated that the per capita housing stock in England was worth between four and five times as much as in Ireland. In some areas poverty was extreme. Thus in 1837 'the worldly possessions of the inhabitants of Gweedore, Co. Donegal, included two feather and eight chaff beds, 16 harrows, one plough, 28 shovels, 32 rakes, seven table forks and 233 stools among a population of 9,000'.

Table 1.4

Real Product Per Capita (UK=100)

	1830	1913	1950	1992	Population growth (%) 1919-1992
UK	100	100	100	100	31[1]
Ireland (South)	40[2]	53[3]	51	73	13
Ireland (North)		58	68		27[4]
US	65	119	170	142	
Denmark	61	80	99	112	57
Finland	51	47	66	96	60
Greece	39[5]	26	27	52	109
Italy	65	49	53	102	60
Portugal	68	22	23	61	54
EU 15			69	102	

Sources: Adapted by author from K. Kennedy, T. Giblin and D. McHugh, *The Economic Development of Ireland in the Twentieth Century,* Routledge, London 1988, pp.14-15; J. Lee, *Ireland 1912-1985,* Cambridge University Press, Cambridge 1989; and R. Summers and A. Heston, *Penn World Tables Version 5.1,* National Bureau of Economic Research, Cambridge MA 1995.
[1] GB only. [2] 1841, all Ireland. [3] 1926. [4] 1984. [5] 1841.

Yet if the country was poor, it was also well-fed, on grain, potatoes and dairy products. After adjusting for fodder and other uses, Peter Solar estimates that in the early 1840s potatoes and grain alone provided about 2,500 calories per person for direct consumption; two-thirds of this was from potatoes. If equably distributed, there was ample food for good health, but problems arose when the potato failed, as it did in the South-West in 1822, in Mayo in 1831 and in Donegal in 1836. Observers at the time generally thought that the Irish were healthy and strong; they grew taller than the typical Englishman or Belgian. Also compensating for low incomes was the wide availability of cheap fuel, in the form of peat.

It has become common to consider the 1815-50 period as one of 'deindustrialisation', during which the importance of industry in the economy fell. This is only partly correct. For the island as a whole industrial output appears to have increased. Large-scale and more efficient production methods were applied to milling, brewing, shipbuilding, rope-making and the manufacture of linen, iron, paper and glass; the road system was improved and reached a good standard; banks were organised along joint-stock lines. Despite these changes, rural industry declined. Thus, for instance, while Bandon boasted over 1,500 hand-loom weavers in 1829, the number had shrunk to 150 by 1839.

The first cause of rural deindustrialisation was that the woollen and cotton industries wilted in the face of competition from Britain. After 1824, when the last tariffs on goods from Britain were removed, and especially after the crisis year of 1826 when British manufacturers dumped large amounts of textiles on the Irish market, these industries declined quickly. A number of writers see this as a case where Ireland would have been better served had it been able to maintain tariffs against goods from the outside. Marx wrote that 'What the Irish need is ... protective tariffs against England'. On the other hand Ireland was not denuded of purchasing power or exports, for otherwise it could not have afforded to buy British textiles.

A second blow to rural industry was the invention of a method for mechanically spinning flax which made hand-spinning redundant, thereby depriving large numbers of families of a supplementary source of income. It also led to a concentration of the linen industry in the North-East, where most of the spinning mills were already located. The weaving of linen was still done by hand, and was boosted by the development. In 1841 Armagh was the most densely-populated county in Ireland, testimony to the importance of cottage-based textiles as a source of income.

Despite the rapid fall in prices after 1815, agricultural exports continued to rise, notably livestock and butter and, most dramatically, grain and flour. By the 1830s Ireland exported enough grain to feed about two million people annually. That the country was able comfortably to feed a rising population, and substantially increase its exports of food, testifies to the dynamism of the agricultural sector, which increasingly used new technologies such as improved seeds, crop rotations, better ploughs, and carts.

The most traumatic event of the period was the Famine. After a wet summer, blight arrived in September 1845 and spread over almost half the country, especially the East. Peel's government provided funds for maize and meal; relief works were set up; and when these proved inadequate more funds were made available. Famine was largely avoided. The Corn Laws, which had kept foreign grain out of the UK with a sliding import tariff, were repealed in June 1846, and Peel's government fell, to be replaced by that of Russell. The potato crop failed completely in 1846, and by December about half a million people were working on relief works, at which stage they were ended. The winter was harsh. By August 1847 an estimated three million people were being supported by soup kitchens, including almost three-quarters of the population of some western counties. The 1847 harvest was not severely harmed, but it was small because a lack of seed constrained the area planted to a sixth of the pre-Famine level. The blight returned in 1848, and in 1849 over 900,000 people were in the workhouses at some time or another. After 1847 the responsibility for supporting the poor had increasingly been shifted from the government to the local landowners who, by and large, did not have sufficient resources to cope. Noting that a few years later Britain spent £69 million on the (futile) Crimean war, Mokyr argues that for half this sum 'there is no doubt that Britain could have saved Ireland'. It is also unlikely that an independent Ireland, with a GNP of £85 million, could have done so without outside support.

As a direct result of the Famine about one million people died, representing an excess mortality of about 3 per cent per annum during the Famine years. The effects of the Famine were uneven. Three-fifths of those who died were young (under 10) or old (over 60), although they constituted just one-third of the population. In hard-hit areas such as Mayo, Sligo, Roscommon, Galway, Leitrim, and Cavan the excess mortality was at least four per cent per year. Labourers and small farmers were hit most severely. Between 1841 and 1851 the number of farms of between one and five acres in size fell from 310,000 to 88,000, while the number of larger farms rose. These unequal effects have led Cullen to argue, controversially, that 'the Famine was less a national disaster than a social and regional one'. We return to this issue below. Serious famines were not uncommon in Europe until the seventeenth century; what was so unusual, and shocking, about the Irish Famine was that it occurred so recently.

Blight struck other countries too. While excess mortality was 3 per cent in Ireland, it was 2 per cent in the Netherlands, just over one per cent in Belgium and somewhat lower in Scotland and England. The higher Irish (and Dutch) rate may represent, as Mokyr has suggested, 'the cost of failing to industrialise'; the more industrialised, and affluent, areas were more able and willing to sustain those whose lives were at risk because of the potato failure. The high excess mortality in the highlands of Scotland marked a turning point there too; population declined in that region for the ensuing century.

The output of potatoes fell by about three-quarters. In response, exports of grain, and pork (which used potatoes), fell by two-thirds, the use of potatoes for animal fodder ceased, and food imports rose very rapidly. As a result the amount of calories available for direct consumption barely fell, on a per capita basis.

This gives credence to Amartya Sen's contention that famines are rarely caused by an absolute lack of food, but rather by a change in the food entitlements of major groups in society. Thus labourers were unable to find employment when blight reduced the need for harvesting and planting potatoes; without income they could not buy food, and so became destitute. It follows that what is usually needed during a famine is income support rather than mere injections of food. This view forces us to focus on the sources and distribution of income, and not on crop failures alone, as part of the explanation of famine. To this we now turn.

Distribution

Pre-Famine Ireland probably had a 'very unequal distribution of income by West European standards'. According to the 1841 census, 63 per cent of the population had access to less than five acres of land, or were 'without capital, in either money, land or acquired knowledge'. A further 32 per cent were artisans, or had farms of between 5 and 49 acres. The remaining 3 per cent were professionals and rentiers, and included the approximately 10,000 proprietors, or 0.12 per cent of the population, who owned at least 100 acres.

There is some evidence that the largely rural proletariat, who constituted somewhat over half of the total population, became worse off during the thirty years prior to the Famine. On balance, witnesses to the Poor Law Commission, which met in 1835, considered that the position of the poor had deteriorated since 1815. This vulnerable group was ravaged by the Famine; between 1845 and 1851 the number of small farms, of between one and five acres, halved.

Rent, including payments in kind, accounted for about £15 million, or almost a fifth of the national income of £80 million. Presumably the bulk of this rent accrued to the wealthiest 3 per cent or so of the population, implying a very great degree of income inequality. Rough calculations suggest that this group probably had per capita incomes averaging over £100 per annum, compared to a national average of £10, and an estimated £4 for poor households.

By 1845 a rudimentary welfare structure was in place, with the completion of 130 workhouses having a total capacity of 100,000. In practice the numbers living in the workhouses rarely exceeded 40,000, except during the Famine.

Historical Debate: Why Did Ireland Remain Poor?

There is no shortage of hypotheses as to why Ireland remained poor, and hence uniquely vulnerable by European standards to the chance failure of the potato crop. Nor does any clear single cause emerge. Perhaps this should not be so surprising. Ireland is but one small region in Europe, and was not unique in undergoing rural deindustrialisation and depopulation. It is possible that the appropriate question is why some areas did industrialise, for in the early nineteenth century this was the exception rather than the rule.

A Malthusian explanation. 'The land of Ireland', wrote Malthus in 1817, 'is infinitely more peopled than in England; and to give full effect to the natural resources of the country a great part of the population should be swept from the soil'. If population growth persists in surpassing the growth of food production 'gigantic inevitable famine stalks in the rear, and with one mighty blow levels the population with the food of the world'. Although the notion that the Famine was inevitable has been consistently popular, the Malthusian explanation has been sharply questioned. Even before the Famine Ireland had more cultivable land per person (1.7 acres) than Belgium

(1.0) or England and Wales (1.5), although less than France (1.9) or Denmark (4.8). Between 1821 and 1841 land reclamation occurred almost as fast as population grew, so that during this period there was very little deterioration in the amount of cultivable land per capita.

Given the rise in food exports, it is unlikely that population was outstripping food supplies in pre-Famine Ireland. Moreover, if the land were overpopulated then incomes should have risen rapidly after the Famine; yet between 1845 and 1854, when the male population on the land fell 24 per cent, output fell fully 17 per cent. The implied 7 per cent improvement in agricultural income per capita is too small to convince one that population pressure severely depressed incomes in pre-Famine Ireland.

In a sophisticated econometric analysis, in which he seeks to explain differences in the average incomes among Irish counties, Joel Mokyr has found that greater population density was not associated with lower incomes. Indeed he even found some evidence to the contrary, and interprets this as refuting the Malthusian view.

Malthus himself later changed his mind, and by 1836 considered that, given enough inputs, Ireland could develop 'prodigious' wealth, perhaps even surpassing England in income.

Insecurity of land tenure. In pre-Famine Ireland most farmers were tenants, and some of them had short leases. If they were to undertake fixed investment in their farms – drainage, reclamation, building outhouses, and so on – they ran the risk that the landlord would raise their rent. So, the argument goes, farmers invested too little in agriculture, except perhaps in Ulster, where thirty-year leases were more common. There an outgoing tenant could sell his or her 'tenant right' to the incoming tenant, thereby recouping some or all of the investment.

At first sight the argument appears plausible. At mid-century perhaps two-thirds of all farmers held short-term tenancies ('at will'), although these were typically the small farms, so that less than half of the land area was held 'at will'. However it is reasonable to doubt the importance of insecurity of tenure in restraining incomes. Most annual tenancies were quite secure, and routinely renewed without significant rent increases; indeed how else can one explain the existence of 'tenant right'? On theoretical grounds it would rarely pay a landlord to be so 'predatory' as to try to expropriate all the benefits from improvements undertaken by their tenants, for else such improvements would not be undertaken. Agricultural growth was not noticeably hampered in earlier or later periods because of the system of tenancies, and did not increase as a result of the shift to owner-occupancy in the early twentieth century. Nor was there any 'sudden aversion to long leases' which might explain the alleged rural stagnation in the pre-Famine decades.

Agrarian violence. In certain areas rural unrest was common, especially in Munster, where secret societies were active. Pre-Famine Ireland has been called 'a remarkably violent country', although it is not obvious that it was more violent than continental Europe in the same period. The violence, or even the perception of it, may have deterred investors, notably landlords, provoking capital flight. It is widely agreed that the main source of this unrest was efforts by landlords, or their major tenants, to clear and consolidate their lands, thereby paving the way for a shift from tillage to grazing, although in Connaught the reluctance of farmers to grant conacre was also a major cause.

Natural resources. One of the most common explanations for Ireland's failure to industrialise is that it lacks extensive deposits of coal. In England 85 per cent of the textile industry was located in coal-mining areas, suggesting that the presence of coal was crucial, and this concentration increased over time. However while the absence of coal may have been a handicap, it need not have been major one. In England coal costs came to about four per cent of the total cost of manufacturing textiles; coal was perhaps two-and-a-half times as expensive in Ireland, thereby increasing costs by six per cent. This was easily offset by lower wages in Ireland. The fact that some industries did succeed, such as the big cotton mill in Portlaw which thrived until the 1860s, suggests that coal was not the indispensable missing ingredient for industrialisation.

Lack of capital. It has sometimes been argued that Ireland lacked capital, and that this hampered its ability to industrialise. However in the aggregate, capital does not seem to have been lacking, particularly for infrastructure. Thus, for instance, Dublin invested more in railways in the six years prior to 1850 than Belfast did in linen between 1800 and 1850. Irish roads were of high quality. In 1860 Irish residents held £40 million in British government stock, and £20 million in Irish banks, a total approaching the value of national income. Merchants do not appear to have been constrained from expanding their trade, and farmers were apparently able to increase the stock of cattle successfully.

Despite adequate amounts of savings, there may still have been shortages, because the system of intermediation, which matched savings with investors, may have been inadequate. Capital did not flow into the fishing industry; rotations were not quickly adopted in farming; housing remained poor. Many industrialists appear to have become landowners rather than reinvest in their businesses, victims of what Lee terms 'the aristocratic cult'. Thus there may have been a shortage of risk capital, although O'Malley cites Hobsbawm with approval when the latter wrote that a great deal of British capital 'was sunk into railways, and much of it was sunk without trace'.

Human resources. Some commentators have argued that Ireland did not industrialise because it lacked key human resources. In this view there were not enough entrepreneurs; the population lacked education; individuals were lazy; and emigration sucked out the best and the brightest.

The idea that entrepreneurs failed the country has a long lineage, and has been argued most recently by The Workers Party. The problem here is one of endogeneity; do entrepreneurs lead development, or do they spring up when opportunities emerge? In some areas, including linen, banking and a number of industries, there were significant numbers of entrepreneurs, although not all of them were Irish. Mokyr has suggested a new twist, that the landlord class failed as entrepreneurs. He argues that they should have been a major force for change and improvement, but too often were absent from their estates to be effective.

In 1841, 54 per cent of men and 41 per cent of women could at least read. This represents a respectable level of literacy, given that all education was private before 1831, being somewhat higher than in richer Spain or Italy, but lower than in France. The establishment of the National Board of Education in 1831 eventually boosted public education, and helped ensure almost universal literacy by the end of the nineteenth century, although the improvement was gradual.

Seasonal unemployment was common among labourers in pre-Famine Ireland, but they appear to have been occupied for on average about 40 weeks annually. Irish labourers abroad were often favoured because of their working abilities, and seasonal migration to England and Scotland was not unusual. The Tatty Pickers, who travelled from Donegal and elsewhere to harvest potatoes in Scotland, have carved a niche in popular lore.

Emigration did impose a cost on the remaining population, since emigrants had to be fed, clothed and housed prior to leaving. The annual cost has been estimated at 1.5 per cent of personal income in the pre-Famine period. Those who emigrated appear to have been slightly less literate than the population at large, and to have come disproportionately from the poorest strata of society. It follows that those who remained were not necessarily the least enterprising or least educated, as has sometimes been supposed.

Competition from Britain. The industrial revolution in Britain made manufactured goods less expensive, and centralised production close to the main markets. Improvements in transport carried these goods to Ireland cheaply. Could Ireland have stood up to such competition?

Not without the ability to impose tariffs on imports, say some, and this provides a major justification for an independent Ireland. Then, reply the critics, how did Scotland manage to industrialise so successfully? And did not Ireland, by specialising and so exploiting its comparative advantage, end up better off than it otherwise would have been? It is clear that the industrial revolution spelled an end to cottage production, but it is not obvious why this had to be due to competition from British, rather than Irish manufacturers. This is why a search for other, deeper explanations of the Irish failure to industrialise is called for.

The outcome of this debate is unsatisfactory. Ó Gráda wrote recently that 'exactly why comparative advantage dictated industrial decline for Ireland is still unclear'. He suggests that capital should have been attracted to Ireland because labour was cheap; yet when capital came later, it is noteworthy that it moved to the higher-wage North-East. He argues that Ireland's lack of coal was a serious handicap. And he suggests that Ireland missed the Industrial Revolution because once it got started in Britain there were strong reasons for industry to stay there, to enjoy external economies in manufacturing. Modern trade theory also emphasises this point, where the main implication is that there is a strong random element in the location and nature of production and trade. But a clearer answer to the question of why Ireland fell behind in the early nineteenth century is still needed, for it goes to the heart of the enormous difficulties which small open economies, such as most of today's less developed countries, have in industrialising in a timely and efficient manner.

4 FEWER BUT RICHER: 1850-1921

The seventy years following the Famine witnessed enormous changes in Irish society and saw the emergence of the modern economy. Over this period per capita incomes more than doubled, and came closer to the British level (see Table 1.3), while the population fell by a third. A rural middle class emerged, replacing the landlords and squeezing out the rural labourers. Within agriculture tillage declined, and the production of dry cattle increased. The North-East became industrialised.

Population
The dominant demographic fact of the period is that population declined, from 6.6 million in 1851 to 4.2 million by 1926. Without emigration the population would have risen, by about one per cent annually in the 1860s, and by half a per cent annually at the turn of the century. This fall in the rate of natural increase was due to a fall in the birth rate, unaccompanied by any fall in the death rate. Since marital fertility remained high, the falling birth rate is largely explained by a falling marriage rate. By 1926 the median marriage age for women was 29, up from 24 in 1861, and remarkably a quarter of the population never married.

Rapid emigration continued, with almost two per cent of the population leaving annually in the 1850s; the pace slowed markedly to under one per cent after 1900. The early emigrants were drawn from all areas of the country, since even for affluent families only the first son was likely to inherit the estate. In later years the bulk of the emigrants came from the poorer, mainly western, districts. After a poor harvest emigration typically rose. Over the period 1820 to 1945 an estimated 4.5 million Irish emigrated to the US, comparable in magnitude to the flows from Italy, Austria and Britain. When the outflow was interrupted during World War I the population increased, despite the loss of 49,000 lives due to the war itself.

Growth and Incomes
Astonishingly, between 1840 and 1913 per capita incomes in Ireland rose at 1.6 per cent per year, faster than any other country in Europe. Where Irish incomes averaged 40 per cent of the British level in 1840, this proportion had risen to 60 per cent by 1913. From Table 1.4 it may be seen that during this period Irish incomes came from behind, and then easily surpassed, those of

Finland, Italy and Portugal. What accounts for this extraordinary record of rising income and falling population?

Part of the explanation is statistical. The Famine, and subsequent high levels of emigration, removed a disproportionate number of the very poor; even if those who remained experienced no increase in their incomes, average income would have been higher than before. However this begs the question of why emigration became relatively more attractive to poor families. The simplest explanation may be that the gap between Irish and foreign wages was greatest for unskilled labour. Table 1.5 shows that in 1844 the wages paid to a skilled builder in Dublin were 14 per cent higher than in London, but the wages paid to an unskilled building labourer were 36 per cent lower. A comparable gap persisted until at least World War I.

Incomes also rose because of dramatic increases in output per worker. The North-East became highly industrialised; in the rest of the country agricultural productivity rose rapidly. This wave of expansion, paralleling that of a century before, was seriously interrupted only by the world crisis of 1874, and a period of agricultural crises after 1877.

Table 1.5

Ratio of Dublin to London Wage Rates

	1844	1886	1891	1905	1934
Unskilled building workers	0.64	0.58	0.63	0.66	1.06
Skilled building workers	1.14	0.82	0.93	0.90	1.13

Source: K. O'Rourke, 'International Migration and Wage Rates in Twentieth Century Ireland' (mimeo), February 1991.

The modern industrial sector grew rapidly, although almost all of the expansion was in the North-East, so that as late as the 1920s two-thirds of the industry in the South was in drink and food processing. While linen output increased slowly, except for a spectacular jump during the cotton famine of the 1860s, it was increasingly concentrated in factories in Belfast and the Lagan valley. Between 1850 and 1875 employment in linen mills and factories rose from 21,000 to 60,000, of which about 70 per cent were women and children. The rapid introduction of power-weaving after mid-century gave the region an advantage over rival linen-producing centres in Britain in this highly competitive industry, and the North-East gradually increased its market share in a product which was steadily losing ground to cotton and other competing textiles. The manufacture of boilers and textile equipment needed in the mills helped diversify the industrial base, and provided the skills and infrastructure which were important for the growth of shipbuilding. Harland and Wolff, the celebrated firm which built the Titanic, employed 500 in 1861, and 9,000 workers by 1900. The shipbuilding industry also provided an impetus for other upstream activities, including rope-making, paint, and engineering.

The growth of Belfast was not confined to linen and ships. The city was also a major producer of agriculturally-based goods such as tobacco, whiskey, and maize flour. One explanation is that Belfast benefited from 'external economies of foreign trade' – regular trade links with markets and suppliers, and a financial system geared towards supporting such links. As a result the population of Belfast, which had reached 70,000 by 1841, rose so fast that by 1901 it rivalled Dublin, with about 400,000 inhabitants. Londonderry became the centre of an important shirt-making industry, employing 18,000 full time workers and a further 80,000 cottage workers at its height in 1902.

By 1907, when the first census of production was undertaken, industrial activity in Ireland as a whole was half as large as agriculture, and employed a fifth of the workforce, making the country at least as industrialised as Italy, Spain or Portugal. Half of all industrial output was exported, Ireland had a worldwide reputation in linen, shipbuilding, distilling, brewing and biscuits, and the volume of trade per capita was higher than for Britain. Hence Cullen's comment that 'along with its large foreign trade, its export-oriented industries and its highly developed infrastructure of banking, commerce and railways, extensive foreign investment yielding a sizeable income made Ireland comparable in some respects with a handful of highly developed countries'.

These industrial changes did not occur painlessly. One major shock was the arrival of the railroads, which expanded rapidly from the 1840s onwards. These made foreign goods cheaper in rural areas, and hastened the demise of the rural textile industry; this was not an inevitable result, since cheaper transport could have made rural industry more competitive.

It is sometimes wondered why Ireland did not become even more industrialised, more like Clydeside than East Anglia. And related to this question, why did the North-East industrialise while by and large the rest of the country did not? Put another way, why did Irish labour emigrate, rather than capital immigrate?

There was no lack of capital, and indeed from the 1880s on Irish residents were net lenders of capital to the rest of the world, investing in British government stock, railways, and other ventures overseas. Interest and dividends from these investments, coupled with remittance receipts, enabled Ireland to run current account deficits on the balance of payments from the turn of the century onwards. The banks may have been cautious at lending, but in this they were no different from their counterparts in England, where industrial development was rapid. Nor is there evidence that skills were lacking. The primary school system expanded rapidly, enrolling 282,000 pupils in state-subsidised schools in 1841, and 1,072,000 by 1887. Whereas 53 per cent of the population was illiterate in 1841, this fraction had fallen to 25 per cent by 1881 and 16 per cent by 1901. Enterprise may have been lacking, although clearly not in the Lagan valley.

The absence of coal probably had some effect, not because this raised costs of production unduly, but because coal itself was a big business; in 1914 a quarter of the British labour force was directly employed in coal or iron and steel. Ireland was next door to, and had free access to, the world's most affluent market.

Some ascribe the growth of industry in the North-East to the role of the Protestant ethic; however industrial development in Europe was not in general tied to Protestant areas. The Ulster custom of 'tenant right' has been given a role, but was neither as widespread in Ulster, nor as exclusive to the province as was once thought. Government investment had a small role, although the efforts of the Belfast harbour board to clear a deepwater channel and reclaim dockland for industrial use turned out to be a key factor in attracting shipbuilders. Perhaps the explanation rests on chance, the idea that once Belfast grew as an industrial centre, accumulating skills, capital and infrastructure, then it became an increasingly attractive location for further investment.

Between 1861 and 1909 gross agricultural output rose by a quarter; since the rural population fell sharply, output per capita in agriculture more than doubled. Cullen reports that the agricultural wage doubled between 1852 and 1912, and concludes that 'rising rural prosperity was evident in post-Famine Ireland. The farmer gained; so too, to an extent, did the farm labourer'.

This growth masks an important change in the structure of agriculture, which shifted from crops to cattle in response to a fall in the price of grain relative to cattle. The decline of tillage, including potatoes, was permanent. From 2.1 million acres of potatoes and 3.5 million acres of grain in 1845, the cultivated area shrank to 0.6 and 1.3 million acres respectively by 1913. Even when the use of copper sulphate spraying, to prevent blight, became widespread by about 1900, the area planted in potatoes did not recover. Correspondingly the area under grass, or in meadow and clover, rose from 11.1 million acres in 1860 to 12.8 million acres by 1900. Cattle exports rose rapidly, from 196,000 in 1847-49 to 847,000 in 1907-09. Exports of sheep also rose, while grain exports fell. The dairying industry was reorganised, with the growth of private and then cooperative creameries. This was partly in response to heightened competition in the British market from higher quality butter from Denmark and New Zealand.

Farmers were not, as is sometimes supposed, slow to change or innovate. For instance, when circumstances demanded it they adopted the creamery system rapidly. Equally importantly, they responded fully to changes in relative prices. This was the basic conclusion of Barrington, in a famous paper delivered in 1926, when he argued that 'there is not a scintilla of evidence ... to suggest that the Irish farmer has regulated his productive activities otherwise than in accordance with the economic tendencies of his time'. More recent research has supported this view. In 1951 Hans Staehl compared Irish with Danish agriculture over the period

1861 to 1909, and found that agricultural output per capita in Ireland grew as rapidly in Ireland as in Denmark, which was considered to have done exceptionally well over the same period. Faced with changing prices and technology 'the response of the Irish agriculturalist ... was rational and normal'.

Ó Gráda, using a partial adjustment model, estimated a supply elasticity for wheat of 0.41 for the period 1850-79, which is fairly high by world standards. He also found 'no strong, clearly discernible trend in responsiveness over time'. This is despite the fact that there was a revolution in land ownership during this period. It appears that those who argued that transferring ownership of land from landlords to tenants would boost Irish agriculture were substantially wrong, although of course the distributive effects were immensely important.

Distribution
The end of the landlords. Between 1870 and 1925 the landed proprietors 'surrendered their power and property', to an increasingly 'comfortable, educated, self-confident rural bourgeoisie', thereby effecting one of the most extensive, and most peaceful, land reforms in history.

As late as 1870, 97 per cent of all land was owned by landlords who rented it out to others to farm. Just 750 families owned 50 per cent of the land in the country. About one landlord in seven lived outside Ireland, and another third lived outside their estates; the remaining half were not absentees. Two-fifths of all landlords were Catholic. Fully a quarter of all land had changed hands under the Encumbered Estates Acts of 1848 and 1849 when many landlords, bankrupted by Famine expenditures and taxes, had to sell. Nine-tenths of these estates were bought by Irish residents, often neighbouring landlords, which reflects the large pool of savings which was available within the country.

The agricultural crisis of the late 1870s meant lower agricultural prices and this, coupled with fixed rents, squeezed tenant farmers. By now they felt confident enough to agitate for the 'three F's' – fair rent, fixity of tenure, and free sale of 'tenant right'. The Land League was founded by Michael Davitt, and forged a link with Parnell and the Irish party in parliament. Their efforts resulted in the Land Act of 1881, which established land courts to hear rent appeals. The courts reduced rents by an average of about 20 per cent, and later courts reduced rents by about another 20 per cent after 1887. In a formal sense this diluted the power of the landlord – Moody refers to it as 'dual ownership' – although it is noteworthy that during the same period real rents fell by comparable amounts in England.

Further efforts prompted legislation which provided tenants with government loans with which to purchase their land. Under the Ashbourne Act of 1885, 60,000 tenant farmers bought out their holdings. The Wyndham Act of 1903 was far more important. It offered loans at an interest rate of

3.25 per cent, repayable over sixty-eight-and-a-half years. Landlords who sold their entire estates received a bonus of 12 per cent, payable out of general government funds. In addition to these favourable terms the Act provided ample financing; between 1906 and 1908, 100,000 tenants bought their land, followed over the ensuing several years by 200,000 more. The result was that 'by 1917 almost two-thirds of the tenants had acquired their holdings'. The inflation of World War I substantially reduced the real cost of the outstanding debt. In 1923 the Free State passed a further law for compulsory purchase, and Northern Ireland did the same in 1925.

Apart from the change in land ownership, the pattern of land holdings changed significantly. The Famine almost halved the number of holdings under 15 acres. The proportion of farms of less than 5 acres continued to decline thereafter, from 24 per cent in 1841 to 12 per cent by 1901, although these tiny farms by no means disappeared. The number of cottiers fell from 300,000 in 1845 to 62,000 by 1910.

Disappearance of landless labourers. In 1841, 1.3 million people classified themselves as 'farm servants and labourers'; by 1911 the number had fallen to 0.3 million. Despite problems of definition, notably in classifying the adult sons and daughters of farmers, it is generally accepted that the period saw the 'virtual disappearance of the hired labourer from Irish agriculture'. Not only did many farm labourers die during the Famine, but they were particularly prone to emigrate. This is hardly surprising, for wages were better elsewhere. In 1900 an agricultural labourer made about ten shillings per week, compared to about sixteen shillings in England and eighteen shillings in Scotland. The change in land ownership had little effect on the labouring class, and the fact that the change took the form it did partly reflects the political impotence of the rapidly shrinking body of farm labourers.

In a succinct summary of these changes Lyons writes that 'the general effect of the economic changes of the second half of the nineteenth century was to substitute a rural bourgeoisie for a rural proletariat' although 'proletarian elements nevertheless remained'. The number of paupers supported in workhouses remained steady at just under 1 per cent of the population from 1860 to the end of the century, but this probably reflects as much on the workhouse system as on the level of poverty itself.

Other divides. The distribution of income can be considered in other dimensions too. Thus, for instance, Protestants maintained their share of national income. This largely reflected the growth of the industrial North-East, which was dominated by Protestant interests, and the fact that Catholics were more likely to emigrate (and more died in the Famine). Catholics did come to fill an increasing proportion of government and professional jobs, although not in proportion to their numbers. The Catholic Church itself grew rapidly, with a spate of church-building between 1860 and 1900, and church-going became much more common. The number of Catholic priests, nuns and other religious rose from almost 5,000 in 1850 to over 14,000 by 1900, making it one of the fastest growing professions during this period.

The small towns stagnated, and so did Dublin until late in the century. In 1861 a third of Dublin workers were 'skilled', but by 1911 this proportion had fallen to a fifth. Dublin's tenement slums were notorious, and probably contained a third of the inner-city population. For the decade 1901-11 the death rate in Dublin was 2.5 per cent per annum, compared to 1.7 per cent for the country as a whole. In 1910 the average weekly earnings of a family in Dublin were between a quarter and a third lower than in Britain, despite the high cost of housing. In contrast to the rest of the country Belfast and Derry grew rapidly. Real wages in Belfast trebled in the sixty years from 1850. The zenith of Belfast's prosperity came during and immediately after World War I, with a boom in shipbuilding and engineering; as David Johnson put it, 'in economic terms the last years of the Union were the best ones'.

Another cleavage was apparent between the poorer western fringe and the rest of the country. One measure is the amount of seasonal migration, largely to Scotland; for example, about half of the workers on the Dillon estates in Mayo/Roscommon routinely migrated for such work. Permanent emigration increased after 1890. In an effort to improve things the Congested Districts Board was established. The area covered by its brief contained a ninth of the total population. Between 1891 and 1926, when it was replaced by the Land Commission, the Board spent £9 million to purchase and consolidate over two million acres, affecting 59,000 farms. It also provided grants to foster local industry and farm improvements.

Historical Debate: Did the Great Irish Famine Matter?
Traditionally the Great Famine has been viewed as the 'great divide' in Irish demographic and economic history. Historian George O'Brien asserted that the Famine 'initiated that great flood of emigration which was to be the dominant feature of Irish economic life in the second half of the century'. Taken literally, this assertion is wrong, but it is undeniable that the pace of emigration accelerated with the Famine. We have also seen that the Famine marked a radical change in agriculture, as the country turned from tillage to grazing.

Challengers to this view believe that the Famine merely accelerated pre-existing trends in the Irish economy. Cullen argues that 'a rise in emigration and a falling population would have been inevitable even if the Great Famine had not occurred'. Crotty considers that the trend from tillage to pasture may be traced to the 1830s or even earlier, and that this shift helped push people off the land since cattle-raising was less labour-intensive than tillage; moreover with the repeal of the Corn Laws in 1846 this trend accelerated. He concludes that the Famine was 'not, as has been frequently claimed, a watershed – at least in any meaningful sense'.

The key to unravelling this complex debate is to focus on the one thing that did undeniably change: the potato blight greatly reduced the productivity of the potato. This raised the resource cost of hiring labour, since now it took more than an acre of conacre to feed a family, and so labour demand fell. At the same time the technology of raising cattle had to be adjusted. In pre-Famine years a third of the potato crop was fed to animals; with the arrival of the potato blight this no longer became feasible, so cattle were raised almost exclusively on pasture. Thus the most profitable technology for producing cattle and other animals changed, from being labour-intensive to being land-intensive. O'Rourke argues that without the blight this would not have occurred, and that the shift to cattle would have been labour-using and not, as claimed by Crotty, labour-saving.

The debate suffers from false advertising. Obviously the Famine 'mattered' to those who died or were forced to emigrate. The slowdown in population growth predates the Famine, as does the rising emphasis on cattle. But the technology of agriculture was changed radically by the arrival of the potato blight; even had there been no actual Famine, this would have led to accelerated emigration, a decline in tillage, and the rise of the modern grazing economy. In Ó Gráda's words, famine was not inevitable, but Ireland was 'desperately unlucky' to face such a 'tragic ecological accident'.

5   FROM INDEPENDENCE TO 1973

When it finally achieved independence, the Irish Free State could count some important assets. It had an extensive system of communications, a developed banking system, a vigorous wholesale and retail network, an efficient and honest administration, universal literacy, a large stock of houses, schools and hospitals, and enormous external assets. By the standards of most of the world's countries the country was well off indeed.

On the other hand the new state faced some serious problems. It had to establish a new government, the Civil War had been destructive and had helped prompt 88,000 people to emigrate in 1921-22, the dependency ratio was high, and the post-war boom had run its course. We now document its subsequent achievements, and evaluate its performance as an independent country.

Population
In 1921 the population of the South stood at 3.1 million. It declined slowly, if unevenly, to a low point of 2.8 million in 1961, and then increased more rapidly to reach a new plateau of 3.5 million by 1986.

The Crude Birth Rate (CBR) measures the number of births in a given year per thousand of population. In the Irish case it remained steady, at about 20, until the 1980s, when it fell to 15 by 1992; this is still high, compared to an EU average of 12. The early stability is deceptive however, as it reflects the outcome of two conflicting trends – falling marital fertility, and a rising marriage rate. Catholics marrying before 1916 had an average of 6.0 children per family; those marrying in the late 1930s had 4.5; Protestant rates also fell, but from 3.6 to 2.7. The implied restraint is all the more remarkable given that the average age of marriage dropped; this had peaked in 1929, when men married at 35, and women at 29, the highest levels in the world at the time.

Thus extensive birth control long predates the arrival of 'modern' methods in the 1960s, although the latter helped reduce the fertility rate (number of children born per women, during her lifetime) from 3.8 in 1961 to 2.0 in 1992. The fertility rate is now below the replacement level (of about 2.3), and below the rate which prevails in the US (2.1) or Sweden (2.1), although it is significantly higher than the low levels of 1.3 or less which are found in Germany, Italy and Spain. This reduction in fertility is typical of countries experiencing similar increases in income.

The Crude Death Rate (CDR) has drifted downwards since 1921, speeded in the 1950s by the eradication of tuberculosis, and now stands at just 9 per thousand. The low rate partly reflects the relatively small proportion of old people. Without migration, the population would have risen by between half and one per cent annually, and would have reached 5.3 million in 1986, or about 50 per cent higher than the actual level. Population growth at this rate, while high by EU standards (where the natural increase is now 0.2 per cent per year), is well below the current rate of world population growth of about 1.6 per cent annually.

Migration remained important, at least until the 1960s. The rate slowed down during the 1930s, when opportunities abroad were limited, and during the 1960s, when more opportunities in Ireland opened up. During the 1970s there was even a net inmigration of 109,000 people, but migration picked up again in the 1980s when the domestic economy turned sour.

An understanding of migration is the key to understanding Irish demographic experience. The explanation is straightforward; when wages rise and unemployment rates fall in Britain, relative to Ireland, emigration increases, and *vice versa*. This means that the labour markets of the two countries are integrated. We thus expect, and find, that wages are essentially the same in Ireland and England, for jobs which require comparable skills. The comparability of wages dates from at least the 1930s (see Table 1.5), and some argue it goes back to the Great Famine. There is an important corollary: Irish wages cannot systematically exceed the British level. Thus Irish economic policy cannot influence the standard of living of those who work, but only the number who work in Ireland.

1921-1932: Agriculture First

The growth model pursued by the Cumann na nGaedheal government was based on the premise that what was good for agriculture was good for the country. Patrick Hogan, the Minister for Agriculture, saw the policy as one of 'helping the farmer who helped himself and letting the rest go to the devil'. This emphasis on agriculture was not surprising. In 1926 agriculture generated 32 per cent of GDP and provided 54 per cent of all employment. The government relied heavily on the support of the larger farmers. The expectation was that not only would agricultural growth raise the demand for goods and services from the rest of the economy, but it would also provide more inputs on which to base a more substantial processing sector. The three major industrial exporting sectors at the time – brewing, distilling and biscuit-making – were all closely linked with agriculture.

The essential elements of the policy, which has come to be known as the 'Treasury View', were free trade, low taxes and government spending, modest direct state intervention in industry and agriculture, and parity with sterling. Free trade was seen as essential if the cost of farm inputs was to be kept low.

The support for free trade was perhaps surprising given that Griffith had argued that one of the main benefits of free trade would be that the country could grant protection to infant industries. On the other hand the government was cautious about making such changes, perhaps for fear of upsetting the financial community, whose opposition to protection was well known, or perhaps because they were, in the words of Kevin O'Higgins, 'the most conservative revolutionaries in history'. The government sought to deflect pressure for stiffer protection by establishing the Tariff Commission in 1926, and appointing members who were, in the main, in favour of free trade. The onus of proof was on any industry wishing to be protected, and the Commission moved slowly on requests, granting few tariffs other than for rosary beads and margarine. After the crash of 1929, and the worldwide recession which followed it, Ireland feared that other countries would dump products on the local market; preemptive legislation was passed in late 1931, but the government fell shortly thereafter. By the end of 1931 the average tariff rate was about 9 per cent.

Government spending was kept low, the budget was essentially balanced, and revenues came to just 15 per cent of GNP in 1931. This was a remarkable achievement, given that military spending had trebled during the Civil War. One serious consequence was that welfare spending remained low, and in the absence of major government assistance, housing for the less well-off remained scarce.

Ideologically the government did not favour taking a very active role in promoting economic development. Despite this it intervened pragmatically in several ways. The Department of Agriculture was greatly expanded, although the impact of this on agricultural output has been questioned. The Congested Districts Board was replaced by the Land Commission, which transferred 3.6 million acres, involving 117,000 holdings, to annuity-paying freeholders during the period 1923-37. Laws were passed to improve the quality of agricultural output, by regulating the marketing of dairy produce (1924) and improving the quality of livestock breeding by registering bulls (1925). The Agricultural Credit Corporation (ACC) was set up to provide credit to farmers. The government subsidised a Belgian company to establish a sugar factory in Carlow, and provided incentives to grow sugar beet.

A major innovation was the establishment of the Electricity Supply Board (ESB) in 1927. This, along with the ACC, represented the first of the state-sponsored bodies which were established during the ensuing years. The ESB successfully undertook the Ardnacrusha hydroelectric scheme, which boosted both its and the country's prestige, and was the most visible accomplishment of the first decade of independence. In due course state-sponsored bodies (SSBs) were set up in many fields – air, train and bus transport, industrial credit, insurance, peat development, trade promotion, industrial development, and so on. By the early 1960s, when the most important of these bodies had been established, they employed about 50,000 people, representing about 7 per cent of the total labour force. The SSBs were not the outgrowth of any particular ideology, but were rather 'individual responses to specific situations'. This, along with their ability to attract good managers, may help explain why they are generally considered to have been successful agents of economic development, especially in the first few decades after Independence, when the private sector did not appear to be very enterprising.

Parity with sterling was the final ingredient in the development model pursued. Few countries at the time had floating exchange rates, and it seemed logical to peg the pound to sterling since 97 per cent of exports went to, and 76 per cent of imports came from Britain. The Currency Act of 1927 established an Irish currency, fully backed by British sterling securities; until 1961 Irish banknotes were inscribed 'payable in London'. By linking the currency with sterling the Free State gave up the possibility of any independent monetary policy, in return for greater predictability in trade with Britain (see Chapter 6).

The economic policy of the Free State in the 1920s was comparable to the typical prescription given by the World Bank to less developed countries in the 1980s. Get the prices right, using world prices as a guide. Reduce budget deficits. Keep government 'interference' to a minimum. Follow a conservative monetary policy. Did it work?

The simple answer is 'in the circumstances, yes in most respects, eventually'. The young nation got off to a rocky start. Between 1920 and 1924 agricultural prices fell by 44 per cent; the Civil War, which only ended in 1923, arrested investment; after Independence, a significant proportion of the skilled labour force left; and the recession in the UK after sterling's return to the gold standard in 1925 reduced the demand for Irish exports. However between 1926 and 1931 real per capita GNP rose about 3 per cent per annum; exports rose 20 per cent, reaching a peak of 35 per cent of GNP in 1929, and a volume which was not exceeded until 1960. Industrial employment rose by 8 per cent. Although agricultural exports rose to a peak in 1930 which was one-third higher than the level of 1925, cattle numbers stagnated, the area in tillage declined, and only sheep and poultry experienced marked growth. This anaemic performance helps explain why emigration continued at a high rate.

1932-1939: Self-sufficiency, Economic War and Depression

Fianna Fáil came to power in early 1932, with an economic policy which differed in two fundamental ways from its predecessor; it was ideologically committed to a policy of greater economic self-sufficiency, and it reneged on paying land annuities to Britain. It also came to power during the darkest hour of the Depression, a time when most countries were erecting tariff barriers.

Why self-sufficiency? It has been argued that there was 'not so much an economic case as an intellectual and cultural case [for protection]. If the country lives almost altogether by a few industries its intellectual life will lack richness and variety ... because agriculture ... did not find employment for large numbers of engineers, electricians, chemists and bacteriologists'. Keynes, lecturing at UCD in April 1933, seemed to support this thrust. 'I sympathise', he said, 'with those who would minimise ... economic entanglement between nations. ... But let goods be homespun whenever it is reasonable and conveniently possible. ... If I were an Irishman I should find much to attract me in the economic outlook of your present government towards self-sufficiency'. Perhaps these remarks are out of context, for he went on to argue that only 'a very modest measure of self-sufficiency' would be feasible without 'a disastrous reduction in a standard of life which is already none too high'.

How self-sufficiency? The main instrument used was more and higher tariffs, which rose to a maximum of 45 per cent in 1936, dipping to 35 per cent by 1938. In 1937, 1,947 items were subject to some import controls, up from 68 in 1931. In Europe only Germany and Spain had higher levels; Irish tariffs were twice as high as in the US, and 50 per cent higher than in the UK. They were introduced piecemeal and so formed an untidy pattern which, in FitzGerald's view, had 'no rational basis'; Meenan considers that they fell more heavily on finished goods, and so provided an incentive for domestic assembly using imported raw materials. The pursuit of self-sufficiency would justify indefinite tariff protection; in this it differs from the views of Griffith, who saw a role for temporary protection to encourage infant industries to take root.

Self-sufficiency was also pursued by introducing price supports for wheat; this was instrumental in raising the acreage planted to wheat from 8,000 hectares in 1931 to 103,000 by 1936, although the total acreage tilled rose less spectacularly, from 428,000 hectares in 1931 to 832,000 hectares in 1936. Bounties were paid for exports of cattle, butter, bacon and other agricultural products in order to expand the volume of exports, and this resulted in a significant rise in the share of government spending in national income. To foster Irish involvement in industry the Control of Manufactures Act (1932) required majority Irish ownership, although in practice exceptions were usually granted upon request. The Industrial Credit Corporation was set up to lend to industry, and issued £6.5 million in its first four years of operation. The Trade Loans Act provided further support for loans to industry.

It is difficult to assess the effect of the policy of self-sufficiency because it became inextricably tangled with the effects of the Economic War. Previous Irish governments had recognised an obligation to pay land annuities to Britain, to cover the cost of money lent under the various pre-Independence land acts. These came to about £5 million annually, or about one-fifth of government spending and almost 4 per cent of GNP.

On coming to office in March 1932, de Valera refused to continue the annuities. In July Britain retaliated by imposing special duties, initially at 20 per cent and later at 40 per cent, on imports of livestock, dairy products and meat, and also imposed quotas, including halving the number of cattle permitted to enter the UK. The Free State countered with tariffs on British goods, including cement and coal – surprising choices for a country bent on industrialisation. After these escalations tempers cooled. Under the Cattle-Coal pacts Irish cattle had easier access to Britain, and Ireland agreed to buy British coal. Initially agreed for 1935, the pact was extended and renewed in 1936 and 1937, and the Anglo-Irish Trade Agreement ended the 'war', with Ireland agreeing to pay a lump sum of £10 million and Britain ceding control of the treaty ports. Given that the capitalised value of the annuities was close to £100 million, this was considered to be a major diplomatic and economic victory for de Valera.

The combined effects of protection and the Economic War were initially dramatic. Industrial output rose 40 per cent between 1931 and 1936. Population stabilised, standing at 2.93 million in 1931 and 2.94 million in 1938 – the first period since the Famine when there had not been a substantial decline – but the amount of unemployment soared, almost quintupling between 1931 and 1934 to about 14 per cent of the labour force by 1935. In part this reflected reduced opportunities to emigrate to the United States. Despite rapid industrial growth, agriculture stagnated, as exports fell sharply. Where exports and imports together amounted to 75 per cent of GNP in 1926, they constituted 54 per cent in 1938, although this decline pales beside the two-third reduction in trade which the US faced in the early 1930s. The existing manufacturing export industries also suffered some decline. By 1936 import-substituting industrialisation had run its course, and industrial output only rose a further 4.5 per cent between 1936 and 1938. It is widely accepted that the slow growth of the economy in the 1950s was largely because of the inefficiency of the industrial sector which developed during the 1930s.

One other event of this period merits a brief discussion. With the onset of the Depression Britain erected tariffs on a wide range of items, including beer. This prompted Guinness to establish a brewery at Park Lane near London. Beer had been Ireland's single most important industrial export, and brewing had accounted for 30 per cent of manufacturing value added in 1926. Once the Park Lane brewery was established, there was little incentive to return to the earlier pattern of concentrating Guinness's production in Dublin. In this case British tariffs led to the establishment of an efficient new factory in England, at the expense of Ireland. It is possible that some Irish tariffs did the same in the other direction, although with a smaller internal market it is less likely to have been common. Using tariffs to promote investment and industry in this way has come under increasing scrutiny by economists in recent years, under the rubric of strategic trade policy.

Historical Debate: Was the Drive for Self-Sufficiency a Mistake?
Joseph Johnston, writing in 1951, argued that but for the Economic War 'our real National Income might well have been 25 per cent more in 1939 than it actually was and 25 per cent more today that it actually is.... The process of cutting off one's nose to spite one's face is sometimes good politics, but always bad economics'. He might have noted that between 1931 and 1938 Irish GNP rose about 10 per cent, compared to 18 per cent in less-protectionist Britain. He might also have questioned how many industrial jobs were really created, noting that while the 1936 census enumerated 199,000 individuals 'involved in industrial occupations', this was only 11,000 higher than the number enumerated in 1926.

 _ Johnston's estimate of a 25 per cent decline has been sharply questioned. Recent research, which tries to recreate what might plausibly have happened in the absence of tariffs, by constructing a computable general equilibrium counterfactual, suggests that the total cost of protection might have been 5 per cent of GNP per year, or £7-8 million annually during the late 1930s, of which perhaps two-thirds is attributable to the Economic War. Against this Ireland gained the treaty ports and received a £90 million write-off on its foreign debt. The expansion of the industrial sector may have provided experience in business management which was valuable in later years.

Having built high tariff barriers, Ireland was slow to reduce them later, and the average rate of effective protection of manufacturing was still an exceptionally high 80 per cent in 1966. If some of the economic sluggishness of the 1950s was the result, then the protection of the 1930s may appear more damaging; perhaps had Johnston been writing in 1960 he would have been closer to the truth. One may also wonder whether a policy of more selective protection, perhaps along the lines favoured by Taiwan or South Korea, might not have proven more valuable.

1939-1950: The War and Rebound
The most important economic result of World War II was that it opened a wide gap between Northern Ireland and the Republic. Between 1938 and

1947 national income grew just 14 per cent, compared to 47 per cent in the UK and 84 per cent in Northern Ireland. Where incomes, North and South, were broadly comparable before the war, by 1947 incomes per head in the Republic had fallen to about 40 per cent of the British level, while in the North they had risen to close to 70 per cent. Why did the South perform so poorly?

Between 1938 and 1943 the volume of exports fell by a half, and imports fell even more. During this period industrial output fell 27 per cent, and industrial employment dropped from 167,000 to 144,000. The main reason was the scarcity of raw material inputs for industry, and the shortage of shipping capacity. Completely reliant on outside shippers until 1941, the government founded Irish Shipping, and moved rapidly to purchase ships, which soon proved their worth. The vulnerability of industry to outside constraints clearly underlined the limits of self-sufficiency for a small open economy. Because of the difficulty of obtaining imports, the country built up significant foreign reserves, but the increase was less dramatic than during World War I, since price controls in Britain were more effective in limiting the rise in the price of those goods which Ireland exported. By 1946 residents had external assets totalling £260 million, approximately equivalent to GNP in that year.

The total value of agricultural output fell during the war period, but net agricultural output – i.e. total output less the cost of non-labour inputs – rose, by 17 per cent between 1938/39 and 1945. This reflected the drastic fall in the use of fertiliser and other inputs, and is generally acknowledged to have exhausted the soil significantly. The structure of agriculture changed, as the area planted in grain and potatoes almost doubled. This was due to the introduction of compulsory tillage, initially set at an eighth and later at three-eighths of arable land. The stock of animals did not decline, with the exception of pigs, which prior to the war had been partly fed on inexpensive imported maize.

During the war real GNP fell, especially initially. Living standards fell further as households, unable to find the goods they wanted, were obliged to save more. The stock of capital in industry became run-down. With emigration to the US blocked, population rose, by 18,000 between 1938 and 1946. The unemployment rate stood at over 15 per cent in 1939 and 1940, but declined thereafter to a little over 10 per cent in 1945. The decrease was due to a sharp rise in migration to Britain, reaching near-record levels in 1942, as people left to work in factories and enrol in the armed forces.

The war was followed by a rebound, and per capita real GDP rose by 4.1 per cent per annum between 1944 and 1950. This occurred despite the fact that agricultural output stagnated, with gross volume falling between 1945 and 1950, and net output shrinking by 5 per cent; an exceptionally poor harvest in 1947 was enough to pull down GNP in that year. Not surprisingly, 70,000 people left agriculture between 1946 and 1951; yet during this period the unemployment rate fell and population increased. Much of this is attributable to the expansion of industrial production, which more than doubled during the same period.

Government spending rose rapidly in the early war years as the army was increased from 7,500 to 38,000 men. After the war government spending grew far faster than national income, increasing its share of GNP from 23 per cent in 1945 to 39 per cent by 1951. In large measure this increase occurred as Ireland sought to emulate the 'social investment' of the Labour Party in Britain, by expanding welfare spending. Alongside this increase was a striking change in the composition of public spending, towards devoting a larger share to capital rather than current spending. While just 5 per cent of government spending went to capital spending in 1945 this fraction rose to 24 per cent by 1950, to pay for housing, roads, hospitals, electricity and telephones.

1950-1958: Decline or Rebirth?

It had become standard to consider the 1950s as a period of stagnation and failure. This is a half-truth. Between 1951 and 1958 GDP rose by less than 1 per cent per year. Employment fell by 12 per cent, and the unemployment rate rose. Irish GDP per-capita fell from 75 per cent to 60 per cent of the EU average. Half a million people emigrated. Yet between 1950 and 1960 real product per capita grew at 2.2 per cent per year, possibly the fastest rate recorded up to then, and industrial output expanded at 2.8 per cent per annum. Output per farmer grew at a respectable 3.4 per cent per year. Rural electrification spread, and the housing stock improved appreciably. Was the glass half full or half empty?

The key to understanding the 1950s is to note that this was the decade when Europe rebounded; Ireland's performance looks disappointing only by the standards of neighbouring countries, not by historical standards. Much of the emigration reflected the lure of improving wages elsewhere, notably in Britain.

Why did output not grow faster in the 1950s? FitzGerald believes that the key problem was a 'failure to reorientate industry to export markets', considering that 'the naiveté of the philosophy that underlay the whole protection policy was not exposed until the process of introducing protection had come to an end'. The quick benefits from protection had been reaped by industrial expansion in the 1930s; the war interrupted further growth, and the post-war boom was transient; by the 1950s Irish industry was supplying as much of the domestic market as it reasonably could, and in order to expand had no option but to seek markets overseas. But since much of the industrial sector could only survive because of protection, it was too inefficient to export successfully, although it was certainly strong enough to lobby against any liberalisation. The persistence of tariffs also hit farmers, sometimes directly. For instance the tariffs which protected wheat and barley raised the cost of feed for pigs and poultry, and the latter both declined.

To switch to exporting, new industries would have to be sought, or existing ones radically restructured; however local enterprise was timid (perhaps understandably so) and wary of initiating such change. To help provide appropriate incentives, export profits tax relief was provided in 1956, and the Industrial Development Authority Act of 1958 granted broader powers to the Industrial Development Authority (IDA), which had been set up in 1949, providing for tax holidays for export-oriented companies if they were to set up in the country. The Shannon Free Airport Development Company was set up in 1959.

One might better view the 1950s as a period of transition rather than one of failure, much as it was in Taiwan and South Korea. It has been argued that the economy was in fact in the process of reorientating itself towards export markets, but that any such change was bound to be slow. As J.J. McElligott put it in the 1920s, when warning of the dangers of protection, 'to revert to free trade from a protectionist regime is almost an economic impossibility'. Exports of manufactured goods rose quite rapidly, accounting for 6 per cent of all exports in 1950 but 17 per cent by 1960. Dramatic as this change was, the increase was from a very low base, and the export sector simply was not large enough to be a potent engine of growth.

An entirely different explanation comes from Kennedy and Dowling, who state baldly that 'the chief factor seems to us to be the failure to secure a satisfactory rate of expansion in aggregate demand'. The main cause of insufficient aggregate demand was unduly restrictive fiscal policy. When balance of payments crises arose, as they did in 1951 and 1955, the government sought to restrain total spending by trying to bring the budget more into balance, thereby lowering the demand for imports. Kennedy and Dowling argue that the government overreacted to such crises, and could easily have borrowed enough to tide the country over. This argument provides an intellectual underpinning for the highly expansionary, and ultimately disastrous, fiscal policy experiment of the late 1970s and early 1980s.

Whatever the causes, the poor overall economic performance created a feeling of pessimism, and this in turn probably deterred investors. As T.K. Whitaker, then secretary of the Department of Finance, put it, 'the mood of despondency was palpable'.

In 1958, at the request of the government, T.K. Whitaker wrote the now-celebrated report Economic Development. Recognising the recent poor performance, characterising agriculture as 'backward', noting the small scale of industry and diagnosing private capital as scarce and timid, the report called for a reorientation of government investment towards more 'productive' uses and away from a primary emphasis on 'social' investment (such as housing). It proposed that tariffs should be dismantled unless a clear infant industry case existed, it favoured incentives to stimulate private industrial investment, and it proposed expanded spending on agriculture, notably for the eradication of bovine TB. On the other hand it warned against the dampening effects of high taxes. With such measures, it suggested, GNP could grow two per cent annually, although it stressed that this was not a firm target. What is most remembered about the report is that it struck an optimistic note in pessimistic times. These measures were incorporated in the First Programme for Economic Expansion which appeared in November 1958, but generally not implemented.

Economic growth during the period of the first plan exceeded anyone's wildest expectations, reaching four per cent per annum instead of the anticipated two per cent. At the time much of this increase was attributed directly to the impact of the First Programme, and support for such indicative planning increased. The Second Programme, introduced in 1963 and designed to run to 1970, was far more detailed and ambitious, forecasting an annual increase in GNP of four per cent per annum; industry was to expand 50 per cent and exports 75 per cent during the plan period. When it appeared that these targets would not quite be met the Second Programme was allowed to lapse. A Third Programme was produced, but quickly sank into oblivion, along with most of the enthusiasm for indicative planning.

1960-1973: Growth Led by Exports and Foreign Investment
Between 1960 and 1973 real product increased at 4.4 per cent per annum, the highest rate sustained either before or since. Immigration began. Per capita incomes rose by three-fifths, kept up with income growth elsewhere in Europe, and significantly outpaced growth in Britain or Northern Ireland.

What sparked, and then sustained, this spurt of economic growth? The bulk of the credit has been attributed to the strategy of export-led growth which the government pursued; less publicised, but perhaps just as important, were several other factors, most notably improving terms of trade (39 per cent better in 1973 than in 1957), expansionary fiscal policy, the boom in the nearby European economy, the fact that solid institutional foundations had been laid in the 1950s, and the optimism generated by the appearance of Economic Development. Once growth is underway it is possible to get a virtuous circle, and this is emphasised by Kennedy. He finds that labour productivity (i.e. output per worker) grew most quickly in those industries which expanded fastest. This higher labour productivity in turn permits firms to raise wages faster than prices, or to restrain price increases and more easily expand to new markets.

The policy of export-led growth stood on two legs – trade liberalisation, and the attraction of foreign direct investment. Trade liberalisation called for reducing tariffs; these, by making inputs dearer and by sucking resources from other sectors of the economy had worked to inhibit exports. Foreign investment, it was hoped, would bring new skills to the country, and help raise the overall investment, and hence growth, rate.

Trade liberalisation was begun in the 1960s as Ireland unilaterally cut tariffs in 1963 and 1964, negotiated the Anglo-Irish Free Trade Area

Agreement in 1965 and subscribed to the General Agreement on Tariffs and Trade (GATT) in 1967. These moves also prepared for eventual membership of the European Economic Community (EEC). (The EEC subsequently became the European Community (EC) and today it is known as the European Union (EU).) It was also recognised that tariff reductions would force some firms out of business, especially in 'traditional' industries such as clothing and footwear where Ireland, as a relatively high-labour-cost country, had lost its comparative advantage. Thus the government provided support for the restructuring of industry, to better prepare it to face foreign competition. In 1965 the Committee on Industrial Organisation was set up, and reported that Irish industry was poorly equipped and managed. On the basis of its recommendations adaptation grants were provided to firms to help them modernise. In 1966 An Chomhairle Oiliúna (AnCO) was established to undertake and promote industrial training. Free secondary education became universal.

With a panoply of tax breaks and subsidies, Ireland successfully induced foreign companies to set up branches in Ireland, and by 1974 new industry accounted for over 60 per cent of industrial output. Indeed the 10 per cent tax on profits in manufacturing has now made the country something of a tax haven.

The final thrust of government policy was wage restraint, viewed as necessary, especially with a fixed exchange rate, to help keep industrial costs at a competitive level. In the 1960s government efforts amounted to exhortation. In the 1970s wage bargaining was centralised, under the National Wage Agreements. Given the option of emigration, the scope for manoeuvre here is small. If real wages were pushed below the British level they would simply stimulate faster emigration, and so could not be sustained.

A consequence of these changes, and a proximate cause of faster growth, was that the investment rate rose from 15 per cent of GNP in the 1950s to 20 per cent in the 1960s, financed mainly by domestic savings (13 per cent of GNP in the 1950s and 16 per cent in the 1960s), but also increasingly by foreign investment.

6 INTO EUROPE: THE ECONOMY SINCE 1973

In 1973 Ireland, along with the UK and Denmark, joined the European Economic Community. The date represents a turning point not only economically, but socially and politically as well, as the country has since turned increasingly towards the European Union, and correspondingly less towards the United Kingdom, in its external relations. The overarching story of Irish economic policy over most of the past quarter-century is one of increasingly tight links with the European Union. Unfortunately the events may still be too close in time to allow for enough historical perspective – this is what F.S.L. Lyons refers to as the dilemma of the contemporary historian – but here we present a broader treatment than the subsequent chapters.

There were two immediate and important implications of membership for Ireland: lower trade barriers, and the Common Agricultural Policy (CAP). The European Economic Community was initially set up as a customs union, with low internal barriers to trade and a common set of external barriers. By joining, Ireland was committed to trading freely with the other member countries, and by 1977 all tariff barriers had been removed. MacDonagh sees an irony in this, writing that 'thus the wheel was to come full circle by 1980. Sixty years after the treaty, the British Isles would once again become a free trade area; economically the Act of Union would be restored!'. The lower barriers were expected to lead to more specialisation in production and more trade. While it was recognised that some of Ireland's industry would wither under the competition, it was also expected that Ireland would become a good platform from which companies from outside the EEC could serve the European market.

These expectations were met. While Irish exports amounted to 34 per cent of GDP in 1963, and 38 per cent in 1973, the proportion had risen to a very high 62 per cent by 1991. This burst of exports paralleled a similar increase in intra-EEC trade which took place in the 1960s, and shows how even small reductions in the cost of trading can have a large impact on the volume of trade. As expected, the destination of exports also changed, with a falling share going to the UK (down to 32 per cent in 1992) and with a rising share going to the other EU countries (rising to 43 per cent by 1992).

Ireland also expected to benefit from the Common Agricultural Policy, which subsidises farm prices. Higher farm prices help farmers at the expense of consumers, but as a net exporter of farm produce, Ireland was expected to gain on balance. This turned out to be true, although the extent of the gain is debated. Net transfers under the CAP during 1979-86 came to between 5 and 10 per cent of GNP annually, but this probably overstates the gains which Matthews puts more realistically at between two and six per cent of GNP. The real income of farmers rose between 1973 and 1979, but fell thereafter to pre-1973 levels and remained there for most of the 1980s (see Chapter 11).

The Great Fiscal Experiment

Membership of the EEC coincided with the fourfold increase in the price of oil (from $3 to $12 per barrel) which resulted from the first oil shock in late 1973; a sharp worldwide recession followed.

The government's response was thoroughly Keynesian (see Chapter 6). The higher price of oil meant that spending was diverted towards imports, thereby depressing aggregate demand for Irish goods and services. The solution adopted was to boost government current spending, and as a consequence the current budget deficit rose from 0.4 per cent of GDP in 1973 to 6.8 per cent by 1975. The result was that despite a difficult international situation, GDP growth during the first six years of EEC membership was robust, as Table 1.6 shows. This counter-cyclical policy probably moderated the rise in unemployment, but did not prevent the rate from rising from 5.7 per cent in 1973 to 9.0 per cent by 1977.

Table 1.6

Measures of Recent Performance

	1960-73	1973-79	1979-86	1986-94
		(annual growth rates, %)		
Real GDP	4.4	4.1	1.5	4.3
Real GNP	4.3	3.4	-0.3	4.3[1]
Gross National Disposable Income	4.9	2.8	0.3	3.2
Gross National Disposable Income per capita	4.2	1.2	-0.4	3.1
Inflation (CPI)		14.5	12.7	1.9[2]
Investment as % of GDP	22.7	27.1	26.2	18.3

Sources: R. O'Donnell, 'The Internal Market', in P. Keatinge (editor), *Ireland and European Community Membership Evaluated,* Pinter, London 1991; J. FitzGerald and P. Honohan, 'Where Did all the Growth Go?', in S. Cantillon, J. Curtis and J. FitzGerald (editors), *Mid-Term Review,* Economic and Social Research Institute, Dublin 1994; and Eurostat.
[1] Author's estimate. [2] Through 1991.

With the passing of recession the appropriate adjustment calls for lowering the budget deficit, and indeed it fell to 3.6 per cent of GDP in 1977. But in 1978 the new Fianna Fáil government, worried about persistent unemployment, strongly boosted government spending once again. This spending was pro-cyclical, and initially had every appearance of success, with rapid economic growth, a reduction in the unemployment rate (to 7.2 per cent in 1979), and significant net immigration for the first time in a generation.

The costs came with a lag. The government had to borrow heavily, and so the ratio of debt to GDP rose, from 52 per cent in 1973 to 129 per cent by 1987, by then easily the highest in the European Union. By 1986 the cost of servicing this debt took up 94 per cent of all revenue from personal income tax. Successive governments initially tried to solve the problem by raising tax rates, especially in 1981 and 1983, but these changes hardly increased tax revenue, suggesting that the country was close to its revenue-maximising tax rates. Much of the additional spending went to buy imports, and the current account deficit widened to an untenable 15 per cent by 1981. Partly as a result, the pound was devalued four times within the European Monetary System in the early 1980s. In 1986 an estimated IR£1,000 million of private capital left the country, anticipating a devaluation; the smart money was right, when the pound was devalued by 8 per cent in August. Between 1979 and 1986 GDP rose by just 1.5 per cent annually, and Gross National

Disposable Income per capita actually fell. The great experiment in fiscal expansion had failed.

Ironically, the new Fianna Fáil government, after criticising the Coalition's austere proposals, introduced a very tight budget in 1987, cutting the current budget deficit to 1.7 per cent of GDP (see Chapter 6). Capital spending was also sharply cut, and by 1992 the ratio of debt to GDP had fallen below 100 per cent. This return to fiscal rectitude was accompanied by a resumption of robust economic growth. Some have argued that this amounted to an expansionary fiscal contraction. The idea is that private investors and consumers, convinced that the government was serious, resumed their spending and triggered a boom. The truth is somewhat more prosaic. The drop in government spending was mainly replaced by a boom in exports, due in part to the 11 per cent devaluation in 1986, along with continued wage restraint (which made Ireland more competitive). Clearly the scope for an independent fiscal policy is now severely circumscribed, which given the history of the 1980s may be all to the good.

From Sterling to EMS

In 1979, in a move which was hailed at the time as foresighted, Ireland broke the link with sterling (which dated back to 1826) and joined the European Monetary System (EMS). The reasoning was straightforward. Ireland had experienced inflation averaging 15 per cent between 1973 and 1979 (see Table 1.6), necessarily the same rate as in the Britain, and it was believed that the key to reducing the inflation rate was to uncouple the Irish pound from high-inflation sterling and attach it to the low-inflation EMS which was dominated by the Deutsche mark (see Chapter 9). Some also argued that Sterling would appreciate with the appearance of North Sea oil, and that this would hurt Irish exports. Although over 40 per cent of exports still went to the UK, about a quarter went to the other EEC countries and so a change in exchange regime was considered feasible.

The adjustment to the EMS was slow and rocky. In the early 1980s inflation actually fell faster in the UK, which stayed out of the EMS, than in Ireland. The slow reduction in Irish inflation towards German levels meant that the Irish pound became overvalued, and had to be devalued within the EMS. Recognising this risk, interest rates remained higher in Ireland than in West Germany throughout most of the decade, although there was gradual convergence. And why did inflation not fall faster? Continued expansionary fiscal policy is part of the explanation; wage increases also continued to be too large to be consistent with very low inflation; and the Central Bank may not have had the nerve to restrain credit enough initially.

But by about 1990 Ireland could boast of low inflation, a tight budget, and a falling ratio of government debt to GDP, and it looked as if the decision to join the EMS was finally paying off. Then in late 1992 the EMS fell apart. High interest rates in Germany, resulting from that country's inflation-fighting strategy, caused the Deutsche mark to appreciate. Sterling devalued, and the Irish pound ultimately followed, because 32 per cent of Irish exports still went to the UK, and in the absence of a devaluation Irish competitiveness in the important UK market would be too severely compromised. The current EMS is a pale shadow of its former self, with hardly enough structure to be distinguishable from a system of floating exchange rates (see also Chapters 6 and 9).

The Rise of Stubborn Unemployment

In 1973 the unemployment rate was 6 per cent. Since 1984 it has never fallen below 13 per cent. In 1994 it stood at 18 per cent, well above the level in the European Union. What are the causes? (See Chapter 8 for a detailed discussion of this issue.)

One could blame insufficient economic growth. Brendan Walsh has found that by the 1980s GDP needed to rise by at least 3.8 per cent per annum simply to prevent the unemployment rate from falling. While it exceeded this rate prior to 1979, GDP grew at just 1.5 per cent per annum between 1979 and 1986, picking up to 4.3 per cent between 1986 and 1994 (see Table 1.6). Just to bring the unemployment rate to the European level of 9 per cent over a period of 5 years would require annual growth of over 8 per cent, which is not likely. Put more starkly, between 1960 and 1990 the Irish economy only increased total employment by 7 per cent.

One could blame demographics. The natural increase in the Irish labour force, at 1.1 per cent in 1970 and 0.6 per cent in 1992, was the highest in the EU. Traditionally a significant proportion of young job-seekers have emigrated. When the usual destinations, mainly the UK and the US, face recession then more people stay in Ireland. Indeed the Irish unemployment rate tracks that of the UK quite closely, and this alone goes a long way towards explaining the surge.

One could also blame a rigid labour market. At a microeconomic level, the incentive to work is weak, particularly for those with relatively low skills. This is because unemployment benefits, defined broadly to include unemployment assistance and other subsidies, replace a high proportion of take-home pay; and unlike the situation in, for instance, Sweden, these benefits may be enjoyed more or less indefinitely. Extensive spending on active training and related policies, to the tune of 4 per cent of GDP recently, do not appear to have had much effect either. In these respects Ireland conforms to the European model of high-wage growth and low-job growth, in contrast with the American model of slow-growing earnings but massive job creation.

Income Distribution

Despite the high unemployment rate, income in Ireland is distributed about as evenly as in other Western European countries. In 1973 the poorest fifth of households shared 7 per cent of household income, compared to 39 per cent enjoyed by the richest fifth. The ratio of the two, at 5.5:1, was lower than in most other countries.

The distribution of income appears to have become more equal over time, at least until the 1980s, in line with the experience of other increasingly affluent economies. There are several scraps of evidence for this. In 1926, 85,000 people worked as servants, which meant that many households were sufficiently rich to be able to afford to hire the poor. This phenomenon has all but vanished – only 6,000 servants were counted in 1981 – reflecting a narrowing of the income gaps between the two groups. And while a skilled construction worker earned 30 per cent more than an unskilled worker in the 1930s, by the 1970s this differential had shrunk to about 10 per cent. Overall employment in agriculture, where incomes are still just two-thirds of non-agricultural incomes, has fallen from over 50 per cent in the 1920s to about 12 per cent now.

At the same time government transfer payments, particularly for pensions and unemployment benefits, have risen over time, and have had a direct impact in improving the distribution of income by maintaining incomes at the low end. Balanced against this is the massive rise in unemployment to over a quarter of a million people. Kennedy, Giblin and McHugh argue that 'inequality of opportunity within Ireland may have been greater than in many other countries', and note that social mobility in Dublin has been found to be less than in Sweden, France, or the UK.

Given its lower average income, it is not surprising that the poverty rate in Ireland is fairly high when compared to the other EU countries, exceeded only by Spain, Greece and Portugal. In 1980, 21 per cent of the Irish population had incomes below a poverty threshold which was set at 40 per cent of average incomes in the EU; this compared with an average of 17 per cent for the EU as a whole. By 1985 the Irish rate had increased to 26 per cent while the EU rate fell to 16 per cent, reflecting the dismal economic performance during this interval. During this period the poverty rate for children rose sharply (from 26 to 35 per cent) and, surprisingly, the rate for the elderly fell dramatically from 34 to 20 per cent, bringing it down to the EU average.

The distribution of income has also changed because of changes in the labour market. Both men and women are entering the labour market later, as they extend their education; and men are retiring earlier. While 96 per cent of men aged 25-44 were in the labour force in 1990, the proportion is just 44 per cent for women, low by EU standards but much higher than the 29 per cent which prevailed in 1979. The increased participation by women mirrors a trend in all affluent countries towards a greater role for women in the labour force.

The Passing of the Irish Growth Model
At least since 1960 the core of the Irish model of growth has been a set of financial inducements to foreign manufacturing industry to set up in the

country. On the surface this worked well, and industrial employment rose from 164,000 in 1962 to a peak of 227,000 in 1980.

During the 1980s the cracks became more evident, as industrial employment fell to 195,000 by 1991. Companies footloose enough to set up in Ireland were also likely to be footloose enough to leave. The policy paid more attention to attracting foreign firms than to strengthening domestic enterprises, and by 1992, 46 per cent of industrial jobs were in foreign firms. The costs also became more evident; direct subsidies were estimated at 3 per cent of GDP during the period 1983-86, equivalent to almost an eighth of industrial value added, and rose to IR£600 million in 1991. With the exceptions of Greece and Italy, Ireland subsidised industry much more heavily than other EU member states. As implemented, the policy had a strong bias in favour of using capital rather than labour, because it subsidised capital and not labour. Until the mid-1970s it also explicitly favoured the creation of jobs for men rather than women.

Convergence?

Ireland is a rich, industrial country. This fundamental fact is often forgotten because of repeated comparisons with wealthier European neighbours. The World Bank ranks Ireland 23rd out of 132 large countries on the basis of a GNP/capita of $12,200 (valued using international prices). The 42 poorest countries, comprising 3,200 million people or well over half the world total, have an average level of GNP/capita of approximately $1,500 (using the same international prices).

At the time of Independence Ireland had an income level comparable to the Western European average, or about half of the level prevailing in the UK. Until 1958 the country continued to lose ground, with a GDP/capita of just three-fifths of the EU average in that year. From then until the mid 1980s Ireland maintained its position relative to the other EU countries, and over the past decade its position has in fact improved, so that now its income (in purchasing power terms) is about 70 per cent of the EU level. This change is important, because it is not guaranteed, and there is as much concern that Ireland, 'on the periphery' would fall behind the dynamic 'core' countries, as there is optimism about convergence (see Chapter 7 for a lengthy discussion of this issue). And the change has occurred against a backdrop of increasing constraints on Ireland's ability to set its own economic policies.

Although GDP/capita is two-thirds of the EU rate, output *per employed worker* in Ireland is 86 per cent of the EU level and is set to move even closer to the European average by the end of the decade; to a large extent this reflects almost total convergence of wages between Ireland and the UK, for any given skill group. Ireland is poorer (i.e. has a lower *per capita* income), thus, because a smaller proportion of the population is in employment and this arises because it has a higher unemployment rate, because a smaller proportion of adults (mainly women) are in the labour force, and because there are relatively fewer adults in the population (because recent high population growth has left a legacy of a young population). Now that the fertility rate has fallen below replacement, and attitudes towards women working have changed, these last two factors are likely to rise towards European levels and further convergence is likely (see Chapter 8).

Contemporary Historical Debate: Has Ireland Failed?

In 1913 Irish real product per capita was twice the Japanese level; by 1985 it was half the Japanese level. This reflects modest progress. But if Ireland faced unusually severe obstacles then even this might indicate a fine performance.

The obstacles were not severe. At Independence Ireland had a literate population, good infrastructure, substantial foreign assets, a functioning bureaucracy. It was close to some of the world's biggest markets. It had substantial natural resources, of soil and sea if not iron and coal. The destruction of war bypassed the country. It was fortunate indeed compared with Denmark, or Austria, or the Netherlands.

One is drawn to conclude that Irish economic performance was unimpressive, not so much in failing to provide a good standard of living as for failing to do so for more people. Why?

Lee has recently offered a provocative analysis of 'the mystery of Irish socio-economic performance'. He considers that the political system has been stable and has served the country well, despite excessive 'localism', but castigates the civil service for being conservative, resistant to new ideas, and overcentralised. He argues that the market for ideas has been sadly limited, paying far too much attention to the British model. He bemoans the ethic of 'begrudgery', where one is distressed at, rather than pleased about, the success of others. And he argues that an ability to speak English was not necessarily an advantage; instead of making the intellectual effort to learn other languages and cultures, the Irish have simply adopted the cloak of anglophone culture. Presumably he has a model such as the Danish one in mind here, rather than, say, Albania or Greece.

The Irish have been more successful than Ireland, and a different answer might be that the easy outlets for emigrants removed the pressure to innovate, and provided a release for would-be entrepreneurs. With the ending and even reversal of emigration from the 1960s, Ireland became much more aware of the outside world. This open-mindedness has been reinforced by membership of the European Union, and the country has now moved into the European mainstream and developed a sophistication which was undreamt of a generation ago.

7 CONCLUDING OBSERVATIONS

The significant events of Irish economic history have been marshalled to support a number of different interpretations.

Nationalists emphasise the ways in which the links between the Irish economy and Great Britain have worked to Ireland's detriment. Writers in this vein have stressed the damage caused by the plantations, the Navigation, Cattle and Woollen Acts, the solid growth during the years of Grattan's Parliament, the lowering of tariffs in the years after the Act of Union, the ineffectiveness of relief efforts during later years of the Famine, and the costs of Ireland's inability to protect its industry from British goods during the second half of the nineteenth century. This approach has typically been used to lead to the conclusion that Ireland would be better off economically with independence.

Support for the nationalist interpretation waxes and wanes with the performance of the economy of the Republic. When independence did not bring a dramatic improvement in growth, and when the import-substitution policy of the 1930s created an inefficient industrial base which stagnated in the 1950s, the advantages of independence came to be seen as less obvious, especially as Northern Ireland appeared to be prospering at the time. However from 1960 to 1980, when growth in the Republic was faster, and dependence on the British market reduced, the nationalist view became respectable again despite, or perhaps because of, the dismantling of tariff protection.

Stripped of its Irish context, this view is comparable to the approach of *dependency theorists,* who emphasise the harmful results of links between peripheral areas and the major industrial powers. The main weaknesses of this approach are that it has tended to neglect the potentially beneficial effects of links with the metropolitan area, and has overestimated the ability of independent states to make wise decisions, as exemplified for instance by Ireland's disastrous fiscal experiment in the late 1970s.

Membership of the European Union has not made the nationalist view completely obsolete, but it has been stripped of its Anglophobic character. There remains space for a nationalism, or perhaps localism would be a better term, to counteract the tendencies of the EU to regulate from the centre what would be better done at a much lower level of government.

Marxists stress the role of the conflict between different classes within the country. Thus, for instance, the Famine and subsequent emigration swept away the greater part of the rural proletariat, paving the way for the emergence of a rural bourgeoisie, which in due course wrested control over land from the aristocracy and provided the leaders of a conservative independent state. In this view the labouring class, whether agricultural or industrial, never achieved enough strength to effect significant social or economic change, and the indigenous capitalist class failed in its mission of creating a dynamic industrial base, thereby forfeiting its right to the perquisites which it continues to enjoy. The conclusion most commonly drawn is that the state needs to take a more active role in filling this entrepreneurial function. Foreign investment by footloose companies is seen as conveying few benefits (see Chapter 12).

The Marxist view fails to explain why largely non-class conflicts, such as that in Northern Ireland, can persist. It typically overstates the ability of the state and public enterprises to create sustainable jobs; once this prop falls, it is not clear what prescription for economic growth remains.

In reaction against the weaknesses of the nationalist and Marxist interpretations, most recent writers have tended to view economic events as having a significant life of their own, being 'substantially independent of political and constitutional issues'. Hence the role of the Cattle Acts, or the Act of Union, or the replacement of tenant farmers by smallholders, are seen as minor. Economic actors are believed to redirect their energies fairly quickly, and seize the available opportunities. This perspective, epitomised in the large body of revisionist writings of Cullen, could be labelled the *classical economics approach*. In the hands of a new generation of economists this approach to history has become increasingly quantitative.

This view too has its faults, in that it can go too far in neglecting political events and institutional arrangements. In the words of Douglas North, 'institutional change shapes the way societies evolve through time and hence is the key to understanding historical change'. North originally believed that inefficient institutions would be weeded out over time, but in his more recent writings he is less sanguine about this prospect. The *institutional approach* complements rather than supplants the classical economics view, and we have drawn on these two perspectives in writing this chapter.

The most interesting lessons from Irish economic history are about growth strategies. Economic growth comes from a multitude of sources such as new technology, capital investment, education and training, land reclamation, enterprise, shifting prices, higher aggregate demand and chance. However these are only the raw ingredients, and must be combined to sustain growth. It is easy to see these ingredients at work. The new technologies of the potato, railways, power-weaving and computers have all been influential. Capital spending is essential at all times, and has increased in recent years. Higher levels of education and improved training have boosted labour productivity. Chance brought the potato blight and two world wars. Land reclamation helped fend off famine in the early nineteenth century. Enterprise was at the heart of the introduction of shipbuilding in Belfast. A secular increase in wheat prices radically changed agriculture in the eighteenth century. Low aggregate demand reined in growth in the 1950s.

Recognising the role of these elements is important, but holds few lessons. The study of growth *strategies* is more illuminating. The policy of *laissez faire* need not guarantee growth, as experience from 1815 to 1850 demonstrates. Nor does a strategy of import substitution necessarily fare better, for while it may have been helpful in the short run in the 1930s, protection left a legacy of inefficient industry in the 1950s. An approach which favours agriculture-led development, such as followed by the Free State in the 1920s, may succeed in raising real incomes, but given the relatively small size of the agricultural sector it is no longer a realistic option. An industrialisation strategy based on attracting foreign capital also has some advantages, but is expensive to implement and risks leaving a country more vulnerable to decisions outside its control.

As a practical matter Ireland has less and less room for pursuing independent economic policies. Fiscal restraint is needed because persistent expansionary fiscal policy does not work well in a small open economy, as the experiment of 1978-87 shows. Monetary policy can only play a passive role once the exchange rate is fixed, whether to sterling or within the EMS. Industrial policy is increasingly circumscribed by the rules which have applied since 1993 to the Single European Market. Recognising the need for greater efficiency, the country has privatised or closed down several state-owned enterprises. As the twentieth century closes, Ireland has become a district of Western Europe, perhaps with a little more autonomy than a typical state of the United States, but with an economic future which is increasingly congruent with that of Western Europe.

That leaves a narrower and more difficult field for local economic policy. The focus will have to be on microeconomic issues, as Blackwell suggests – bending to such tasks as gearing society to produce entrepreneurs and vitalising indigenous enterprise, evaluating enterprise, evaluating public investment more thoroughly, introducing flexibility into the labour market, and reducing the disincentives to do unskilled jobs.

Since wages in Ireland are closely linked with those in Britain (and, increasingly, Europe), once individuals have been equipped with education, economic policy has remarkably little influence on the standard of living they will enjoy in Ireland. What it can still influence to some limited degree is the number who enjoy that standard of living in Ireland rather than elsewhere.

Suggestions for Further Reading
The literature on Irish economic history is already enormous. A few suggestions for further reading are given here, and much of the information in this chapter comes from these sources. A fully annotated version of the chapter is available from the author.

General History
1 R.F. Foster, *Modern Ireland 1600-1972*, Allen Lane, London 1988.
2 J.J. Lee, *Ireland 1912-1985*, Cambridge University Press, Cambridge 1989.
3 F.S.L. Lyons, *Ireland Since the Famine*, Weidenfeld and Nicolson, London 1971.
4 T.W. Moody and F.X. Martin (editors), *The Course of Irish History*, Mercier Press, Cork 1967.
Economic and Social History
1 R.C. Crotty, *Irish Agricultural Production*, Cork University Press, Cork 1966.
2 L.M. Cullen, *An Economic History of Ireland Since 1660*, Batsford, London 1972.
3 M. Daly, *Social and Economic History of Ireland Since 1800*, Educational Company, Dublin 1981.

4 K. Kennedy, T. Giblin and D. McHugh, *The Economic Development of Ireland in the Twentieth Century,* Routledge, London 1988.
5 A. Leddin and B. Walsh, *The Macroeconomy of Ireland* (third edition), Gill and Macmillan, Dublin 1995.
6 J. Mokyr, *Why Ireland Starved,* Allen and Unwin, London 1983.
7 C. Ó Gráda, *The Great Irish Famine,* Macmillan, London 1989.

PART I

POLICY
OBJECTIVES

CHAPTER 2

Primary Policy Objectives

*Andrew John**

1 INTRODUCTION

The aim of this chapter is to provide a framework for thinking about economic policy objectives. It is suggested here that the principal economic objectives of policymakers can be summarised in terms of policies that ensure efficient use of economic resources, both at a point in time and through time; and policies concerned with the distribution of output at a point in time and through time. The success or failure of economic policies can be assessed in part using measures of employment, equity, and growth.

Section 2 presents the key assumptions of the chapter and introduces the concept of economic efficiency. The role of markets in achieving efficiency is explained, and other arguments for a free-market economy are evaluated. The section then explains how economic policies can be used to correct deficiencies of the market. Finally, the assumptions of the analysis are critically examined.

Section 3 argues that economic efficiency does not provide a sufficient basis for economic policymaking. Policy should also address intragenerational and intergenerational distribution. This section therefore considers the determinants of distribution in a market economy, as well as arguments for increased equality.

Section 4 suggests that the policymaker's problem can be formulated, and her achievements evaluated, in terms of proximate objectives that capture different dimensions of policy. Full employment and economic growth are considered in detail. For both aims, there is a discussion of measurement issues and the correspondence of the best available measure with the theoretical ideal. This is followed by consideration of whether or not policy intervention is desirable, which involves comparing the outcome in the absence of intervention (the free-market outcome) with some ideal outcome. Both efficiency and equity issues arise in each case. Section 5 concludes the chapter.

* The author's gratitude continues to be extended to Tim Callan, Adrienne Cheasty, John Clark, Isabel Harrison, Seán Nolan and Maeve O'Higgins for their comments on earlier versions of this chapter. Responsibility for errors and opinions is the author's.

2   ECONOMIC EFFICIENCY, ECONOMIC POLICY, AND THE MARKET MECHANISM

The analysis begins with a few standard assumptions that are maintained throughout the chapter. From these assumptions, *Pareto-efficiency* is established as an aim of economic policy. Next, the case for a free-market economy is considered. Specifically, it is shown that freely-operating markets can play an important role in attaining economic efficiency. Other arguments for a market economy are also evaluated. Economic theory suggests that there are circumstances under which free markets will not achieve efficiency; these are discussed in the third subsection. The associated rationale for government intervention is developed in the fourth. The final subsection considers criticisms of the assumptions and methodology of this analysis.

Pareto-Efficiency
Consider the following five assumptions:
  (i)   the aim of policymakers is the maximisation of social welfare;
  (ii) social welfare depends positively upon the welfare of all individuals in society, and nothing else;
  (iii) the welfare of individuals depends positively upon the goods and services that they consume;
  (iv) individuals are the best judges of their own welfare and act in their own self-interest;
  (v)   firms maximise profits.
For the present, these are simply taken as given.

Now suppose that policymakers can choose between two allocations of resources (labelled A and B) with the property that all individuals are at least as well off (in terms of overall utility, or satisfaction) in B as in A, and at least one individual is strictly better off. Then B is said to be *Pareto-superior* to A. If, by contrast, some individuals are better off and some are worse off, then the two situations are *Pareto-non-comparable*. If a given situation has the property that there is no feasible Pareto-superior outcome (so policymakers cannot make some people better off without making others worse off), then that situation is said to be *Pareto-efficient*, or, for brevity, simply *efficient*.

Assumptions (i) and (ii), taken together, imply that policymakers should aim for efficiency. The desirability of efficiency is a weak proposition that would be acceptable to most people as a guiding principle of policy. It underlies most welfare analyses undertaken in economics, and is probably the only normative proposition that commands general assent among economists.

Pareto-efficiency can be decomposed into *efficiency in production* and *efficiency in exchange*. Assumption (iii) states that individuals derive satisfaction from the goods and services they consume. Since the production of goods and services requires resources, and since resources are limited, society should seek to make the best use of the limited resources at its disposal. In particular, if resources can be reallocated in such a way as to produce more of at least one desired commodity and at least as much of all other desired commodities, social welfare can be increased. Efficiency in production is achieved when no such reallocation is possible.

Efficiency in exchange concerns the allocation of existing goods and services. Given a fixed amount of goods to be distributed among consumers, an allocation is efficient if no Pareto-improving redistribution is available. If agents are the best judges of their own welfare (assumption (iv) above), then an efficient allocation can be achieved by voluntary exchange of goods. Put another way, an allocation is not efficient if there exist mutually beneficial trades that have not been consummated.

The Role of Markets

A fundamental result of economic theory is that efficiency in both the production and exchange of goods and services can be achieved in an economy characterised by perfectly competitive markets for all goods and services in all time periods. Further, any Pareto-efficient outcome can be attained in such an economy, by means of appropriate initial redistributions. These results are known as the *first welfare theorem* and *second welfare theorem*. They provide a rigorous theoretical justification for the belief that the price mechanism is an efficient allocator of resources.

Consider first efficiency in exchange. Suppose that individuals start off with a given quantity of goods and can buy and sell as much as they want of these goods and the goods of others, at prices that they take as given. It can be shown that, at some set of prices, the desired transactions of everyone in the economy are mutually compatible. Further, in carrying out these transactions, individuals effectively trade with one another up to the point where all benefits from exchange are exhausted. That is, they achieve an efficient point at which no further mutually beneficial trades exist; there is no conceivable swap of goods between any two individuals that both would favour.

The intuition for this result is easily understood in terms of the economist's favourite tool: supply and demand. First, remember that exchange is voluntary: buyers and sellers choose to participate in markets because their exchanges make them better off. If they weren't going to gain, they wouldn't be buying or selling. So there is benefit from each exchange. A moment's reflection on supply and demand should also make it clear that more of a product is traded at the equilibrium price than at any other price. If the price were higher, demanders would be willing to buy less. If the price were lower, suppliers would be willing to supply less. At the equilibrium price, therefore, the maximum possible number of mutually beneficial exchanges occurs. If markets exist for all goods and services, then this logic applies in every market and all the possible gains from exchange will be exhausted.

Efficiency in production is achieved under free markets given the assumption that producers maximise profits. (If producers are simply individuals, or act solely in the interests of their shareholders, then this assumption can be viewed as a corollary of assumption (iv).) If a firm can obtain more output using the same quantity of inputs, then it can increase its profits. Moreover, any firm that uses resources inefficiently will be unable to compete in a free market. With production, there is still a set of prices such that everyone's transactions are mutually compatible.

The import of these results is striking. If individuals transact in competitive markets, then, although they act purely in their own self-interest, they arrive at an outcome with the desirable social property of Pareto-efficiency. Freely-operating markets provide the incentives for firms to produce the right quantities of goods and services, and also provide the mechanism whereby individuals can carry out mutually beneficial exchanges.

These results turn out to be less powerful than they might at first appear. None the less, they do suggest that a free-market economy is the appropriate starting point for the systematic analysis of economic policy. They also provide the strongest theoretical argument in favour of the free-market economy. Other justifications for free markets have also been proposed, though, and will be considered briefly here.

One argument for free markets is that they provide *consumer sovereignty.* This is the idea that, in a free-market economy, production of commodities is designed to meet demand, with the function of producers being solely to respond to the wishes of consumers. Proponents of the consumer sovereignty argument sometimes describe it as 'economic democracy'.

A certain amount of mystique surrounds the consumer sovereignty proposition, given that it is really no more than a recognition of the fact that consumer preferences have an effect on the economic system; one could as easily speak of 'technology sovereignty'. But the idea does embody one important insight: when firms do respond to market pressures, the tastes and preferences of consumers matter. If consumers do not wish to purchase a good, it will not be produced; should demand for a good increase, production will respond. This stands in contrast to centrally-planned economies, for example, where there is no such necessary link between consumer preferences and output.

Ireland is a small open economy, though, so consumer sovereignty does not imply that the preferences of Irish consumers give rise to the pattern of Irish output. Instead, the preferences of American, British, European and other consumers ultimately determine much of the pattern of output in

Ireland. Equally, the preferences of Irish consumers have a negligible effect on the pattern of world production. The appeal of consumer sovereignty as economic democracy is perhaps lessened somewhat. In any case, implicit in the consumer sovereignty principle is that the preferences of the rich are given much more weight than those of the poor, so the idea would be better described as plutocracy.

A second argument for free markets derives from the possibility that the existence of choice may, in itself, be a source of welfare. In other words, it may be the case that competitive markets are not merely a mechanism whereby individuals can maximise their utility and achieve efficiency in exchange, but also are an independent source of welfare. Suppose an individual is given a choice between two commodities – a loaf and a fish – and chooses the fish. Does this differ, in terms of the individual's welfare, from the situation where she is simply presented with the fish? If utility is derived only from consumption, then the two situations must be identical. Intuition suggests, though, that having the chance to choose is preferable. Conversely, choosing may be a source of disutility, if there are costs associated with decision-making.

While neither the consumer sovereignty argument nor the utility-from-choosing argument is that compelling on its own terms, they together contain an element of truth. Free markets allow Pareto-improving transactions to occur with a minimum of information. A high price for a product conveys the information to producers that the product is desired by consumers. Nobody has to survey consumers and ask them what they want; they reveal their preferences by their transactions in markets. Likewise, the consumer of the previous paragraph knows that she prefers the fish to the bread. If she is allowed to choose, then she will get the fish without anyone else needing to know her preferences.

One final argument for a free-market economy is the assertion that economic freedom – the right to buy and sell goods and services in competitive markets – is a precondition for, or a part of, wider political freedoms.[1] It is true that a market economy rests on the right to buy and sell goods and services, and so requires a legal system that upholds private property and contracts. So the argument essentially comes down to the question: is private property necessary for freedom? When put this way, there does not appear to be a good *prima facie* reason for associating freedom and private property. Private ownership implies an exclusive right to benefit from the flow of services from a good, which by definition restricts the freedom of others to benefit from that flow of services. It is certainly not self-evident that political freedom is automatically associated with a fully market-oriented economy. It would instead seem reasonable to suggest that, for some goods (say, wristwatches), freedom is well served by private ownership, while private ownership may imply undesirable and unnecessary restrictions on freedom in the case of other goods (such as beaches).

Market Imperfections

The efficiency of competitive markets derives from a set of restrictive assumptions that does not describe any actual economy. Free-market economies in practice do not accord with the idealised abstraction of perfectly competitive markets. Four departures from the free-market ideal are addressed here: externalities, public goods, information imperfections and non-competitive behaviour.

Externalities are costs or benefits that arise from production or consumption of a good, but accrue not to the producer or consumer, but to others. Externalities can be positive or negative: they are said to be negative if one agent's actions impose costs on others, and positive if the agent's actions confer benefits on others. Either way, they result in a misallocation of resources.

The classic example of a negative externality arising from production is pollution. If a power plant emits sulphur dioxide into the atmosphere, causing acid rain, it is imposing a negative externality. An example of a positive externality from production is knowledge arising from research and development. For example, if advances in technology, due to the research of a particular firm, benefit other producers who did not pay for the research, then there is a positive production externality. Examples of negative externalities from consumption are second-hand smoke from cigarettes and pollution from cars. Conversely, if smoking makes someone less irritable and thus more pleasant company, then this is a positive consumption externality.

If an activity is a source of negative externalities, then, from a social perspective, too much of that activity will occur. Individuals driving cars have no incentive to worry about the air pollution that they cause. The cost to society of their activity is greater than the cost they bear privately. Hence people will drive too much, from a social point of view. Similarly, if an activity generates positive externalities, then there will be too little of that activity from a social perspective. If a firm that engages in costly research and development knows that its discoveries will be quickly appropriated by others, then the benefit to society exceeds the benefit to the firm. There will be too little R&D, from a social point of view.

The welfare theorems assume no externalities (or, more precisely, assume that markets are introduced for all external effects). The presence of externalities in the real world means that free markets will not result in an efficient allocation of resources: market prices of goods in real economies frequently do not reflect their true social costs.

A second and related problem with free-market economies in practice arises from the existence of *public goods*. Public goods have two characteristics. First, they are *non-excludable:* no-one can be excluded from the benefits they confer. Second, they are *non-rival:* one person's consumption of the good does not affect the consumption of others. The classic example of a public good is national defence. Clean air and knowledge also are – at least to some degree – public goods. Contrast these with a private good: say, a bar of chocolate. If you own a bar of chocolate, then others are excluded from enjoying it unless you choose to share it. Moreover, if you eat a piece of chocolate, then no-one else can eat that same piece.

The distinctive characteristics of public goods mean that they will not in general be supplied in a pure market economy. But individual welfare depends upon a number of goods that possess some or all of the attributes of public goods. And the market mechanism does not easily allow consumers to express a preference for clean air or greater national defence. Hence social welfare cannot necessarily be equated with welfare arising from consumption of consumer goods only.

Another reason why free markets may not perform quite as advertised in real economies is that firms and consumers are not perfectly informed about the economy. Producers must make decisions based on incomplete knowledge of consumers' tastes, and consumers will in general lack information on both the prices and the quality of the goods they wish to purchase. As mentioned above, markets themselves supply some of this information through the prices that they generate. Still, lack of information means that mistakes will be made and resources will be misallocated.

Lack of information on quality is particularly significant in the case of goods (such as consumer durables) that are relatively expensive and are bought infrequently. The less frequently a good is bought, the less sensitive is the market mechanism, for there is no immediate way in which the dissatisfied consumer can convey this dissatisfaction in the market. Lack of information is also a problem where the costs of an uninformed choice are high. Suppose, for example, that an airline is lax about training and safety procedures. It is true that, after a few crashes, market forces would probably operate to put it out of business, but the adjustment to equilibrium is costly. To put these points another way, since market processes operate in real time and adjust over time, uninformed consumers may sometimes engage in inefficient out-of-equilibrium trades.

All of this suggests that information should be viewed as an economic good that is bought and sold like other commodities. To a large extent this true – think of Which? magazine, or think of market research firms. But there are many reasons for expecting the markets for information to be imperfect. There may be economies of scale in information gathering, implying that single individuals cannot acquire the information they need. Information also has many of the attributes of a public good. Finally, some information may be inherently private. Suppose, for example, that a worker wishes to know the safety record of the firm at which she is applying for a job. The firm may not have the incentive to tell the truth and the worker may be unable to verify the information received. (There is now a vast literature on the economics of information that unfortunately cannot be surveyed here.)

Perhaps the most obvious divergence between the theory and reality is that real-world markets are usually not characterised by perfect competition. Many markets in Ireland possess the characteristics of monopoly, oligopoly or imperfect (monopolistic) competition (see Chapter 10). In such cases agents possess market power; they do not take prices as given but can instead influence the prices of goods they buy and sell. This means that firms will tend to reduce the quantity they produce in order to increase the price they receive for their output. The level of output that generates maximum profit for the firm will then be less than that required for an efficient equilibrium.

Economic Policy
The weaknesses of a free-market economy that have just been noted – externalities, public goods, information problems and market power – amount to a criticism of the institutional assumptions of the competitive markets model. That is, they describe problems that arise in real economies but are excluded by the assumptions of the first and second welfare theorems. Their import is that unfettered markets will in general not allocate resources in an efficient manner.

These weaknesses can be viewed in a more constructive light, however, whereby they provide a basis for a systematic theory of policy intervention. When existing markets correspond closely to the competitive ideal, theory suggests that free operation of such markets will lead to efficient allocations. Intervention is then unnecessary. Conversely, when markets are characterised by one or more of the problems just noted, economic theory suggests that policy intervention is required, and should be designed to correct the distortion. That is, policymakers should intervene in such a manner as to make markets correspond as closely as possible to the competitive ideal, and hence encourage an efficient outcome.

Theory suggests, for example, that policymakers should intervene to correct for externalities. For example, taxes on petrol are a means whereby policymakers can try and bring the private costs of driving in line with the social costs. Subsidies to research and development activity might likewise be a means of encouraging firms to put more resources into the acquisition of knowledge. Theory also suggests that policymakers should ensure the provision of public goods.

Information problems might also suggest a role for policy. For example, imperfections in the markets for information could justify a role for policymakers in the collection and dissemination of information. Policymakers might also regulate safety standards in the workplace or elsewhere because of the problems generated by private information: workers cannot easily monitor the safety of their workplace; consumers cannot monitor the safety of their airlines. Finally, policymakers should also intervene, according to this theory, to offset the distortionary effects of market power. For example, policymakers can enact anti-trust laws and other regulations on monopolies. Policymakers can also use tax and subsidy schemes to encourage increased production by firms with market power.

Policymakers can also play a role by encouraging the development of markets and by providing a secure legal framework to enforce contracts. For example, patent laws allow firms to retain the profits from research and development. Some governments have also developed market-based responses to environmental problems. The Clean Air Act in the United States, for example, allows firms to buy and sell permits that bestow a right to emit a certain amount of pollution. Total pollution is controlled by controlling the total quantity of permits, but firms can trade permits so that pollution abatement is carried out by those firms able to limit their emissions most easily and at lowest cost. Some public goods can also be incorporated – at least in part into the market mechanism: national parks and toll motorways are examples. The practical details of such policymaking are covered in greater detail in Chapter 4.

This approach to policymaking is thus based on the idea of exploiting the known efficiency properties of competitive markets. In itself, the theory gives no indication of whether government policy should be highly interventionist or based principally on *laissez faire;* that decision requires judgements on the empirical incidence of the different problems noted and of the costs of intervention.

A couple of reservations about this approach to public policy can be noted. First, an important result, known as the *Theory of Second Best,* indicates that if there is a distortion in one market (that cannot be corrected directly), then it may no longer be optimal for other markets to be perfectly competitive.[2] As an example of this, consider the case of a polluting monopolist who is induced to produce the competitive level of output. The result is a more severe pollution problem. The Theory of Second Best might appear devastating, for it could suggest that the proposed approach to policymaking is worthless. A more sanguine interpretation notes that the second-best argument requires that different distortions should be offsetting; hence it can be argued that the theory should be considered to be applicable unless the existence of offsetting distortions can be demonstrated explicitly.

Actual economies may also diverge from the competitive ideal in ways that cannot be corrected by policymakers. For example, one notion underlying competitive markets is price flexibility. If prices are flexible, then they will respond to shocks in such a way as to ensure that demand and supply are always equal. If some prices are sticky, though, then demand and supply may not always be equal at the price prevailing in the market. Some mutually beneficial trades will then not be realised. The welfare theorems also assume the existence of markets for all goods in all time periods. This assumption is palpably false: try and find someone willing to quote a price for a promise to deliver kiwi fruit in Galway on 16 February, 2060. Mutually beneficial trades may go unrealised because markets are missing.

Policymakers, however, do not have it in their power to order prices to be more flexible. Similarly (patent laws and pollution permits notwithstanding), policymakers cannot in general simply establish markets that are missing. (Introducing an extra market when other markets are missing actually need not be welfare-improving, for second-best reasons.) Furthermore, there may be reasons why prices are rigid or markets missing; without understanding these, the consequences of economic policies cannot be predicted. These are among the deepest questions in economics, and it is not possible to do justice to them here. The important lesson for current purposes is that there are substantial constraints upon policy.

There are practical as well as theoretical difficulties with this approach to policy. Economists and politicians possess only an imperfect knowledge of the economy, so inefficiencies are not always easy to identify, effective policies may be hard to design and implement, and the consequences of policy actions may be unpredictable. Much work in economics also emphasises the importance of expectations and credibility for successful policy. Private agents form expectations about government policies, and these expectations themselves influence the impact of policy. For example, the effects of a tax cut depend crucially on whether it is expected to be temporary or permanent. Policymakers have more influence if they can influence the public's expectations by credibly committing to policies in advance, but such credibility may be hard to acquire.

The economic influence of policymakers in Ireland is also limited by the fact that the economy is 'open' (closely linked to the world economy through trade) and 'small' (so that economic events in Ireland have a negligible influence on the world economy). Much of what happens in the Irish economy is thus determined by developments in the outside world, beyond the realm of domestic policy.

Criticisms

The argument developed so far is based on behavioural assumptions to which some may object. Recall that it was assumed that policymakers seek to maximise social welfare; that social welfare depends upon individual welfare (and nothing else); that individual welfare depends upon the consumption of goods and services; that individuals are the best judges of their own welfare; and that firms maximise profits.

There are certainly valid criticisms to be made of assumption (i) – that policymakers seek to maximise social welfare. Although a useful simplification, the assumption is based on a rather idealised view of the political process. It ignores other possible aims of governments, such as maximising their probability of re-election, or satisfying particular interest groups and constituencies, or maximising the post-tax salaries of cabinet ministers! Certainly, the complexities of decision-making in the political process are hardly captured by an assumption that all political decisions are made by a benevolent government in the best interests of society.

Some economists have argued that the political process should be evaluated in strict economic terms – that is, in terms of agents acting purely in their own self-interest. When carried to its limit, such an argument leaves little room for the more orthodox view that governments may act in society's interest. The view adopted here is less cynical and more hopeful: policymakers can and (often, if not always) do carry out policies in the public interest.

Assumption (ii) is that social welfare depends positively on the welfare of the individuals in society and nothing else. It therefore explicitly suppresses the possibility that other (non-economic) objectives, such as human rights, may have a direct influence on social welfare. Sen has argued persuasively that an exclusive stress on the levels of the welfare of individuals is insufficient for policy purposes, and that other 'non-utility' information should also be used.[3] The emphasis on individual welfare in this chapter should not be interpreted as necessarily excluding the admission of non-utility information in policymaking; rather, such considerations are ignored for purposes of clarity and simplicity.

Criticisms of assumption (iii) – that individual welfare must always depend positively on the consumption of consumer goods – cut to the heart of the economic method. Critics of this assertion reject the consumerism that underpins the capitalist system (do we really need so many brands of toothpaste?). A related point is that individuals' welfare depends upon more than just consumption of consumer goods. This is discussed further in the next section.

Assumption (iv) asserts that individuals act in their own self-interest and are the best judges of their own welfare. This is an assumption of rationality. While superficially reasonable, there are many criticisms of this assumption. First, there is evidently some question about the inclusion of certain individuals, such as children or the mentally-ill. Second, work in economics and psychology suggests that not all behaviour is easily explained or characterised in terms of economic rationality.[4] Third, although this argument is anathema to most economists, it is sometimes argued that policymakers should be paternalist in certain cases. Debates over the legalisation of drugs, for example, are largely debates about this point.

Another influential set of arguments countering assumption (iv) denies that the preferences of consumers can be viewed as a primitive concept; rather, it is necessary to consider the ways in which consumers' preferences may be altered. The possibility of artificially created demands and desires was perhaps given its fullest exposition by Galbraith.[5] By means of advertising and other forms of sales promotion, Galbraith argues, wants may be actively created by producers. If one accepts the premise that consumer demand can be manipulated, then producers certainly have an incentive to do so within a market system.

There are arguments to be advanced against this, however. First, advertising may play an important role in providing information to consumers. Second, firms may have other incentives to engage in advertising, such as a wish to create barriers to entry in a particular industry. Third, it is evidently not the case that Galbraithian arguments are applicable in all cases or to all goods. The public clearly cannot always be persuaded to behave as producers might wish. Most current readers may never have heard of – or may have forgotten – 'Guinness Light', a product which failed dismally a few years ago despite extensive promotion. 'New' Coca-Cola in the United States suffered a similar fate: public response to a change in the Coca-Cola formula forced the company to continue production of the original product.

Finally, assumption (v) – that firms maximise profits – represents a somewhat naive view of the theory of the firm. There is an extensive literature in economics that explores the problems arising from private information and *agency problems* – the difficulties of ensuring that a subordinate has the incentives to behave as his manager would wish. Discussing such matters goes well beyond the scope of this chapter.

3 DISTRIBUTION

Recall the argument so far. A few fairly plausible assumptions imply that policymakers should strive for Pareto-efficiency. The assumption that individuals are the best judges of their own welfare implies that voluntary market trades are Pareto-improving. A complete system of perfectly operating markets will therefore give rise to a Pareto-efficient allocation. In reality, there are a number of significant departures from the ideal of perfectly competitive markets. Hence, policymakers can attempt to correct for these departures and so bring the economy towards a Pareto-efficient allocation.

But there is a slight problem with this reasoning. In practice, few if any policy proposals will be Pareto-improving. Almost any policy change will make some people better off and others worse off. Tougher regulations on polluting firms make those firms worse off, even if such regulations lead to a cleaner environment. Anti-trust laws hurt monopolists even though they benefit consumers. So if policymakers were restricted to Pareto-improving policies only, the scope for policy would be very limited. (It is sometimes possible to design combinations of policies that mitigate such effects – for example, a policy that will adversely affect employment in a particular industry could be accompanied by policies to retrain and relocate displaced workers. Still, realistically, any package of policies will leave some worse off.)

To put the point another way, it is emphatically not the case that all Pareto-efficient allocations are preferred to all allocations that are not efficient. Most allocations are Pareto-non-comparable, and the Pareto criterion provides no guidance for choosing among them. Moreover, there are many different Pareto-efficient allocations, and the Pareto criterion again is of no help in choosing among these.

In brief, efficiency takes no account of distributional issues. A society where millions are starving while its ruler lives in unimaginable luxury may be using and distributing its resources efficiently. Taking a pound from the richest person in society and giving it to the poorest cannot be justified on the grounds of economic efficiency, since even if the poorest person is saved from starvation, the sybarite may be made worse off by having to consume champagne of an inferior vintage.

Beyond Pareto-Efficiency

There are three responses to the limitations of efficiency. First, it can be argued that the weakness of the Pareto criterion is unfortunate, but that economic analysis simply has nothing to contribute in choosing among Pareto-non-comparable outcomes. Second, it is possible to consider *potential Pareto-improvements* – cases where some are made better off by a policy and some worse off, but where the gainers could conceivably compensate the losers. Third, it is possible to include explicit consideration of distribution in formulating policy.

Many economists reject the notion that economic analysis should go beyond efficiency and consider questions of distribution. One of the greatest strengths of economics is that it derives interesting and significant policy results on the basis of the single value judgement that economic efficiency is desirable. Economists are understandably reluctant to introduce other, more controversial, value judgements into their world. Still, the desirability of efficiency is a value judgement; furthermore, it is the value judgement that economists have chosen to emphasise. It is not self-evident that all members of society would accept this judgement, and it is far from obvious that they would view it as sufficient for policy analysis.

To put the point more forcefully, consider the extreme (and paradoxical) case where society contains an anarchic individual who is vehemently opposed to economic reasoning – so much so that any use of economic methods in policy evaluation drastically reduces this person's welfare. Then anyone who believes that Pareto-efficiency is the only basis for policy analysis would be forced to conclude that economic methods could be of no assistance at all to policymakers.

Potential Pareto-improvements have superficial appeal as a way out of the non-comparability dilemma. Under this approach, a policy is judged desirable if its benefits outweigh its costs, irrespective of who gains or loses. If a policy would make the richest person in society two pounds richer, and the poorest person one pound poorer, the policy is potentially Pareto-improving. But this approach actually introduces an additional value judgement implicitly, by asserting that distributional considerations should be irrelevant for economic policy (which is not the same as arguing that economics can say nothing about distribution). Alternatively, one can argue that economists can usefully identify potential Pareto-improvements without recommending them; the ultimate decision is then left to a policymaker who takes account of distributional issues. This is really nothing more than a restatement of the view that matters of distribution are outside the purview of economics.

The position adopted here is that the introduction of further value judgements for policy analysis is legitimate and indeed desirable, provided these are made explicit. In moving beyond the Pareto criterion, however, less consensus on policy aims is likely. Mainstream economic analysis also has less to contribute, since most economists concern themselves only with questions of efficiency.

Start, then, from the recognition and acceptance that any given policy will not be Pareto-improving: all policies generate winners and losers. If policymakers have explicit distributional goals, however, then policies can be judged both on efficiency grounds and on their distributional impact. A policy deemed desirable on efficiency grounds would be judged acceptable if it also moved the economy in the direction of some desired level of overall distribution. If, as will often happen, the dictates of efficiency and equity are in conflict, then policymakers must evaluate the relative merits of the two factors.

Distribution of What?

Given a need or desire to formulate explicit distributional goals for policymakers, the next problem is to decide what measure or measures of inequality would be suitable. The assumptions of Section 2 focused on individual welfare. So a natural starting point is to think about the determinants of individual welfare.

Economists frequently represent the lifetime utility, or satisfaction, of an individual as follows:

$$(1) \qquad U^i = \sum^T_{t=0} \beta^t u (c_t^i , n_t^i ; x_t^i , X_t^i)$$

where U^i is lifetime utility of person i, $\beta < 1$ is a discount factor, c_t^i is consumption of this person in year t, n_t^i represents leisure in year t, x_t^i represents other factors specific to person i that influence her welfare, and X_t^i represents other influences on welfare that affect both this person and others in the economy.

The equation looks formidable, but is actually quite straightforward. Think about an individual who has T years to live. Each year she chooses how hard to work, and she chooses how to divide her income between consumption and saving. These choices are primary determinants of her utility in that year: higher consumption gives her more utility; higher labour supply means less leisure, and so lower utility that year. Her utility also depends on other things, both specific to her – for example, her health – and more general – for example, public goods such as the quality of the environment. These other factors may be partially or completely outside her control. Her utility in a given year is given by the function u( ). Lifetime utility is just the sum of utilities in each year of life, except that future years are given less weight than current years (because of impatience, or because of uncertainty about the future); this is captured by the number b, which is less than one.

The agent's choices about working, consuming and saving depend on her resources. Each year she faces a budget constraint that describes the evolution of her wealth (assets):

$$(2) \qquad A_{t+1}^i = A_t^i (1 + r_t) + w_t^i n_t^i - c_t^i .$$

Here, A_t^i is assets at the beginning of year t, w_t^i is the wage she earns, and r_t is the interest rate. So each year she enters with a stock of assets that depends on past saving decisions (and inherited wealth). Over the course of the year she earns interest income on those assets. She also earns income from working. If her income exceeds her consumption then she is saving and hence building up her stock of assets.

Armed with this stylised description of individual welfare, consider distribution in the economy. The ideal comparison is probably of distributions of the lifetime welfare of all individuals in the economy. But this immediately causes an obvious problem. It is difficult – perhaps impossible – to compare the welfare of different individuals. After all, is it really possible to say for sure that one person is happier than another? Is such a statement even meaningful? This question of *interpersonal comparison of utility* has long bedevilled economists who consider problems of distribution and fairness. (It is captured in the equation by the x_t^i terms, which might include things that are not observable or measurable; alternatively, the utility functions could be different for different individuals.)

As discussed below, some economists argue that interpersonal utility comparisons need not be ruled out. Still, it is evidently easier – at least for the present – to ignore the differences among individuals captured by the x_t^i variables, and proceed instead in terms of things that are more easily measurable but that still contain information about individual welfare. Here are some contenders.

Discussions of inequality often focus on the distribution of income and wealth. From the perspective of an individual, neither income nor wealth necessarily provides good information about welfare. The reason is that both are likely to vary considerably over the course of a person's lifetime. Young people typically have low incomes and little wealth. Older people with more skills and experience are likely to have higher incomes and are also likely to have accumulated wealth. Retired people living off past saving may have high wealth but low incomes.

When thinking about how the overall distribution of income or wealth is evolving over time, however, these problems are less serious. Provided that the age structure of the population is roughly constant, the proportions of young, middle-aged, and old people will stay about the same. Then, even though income and wealth vary over the life cycle of individuals, this would not affect the overall distribution.

In principle, a better measure of the welfare of an individual would be *permanent income*. This is, roughly speaking, the amount of income that an individual can sustain over an entire lifetime. In practice, permanent income is difficult to measure directly. A good proxy might be to measure consumption, however. Economic theory suggests that individuals seek to keep consumption smooth over their lifetimes, implying that their consumption will be approximately equal to their permanent income.

A problem with consumption as a measure of welfare, though, is that it ignores the transmission of wealth across generations. Suppose two individuals have identical income and consumption paths. Suppose, however, that one also came into life with a large inheritance and bequeaths the same sum, plus interest, to his heirs. The wealthier person might enjoy higher welfare, for a number of reasons. Perhaps he obtains utility from leaving a large bequest. Perhaps his wealth brings additional security. Perhaps wealth is also a source of power and influence. If any or all of these effects is important, then wealth should be included as part of x_i, and consumption will not adequately measure welfare.

Measures of consumption, income, and wealth also share the problem that they do not account for the value of leisure. One individual may choose to work long hours in order to enjoy high consumption. Another may choose to live a simple life in the woods, work and consume little, and enjoy leisure. Comparisons of income, consumption, or wealth would all misrepresent welfare in this case.

Note that measures of consumption, income or wealth may not accurately reflect individual welfare because of the presence of the X_i variables. For example, the welfare of all people might be influenced by certain environmental variables, such as the extent of air and water pollution. These have implications for the distribution of welfare if the burden of such pollution is born disproportionately. For example, poorer individuals may have to live in smog-filled cities while rich people can escape to clean country air. (There is a subtlety here, however. The better environment in the country might be reflected in, say, higher housing prices, in which case this environmental disparity would be captured, in part at least, by consumption measures.)

Notwithstanding all these difficulties, there are a number of possible measures of inequality at a point in time. The simplest of these are summary statistics on income and wealth distribution. For example, it is possible to examine the range of incomes (or wealth) in the population being studied, or the standard deviation, or the coefficient of variation. Statistical measures have also been designed specifically with inequality in mind, such as the Lorenz curve and Gini coefficient, and other more sophisticated measures.[6]

Distribution for Whom?

All of the above discussion presumed that the appropriate unit of analysis was the individual. But, at least for some issues, it may make more sense to think about households rather than individual agents. For example, household distributions may convey more information about poverty, the welfare of children, and so on. Nothing in the discussion so far precludes interpreting the utility function as summarising the well-being of a household rather than a single individual, although the specification is obviously not rich enough to capture all the details of household decision-making.

More significantly, the discussion to this point has avoided the question of who should be included in distributional objectives. First, while inequality is almost always considered at a national level, there is no obvious logical reason why this should be the case. It is true, of course, that Irish policymakers can have a greater influence on national distribution than they can on worldwide distribution. But almost the entire discussion of inequality in this chapter could be applied globally as well as nationally. And while efforts are often made to reduce inequality within a nation, aid from the industrialised nations to less developed economies is minimal, given the extent of inequality between them.

Second, policies presumably need to be judged not only in terms of their effects on the distribution of resources today, but also in terms of the welfare of future generations. Although they are answerable directly only to those currently alive, policymakers clearly do not pursue policies without regard to long-term consequences. But it is not at all obvious how much weight policymakers should place on the welfare of future generations.

Such concerns arise forcefully in a number of contexts, such as policies directed towards the environment and policies that affect long-run economic growth. Further, as will be clear from the discussion in the next subsection, there are forces that generate considerable persistence of inequality. Bequests are an obvious mechanism for inequalities to be transmitted from one generation to the next. Different qualities of schooling for the rich and the poor might be another. For now, simply note that a complete analysis of economic policy must therefore address the efficient allocation of resources both at a point in time and through time, and consider both intragenerational and intergenerational equity.

Determinants of Distribution

The previous subsection considered a number of measurable variables that contain at least some information on individual welfare. But what actually determines the distribution of these variables? The starting point again is the lifetime utility of an individual. It was already noted that age (position in the life cycle) will affect measured inequality. Differences in work effort will also obviously affect income received; this is immediately evident from the agent's budget constraint. And different consumption-saving decisions will affect the individual's lifetime wealth profile; again, this is easily understood by thinking about the agent's budget constraint.

The point is simply that, because people have different preferences, they will make different choices when faced with the same opportunities. An impatient person will save less and so have lower wealth over her lifetime. An ascetic will work less and so have lower income and wealth. Even when individuals face the same opportunities, in that sense that they face the same budget constraints, inequalities will emerge.

The analysis gets a little more complex given that agents also face different budget constraints. In reality, people evidently do not all face the same wage. (For that matter, people do not necessarily face the same return on saving.) Wages differ across individuals for many reasons. One is that different individuals have different innate talents. A talented footballer or rock musician may command a very high wage, while an unskilled worker commands a low wage.

A second source of differences in wages is differences in acquired skills and knowledge. Economists refer to such skills as *human capital.* Individuals may differ in their human capital because of the quality of schooling they receive. This includes learning at home: children are more likely to have high human capital if they are born to parents who themselves possess high human capital. Individuals can also invest in the acquisition of human capital as adults. Those who go to college have higher human capital than those who leave school at 16, and those who have post-graduate education have still higher human capital. In practice, differences in human capital are a significant source of inequality.

Differences in human capital therefore arise in part from investment choices made by the individual, and in part from factors beyond the individual's control. The human capital of someone fortunate enough to have attended a good school and to have had involved and educated parents will probably be higher than that of someone who attended a poor school and had parents disinterested in her education. Such differences are essentially beyond the child's control. But the decision to pursue an MBA, or to be trained as a lawyer, accountant, plumber, airline pilot, or doctor, is one that is made by adults in recognition of the fact that it will ultimately lead to higher human capital and higher income.

The fact that some individuals choose to invest in human capital while others do not may reflect differences in preferences (perhaps those who pursue a PhD place little value on leisure), or may be itself be a result of differences in innate talents or in human capital acquired as a child. The *return* to investment in human capital, in other words, differs across individuals, and so different incentives to acquire human capital will give rise to a distribution of human capital across individuals.

Incomes also vary across individuals purely because of luck or chance. A talented footballer born in the US might never discover his skills and so could miss out on the high income he could have earned in Europe. Likewise, there might be Irishmen who could have earned millions of dollars as baseball pitchers in the US, if only they had had the chance to play baseball as children. Similarly, history abounds with examples of artists and musicians who earned little in their lifetimes because their genius was only recognised posthumously. Mozart died in poverty. Mozart's sister never realised her potential because there were few opportunities for women composers and musicians in her time. Conversely, one might easily imagine that the members of U2 would not have been multimillionaires had they been born fifty years earlier, or in a different country.

On a more prosaic level, technological advances reduce the value of certain skills. The advent of the car reduced the value of the human capital of blacksmiths; the advent of the personal computer reduced the value of the human capital of accurate typists; the advent of automated switchboards reduced the value of the human capital of telephone operators, and so on.

The value of human capital thus depends on investment choices and on luck. Other investment choices are also sources of inequality, as are other kinds of luck. Individuals who are talented enough or lucky enough to invest well in the stock market will enjoy higher incomes than those who invested poorly and/or were unlucky. To make matters more complicated still, different attitudes towards risk play a role as well. One might expect to see greater inequality among people who are more willing to take risks.

Finally, and very significantly, the distribution of income and wealth naturally depends upon inheritance. Individuals born of wealthy parents will have higher income and wealth than individuals born of poor parents. In sum, measured inequality depends upon, at least: position in the life cycle, work effort, innate talent, human capital, investment decisions, inheritance, and luck. Once policymakers enter the picture, of course, government actions (taxes, transfers, etc.) also influence the degree of inequality.

Desired Inequality

It is now necessary to enter the realm of value judgements about inequality. The discussion in the previous subsection provides a framework that allows an individual to assess his or her personal views on inequality. Most people would probably agree that it is reasonable to accept the differences in income, consumption, or wealth, that arise from different consumption-leisure or consumption-saving choices. Even the most avid egalitarian would be likely to accept that inequalities may justifiably arise from people's choices. But beyond that point, opinions certainly differ.

The reader can ask herself or himself the relevant questions: should inequalities arise because of inherited wealth? because of inherited human capital? because of acquired human capital? because of talent? because of luck? Ideally, the policies pursued by Irish policymakers should somehow reflect the views of all individuals in the economy on such questions. Of course, people's views on such issues are likely to be coloured by where in the distribution they find themselves.

Philosophers, economists and others have developed some approaches to inequality that can help to clarify one's thinking on these matters. Some have also presented strong arguments for egalitarianism. This section briefly considers some such arguments. As is often the case in this chapter, however, there is a huge literature to which the current discussion does not do justice.

The first and simplest argument for equality is simple *utilitarianism*. This argument rests on interpersonal utility comparisons and starts from the strong assumption that all individuals have identical utility functions (that is, identical capacity for the enjoyment of goods and services, or, in terms of the earlier equation, identical x_i^j variables). It is assumed also that the utility functions exhibit diminishing marginal utility, and that the goal of policymakers is to maximise total welfare. Then the optimal distribution of output will be egalitarian. Utilitarianism is subject to many objections, though. In particular, once the assumption of identical utility functions is relaxed, this criterion is likely to dictate redistributions that exacerbate inequalities of welfare. (If average and marginal utilities are positively correlated, then, under this approach, resources will be taken from the less well-off and transferred to the better-off.)

A second simple argument for equality, due to Lerner, runs as follows.[7] Suppose there is an ideal, but unknown, distribution of income corresponding to the ideal level of inequality. Then total equality of income will minimise the maximum possible arithmetic divergence from this ideal; similarly, beginning from a position of inequality, measures to decrease inequality are more likely to move the distribution closer to the ideal than away from it.

A number of influential arguments for equality are based on the idea that distribution should be determined according to principles that individuals would choose in an 'original position'; that is, prior to their being randomly allocated a place in society. The idea here is to create a thought-experiment that allows people to think about inequality in a disinterested manner.

One such argument is based on an assumption of risk-aversion: the idea that people dislike uncertainty. Consider the situation where, in the original position, an individual has to choose among possible worlds that differ in the distribution of utility across individuals. Suppose, however, that in each possible society the average level of utility is equal. If the individual is risk-averse, then she will prefer a distribution where the utility of all individuals is equalised.

A closely-related argument is that of Rawls' *Difference Principle*.[8] Rawls suggests that individuals in the original position would adopt a maximin criterion, whereby the optimal social state is one in which the welfare (or income) of the worst-off individual is maximised. In the terms of the previous paragraph, this amounts to assuming that individuals are infinitely risk-averse: the Rawlsian thought-experiment effectively removes the restriction that expected utility is constant in all states of the world. For example, the Rawlsian principle would suggest that a social state where all individuals received an income of IR£100,000 would be preferred to a state where one individual received IR£99,999 and everyone else received IR£110,000.

Individuals may also have a preference for some redistribution. In terms of the earlier discussion, the overall distribution of income might directly affect individual welfare (that is, it could be one of the X_i variables). This might be for altruistic reasons or for pragmatic reasons: marked inequalities often generate social tensions that have high costs. Inequalities between readily identifiable social groups may be particularly likely to lead to social unrest; examples of this might be Northern Ireland, South Africa, and, more generally, workers' revolutions and general strikes. In such cases the affluent may have a definite interest in redistribution.

Finally, there is simply the argument that some redistribution may be ethically desirable. Earlier, it was noted that it is difficult to discuss distribution in terms of welfare, because that requires interpersonal comparisons of utility. But inequalities of income, wealth, or consumption surely miss important individual determinants of welfare (x_i variables). For example, individuals who are disadvantaged – say, handicapped persons, or the elderly – may require more income to bring them to the same level of welfare as those who are not. It can then be argued that society should seek to help such individuals and compensate them for this disadvantage, rather than hinder them. In its most direct form, this is Marx's proposal in *A Critique of the Gotha Programme:* 'from each according to his ability, to each according to his needs'.

Measurement of needs obviously poses problems, but it is actually likely that there is some consensus on such matters. Sen has proposed a needs-based system of distribution in which he suggests the thought-experiment of deciding whether one would prefer to be individual A (say a healthy person) with a given income or individual B (a handicapped person) with the same income, in order to make a judgement on relative needs.[9]

In opposition to such arguments, Nozick argues that distribution at any time should depend upon historical factors that determine individuals' entitlements, and that it is therefore invalid to consider distribution at a point of time, independent of these entitlements. The approach of welfare economists, he argues, is inadequate because it cannot take account of such factors.[10] While Nozick is correct to point out that static measures of distribution are highly imperfect, it is not true that the economic approach is inherently static, as should be abundantly clear from the preceding discussions. The significant question is the one that has already been asked: which historical factors should be viewed as legitimate sources of inequality?

If any or all of the preceding arguments for equality is perceived to have merit, then there is no particular reason to expect that the socially desirable level of inequality will be given by market forces. Policymakers then should take account of distributional goals in the formulation of policy.

There are few constraints in principle upon the ability of policymakers to achieve redistributions by means of taxes and transfers. But redistribution has costs. If policymakers wish to redistribute resources (either at a point in time or intertemporally), then they will have to levy taxes and pay out subsidies. Taxes and subsidies alter behaviour, however – they are *distortionary*. Redistributions will thus in general cause some loss of efficiency.

The design of policies to achieve distributive goals must therefore recognise that taxes and transfers alter work incentives. The disincentive effects of income taxation are actually unclear, since income and substitution effects have opposite effects. If individuals wish to maintain a given standard of living, then increased marginal tax rates could increase work input. The importance of financial incentives is also lessened by the fact that well-paid jobs tend to be more pleasant, and yield greater job satisfaction, than low-paid work. The available evidence does not suggest that moderate levels of taxation have strong incentive effects on work effort. Higher tax rates may also encourage tax avoidance and tax evasion, though (see Chapter 5). The relevance of this is borne out by the undoubted importance of the underground economy in Ireland.

4   EVALUATING PUBLIC POLICY

Sections 2 and 3 argued that policy should be directed both toward efficiency and distributional goals. Popular discussion of policy aims is of course not usually cast in the rather abstract language of those sections. The ultimate aim of this section is to consider how the analysis so far might be used to shed light on more familiar goals, and how the success or failure of policy can be evaluated.

Proximate Policy Objectives
The starting-point here is the first two assumptions made in Section 2: policymakers seek to maximise social welfare, and social welfare depends upon the welfare of individuals. To turn this into a well-defined policy aim, it is necessary to be more precise about how social and individual welfare are related. That is, it is necessary to aggregate the welfare of individuals.

One method of aggregation is the formulation of *social welfare functions.* The idea is that aggregate social welfare can be described by a single number. The simplest form of social welfare function expresses aggregate welfare as a function of the welfare (utility) of all the different individuals in society. The idea is conceptually straightforward and provides an extremely useful way of thinking about the policymaker's problem. Social preferences over distribution can be built directly into the form of the function, and policies can be judged by whether or not they increase the value of the function.

One way of making the social welfare function more operational is to consider the aggregation problem in stages. Specifically, the idea is the following: social welfare is taken to depend upon a few target variables, which themselves represent aggregate indices of individual welfare. The usefulness of this approach obviously depends upon the selection of appropriate aggregates. Ideally, the aggregates chosen should possess a number of characteristics: they should be well-defined, measurable, and related to individual welfare; and they should offer a means of evaluating policies and assessing their overall impact on welfare.

One possibility is to choose as aggregates groups of individuals with identifiable characteristics, and then consider social welfare as a function of the welfare of those groups. In practice government policies often take this form, and in many contexts this seems sensible: resources might be devoted to provisions for the handicapped, for example. This method of aggregation might be particularly appropriate if distributional considerations were at the forefront of government policy.

The approach also has disadvantages. It leaves the question of measurement of group welfare unanswered; there are no obvious criteria for the selection of groups; and it is necessary to pay particular attention to the influence of particular groups upon policy. For these reasons, this is not the method of aggregation adopted here. None the less, policies aimed at different groups are still of interest, for they can be interpreted as policy instruments that may be used in the pursuit of other objectives. The discussion in Chapters 11 and 12 can be interpreted in such terms.

The aggregation utilised here is instead that of selecting *proximate objectives* of economic policy. These are aims that embody distinct aspects of economic policy decisions. While there is some arbitrariness in the choice of proximate objectives, the discussion so far suggests that the aims should be chosen to reflect efficiency, intragenerational equity, and intergenerational equity. As noted earlier, a secondary aim is to discuss goals that receive public attention. Specifically, the discussion here focuses on the familiar macroeconomic goals of full employment and growth. Full employment is useful as an indicator of overall efficiency. Growth captures intertemporal trade-offs. In addition, for the reasons set out earlier, an goal of equity should be explicitly included.

To implement this approach, measures of full employment, growth and equality must be selected. Policymakers are presumed to have some desired (ideal) value of each of these measures, derived in some manner from individual preferences. (Policymakers are assumed to recognise and respect resource constraints in formulating these ideals; they do not hope for infinite growth, for example.) The aim of policy is then to get as close as possible to these ideal values. This entails a comparison of the ideal with the outcome that would occur in the absence of intervention – that is, in a free-market economy possessing the distortions noted in Section 2.

Other goals could certainly be included in the objective function, and one objective is perhaps particularly notable by its absence. Full employment and growth are two traditional aims of macroeconomic policy. The other standard aim of macroeconomic policy is low inflation. People care about the level of inflation – in the earlier formulation, the inflation rate is an X_i variable. Policies towards inflation are also influenced by questions of both efficiency and distribution. Discussion of inflation is deferred until Chapter 3, however.

Before proceeding, one final difficulty with the use of social welfare functions should be noted. In keeping with economists' preferences for minimising value judgements, welfare economists were reluctant to assume that utility was measurable and that comparisons of utility across different individuals were possible. In the development of welfare economics, much attention was therefore given to the problem of formulating social welfare functions without making such assumptions. Ideally, one might wish to find a social welfare function that aggregates everybody's preferences over different possible social states.

Unfortunately, a very important result in social choice theory – Arrow's *impossibility theorem* – indicates that there is no generally applicable way of deriving such a 'social preference ordering', if certain fairly weak assumptions are to be satisfied.[11] Arrow's result effectively implies that the use of social welfare functions requires interpersonal utility comparisons. To proceed in welfare economics, the real issue is then not whether interpersonal comparisons should be made, but how.

The main import of the theorem here is as follows. The preferences of individuals in society are partially revealed by their market transactions. Market mechanisms, however, do not permit preferences to be articulated on all facets of economic policy. Arrow's theorem indicates that, unfortunately, it is difficult to use a consistent notion of social preferences. There is some difficulty in speaking of, say, a social preference for 3 per cent economic growth. With some apology, the chapter does not address these issues; to do so would require an extensive survey of the theory of social choice. Instead, it is taken as given that social preferences on certain matters can be articulated, albeit imperfectly, through the political process.

Full employment and growth are discussed in turn. For each objective, the foregoing theory of efficiency and distribution provides guidance for policy. Measurement of inequality and arguments for reducing inequality were already discussed in detail in Section 3, and so are not discussed in this section.

Full Employment
Many policies directed towards efficiency will be microeconomic in nature, since the emphasis of such policies is the correction of distortions in individual markets. There are thus no simple measures of the extent to which efficiency is being achieved in practice; a case-by-case analysis of all interventions is required. There are, however, useful indicators of efficiency for the economy as a whole. In particular, the definition of productive efficiency suggests that there are inefficiencies present when economic resources are lying idle. Hence a necessary – though far from sufficient – condition for efficiency would appear to be that all economic resources should be in use.

Given this, it is natural to consider the extent to which resources are employed as one indicator of economic efficiency. It is possible to consider the utilisation of various resources; for example, the level of capacity utilisation is an indicator of the efficient use of the economy's stock of capital. The discussion here focuses only on the employment of labour in the economy.

Many people might feel that full employment does not require explicit justification as a policy objective: it may seem obvious that unemployment is undesirable and inefficient. But matters are actually not quite so simple. First, as was noted in Section 3, leisure is a desired commodity. In the labour market, workers exchange leisure for the ability to purchase other goods and services that they want. Efficiency therefore dictates that individuals should be able to work up to the point where the value of additional leisure equals the value (in terms of other commodities) of additional work. If everyone can do so, then all unemployment is voluntary and does not signal inefficiency.

Conversely, if some individuals would like to work at the going wage, but are unable to do so (the supply of labour then exceeds the demand for labour at the given wage), then they are said to be *involuntarily unemployed*. Involuntary unemployment is the concept that ideally should be captured by an unemployment measure. Unfortunately, it is not clear to what extent available measures capture this notion. Also, note that a concentration on employment at a point in time suppresses much information about employment and unemployment statistics over time. A more detailed and accurate evaluation of the data requires consideration of quit rates, lay-off rates, unemployment duration and labour force turnover (see Chapter 8).

As an aside, some economists argue that the notion of involuntary unemployment is not very meaningful. They claim that an unemployed person can always find some kind of job – for example, an unemployed neurosurgeon could get a job as a janitor. In fact, it is not completely obvious that she could: employers are reluctant to hire applicants whom they perceive as overqualified and so likely to quit as soon as a better opportunity comes along.

Those members of the population in work or actively seeking work are called the *labour force*. Those in work are *employed;* those out of work and seeking work are *unemployed*. The unemployment rate is defined as the number of unemployed people divided by the number in the labour force. A problem is that some individuals may withdraw from the labour force in times of recession. These are referred to as *discouraged workers* (see Chapter 8). The tradition of emigration from Ireland reinforces this problem: Irish labour is internationally mobile and so people unable to find jobs in Ireland may seek work overseas. Note also that some individuals engaged in productive activity are not registered as employed; the obvious example is that of women and men doing unpaid housework.

Since labour is not homogeneous, aggregate unemployment measures may conceal marked divergences in unemployment rates for different sectors of the economy. This in turn makes the pursuit of full employment more difficult, for certain types of labour may be in excess demand while others are in excess supply. That is, there may be overemployment and unemployment in certain sub-markets even if aggregate measures indicate relatively low unemployment. The unemployment rate generally differs markedly across regions, but this is not revealed by aggregate unemployment measures.

Another problem arises because inefficiencies may take the form of *underemployment* rather than unemployment. For example, if an individual has a job, but would like to work more hours and is unable to do so, then this is inefficient underemployment that will not find its way into official measures. A redistribution of a fixed quantity of work across the labour force could have marked differences in measured unemployment.

The 'ideal' level of unemployment is often described as *full employment,* although the terminology may be misleading because that term is also used to describe the long-run (or *natural rate*) level of employment. There is no necessary presumption that the long-run level of unemployment is efficient. Full employment does not mean zero unemployment, for that would imply a static economy with no labour force turnover. There will always be some unemployment associated with job search, turnover, and entry and exit from the labour force. This is known as *frictional unemployment*. Some frictional unemployment is necessary for the efficient functioning of the economy, and the amount of frictional unemployment is not necessarily constant over time. It depends, for example, upon the mechanisms which exist for matching supply and demand (employment agencies, etc.) as well as the generosity of unemployment benefits.

The extent of frictional unemployment also depends upon the growth rate of the economy. Increased economic growth will in general require increased labour mobility and hence higher labour turnover. Frictional unemployment will therefore tend to increase if the economy grows more rapidly, implying that the full employment rate of unemployment will be higher. If growth is accompanied by increasing specialisation and an increase in the size of firms, this effect may be exacerbated by a decrease in loyalty (on the part of both firms and workers) and hence increased quit rates and lay-offs. The main point, though, is that those who are frictionally unemployed should probably not be viewed as involuntarily unemployed.

Workers may lose their jobs because of changes in technology or changes in demand for the output they produce. Section 3 noted that technological changes can significantly affect the value of certain forms of human capital. Workers who possess relatively specialised skills will evidently be hard hit if technological advance renders those skills obsolete. The resulting loss of jobs gives rise to *structural unemployment.* Unlike the frictionally unemployed, structurally unemployed workers are frequently out of work for long periods – months or even years.

Active government intervention may be justified if there is involuntary unemployment and if government policies can be used to eliminate it. There are two distinct types of inefficiency. First, the long-run level of employment need not be efficient. Second, short-run fluctuations in the economy (the business cycle) may result in inefficient short-run variation in employment.

There are many reasons to believe that the long-run equilibrium level of unemployment need not be efficient. First, firms and workers expend time and effort searching for each other. When a worker is successfully matched with a firm, both the firm and the worker benefit. Thus the search efforts of both the worker and the firm generate external benefits for the other (and perhaps also external costs and benefits to other workers and firms). Externalities create a presumption of inefficiency. Unfortunately, there are many externalities – both positive and negative – associated with the search process, so it is difficult to judge with confidence whether they result in too much or too little unemployment.

Efficiency wage theories also suggest that the long-run level of unemployment may be inefficient. The idea of these theories is that there is a positive relationship between wages and productivity. If a firm pays its workers a higher wage, this may cause those workers to be more motivated, harder working, more loyal and less likely to quit the firm. In order to obtain these benefits, firms may pay a wage higher than would be consistent with equilibrium in the labour market. Some workers may then be unable to find jobs and will be involuntarily unemployed. Finally, imperfect competition in the markets for goods, implying that firms produce less than the socially desirable level of output, shows up as unemployment or underemployment in the labour market. Such distortions suggest that there are many microeconomic interventions that might be implemented to correct these and other market failures (see Chapters 8 and 10).

The argument that policymakers should intervene to stabilise the economy in the short run is based on the proposition that market failures result in large amounts of involuntary unemployment. Most notably, if prices are *sticky*, rather than perfectly flexible, then markets will no longer allocate resources efficiently and there may be room for welfare-improving macroeconomic policies. For many years, the consensus among macroeconomists was that wage- and price-stickiness were prevalent, so that such *Keynesian or cyclical unemployment* was widespread. Hence it was often argued that active *demand management* policies could be profitably used to achieve full employment. Since Ireland is a small open economy, though, the ability of Irish policymakers to bring about full employment by means of aggregate demand management is extremely limited (see Chapter 6).

Some economists *(New Classicals)* deny the existence of Keynesian unemployment, and argue instead that prices are flexible and markets do in general work efficiently. On this reasoning, unemployment is voluntary, arising solely because individuals value leisure, and hence policymakers should not intervene to seek full employment. The branch of new classical economics known as *real business cycle theory* – at least in its purest incarnation – asserts that economic fluctuations are simply the efficient response of the economy to real shocks, such as improvements in technology. New classical economists argue that, at most, the economy can only be moved from full employment transiently, as a result of unanticipated monetary shocks. Under these arguments, policymakers should not intervene to ensure full employment, cannot do so successfully anyway, and are likely to make matters worse if they try. While space precludes detailed assessment of these theories, New Classical theory does not appear to provide a good explanation of short-run variation in employment (see Chapter 6).

Recent research in the Keynesian tradition provides better explanations of price and wage rigidities, which were simply assumed in earlier Keynesian work. *New Keynesian* economics has also shown that *coordination failures* may arise from imperfect competition and/or search externalities.[12] When such imperfections are present, economies may get stuck at inefficient levels of output and employment. Theories of *hysteresis,* meanwhile, argue that unemployment is particularly costly and likely to persist because unemployed workers may lose skills and become less productive. These and other theories provide increased support for the view that active government policies directed at full employment can be justified on efficiency grounds (see Chapter 8).

Unemployment has distributional consequences also. When the economy goes into recession, most workers retain their jobs and so are not directly affected by the downturn. (Real wages do not appear to fall much in recessions, so workers are not hurt in terms of pay, though they may of course feel less secure about their futures.) But those who are laid off in recessions suffer substantial costs. Thus, in practice, the costs of recessions appear to be borne disproportionately by the unemployed. There are also non-economic costs of unemployment that exacerbate this problem: employment can carry with it job satisfaction and a sense of contributing to society, while unemployment may bring low self-esteem and low social standing. Consequently, promoting full employment is likely to be consistent with reducing inequality.

Even among the unemployed, the burden of unemployment is spread unequally. Much measured unemployment is accounted for by the long-term unemployed – that is, those who, once unemployed, remain out of work for long periods. In practice, the distributional impact of unemployment is probably one of the most important reasons for the pursuit of full employment.

Economic Growth
As with full employment, the desirability of economic growth is apparently taken as self-evident by many commentators. But it is not at all clear that increased growth should in fact be pursued by policymakers. The critical feature of growth is that it embodies a choice or trade-off between consumption in the present and consumption in the future. Decreased consumption today permits increased consumption at some future date, and *vice versa.*

When thinking about the allocation of an economy's resources over time, the question is thus: how much of society's output should be consumed and how much should be saved for purposes of future consumption? Society's resources are consumed by private individuals and by the government. Choices about saving are likewise made by both individuals and government, and total national saving is the sum of the saving of individuals and of the government. If the government runs a deficit, then, other things equal, total saving is decreased. Thus government policies have a direct effect on saving. Government policies (particularly on taxes) also affect individuals' consumption-saving decisions and so influence national saving through that channel.

In a closed economy, saving finances investment. Investment in turn increases the capital stock, allowing more output to be produced in the future. Low consumption today thus permits higher consumption in the future and *vice versa*. The link between saving and growth is subtle, however. Standard theory (as embodied in, say, the Solow growth model or neoclassical growth model; see Chapter 7) suggests that the long-run rate of growth does not depend upon the rate of saving, although the long-run level of output and consumption per person does depend upon the rate of saving. In other words, a society that chooses to save a larger percentage of its output will, in the long run, enjoy a higher standard of living, but not a permanently higher growth rate. The growth rate of output per person depends primarily on the rate of technical progress. The long run in this case is measured in decades, however. If individuals choose to save more and consume less at some point in time, then the short-run effect of this change will indeed be a higher rate of growth.

In a small open economy, matters are more complicated, because there is no longer a simple link between saving and investment. Irish people can save by holding foreign assets; foreigners can own Irish capital. The rate of capital accumulation in a closed economy depends primarily on the saving rate, but increased saving need not imply increased growth, even in the short run, in an open economy. A corollary is that intergenerational redistribution is possible without necessarily affecting the growth rate. For example, the government can increase taxes today and cut taxes in the future without changing the level of investment. These topics are considered in more detail in Chapter 7.

Economic growth is an increase in the output of the economy. Output, in turn, is the production of goods and services in a given time period. Obviously, changes in population would certainly be expected to influence the extent to which increases in output can be associated with increases in individual welfare. This suggests that changes in output per capita provide the most appropriate measure of economic growth. Yet there are deficiencies of this measure. The fundamental reason for believing that output per capita and economic welfare are related is assumption (iii) from Section 2: economic growth permits increased consumption, and the welfare of individuals depends upon the goods and services that they consume. But recall also that there are other influences on welfare – leisure, and also the $x_i{}^i$ and $X_i{}^i$ variables). If measured economic growth also affects these variables, then economic growth need not imply increasing welfare.

For example, suppose economic growth is brought about by increased labour force participation. The implied decrease in leisure time represents a cost that is neglected by the growth measure. Voluntary participation in the labour market does indicate that the increased real income more than compensates for the decreased leisure, but changes in output do not measure the net gain.

Externalities pose an even more severe problem. Earlier it was noted that consumption and production can give rise to costs and benefits that are not included in measured economic growth. If growth leads to environmental degradation, for example, then the growth rate of output per person does not accurately measure changes in welfare. Perverse associations are even possible: increased medical costs arising from, for example, pollution externalities or work-related accidents would show up as increases in output.

Fortunately, analyses of economic welfare that take account of the value of leisure and of externalities provide some evidence that growth in output is probably fairly closely associated with improvements in welfare. On balance, in other words, the effects of various externalities and of changes in leisure more or less cancel out. Environmental economists are also developing measures of output that take explicit account of environmental externalities and changes in stocks of natural resources.

The next question is how the socially-desired level of growth compares with the free-market level. A number of arguments suggest that free markets may lead to inefficiently low growth. First, there may be important market failures in those markets linking the present and the uncertain future, implying that policymakers should target growth as a proxy for the infeasible task of correcting all the deficiencies of the market. The principal market failures are probably in capital markets and markets for insuring against risk, and it can be argued that the net effect of these is likely to be insufficient growth.

A second argument recalls that technical progress is the key determinant of economic growth. There may be substantial positive externalities associated with technological advance, since the returns to invention and innovation may not always accrue solely to the inventors and innovators. Technological progress is the accumulation of knowledge, and knowledge possesses public good characteristics. As a consequence, there may be insufficient investment, from a social point of view, in research and development, and so the growth rate of the economy may be sub-optimal. Much work on growth theory in the last decade has emphasised such externalities (see Chapter 7). (Some of these theories also suggest that the steady-state growth rate may in fact depend upon the saving rate, implying that there may be long-run arguments for encouraging saving.)

Conversely, an influential body of opinion emphasises the negative externalities associated with growth. It is often argued that economic growth uses up precious natural resources and brings about the degradation of the environment. Such issues have been brought into the European political arena by (for example) the Ecology Party in Britain and the Green Party in Germany.

Although loss of natural resources and damage to the environment are often talked about as if they were the same problem, it is important to distinguish between them. Both history and economic theory give cause for optimism when thinking about the loss of natural resources. When a resource becomes increasingly scarce, its price rises. Higher prices provide incentives for producers to switch to substitute resources and for inventors (research and development teams) to develop alternative technologies that do not require the resource. For example, in the 1970s, there was much concern that the world would run out of oil. But higher oil prices led to a shift to more energy-efficient means of production and less demand for oil. Many – perhaps most – so-called scarce resources have actually been becoming cheaper over time as technological progress has made them less essential (the development of fibre optics greatly reduced the demand for copper, for example).

There is less reason to be sanguine about environmental degradation, however. The problem of scarce natural resources (such as oil or copper) can be handled well by market mechanisms because such goods can be privately owned. But problems of bio-diversity loss, ozone depletion, air pollution, ocean pollution and the like will not in general be handled well by market mechanisms. The reason is that species diversity, the ozone layer, clean air and clean water are all public goods (often global public goods). Freely-operating markets are unlikely to handle such concerns effectively.

Still, it is not correct to conclude that economic growth necessarily harms the environment. The evidence on the links between environmental problems and growth is subtle. Some environmental problems – such as lack of clean water and sanitation – are worse in developing countries and better in developed economies. Other problems – such as accumulation of waste in landfills, or emissions of carbon dioxide (which might cause global warming) are more severe in developed economies than they are in developing economies. Still others – such as air pollution – appear to be worst in middle-income countries: developed economies can and do spend resources on the preservation of the environment. The experience of Eastern Europe illustrates very graphically that there is no obvious simple relationship between pollution and growth.[13]

Perhaps the main lesson is that, although environmental degradation is a real problem that should be a priority for policymakers, it is a problem that should be addressed directly. Limiting growth is an extremely indirect and inefficient approach. As Solow has put it: 'what no-growth would accomplish, it would do by cutting off your fact to spite your nose'.[14]

Now consider growth and distribution. Issues of both intra- and intergenerational equity arise here. In one sense, growth and intragenerational equality are highly complementary. Growth, which implies relatively higher income in the future, may make intragenerational redistributions possible with changes in relative incomes only. Increased equality may be possible without any reductions in anyone's absolute standard of living, so it may be possible for redistribution to occur without violation of the Pareto principle. This is a persuasive argument for economic growth.

The validity of this argument really depends on whether one thinks of the extra income from growth as accruing directly to individuals or to society as a whole. Obviously, if individuals receive the extra income from growth, then redistribution still means that some gain and others lose. The argument that increased growth facilitates redistribution then rests on a presumption that individuals are prepared to accept higher marginal tax rates as their incomes increase. While this is not self-evident, it does seem probable that redistribution is easier when incomes are growing; people are probably more aware of a cut in their living standards than of the fact that their incomes are growing more slowly than they might otherwise be. And, in passing, it might be noted that even if growth does not lead to greater equality, it will still usually imply that the absolute standard of living of the poor will increase.

There is one argument that suggests a trade-off between growth and equality. Saving is necessary to provide funds for the investment in capital that leads to increased future incomes. Further, it is sometimes argued that the marginal propensity to save is higher at higher income levels. If so, increased equality will imply a reduction in investment and hence a reduction in growth. Note, though, that this reasoning merely suggests that some inequality of income is necessary; it has no logical connection to any particular distribution criterion. In particular, the argument does not justify existing inequalities. And recall again that there is no direct link between saving and investment in a small open economy, provided that financial markets operate efficiently. Thus one of the most common justifications for inequality in a capitalist society is probably wholly inapplicable in Ireland. Available evidence, moreover, does not indicate a positive correlation between inequality and growth.

Turning now to growth and intergenerational equity, note that individuals in society do make intertemporal choices. People decide upon their present level of consumption and the amount they wish to save for future consumption. In a well-functioning (closed) economy these saving decisions would generate the right amount of investment, at least from the point of view of the current generation. It would then not be appropriate for policymakers to intervene and affect the rate of growth, as far as these individuals were concerned.

If individuals lived forever, there would only be one generation to worry about. Since they do not, it is necessary to think about how the actions of current generations affect those who will be alive in the future. Because an individual's welfare may depend in part upon the welfare of her children (and, by implication, grandchildren, great-grandchildren, etc.), the interests of future generations are not completely excluded when decisions are made in the present. Indeed, if altruistic links between generations were strong enough, individuals might effectively behave as if they lived forever. There would then be no immediate reason to conclude that intervention to encourage or discourage growth is socially desirable. The reality, however, is that different generations almost certainly have different interests. If current generations save more and consume less, that will increase the capital stock and hence the production possibilities of future generations. If current generations destroy the ozone layer and cut down the rainforests, that reduces the welfare of future generations. As discussed earlier, policymakers must thus decide how to weight the interests of future generations as against the current generation.

Finally, the expectation of continued technical progress and thus continued growth, outside the influence of Irish policy, raises the provocative question of why current Irish consumption should be limited to promote the interests of future generations. The appropriate redistribution may be from future generations to the present. 'Why should we poor folk make any sacrifices for those who will in any case live in luxury in the future?'[15]

5 CONCLUSIONS

Coherent economic policymaking requires that policies be directed towards the efficient allocation of resources at a point in time and through time, and also toward both inter- and intragenerational distribution. This chapter has presented an approach to policymaking that emphasises such concerns. Throughout the analysis, the value judgements and institutional assumptions needed for the arguments were made as explicit as possible, and some attempt was made to indicate the weaknesses and deficiencies of the assumptions. Whether or not the violation of these assumptions in real economies leads to substantive differences in the conclusions drawn is partly an empirical matter, and partly a matter of individual judgement.

Ideally, policymakers should have an understanding of the ultimate aims of policy, of the relative social evaluation of these aims, and of the ways in which different policies interact and limit the policy decisions that can be made. Further, good policy decisions obviously require knowledge of the policy instruments that exist and the ways in which they can be used to achieve these aims. It is important to remember that, in Ireland, the effects of almost all policy instruments are influenced by the smallness and openness of the economy. The relevance of this for Irish economic policy will become even more apparent in subsequent chapters.

A theme of the chapter is that Pareto-efficiency does not provide a sufficient basis for economic policy analysis. It is desirable also to have well-defined distributional aims. Policies should be directed both at efficiency and at distribution; policies which are designed to achieve efficiency alone will not be sufficient to achieve the aims of policymakers. If it were the case that the objectives discussed here could all be pursued independently of one another, then the existence of different objectives would not pose major difficulties for the design of economic policy. Unfortunately, the existence of trade-offs between objectives implies that policy aims do conflict.

An implication of policy trade-offs is that it is almost certainly undesirable to pursue one aim irrespective of the costs in terms of other objectives. For example, it is evident that it would not be optimal to direct all economic policy and economic resources to faster growth. This observation applies as much to the aim of economic efficiency as any other. If productive efficiency can only be achieved at a cost in terms of divergences from socially-desired redistributions, then complete productive efficiency is unlikely to be optimal. By implication, even a system of perfectly competitive markets will be sub-optimal. Further, it may be the case that policies designed to correct market failures will have costs in terms of other objectives. The lesson of all this is that particular policies should be assessed in terms of their implications for all objectives, and no objective should be given absolute priority.

A corollary is that it is inappropriate to criticise a particular aim of policy on the grounds that it would be undesirable to exclude other considerations in practice. For example, economic efficiency should not be dismissed as an aim of policy because it implies no concern with distribution; similarly, increased economic equality should not be argued to be undesirable simply because it may generate some inefficiency. This point is obvious, yet must be made because it is so often neglected in popular discussions of policy.

It is also worth noting that difficulties of measurement do not provide a good reason for dismissing an objective; it may be possible to make progress towards a policy gain even when the gains cannot be measured precisely. Equally, the fact that policy measures are sometimes crude and ineffective in practice does not imply that the aims of policy have been incorrectly selected; rather, failures of policies in practice are a source of information for the design of better policy in the future.

Finally, it should be emphasised again that there are substantial problems in the articulation of social preferences over different objectives. But, while the derivation of social preferences is not straightforward, political mechanisms do exist, however imperfect they may be, to allow individuals to express such preferences. There is no particular reason why such opinions should be the same as those revealed in economic markets, and there is no reason to dismiss economic preferences voiced through the political process.

All individuals are entitled to their own value judgements on the objectives considered here, and to express their preferences through all available mechanisms. This chapter has sought to clarify some of the strengths and weaknesses of various arguments for different objectives. But, ultimately, the appropriate choice of policy depends upon the value judgements of individuals in society.

Endnotes

1 For this argument, see M. Friedman, *Capitalism and Freedom*, University of Chicago Press, London 1975, and F. Hayek, *The Road to Serfdom*, University of Chicago Press, Chicago 1944. See A. Okun, *Equality and Efficiency: The Big Trade-Off*, Brookings Institution, Washington DC 1975, for a discussion.
2 See R. Lipsey and K. Lancaster, 'The General Theory of Second Best', *Review of Economic Studies*, October 1956.
3 See A. Sen, 'Personal Utilities and Public Judgements: or What's Wrong with Welfare Economics?', *Economic Journal*, 89, 1979.
4 For useful discussions, see C. Plott, 'Psychology and Economics', in J. Eatwell, M. Milgate and P. Newman (editors), *The New Palgrave: A Dictionary of Economics*, Macmillan, London 1987; and M. Machina, 'Choice Under Uncertainty', *Journal of Economic Perspectives*, Summer 1987; and the references cited in these articles. This research has focused in particular on criticisms of the economic approach to decision-making in the presence of uncertainty.
5 J. Galbraith, *The Affluent Society*, Penguin Books, Harmondsworth 1962. For some different critical perspectives on the economic theory of the consumer, see also: T. Scitovsky, *The Joyless Economy*, Oxford University Press, Oxford 1976; A. Sen, 'Rational Fools: A Critique of the Behavioural Foundations of Economic Theory', in H. Harris (editor), *Scientific Models and Man*, Oxford University Publications, Oxford 1978; and J. Robinson, *Economic Philosophy*, Penguin Books, Harmondsworth 1978.

6 See A. Atkinson, *The Economics of Inequality* (second edition), Clarendon Press, Oxford 1983, Chapter 3. This book provides a very thorough analysis of many economic aspects of equality, including detailed statistical evidence for Britain. It also contains an extensive set of references. See also A. Sen, *On Economic Inequality,* Clarendon Press, Oxford 1973, Chapter 2.

7 This type of 'ignorance' argument was first propounded by Lerner; see A. Lerner, *The Economics of Control,* New York 1944.

8 See J. Rawls, *A Theory of Justice,* Harvard University Press, Cambridge MA 1971. This interpretation of Rawls is somewhat simplified, and does not exactly characterise the Rawlsian thought-experiment. Note that Rawls does not actually present his arguments in terms of utility, but rather in terms of access to social primary goods.

9 See Sen, *On Economic Inequality,* op. cit.

10 R. Nozick, *Anarchy, State and Utopia,* Basic Books, New York 1974.

11 See K. Arrow, *Social Choice and Individual Values,* Wiley, New York 1951.

12 See R. Cooper and A. John, 'Coordinating Coordination Failures in Keynesian Models', *Quarterly Journal of Economics,* August 1988.

13 See World Bank, *World Development Report 1992: Development and the Environment,* Oxford University Press, Oxford 1992. A. John and R. Pecchenino, 'An Overlapping Generations Model of Growth and the Environment,' *Economic Journal,* November 1994, presents a theoretical model consistent with these findings.

14 R. Solow, 'Is the End of the World at Hand?', *Challenge,* 1973, reprinted in E. Mansfield (editor), *Principles of Macroeconomics: Readings, Issues, and Cases,* Norton, New York 1974.

15 Solow, *op. cit.,* p.179.

CHAPTER 3

Secondary Policy Objectives

Dermot McAleese*

Politicians and the media frequently advert to price stability and the balance of payments in such a way as to suggest that these factors are key components of economic welfare. Yet here they are being discussed as secondary policy objectives (i.e. not as ends in themselves). The significance of these secondary objectives, however, is that their attainment may be crucial to the achievement of the primary objectives. In this light the importance accorded them is understandable.

This chapter begins with a discussion of inflation. It is defined as a sustained increase in the general price level. The determinants of inflation are analysed, distinguishing between the proximate causes (excessive increase in money supply or a slack exchange rate regime) and the ultimate causes (what makes governments acquiesce in a particular monetary or exchange rate policy). The adverse economic effects of inflation are surveyed. They arise chiefly, but not exclusively, because of the unpredictability of inflation and the uncertainty which is thereby created in economic transactions. Note is also taken of the adverse effects on output and employment of policies designed to eradicate inflation. Inflation and deflation both bring problems – and both can be avoided only by maintaining price stability.

The balance of payments is analysed in the second section. The economic significance of its various subheadings is evaluated. The balance of payments always balances – in the same sense as saving 'always' equals investment – but it may not balance in a manner conducive to growth and free trade. The distinction between current and capital account transactions is important in balance of payments analysis. The reason for concern about the balance of payments is that a smoothly functioning foreign payments system is a necessary precondition for the orderly and liberal exchange of goods, services and factors of production between countries. International trade and factor movements, in turn, exert a favourable impact on growth, employment, efficiency and choice.

---

*   The author would like to thank Fiona Hayes and John O'Hagan for helpful comments and
    Patricia Dowling for research assistance.

1 INFLATION

What is Inflation?

Inflation is a rise in the cost of living resulting from a *persistent* rise in the *general* level of *money* prices.[1] It is defined by reference to the total money price of a particular *fixed* combination of consumer goods (sometimes called a basket of goods). Three factors affect the accuracy of the figures. First, the number of goods in the sample basket is an incomplete inventory of the economy's goods *(composition bias)*. Also, new products can contribute to welfare in ways that are often not fully incorporated in measured price indices. Second, there may be changes in the quality of goods which are not accurately incorporated in the price index *(quality bias)*. Third, no account is taken of the fact that people may make substitutions from high-priced goods to lower-priced goods *(substitution bias)*. That is, the composition of the average consumer's basket of goods and services changes with each change in relative prices. A doubling in the price of potatoes, for example, would raise the Irish Consumer Price Index (CPI) by nearly one percentage point (potatoes carry a weight of 0.78 per cent) but this takes no account of availability of close substitutes such as rice and farinaceous foods. As time goes by, people switch their buying to products which have increased less in price: but the base weights (the CPI is a Laspeyres index) take insufficient account of this switch.[2]

The precise empirical importance of these various sources of measurement bias is not known. Studies of the consumer price index in the US and Canada suggest a total measurement bias of between 0.5 and 1.0 percentage point each year.[3] Although this bias may seem reasonably small, one cannot be certain that the degree of bias is as low in other countries. In any case, even a bias of +/- 1 per cent is enormous with an inflation rate of, say, 2 per cent. These results suggest that policy should target an inflation rate in excess of zero – in practice most countries aim for a rate of 0 to 2 per cent.

Measures of inflation, therefore, are not quite as straightforward as they might appear. The consumer price index is an extremely sensitive index from a political point of view.[4] The basket of goods and services on which it is based represents an average pattern of spending. This may not be a good representation of the spending patterns of each individual section of the community. Thus the spending pattern of a senior executive will differ significantly from that of an unemployed social welfare dependant. The poorer person's consumption will contain a higher proportion of basic necessities than the executive's. In a time of high inflation, most prices will rise more or less proportionately and the biases arising from these different consumption patterns may not prove too distortionary. Nevertheless, a common complaint from the public about the consumer price index is that it does not match their own experience.

What Causes Inflation?

Inflation occurs when the growth of the money supply persistently exceeds the growth of real output. If each of us awoke today with twice as much money as yesterday, we would spend some of the extra money on goods and services to celebrate our good fortune. In technical terms, we would reduce the excessive proportion of our wealth held as money. The demand for goods would rise. Prices – and wages – would be 'driven' or 'bid' up. Since spending does not reduce the *total* holding of money but merely transfers money from one person to another, nominal money stock remains at twice its original level. As prices rise, however, the real purchasing power of that money declines. Eventually equilibrium is reached when prices and income in money terms are about twice as high as they were, because only then would we want to hold that doubled amount of money. This explains why inflation cannot continue without a sustained increase in the money stock, and why continued excessive increases in the money stock are invariably followed by inflation. But how and why does the money stock increase so rapidly?

The issue has been debated for many years. Inflation can happen if the monetary authorities fail to control the growth of the money supply. Excessive credit expansion due to deregulation and loss of restraint on financial institutions fuelled British inflation in the late 1980s, notwithstanding that country's sound fiscal policies. Hence emphasis should be placed on having an efficient and independent central bank with clear anti-inflation objectives.

Another cause of inflation is government budget deficits financed by monetary expansion. But what causes the government (i) to run budget deficits and (ii) to finance them by monetary means? Some argue that governments find it easier politically to print money or to borrow abroad than to levy extra taxes in order to finance increased public sector spending. Another explanation is that the inflation which follows excessive government spending eases the financing constraint by enabling the government to increase the tax burden without explicit tax increases – by the simple expedient of not indexing income tax bands to the inflation rate. Others argue that the reasons are more deep-seated: that governments validate inflation which arises because of inflationary wage demands (caused, for example, by dissatisfaction with the status quo) or because of supply-side shocks (for example, energy price increases). The government chooses to validate inflation because it believes that the short-run costs of not doing so in terms of civil strife, unemployment and disruption are greater than the economic costs of inflation itself (about which more later).

Some further modification of the analysis is required to explain inflation in small open economies (SOEs). These economies, being heavily dependent on trade, are as much exposed to external inflationary pressures as to internal pressures. The extent to which inflation is imported from the rest of the world, then, hinges crucially on the exchange rate regime adopted by the small country. If the exchange rate is *fixed* relative to a weighted average of its major trading partners, inflation will largely depend on what happens in these countries. If they have high inflation, it will be transmitted to the small country; if they have low inflation, the small country will have low inflation. The *inflation-transmission mechanism* operates through a number of avenues. First, through international trade in goods and services – the SOE is a price taker which means that its export and import prices are fixed in foreign currency. If the dollar price of imported oil, raw materials and intermediate goods rises, and the exchange rate is fixed, the domestic price in the small country's currency must also rise. Second, if there is free movement of labour between markets (as is the case between Ireland and the UK), wage trends in the larger country will be followed in the smaller country. If they are not, labour will move towards the market with the higher wage so bidding up the price of labour. The transmission mechanism also works through capital markets. High inflation in the larger country means high nominal interest rates which, if a capital outflow is to be avoided, must be followed by interest rate increases in the small country. A third possible mechanism comes into operation if the higher inflation in the larger country leads to the generation of a balance of payments surplus in the small country. In so far as this results in an increase in the latter's money supply, inflationary pressures are generated. The relevance of this third factor increases to the extent that price adjustment through the international trade mechanism is slow and interest rate adjustment rapid.

This explains why a small open economy with a fixed exchange rate might be expected to import inflation from its major trading partners. A classical example of this process was the conformity between Irish and UK inflation rates under the sterling parity system (see Chapter 6). Canadian prices also followed US prices closely during the period when the exchange rate between the two countries was fixed. But there are many SOEs where the inflation rate is a good deal less, and others where it is considerably greater, than the weighted average of their main trading partners. Switzerland and Austria have experienced lower inflation than their trading partners, while many Latin American countries have in the past inflated much faster than their trade partners. The reason for the difference was that these countries had *flexible exchange rates*. Thus, Switzerland has insulated itself from external inflationary pressure by periodic revaluations of the Swiss franc. By contrast, Latin American countries exacerbated external inflationary pressures by frequent devaluations. In these instances, the causes of inflation must be discussed in the context of exchange rate policy as well as monetary policy. Why is it that a government in one country is able to revalue its way out of inflation while another adds fuel to inflation by devaluation? Again one reverts to considerations beyond the confines of economics, e.g. the public's attitude to inflation, the political stability of the government, the degree of consensus in society and the public's response to adverse shocks to the economic system.

One frequently hears of the *inflationary spiral.* Inflation feeds on itself. Higher prices lead to higher wage demands which cause higher prices which result in even higher wage claims next round, and so on. At the end of the 1980s, at least four countries were experiencing runaway inflation in excess of 1,000 per cent per annum (Argentina, Nicaragua, Peru, Yugoslavia). In 1994, Brazil recorded an inflation rate of over 5,000 per cent and inflation has been growing rampantly in Russia and the Ukraine. Once caught in a spiral it is hard to escape. It is a good reason for staying off the spiral in the first place.

The proximate economic causes of inflation are comparatively easy to analyse. Its ultimate causes are more complex. Nobody believes anymore that inflation is exclusively associated with excess aggregate demand – the prevalence of *stagflation,* i.e. recession combined with inflation, has seen to that. Nor can inflation be associated exclusively with poor countries. High rates of inflation have at various times since the Second World War affected both developed and developing countries.

Inflation and Primary Policy Objectives
Inflation has implications for efficiency, growth and income distribution. The precise dimensions of these implications, however, is a matter of continuing debate. As Dara McCormack of the Central Bank observed:

> It has been said, with some justice, that 'most people think inflation is a bad thing for very bad reasons'. There is no consensus on the matter in the economics profession; some economists seem to suggest that since over time it will tend to be largely anticipated, inflation involves little more than 'changing the unit of account' and has, therefore, negligible economic effects. Others have argued that the layman's intuition is correct, that inflation is indeed a bad thing, and have sought to give cogent reasons as to why this is the case.[5]

In the conclusion of this chapter, McCormack comes down firmly on the side of the anti-inflationists. The World Bank's assessment is also unambiguous:

> Rapid and accelerating inflation undermines allocative efficiency because it increases uncertainty and induces savers to invest in unproductive 'inflation hedges' such as real estate, consumer durables, gems and foreign currency deposits. Some countries have developed complex systems for indexing wages and prices to compensate for inflation, though this is administratively costly and tends to penalise those (mostly poor) people outside the indexation system. Where indexation does not exist, the 'inflation tax' contributes to a growing sense of social and economic injustice.[6]

Even if a debate of sorts exists about whether or not, or to what extent, inflation is damaging to economic 'health', no reputable economist has argued that high inflation is positively beneficial to efficiency and growth.

Modern analysis of the effects of inflation makes a sharp distinction between inflation which is anticipated and that which is unanticipated or which comes as a 'surprise'. The principal welfare costs arise only when inflation is not fully anticipated. These effects would disappear if inflation were to continue at a steady (or otherwise predictable) rate which the public would learn to anticipate, and if institutions adapted fully to this anticipation. Perfectly anticipated inflation is a limiting case. By examining the theoretical assumptions underlying this case, and progressively relaxing them, light is shed on the more fundamental effects of inflation.

Perfectly Anticipated Inflation. Inflation is fully anticipated when each and every transactor correctly forecasts what the rate of inflation turns out to be and can adjust their economic behaviour appropriately to the anticipated inflation. There are thus two main elements involved: first, the formation of correct expectations and, second, the absence of any institutional rigidities which would limit transactors' ability to allow for inflation. The latter would include any degree of official or unofficial price controls, ceilings on interest rates as well as institutional conventions and rigidities such as contracting in fixed nominal amounts (as in most insurance policies). There would have to be, in effect, a fully indexed economy implying, among other things, a comprehensive system of wage and salary indexation, indexing of tax brackets and allowances, taxation of real rather than nominal returns on assets, etc. In brief, all prices for goods and services, including labour services, would have to be perfectly adjustable. This would be an example of what has been called the 'flexprice' economy. In such an economy, when inflation is accurately anticipated there is only one pure welfare cost to inflation and this arises from the nature of money itself.

Cash balances yield an implicit social return by virtue of the convenience they afford in making transactions. Inflation can be regarded as a tax on cash balances: the negative yield on cash balances is equal to the rate of inflation. The higher the rate of inflation, the larger is the negative yield and the opportunity cost of holding cash. Holders of cash balances will, therefore, shift into less liquid and convenient but income-yielding assets. This substitution involves a further loss of efficiency in so far as cash balances, which are virtually costless to produce, are economised on in favour of more frequent transactions in less liquid and intrinsically valuable assets.

The deadweight loss or excess burden of the inflation cost on cash balances, known as the 'shoe-leather cost' of inflation, can be measured (subject, of course, to a daunting list of caveats) as the area of the triangle under a demand for narrow money or currency function. A number of estimates of the magnitude of this cost have been made for the United States. Although lower than the cost of redistribution of income and wealth when inflation is unanticipated, the cost of anticipated inflation was found to be on a par with the welfare cost of the US corporate tax system, even at levels of inflation as low as 5 per cent. Moreover, the welfare cost of inflation was found to increase rapidly with the size of the rate of inflation.[7]

In addition to this pure welfare cost, anticipated inflation will also impose the so-called 'menu cost' of actually changing prices in what have been called 'customer markets', i.e. those markets in which prices are set and, in the normal course of events, kept unchanged for some time, such as labour markets, retail and wholesale trade, pay telephones and parking meters. Obviously, these menu costs are greater the higher the rate of inflation and, at some very high rate, nominal pricing would presumably be abandoned altogether in favour of some alternative indexation agreements.

The welfare costs of anticipated inflation may appear arcane and insignificant. Yet, as mentioned, some studies have suggested that these costs are quantitatively significant relative to other distortions, even at relatively low rates of inflation. Thus, under ideal conditions, impossible to match in practice, there are non-trivial welfare costs associated with even a steady, fully anticipated inflation and these costs increase as the rate of inflation increases.

Accurate Expectations with Institutional Rigidities. In the theoretical long run, it is certainly inconceivable that, in the face of accurately predicted inflation, institutional rigidities based on transactions being conducted on a nominal basis would survive for very long. For such rigidities to survive, 'money illusion' would have to be widespread and there is little evidence of that being the case. However, if inflation were to proceed at, say, 5 per cent per annum over a number of years, this rate would come to be expected without there having to be any radical restructuring of payment habits, financial conventions, contract periods and so on. The reasons for this apparent inertia lie in the nature of most markets, where prices do not fluctuate greatly from day to day. (Foreign exchange and commodity markets are possible exceptions to this rule.) Most markets are what Hicks calls 'fixprice' markets where prices have to be 'made': Okun's 'customer markets' are essentially the same thing.[8]

In such markets, it is easier to 'make' prices if, as Hicks puts it,

> substantial use can be made of precedent: if one cannot at least start the bargaining from some presumption that what has been acceptable before will be acceptable again. When prices in general are fairly stable, this is often rather easy. The particular prices which result from such bargains may not be ideal from the point of view of the economist, but the time and trouble involved in improving them is simply not worth the candle. To be obliged to make them anew, as one is obliged to do so in continuous inflation, involves direct economic loss and (very often) loss of temper as well![9]

Costly information-gathering and research activities are reduced considerably by reliance on such precedents and conventions.

Unanticipated Inflation. Actual experience shows that inflation tends to be extremely variable from year to year and from one period to another. The sharp acceleration in the rate of price increases from the late 1960s to the 1970s could not have been anticipated correctly by extrapolating past experience. Inflation has not proceeded at a steady pace. Rather it has been uneven and sporadic. From this feature springs the most serious welfare losses.

First, uncertainty about the inflation rate undermines the role played by money in economising on transaction costs. Fixed-price orders, leases and other explicit long-term contracts, fixed-time schedules for price changes and the broad general commitment to continuity of offers by suppliers are important ways of assisting forward planning. Uncertainty about the future price level shortens the time horizon of such agreements, thus imposing a welfare loss on society. These losses, though small in any one year, can accumulate over time into a significant aggregate loss. In addition, inflation has a tendency to create shorter-term investment horizons diminishing the attractiveness of long-term commercial investments.[10] Investment in 'inflation hedges' such as property increases at the expense of long-term investment in industry. Thus inflation can have adverse consequences for economic growth. The International Monetary Fund (IMF), in an extensive multi-country study of inflation and growth, found that the evidence supported two main conclusions: (a) low inflation is associated with stronger growth performance and (b) hyperinflation is associated with economic failure.[11] For countries with moderate rates of inflation, statistical analysis is less conclusive. More firmly-based evidence from recent studies indicates that productivity growth falls by between 0.05 to 0.10 percentage points for each additional percentage point of inflation.[12] These results imply quite significant long-term losses for the economy.

Second, uncertainty about future price levels results in a whole range of arbitrary redistributions of income and wealth. A faster than expected inflation rate, for instance, will tend to discriminate against creditors in favour of debtors: to redistribute income among various categories of asset holders from those whose incomes are fixed in nominal money terms or which typically lag behind inflation (pensioners, annuity-holders) to those whose incomes are more easily adjustable to inflation, such as unionised wage earners and owners of capital. Another, perhaps less familiar, redistribution is the probable redistribution of real wealth from the old (who have accumulated assets) to the young who are, in general, net debtors. Most of these redistributions reflect either a complete inability to adjust to a higher rate of inflation or, more likely, a lag in adjustment.

The haphazard nature of the income distribution effects can lead to social unrest and general discontent as people find it increasingly difficult to assess the progress in their real incomes and to predict what their real earning will be in the future. Okun remarked that, 'people are not thought to store the consumer price index in their memory banks'![13] In a period of 1 per cent inflation, people who receive pay increases of 4 per cent recognise clearly that they have gained in real terms. In a world of 13 per cent inflation, those fortunate to receive pay increases of 16 per cent are likely to be much less confident about how they are faring. That loss of information is a genuine subtraction from welfare. Prices cease to fulfil their signalling function as the effects of relative shifts in prices are blurred by the general rise in the price level. A more graphic assessment is given by Keynes (who draws in turn on Lenin):

> There is no subtler, no surer means of overturning the existing basis of society than to debauch the currency.[14]

2 THE BALANCE OF PAYMENTS

What is the Balance of Payments?
The balance of payments is, by definition, a record of all commercial transactions between residents of one country and residents of another. There are a number of ways of classifying these transactions but, for simplicity, only three basic concepts are considered here. First, there is the *balance of trade,* representing the balance between the value of merchandise exports and imports. Second, the *balance on current account* is obtained by adding 'invisible' items such as net tourism receipts, emigrants' remittances, repatriated profits, interest on foreign debt, transportation charges, etc. to the balance of trade. It is customary nowadays to divide invisibles into two groups: services and international transfers. Third, there is the *balance of autonomous transactions* which equals the current account balance plus net long-term capital inflows. Thus if the current account registers a deficit of IR£100m and net long-term capital inflow equals IR£150m, the balance of autonomous transactions is in surplus to the value of IR£50m. In deciding whether a country has a balance of payments 'problem' or not, the balance referred to ought, in most normal circumstances, to be the balance of autonomous transactions or, simply, the *basic balance.*

The remaining items on the balance of payments account include changes in external reserves and short-term capital movements. These are referred to in the literature as *accommodating* items on the grounds that they react passively to changes in the balance of autonomous items. Thus if the country has a deficit on the balance of autonomous payments, equality between supply and demand for foreign exchange can be brought about either by a reduction in the level of external reserves or by short-term foreign borrowings. The change in accommodating transactions is viewed as the direct consequence of the deficit in the balance of autonomous payments.

A country can be said to have a balance of payments *problem* when the basic balance is in deficit (or in surplus) for a sustained period of time in conditions of free trade and 'full' employment. The time dimension is important since a transitory deficit (due to a dock strike or a bad agricultural harvest, for example) presents fewer problems than one which is expected to persist. Free trade conditions must be insisted upon since it is always possible to rectify a deficit by a government decision to limit imports through tariffs or quotas or other administrative measures. Similarly a deficit can always be reduced by policies which restrain the growth of economic activity and the level of employment. Where protection or deflationary policies are used to correct a deficit, conflict appears between the primary policy objectives of growth and full employment and the secondary objective of balance of payments equilibrium. It is the task of economic policy to resolve this conflict to the utmost extent possible. The available policy instruments – competitiveness, the exchange rate and commercial policy – are discussed in Chapter 9.

It might be thought easy to state whether a country has or has not a balance of payments problem, but in practice this is not so. First, judgement has to be exercised in distinguishing transitory from permanent influences on the balance of payments. Second, opinions differ as to the precise definition of 'free trade' and 'full employment'. Third, there are thorny statistical and conceptual problems in defining the basic balance.

An example of conceptual problems is the treatment of capital inflows. Some might interpret foreign purchases of long-term Irish bonds as a long-term investment decision. A contrasting view would be that such inflows were motivated by the expectation of a short-term gain, perhaps because Irish interest rates were temporarily higher than EU rates. In the former instance, the capital inflow is autonomous; in the latter it is accommodating. An assessment of a country's balance of payments position, therefore, requires judgement and a knowledge of how the economy works.

Statistical limitations are a feature of most aggregates which economists deal with. Statistics on the capital account of the balance of payments are particularly prone to error. Mistakes on the capital account often entail consequential errors in the current account balance. For example, because of the incomplete coverage of data on profits earned by overseas subsidiaries in Ireland, outflows under this heading can be underestimated. Since the overall balance of payment must always balance, an underestimate of a *current* outflow implies an overestimate of a *capital* outflow or, more likely, an excessively high residual item. Discrepancies of considerable size can arise in this way. They pose problems not only for the Irish authorities but also for the International Monetary Fund which regularly records a large overall statistical discrepancy of about $100 billion. Hence its prudent warning that 'a degree of caution is well warranted in interpreting current account developments as depicted by the available statistics'.[15]

Growth, Efficiency and the Balance of Payments

The balance of payments is relevant to growth because sustained imbalances tend to inhibit growth and to engender inflation. Imbalances include surpluses as well as deficits. By definition, one country's surplus is some other country's (or group of countries') deficit. While surpluses can sometimes create problems for the surplus country (in the form of restrictions on its exports, or pressures to import more or to invest more abroad), the most pressing difficulties are likely to be felt by the deficit country. In every year between 1982 and 1995, the Japanese have recorded a large current account surplus and the Americans an even larger deficit. Most would accept that the US deficits are more problematic than Japan's surpluses. Because of this asymmetry, the focus of the analysis below is on the effects of deficits.

When a country runs a current account deficit this means that it is absorbing more goods and services from foreigners than it is earning from export of goods and services to them. In this limited sense, a deficit signifies that a country is 'living beyond its means'. Suppose, however, that the deficit is being used to purchase capital equipment which will enhance the country's future earning capacity. In that case, running a deficit might make good economic sense. The deficit should then be financed by long-term capital inflows through the public or private sectors. The *basic balance* will be zero and there will be no balance of payments problem – or rather, in most normal circumstances, there should be no problem, provided there is a reasonable expectation of long-term capital inflow being used to productive effect.

This interpretation of a balance of payments deficit was much favoured by US President, Ronald Reagan and Nigel Lawson, Britain's former Chancellor of the Exchequer, in the 1980s. They attributed the deficits of the US and UK respectively to the strength of their economies. According to this perspective, the prospect of attractive rates of return in the two countries led to capital inflow, higher investment, more demand for imports and, consequently, a current account deficit. In Mr. Lawson's words:

> Some see a current account deficit as a sign of economic weakness: 'Britain in the red' as the newspapers are wont to put it. But of course a current account deficit is manifestly not at all like a company running at a loss. A better analogy is with a profitable company raising money overseas – either borrowing, or reducing its holdings of overseas assets, or attracting new equity. A company with greater investment opportunities than it could finance from retained profits would look for additional funds from outside. A country in a similar position will draw on the savings of the world, particularly in today's global markets.[16]

Mr Lawson took what in hindsight might appear an unduly complacent view of what was to become a series of UK current account deficits amounting to a cumulative total of £100 billion between 1988 and 1991. Eventually this excess of expenditure over income had to be squeezed out of the system by restrictive monetary and fiscal policies, leading to lower growth and higher unemployment.

From a growth perspective, the objective must be to maintain a sound credit rating so that, in the event of unforeseen emergencies, a country can borrow abroad without the disruption of its investment plans which might otherwise be necessary. This can only be achieved if a sustainable basic balance position is maintained over time. Long-run current account deficits must therefore be matched by levels of profitable investment which will repay directly or indirectly the costs of financing them.

Efficiency and the balance of payments is another important link between primary and secondary policy objectives. A country in balance of payments difficulties will frequently feel it necessary to resort to protection. Protection, by inhibiting international trade, brings static and dynamic losses.

Every first-year textbook has a section on the law of comparative advantage. The law states that a country gains from trade by exporting the goods in which it has a comparative advantage and importing those in which it has a comparative disadvantage. The essential insight of Ricardo's law is as valid today as it was when first enunciated nearly two hundred years ago. It is particularly relevant to small countries because small size places obvious limitations on the number of products which can be manufactured efficiently at home. In addition to extending the market for domestic production, trade also brings substantial benefits through extending the range of product choice available to consumers.

The above 'static' gains from trade are complemented by 'dynamic' effects. First, access to foreign markets makes it possible for a country to specialise to a vastly greater degree than if it were catering only for the domestic market. The resultant economies of scale are directly attributable to international trade. They help to explain why Ireland has become a major producer on a European scale of tennis balls, hospital disposable products, computer-related office equipment and liqueurs. Only a fraction of the output of the Irish plants producing these goods is absorbed on the domestic market. Large plants employing vast workforces are not needed to avail of economies of scale. Horizontal specialisation simply requires that moderate-sized plants (often in the 100-200 worker category) are allowed to specialise to a very high degree in a limited product range.

Second, a major dynamic gain arises from the stimulus to international competition given by exposure to foreign trade. Protection in a small state tends to foster monopoly – an argument stressed by Frederick List over a century ago and one which led him to describe the union of Britain and Ireland as 'a great and irrefragable example of the immeasurable efficacy of free trade between united nations'.[17] Firms exposed to external competition must keep up to date technically and have to operate at a high level of efficiency: otherwise they will not survive. The main beneficiary of this pressure on performance is the domestic consumer.

Third, although efficiency has been analysed separately from growth, there is an interaction between them. More efficiency in the use of existing resources makes it easier to attain growth. A smoothly functioning world payments system makes it easier to attain both efficiency and growth. Adoption of a proper balance of payments policy by each country helps to ensure that the world payments system actually works smoothly. Balance of payments equilibrium is not desired for its own sake. People are concerned about it only because they are concerned that the benefits of trade and international factor movements should be maximised. Countries which have in the past opted for an inward-looking, closed-economy approach to policy, such as the former Soviet Union, Albania and Vietnam, did not have balance of payments problems – but neither did they enjoy the benefits of expanding trade.

3 CONCLUSION

A clear link exists between the primary policy objectives and the secondary objectives of balance of payments equilibrium and price stability. Failure to achieve either or both of the secondary objectives has adverse consequences for efficiency, growth and income distribution. The nature of these effects has been outlined.

Although it has occupied the centre stage in economic discussion for many years, inflation has now become less of a problem. 'Is inflation dead?' is a question that has been posed in scholarly publications as well as in newspapers and popular journals. Prices in the industrial countries in the first half of the 1990s were increasing by only 3 per cent per annum compared with 9 per cent in the period 1972-81. A banner headline in *The Independent* of 18 August 1994 reported the UK's success in controlling inflation with the celebratory headline: INFLATION HITS 27-YEAR LOW. Forecasts for 1996 indicate that, of all industrial countries, only Italy will have an inflation rate above 5 per cent. The corresponding forecasts for the UK and the US are 4.2 per cent and 3.8 per cent respectively. Europe's low-inflation core is forecast to continue to have inflation of less than 3 per cent per annum.

One explanation for lower inflation is that politicians, by attaching more priority to this policy objective, have made it easier to implement appropriate policies. As Browne and Fell express it:

> There is now more conviction among politicians of the electoral
> advantages of running an economy in a way that keeps inflation

under wraps, with ageing populations in many countries providing a growing constituency in favour of low and stable inflation. Politicians seem increasingly more content to leave monetary policy to independent central banks. This favourable political background is enabling central banks to engage in pre-emptive strikes against inflation – a strategy that is, in the long run, likely to be much less painful than allowing inflation to emerge (possibly into double figures), then applying hard on the brakes and bringing the economy crashing to a sudden halt. This new approach can only be good for inflation and, since low inflation and high output growth go together in the medium to long run, good for the overall economy.[18]

However, rising prices are still a major source of concern in some Latin American countries and in parts of the former Soviet Union. Furthermore, experience in the 1980s demonstrates an important lesson: inflation is always ready to oblige with an encore. The spectacular decline in the UK inflation rate from around 16 per cent in 1980 to under 4 per cent in 1986 was succeeded by a regression to higher inflation in the late 1980s and early 1990s – solely as a result of careless macroeconomic policy.

Has this decline in inflation been associated with a demonstrable improvement in economic efficiency and social stability? Most would believe that it has. The maintenance of price stability has been enshrined as a major objective of the EU as it progresses towards monetary union and the single currency. The newly-liberated countries of Eastern Europe are alarmed by the potentially harmful effects of inflation in their nascent democracies.[19] At a theoretical level, economists have become increasingly of the view that inflation must be confronted rather than be adjusted to by devices such as inflation-indexing. Although these indexes act as a palliative to the adverse efficiency effects of inflation, they tend to undermine the credibility of a government's anti-inflation policies, as well as weakening important sources of political opposition to inflation.[20]

Recent experience draws attention to the painful withdrawal symptoms which accompany the lowering of inflation. These occur because of sluggish adjustment in labour and commodity markets to the lower rate of inflation and to continuing uncertainty about whether this rate will be maintained. Writing sixty years ago, Keynes observed that 'each process, inflation and deflation alike, has inflicted great injuries... Each has an effect in altering the distribution of wealth between different classes ... *Both evils are to be shunned'*.[21] Inflation creates problems; curbing inflation creates problems. The solution for governments is to ensure that price stability, once restored, is thereafter maintained.

Balance of payments problems remain a serious constraint on development in many countries. The problem of huge OPEC surpluses dominated discussion in the 1970s. Balance of payments policy in the 1980s and 1990s has been preoccupied with the Japanese surplus, the US deficit and financing problems of heavily-indebted third world countries. Recently, attention is being focused on problems of international policy coordination.

In the more stable price environment of the 1990s, the main themes of debate focus on automatic versus policy-induced adjustment mechanisms, optimal levels of foreign borrowing, interdependencies between countries participating in the international trade system and international coordination in the field of exchange rates and monetary policy. Since one country's surplus is another's deficit, the best approach of finding optimal paths to a sustainable equilibrium is by cooperation between the countries concerned. This is particularly the case for the large industrial countries. A stable macroeconomic framework in the developed world, in turn, would be helpful to developing countries as they strive to contain their foreign debt and achieve faster growth without being held back by a balance of payments constraint.

Endnotes

1 A. Alchian and W. Allen, *Exchange and Production: Competition, Coordination and Control* (third edition), Wadsworth, California 1983.
2 Changes in the broad pattern of expenditure, however, tend to occur relatively slowly over time and the weighting basis has, in fact, been changed on five occasions since the foundation of the state, the most recent being November 1989.
3 These figures are taken from, 'Inflation Objectives in the Medium to Longer Term', *OECD Economic Outlook,* Paris, June 1994.
4 So much so as to cause the resignation of Brazil's Finance Minister in September 1994. In a private conversation mistakenly broadcast by satellite television to all of Latin America he remarked that when it comes to inflation indices: 'I don't have any scruples. What is good, we use – what is bad, we hide.', *Financial Times,* 5 September, 1994.
5 D. McCormack, 'Inflation: Anticipated or Unanticipated', in D. McAleese and L. Ryan (editors), *Inflation in the Irish Economy: A Contemporary Perspective,* Helicon, Dublin 1982, p.31. A useful up-to-date survey of the source, costs and solution to inflation is available in International Monetary Fund, *World Economic Outlook,* May 1990, Chapters III and IV.
6 World Bank, *World Development Report 1983,* Washington DC 1983, p.59.
7 J. Tatom, 'The Welfare Cost of Inflation', *Federal Reserve Bank of St. Louis Review,* November 1976.
8 J. Hicks, *The Crisis in Keynesian Economics,* Blackwell, Oxford 1974; and A.M. Okun, *Prices and Quantities: A Macroeconomic Analysis,* Blackwell, Oxford 1981.
9 Hicks, *op.cit.,* pp.78-79.
10 P. Neary and F. Ruane, 'Inflation and Growth', in McAleese and Ryan, op.cit. Recent cross section analysis of developing countries shows a significant negative correlation between growth and between inflation and investment ratios. (See IMF, *World Economic Outlook, op. cit.,* p.56 and R. Dornbusch and A. Reyneso, 'Financial Factor in Economic Development', *American Economic Review,* May 1989.)
11 International Monetary Fund, *World Economic Outlook,* May 1990.
12 A. Grimes, 'The Effects of Inflation on Growth: International Evidence', *Weltwirtschaftliches Archiv,* 1991, and A.S. Englander and A. Gurney, 'Medium-Term Determinants of OECD Productivity', *OECD Economic Studies,* No. 22, 1994.
13 Okun, *op.cit.,* p.287.

14 J.M. Keynes, 'Economic Consequences of the Peace', in *Collected Economic Writings,* Vol.II, Macmillan, London 1971, p.149.

15 International Monetary Fund, *World Economic Outlook,* Washington DC 1983, p.161.

16 Nigel Lawson, Chancellor of the Exchequer's Special Lecture to the Institute of Economic Affairs, London, 21 July 1988.

17 The quote is from F. List, *National System of Political Economy* (translated by S.S. Lloyd), Longmans, Green and Company, London 1904, p.100. Arthur Griffith once expressed the wish to see this book in the hands of every Irishman in the belief that arguments for protection therein would support the Sinn Féin case. Had this wish been granted, the result might not have been as favourable to the protectionist cause as Griffith imagined.

18 F. Browne and J. Fell, 'Inflation – Dormant, Dying or Dead?' (Technical Paper, Central Bank of Ireland), October 1994.

19 The eminent Hungarian economist, Janos Kornai, describes inflation as a disaster which 'descends mercilessly on the population, leading to perpetual unrest as people see the savings they have scraped together melt away in their hands'. Janos Kornai, *The Road to a Free Economy,* Norton, London 1990, p.108.

20 S. Fischer and L.H. Summers, 'Should Governments Learn to Live with Inflation?', *American Economic Review,* May 1989.

21 J.M. Keynes, 'The Social Consequences of Changes in the Value of Money', in *Collected Economic Writings, op. cit.,* p.60.

PART II

POLICY IMPLEMENTATION

CHAPTER 4

Government Intervention

Philip R. Lane

Part I of this book established five economic policy objectives: full employment, equality, economic growth, price stability and external balance. The government, on the premise that it indeed cares about national welfare, is responsible for the pursuit of these goals: as an economic actor, it is characterised by special features, such as its powers of compulsion, that permit it to influence economic activity by methods that are not available to private actors such as firms or consumers. In this chapter, the role of government in pursuing the policy objectives identified in Part I is first described. Second, the instruments available to the government in fulfilling this role are explored. The success of government intervention depends on how efficiently it employs these instruments.

The rest of the chapter is organised as follows. In Section 1, the government's role in attaining the policy objectives identified in Part I is described. Section 2 examines public expenditure, the most visible policy instrument available to the government. Section 3 is concerned with alternative policy instruments, including regulation, state-owned enterprises, planning and social partnership and international policy coordination. Section 4 concludes the chapter.

1 THE ROLE OF GOVERNMENT INTERVENTION

This section describes the functional role of the government. There are a number of classic arguments providing a rationale for government intervention in the economy. The starting point is to recognise the absurdity of a no-government economy. A central authority and a legal system is necessary to permit the creation of the (explicit or implicit) contracts that govern all economic activity, for example through the design and enforcement of corporate and labour laws. From cross-country evidence and historical examples, it is clear that anarchy and the absence of a 'rule of law' result in very poor economic performance (and the emergence of private contract-enforcement systems, such as Mafia-style organisations).[1] We can interpret economic activity as an elaborate game: as with any other game, a set of rules and a referee are required. The government is responsible for designing and enforcing the rules determining what is permissible behaviour on the part of firms and consumers (the 'players' in the economy).

A second function relates to the efficient allocation of resources. In Chapter 2, it was shown that the efficiency properties of a free market economy depend on highly restrictive conditions. Pure public goods, that is goods collectively consumed (e.g. national defence), will not be supplied by private markets. Second, many private activities generate external effects that are not included in market prices so that activities generating positive externalities are underproduced by the market and those generating negative externalities are overproduced.

A third problem is that markets are often imperfectly competitive. Producers with monopoly power will charge too high a price and produce too little relative to what is socially optimal. A fourth problem is that imperfect information, for example in calculating the likelihood that a borrower will repay a debt, can lead to the absence of many markets, in particular credit and risk-sharing markets. While there is consensus that the government has a valid role in the provision of public goods and correcting some externalities, there is more controversy about its ability to correct the third and fourth problems. These market failures, however, do highlight the inadequacy of the market economy in optimising social welfare and provide an a priori basis for government intervention. The costs of market failures are potentially huge. As an illustration, it is widely believed that there are positive externalities to education and R&D. If correcting underinvestment in these activities raised the annual economic growth rate by two percentage points, the result would be a doubling of national income in thirty-five years.

Even if all such market failures were successfully corrected, a third function for government intervention would remain. The income distribution attained by a market economy is conditional on the initial distribution of endowments (both monetary and personal). For example, someone with rich parents and good health will likely do better than a person lacking such advantages. It also has a random element: for example, the weather can determine the success of many agricultural projects. If society believes that moral or ethical criteria require a 'levelling of the playing field' and a reallocation of incomes, such redistributive activity has public good characteristics and hence is most appropriately performed by the government.

A fourth function of government intervention is to stabilise the economy. Expectations of a recession can be self-fulfilling: if investors fail to initiate projects because they believe there will be a lack of demand, their prophesies may well turn out to be correct *ex post*. Symmetrically, an economy can fall victim to an euphoria effect, with a general belief that the level of economic activity can only continue to increase. An example of the former case is the

Great Depression of the 1930s. Both these cases are arguably detrimental to national welfare, as decisions are made using flawed criteria and levels of activity fluctuate violently. The government, by setting monetary and fiscal policies to 'lean against the wind', can help avoid such extreme outcomes. One stabilisation technique is to run a budget surplus when output is temporarily high and a deficit when output is temporarily low.

In order to fulfil its role, the government has available to it a range of policy instruments. We first examine public expenditure before turning to other policy instruments.

2 PUBLIC EXPENDITURE

In this section, the measurement of public expenditure is first discussed. Next, we turn to the role of public expenditure as an instrument of policy and its composition. The determination of the level of public expenditure and methods of financing public expenditure are then addressed.

Measurement

The ratio of public sector expenditure to national income provides a measure of the importance of public expenditure as a policy instrument. Normalising by the level of national income is appropriate: in a wide class of economic models, the value of government services is approximately proportional to the level of output.[2] In Table 4.1, the ratio of general government expenditure to GDP is reported for Ireland, the UK, the EU, the US and Japan for a number of years. From the table, it is clear that all countries shared a strong upward trend in government spending over 1960-80. It is noteworthy that government spending is significantly higher in Europe than in the US or Japan. In the 1980s and early 1990s, the rate of increase was moderated but generally not reversed. Ireland is an important exception, with significant reductions in the ratio of government expenditure to GDP after 1987. However, in the early 1990s government spending in Ireland gradually started to increase again.

Table 4.1

General Government Expenditure as a
Percentage of GDP, 1960-93

	Ireland	UK	EU	US	Japan
1960	28.0	32.2	32.3	27.0	n.a.
1970	37.4	36.8	37.4	31.6	19.3
1980	50.5	43.1	46.8	33.7	32.6
1990	42.0	40.0	48.1	36.7	32.3
1993	43.8	45.1	51.5	38.5	n.a.

Source: European Economy Annual Report 1994. EU data exclude the six countries joining after 1973. General government includes national, state and local levels of government.

Theory and Composition

Public expenditure can be disaggregated into three categories: public consumption, public investment and transfer payments. Public consumption pertains to government purchases of goods and services, which may be produced privately or in the public sector. Major components of public consumption include spending on health care and education. Public consumption also includes items such as national defence, the provision of a police force, a legal system and a fire safety system. These items are in the public goods category, with the consequence that public provision is necessary for the efficient allocation of resources. A police force and a legal system are also necessary for the government to perform its functions as designer and enforcer of the rules of the economic game.

Public investment by the central government includes both provision of infrastructure such as the road network and capital inputs used in the production of publicly-provided goods and services (e.g. military equipment, publicly-owned schools and hospitals). Much infrastructure has public goods characteristics: for example, everyone benefits from the roads network. Private provision of infrastructure (e.g. toll bridges) occasionally occurs but is invariably dependent on an agreement with the government, which grants the provider special exemptions from normal property laws.

Transfers are a large and growing component of public expenditure in many countries. Transfers include payments to individuals and subsidies to firms. Important kinds of transfer payments include unemployment assistance, old-age and disability pensions and interest payments on public debt. While transfers do not represent direct control of resources by the government (the recipient decides how a transfer is spent), they have to be financed by taxation or public borrowing and hence are properly counted as a component of public expenditure.

In Table 4.2, major components of public expenditure for selected countries are reported. While Ireland spends comparatively little on defence, especially relative to the US, the allocations to education, health care and welfare are broadly in line with other countries. A high proportion of Irish

Table 4.2

Composition of General Government Expenditure (Major Items)

	Ireland	UK	Germany	US
Defence	.026	.076	.045	.112
Education	.117	.106	.074	.177
Health	.210	.132	.147	.159
Welfare/SS	.222	.273	.362	.216
Interest	.145	.062	.037	.104

Source: IMF Government Financial Statistics Yearbook 1994. Data are from 1991 for Ireland and the UK, 1990 for Germany and 1992 for the US. SS are Social Security payments.

public spending is committed to servicing the interest on the national debt. It should be noted that in some countries, such as Germany, much spending on health care is counted as a form of welfare payment.

Health Care

Government intervention in the health care market is motivated by both efficiency and equity considerations. The market for health care is widely regarded to be especially plagued by information imperfections: patients (i.e. consumers) must rely on medical professionals (i.e. producers) for assistance in decision-making, introducing important distortions in the incentives facing producers of health care services. Second, the random element in the occurrence of ill-health and the high cost of many treatments means that private health care systems are typically financed by insurance. Insurance markets suffer from special problems: one problem is that both producers and consumers may choose unnecessarily expensive treatment methods when the bill is paid by a third party, the insurance company. In this situation, a competitive insurance market may be inefficient as no single actor has the capability to control costs. A public health care system may be more efficient because a 'single payer' is better able to impose discipline on the choices made by producers and consumers of health care services. An alternative course of action would be to allow for a private monopoly provider of health insurance but here the government would still have an active role in regulating the behaviour of the monopoly insurance firm. Government purchases of health care services may also be justified by ethical criteria, if society makes the value judgements that low incomes should not be a barrier to good health and/or that sufferers from chronic conditions (e.g. diabetes) should not also have to suffer a monetary penalty by bearing the costs of treatment privately.

Education

Public expenditure on education is also motivated by both efficiency and equity criteria. It is debatable whether education spending should be interpreted as consumption: if we interpret education as investment in 'human capital', it should more properly be counted as an investment item.[3] Intervention on efficiency grounds is justified by market failures in both education and credit markets. Even if the education market were perfect, typically the income gains from education are obtained only after the education process is completed while the costs are incurred up front. This means that many students (or their parents) must borrow in order to finance their education. Credit markets, however, are plagued by information problems: lenders do not know for sure that a borrower will repay and typically demand collateral for a loan. In the mortgage market, the borrower offers the property as collateral and the bank can reclaim the property in the event of a default. In contrast, a borrower cannot offer her 'human capital' as collateral for an education loan: a person's knowledge and skills cannot be reclaimed by the bank. These considerations may justify government purchases of education or, at the least, provide a scheme of credit subsidies to purchasers of education. The abolition of third-level fees in 1995 is another method to solve this problem but is crude in that it is not linked to a 'graduate tax' on beneficiaries of the system. In this sense, the abolition of fees is a transfer from those who do not attend college to students, which is likely to be regressive in its distributional effect.

Even if credit markets were efficient, however, it is likely that imperfections in the education market may justify government intervention. It is widely believed that education has positive external effects. If one person acquires some skills, it is likely that she will benefit co-workers as her new skills also make others more productive. This provides a rationale for subsidising education as the gains do not solely accrue to the student. This externality effect moderates the criticism made earlier of the abolition of third-level fees. The externality benefit is also much reduced if a graduate permanently emigrates: one solution would be an 'emigration' tax on graduates that accept jobs overseas. To the extent that migration is mostly within the European Union (EU), the first-best solution would be education subsidies from the EU to countries that suffer net emigration of graduates.

Equity considerations also provide a rationale for government financing of education. It is indisputable that education is a key determinant of income. Low-income households may not have the resources to finance education for their children, leaving them at a disadvantage in the labour market. In addition, children whose parents are highly educated appear to do better in later life. In order to provide a more equal distribution of opportunities, government subsidies to the education of children from low-income households may be justified. It is unclear, however, that the government need also be the provider of education services: it is possible that a system in which schools and colleges are privately-run but students receive public subsidies might do as well in attaining the government's objectives.

Transfers
Some transfers can be justified by imperfections in insurance markets. For example, it is likely that only a monopoly provider could provide insurance against unemployment given the need to pool risk across as many workers as possible. Perhaps the strongest efficiency argument in favour of public old-age pensions is that people tend to behave in a 'dynamically inconsistent' manner: although they know they should save for retirement, it is difficult for many to have the discipline to save for an event that is far in the future. This provides an argument for a compulsory savings scheme but not necessarily for government operation of such a system. The example of Chile, where the

government requires people to participate in one of a set of alternative pension schemes offered by private providers but does not itself run such an operation, is being closely watched to discover whether alternatives to government-run pension systems can succeed. Equity considerations, however, may justify public subsidies to those who earn too little to save enough for even a minimal pension.

More generally, a value judgement that every member of society deserves a basic standard of living justifies the bulk of transfers made to individuals. A potential cost, aside from the need to levy taxation, is that the existence of a safety net may distort incentives: some people may not try hard enough to find a job or save for old age in the knowledge that a minimal standard of living is guaranteed by the government.

Producer subsidies are another kind of transfer. Subsidies to firms are high in Ireland relative to many other countries. In theory, producer subsidies can be justified if firms would not otherwise locate in Ireland and attracting these firms generates benefits exceeding the costs of the subsidies (see also Chapter 12). The availability of subsidies, however, may distort incentives. A firm can invest resources in improving efficiency or in lobbying the government for a handout: by allowing the second option, the government may unwittingly reduce the competitiveness of domestic producers. Another problem is that Ireland competes with other countries, especially other peripheral EU regions, in attracting footloose firms: this bidding war may result in the successful country suffering a 'winner's curse', having to offer a subsidy larger than any potential benefits.

Interest payments on the public debt is another important category of transfer payment. While payments on foreign-owned debt represent a net loss to the Irish economy, payments on domestically-held debt are just like other kinds of domestic transfers. The government always has the option to default on its debt but this may be regarded as unfair to debt-holders and would raise the cost of any future public borrowing.

The Determination of Public Expenditure

Both technical and institutional/political factors determine the actual level of public expenditure. Some elements are common to all countries and others are specific to Ireland. Until 1987, the focus was on explaining the upward trend in public expenditure. The fiscal reforms initiated in 1987 significantly reduced public expenditure, although there has been some weakening of fiscal discipline in the early 1990s.

Technical Factors

The technical approach regards the level and composition of public expenditure to be largely predetermined and, to a significant degree, independent of the ideological position of the government. A rising trend in public expenditure as a share of national income as a country grows richer is a pattern observed in many countries and is termed 'Wagner's Law'. One reason is that public subsidies to health care and education and old-age pensions may be regarded as luxury commodities, with an income elasticity of demand greater than unity. As incomes grow, society demands more of these services and public expenditure inexorably rises. However, it is also true that taxation cannot rise forever – excessively high tax rates would too severely distort production – which imposes an upper bound on the ratio of public expenditure to GDP in a market economy. The fiscal reforms attempted by many countries in recent years may be a result of having approached this upper bound.

Another explanation for the upward trend in public expenditure is the so-called 'Baumol's disease', named after the economist who proposed the hypothesis.[4] Baumol's hypothesis is that an economy can be divided into progressive and non-progressive sectors. Productivity gains in the progressive sector, achieved, for example, by increasing capital intensity, drive up wages which must be matched by the non-progressive sector if it is to attract labour. Provision of education and health care services likely falls into the non-progressive sector, on the basis that productivity growth in such labour-intensive sectors is limited: it follows that the implicit relative price of producing these services must increase. If the income elasticity of demand for these services exceeds the price elasticity of demand, the ratio of public expenditure to GDP will automatically increase in this case even though the actual quantity of publicly-financed services does not increase, due to the increased cost of providing these commodities. It may be wrong to assume, on the other hand, that productivity growth in these sectors is not possible, as another explanation for slow productivity growth in publicly-financed sectors is the lack of competitive pressure to produce efficiently. Stronger cost controls and the contracting-out of some services may help in forcing more rapid productivity growth in these sectors (see Chapter 10).

An important dimension of high costs in publicly-financed sectors pertains when the government is the direct provider of goods and services. Unions know that the government is driven by political criteria and will not go bankrupt if it pays high wages or offers generous benefits to employees (i.e. the government faces a 'soft budget constraint' in that it can raise taxes or borrow to finance a higher public sector wage bill). This may result in the public sector payroll being higher than if the same activities were contracted out to privately-owned producers. Against this view, this problem may arise whenever the government is the final payer and therefore may not be special to sectors in which the government is the direct provider of goods and services. As an example, US defence contractors famously charge high prices for government contracts.

Demographic trends pre-commit a certain amount of public expenditure. In the 1970s and 1980s, Ireland had an unusually high number of people of school-going age so that the education budget of necessity had to increase. In the same fashion, an increase in the proportion of old people places heavy pressure on health care and pensions expenditure. By an argument of symmetry, reductions in the number of young people or retirees automatically reduce public expenditure so that such pre-commitments do not imply an inexorable upward trend in government spending. The sharp decline of the Irish birth rate in the 1980s will mean a substantial reduction in the school-going population over 1996-2006, relieving demographic pressure on education spending. Moreover, while the impact of the 'greying' of the population on public expenditure will soon be a major issue in many countries, such as Japan, the US and Germany, it is not expected to hit Ireland until 2010-2025.[5]

Welfare payments is another area in which much public expenditure is pre-committed: all qualified individuals, once legislation is enacted, are entitled to receive benefits. It follows that an increase in unemployment, for example, automatically increases public expenditure as more unemployment assistance must be paid out. However, it may also be argued that if such forces do point to a persistent increase in spending, the scale of benefits and services should be correspondingly reduced, given the taxation cost of financing this expenditure. The OECD has also pointed out that the level of benefits in Ireland appears too high relative to the level of development. This is to ignore, however, a powerful international demonstration effect, with strong social pressure existing to match the level of benefits available in other EU countries.

Another important technical factor in determining public expenditure is the level of the public debt. Budget deficits incurred in previous years result in the commitment of funds to interest payments on that debt in the current year. A cynical view is that that accumulation of public debt can be a device whereby a government is able to constrain its successors' choices about public expenditure.[6] It is again the case that reducing the public debt creates a virtuous cycle in that the predetermined component of public expenditure is also reduced in subsequent years.

Finally, it is important to distinguish between the trend component of public expenditure and the temporary component. While increases in the trend component indicate the need to increase taxation proportionally, temporary bulges in public expenditure do not.

Institutional/Political Factors

The preceding analysis has been based on the assumption that the government acts to maximise social welfare. While the bulk of public expenditure decisions may usefully be interpreted in this way, a substantial component is influenced by a more overtly 'political' process, in which public expenditure allocations are the outcome of a struggle between the electorate, interest groups, civil servants and politicians. This process may produce outcomes that are contrary to social welfare: that is to say, government failure may be as important as market failure in failing to achieve desirable outcomes.

One reason why social welfare is not maximised is voter ignorance of the true costs of public expenditure. The so-called Downs paradox (individual voters have no influence over the result of an election) suggests that it is not worthwhile for the electorate to learn much about the costs of different public spending programmes. In contrast, some groups within society will have a vested interest in specific areas of public expenditure (e.g farmers and agricultural subsidies) and will act collectively to promote these specific areas of expenditure. The net result is an overallocation of resources to public expenditure. In a famous book, Mancur Olson pointed out that such interest groups are easier to organise in a rich society and hence this problem will increase over time.[7]

This 'fiscal illusion' argument applies most forcefully when the costs of public expenditure are deferred, i.e. when expenditure is financed by borrowing rather than current taxation. A good example was the Irish experience in 1977-82, with increases in public expenditure financed by debt and there was, as one commentator has put it, 'a grim tale of financial irresponsibility as the Irish insisted on living in a dreamland'.[8] Fiscal illusion diminishes over time as higher taxation at some point becomes inevitable. A learning process therefore takes place – however, the damage caused by even a short period of fiscal illusion can have prolonged effects, given the pre-commitment of public expenditure to debt servicing in subsequent periods. In systems in which increases in expenditure must be approved by referendum, in contrast, fiscal illusion may work in reverse with the cost of public spending overstated and the benefits understated (e.g. a number of states in the US).

The characteristics of the civil service bureaucracy can also contribute to government failure. Civil servants act as agents for the government in evaluating and monitoring the usefulness of different public expenditure programmes. The information advantage this gives them may lead to an excessive amount of public spending. An influential hypothesis is that bureaucrats like to maximise the size of their departmental budgets, as this is associated with greater power and status. With each department seeking to promote its own expenditure programmes, the net result is to place upward pressure on the level of public expenditure. A counter-argument is that if civil servants are rewarded for achieving efficiency gains in their departments, this may provide an incentive not to overstate the virtues of particular programmes.

Much current research is devoted to analysing the impact of the structure of the political system on public expenditure decisions. For example, it has been suggested that a political system that produces governments that are coalitions of parties with significantly different economic philosophies and short tenures in office is less able to control public expenditure.[9] Each party in a coalition has a veto on reductions in its favoured areas of expenditure so that a prisoners' dilemma situation results – it is in the collective interest of the government to control public expenditure but no single party has the incentive to accept unilateral expenditure reductions. Short tenures make it infeasible to implement spending controls as it will not have the time to enjoy the benefits before the next election. In these circumstances, it seems that fiscal control can only occur under 'crisis' conditions, with the level of the public debt so high that there is no alternative to reforming public expenditure. Often, this requires suspension of normal political rivalries and the formation of a government of national unity. Elements of this story ring true for the Irish experience during 1982-87. More recently, the formation of a left-right coalition in 1994 will make it harder to control public spending, according to this analysis.

Another manifestation of politics-driven fluctuations in public expenditure is the widely-documented phenomenon of the political business cycle.[10] This refers to the phenomenon of increases in visible public expenditure projects, coupled with tax cuts, in the run-up to political elections. The timing of these fluctuations suggest such spending has little basis in terms of social welfare criteria but rather is directed at winning favour for the incumbent government.

In summary, both technical and institutional/political factors are helpful in understanding the determination of public expenditure. As we have seen, there are strong forces placing upward pressure on the level of public expenditure. (It should be noted that many of these forces also influence other methods of government intervention, as we will see later in this chapter.) We have also learned that virtuous cycles are possible in which a decline in unemployment or borrowing, to list two examples, can lead to further reductions in public expenditure. At some point, an upward trend in public expenditure must come to a halt as the public debt spirals out of control or the tax burden becomes too onerous but it remains to be seen whether a persistent reduction in the level of public expenditure is possible. Once a period of fiscal crisis is over, the underlying forces promoting higher public spending may well re-emerge.

Financing Public Expenditure

The government must finance public expenditure by imposing taxation, borrowing, printing money or receiving international transfers. In the previous section, some reference was made to the fact that the optimal level of government spending cannot be determined without reference to the costs of financing public expenditure. (To calculate the full social cost of public expenditure, we should also include the costs incurred by interest groups in lobbying for particular spending programmes.) We can think of the optimal level of the public expenditure as that level at which the marginal social benefit of public expenditure just equals the marginal social cost. The direct cost of financing public expenditure is the level of taxation imposed on the economy: public consumption and investment and payments on the foreign component of the national debt leave a smaller share of income at the disposal of the non-government sector of the economy. Taxation also distorts the choices faced by firms and consumers (see Chapter 5). These indirect costs ought not to be ignored when considering the desirability of a given level of public expenditure.

Taxation

In Table 4.3, data on government current receipts as a ratio to GDP are reported. As with public expenditure, there is a substantial upward drift in the share of GDP accruing to the government in the form of tax revenues. Europe is significantly higher taxed than the US or Japan. Tax revenues as a share of GDP in Ireland actually peaked in 1984 with the expenditure reductions since 1987 allowing some decline in taxation. Notice also that taxation in Ireland has consistently been below the EU average. The trend increase in taxation in Ireland was significantly lower than for public spending, especially in 1977-82, which implied a rapid accumulation of debt (as was also the case in countries such as Belgium and Italy).

Table 4.3

General Government Tax Revenue, 1960-93

	Ireland	UK	EU	US	Japan
1960	24.8	29.9	32.3	27.6	n.a.
1970	33.2	39.8	37.5	30.5	21.1
1980	37.8	39.7	43.2	32.4	28.1
1990	39.5	38.7	44.3	34.2	35.2
1993	40.8	36.8	45.8	33.7	n.a.

Source: As for Table 4.1.

Taxes distort economic choices. Income taxes distort the choice between work and leisure and the choice whether to work at home or overseas. Capital taxation reduces the incentive to save for the future. Taxes on particular types of goods distorts consumption choices. A key principle of optimal taxation is that the tax system should minimise the distortionary costs of a given amount of tax revenue. This does not imply equal taxes on all types of goods and activities: rather, it is less distortionary to tax more heavily goods and factors that are inelastically demanded (e.g. alcohol or cigarettes) or inelastically supplied (e.g. land). Taxes on some activities can be interpreted as 'negative subsidies', e.g. we can interpret taxation on petrol as in part an attempt to discourage the negative environmental externality generated by car use.

Ireland's tax system is far from optimal. The range of goods and factors that are taxed is relatively narrow (e.g. property and capital are taxed lightly) with the consequence that high taxes have to be imposed on labour and

115

consumption (see Chapter 5). The narrowness of the tax base and the consequent high rates of taxation are arguably highly distortionary. Serious distortions include the 'tax wedge' that creates a gap between the labour costs facing employers and employees' take-home pay (which reduces employment), the strong incentives for skilled workers (e.g. new college graduates) to emigrate and overinvestment in housing. Such a tax system increases the marginal social cost of taxation, even if the average level of taxation is not extraordinary by OECD standards. Conversely, efforts to widen the tax base and hence allow a reduction in marginal tax rates would reduce the costs associated with public expenditure. Tax reform, however, is politically difficult as those groups gaining from the current system will typically resist changes in the tax code.

Public Debt
The counterpart to Ireland's low level of taxation relative to public expenditure during 1972-87 was a sharp increase in the national debt. From Table 4.4, it is clear that debt/GDP ratios can experience sharp changes in relatively short periods of time, depending on the paths of primary fiscal deficits, interest rates and GDP growth (see also Chapter 6). Since its peak in 1987, Ireland has successfully reversed the growth of the debt/GDP ratio, in contrast to countries such as Belgium and Italy that failed to make fiscal reforms. The debt/GDP ratio is still at a relatively high level.

Table 4.4

General Government Gross Public Debt
as a Percentage of GDP, 1980-96

	1980	1987	1993	1996
Belgium	81.6	135.6	142.2	137.3
Germany	32.8	43.8	50.2	60.4
Ireland	*71.3*	*116.0*	*92.7*	*79.7*
Italy	59.0	92.6	119.4	126.1
Japan	52.0	74.9	73.7	88.2
UK	54.1	48.6	47.1	54.1
US	37.7	52.0	64.3	65.0

Source: OECD Main Economic Outlook, December 1994, Table A33. 1996 figures are projections.

Public borrowing can be justified in several situations. First, if government spending increases temporarily, it is less distortionary to borrow than to increase taxation temporarily. To see this, consider what would happen if the government followed a policy of raising taxation during a recession (when government spending naturally increases) and lowering taxation during a boom – this would be destabilising, further depressing output in the recession and unnecessarily raising output in a boom. Second, if a public investment project increases future national income by raising productivity, borrowing is again justified as debt repayments can be made out of higher future income without having to increase tax rates. Third, borrowing to finance some proportion of even public consumption or transfers may be justified on the grounds that future generations are likely to be richer than the current generation and borrowing is a mechanism to transfer wealth from future generations to ourselves. (The ethical basis for this last argument is controversial.)

A problem with these criteria is that they are hard to implement in practice. It is often difficult to know whether an output decline is temporary or permanent or whether a given public investment project will indeed increase future national output. If fiscal illusion exists, the option to defer the costs of public expenditure via borrowing may be very tempting for politicians. This is especially the case for an open economy such as Ireland that can borrow from abroad as, in this case, the initial cost of public expenditure is paid by foreigners. (The flip side is that debt repayments also accrue to foreigners.) The accumulation of debt also makes the government vulnerable to interest rate increases, which are largely driven by external factors: this gives financial markets tremendous influence over budgetary decisions. It is arguable that this is a beneficial effect, disciplining politicians who would otherwise always prefer to increase public spending. A high public debt creates special problems as investors fear the government will resort to debt default, high inflation or high taxation of assets in an attempt to reduce the burden of interest payments. In the run-up to the 1987 fiscal stabilisation, the public debt overhang presented a serious deterrent to domestic investment for these reasons (see Chapter 6). Conversely, the public expenditure reductions implemented in that year served to improve investor confidence and reduce fears of high future taxation: the result was that a sharp contraction in government spending was accompanied by a turnaround in economic activity, with a large improvement in the growth rate of output.

Money Creation
The government has a third option in financing public expenditure: printing money. The government has the right to create money, via the central bank. This option is inflationary but inflation has other beneficial effects, in terms of financing public expenditure, such as depressing the real value of outstanding nominal public debt. This has been a popular method of financing in Latin America and many developing countries, which lack proper tax-collection systems, and is typically the root cause of hyperinflationary episodes in these countries. Such an inflation tax, however, is highly distortionary as people must spend time and resources in reducing their reliance on money for transactions and as a store of value (see Chapter 3). Ireland has relied comparatively little on this source of financing. One reason is that it is

inconsistent with maintaining a pegged exchange rate, which has long been a main instrument of our macroeconomic policy (see Chapter 9). Another is that dependence on foreign borrowing limits the effectiveness of this option: foreigners will refuse to hold Irish-pound-denominated bonds if the inflation rate is excessive. In addition, domestic inflation depreciates the Irish pound and makes repayment of foreign-currency-denominated debt more expensive.

International Transfers

Ireland receives substantial fiscal transfers from its EU partners (see Chapter 9). Grants from the European Social Fund averaged 2.3 per cent of GDP during 1990-93 and will average 6.2 per cent of GDP over 1994-96. Such transfers are a cheap method of financing public expenditure and as such help lower the social cost of a given level of public expenditure. However, because they must be applied to only approved projects, the transfers also distort public expenditure choices and make feasible projects that would not otherwise be chosen. The desirability of this feature depends on the quality of the EU decision-making process relative to that employed for domestically-financed public expenditure projects. It should be noted that the once-off nature of these grants indicates that they should largely be used for investment purposes, rather than financing recurring items of expenditure.

In summary, determining the optimal level of public expenditure requires an evaluation of the costs of financing public expenditure. Taxation is distortionary but the Irish tax system fails to minimise these distortions, increasing the marginal social cost of any given level of public spending. Public borrowing can be justified by a number of criteria but may be too tempting an option, artificially reducing the current costs of increasing public expenditure. A third financing option – printing money – is little used in Ireland, being incompatible with a pegged exchange rate and dependence on foreign borrowing. Finally, EU transfers have been an important source of financing in recent years but cannot be relied upon as a permanent option.

3 OTHER METHODS OF INTERVENTION

In this section, the government's ability to affect the behaviour of the economy via policy instruments other than public expenditure is examined. These alternative policy instruments include regulation, state ownership of commercial enterprises, planning and social partnership, and cooperation with other sovereign governments. The theoretical bases of these intervention mechanisms, and their role in government intervention in the Irish economy, are explored in detail in this section.

Regulation

The government's rule-setting function was described in Section 1. Its legislative powers can also be used to influence the allocation of resources and the distribution of income. By passing and enforcing laws concerning the setting of prices, the quality of a product and/or the market structure of an industry, the government is able to direct private economic behaviour in order to promote its policy objectives.

Regulation can be justified on a number of theoretical grounds. One justification is the presence of monopoly power: if, by virtue of increasing returns to scale, an industry is characterised by monopolistic competition, economic theory predicts prices will be set above marginal cost and production will be below the competitive level. It is possible that government regulation of pricing behaviour in such industries can force monopolistic firms to behave more competitively. However, this is difficult to achieve in practice. One reason is that although monopoly profits may appear inefficient in a static framework, such profits may be efficient in a dynamic sense as the reward for innovation. A good example is the pharmaceutical industry. Firms compete intensively to introduce new drugs and must invest heavily in R&D. Those firms that successfully invent new drugs receive patents that give them monopoly rights to the new drug and allow them to recoup the costs of R&D investments via a period of high prices relative to marginal costs. Requiring such firms to price more competitively would reduce the gains to innovation and the net result would be a slower rate of invention of new drugs.

A second reason is that monopoly power may actually be the result of government regulations. Barriers to entry are often enshrined in law, such as the restrictions on the number of liquor and taxicab licences or tariffs on imports. In these cases, what is required is government deregulation or trade liberalisation in order to improve the intensity of competition. A third reason is that the regulated firm will have more information about its cost structure than the government and hence it is difficult for the government to know what the competitive price should be. The regulating agency may be manipulated by the firm in this case, a situation known as 'regulatory capture'. Finally, even if only one firm is active in a sector, it still may be forced to behave competitively because it is disciplined by the threat of potential entry by other firms into the industry: it is sometimes difficult to know whether a sector truly suffers from monopolistic behaviour (see Chapter 10 for a more detailed analysis).

These theoretical arguments are very relevant in the context of the Irish economy. As will be argued in Chapter 10, many sectors in the Irish economy are protected by legislative barriers to entry. Deregulation of public houses, taxicabs, telecommunications and the market for lawyers could substantially improve competitiveness in these sectors, leading to greater efficiency and lower prices. The international trend is towards trade liberalisation and deregulation of protected sectors, in the hope that monopoly positions will be weakened and inefficient practices eliminated.

Safety standards are another justification for regulation. Product liability laws by which a firm can be sued if its products harm consumers may be an inadequate guarantor of safety, given that it is costly for victims to bring law suits. In addition, firms may find it hard to market new products with unknown safety characteristics. For these reasons, public safety standards may suit both producers and consumers. A third justification for regulation concerns production or consumption activities that generate external effects. The government may choose to place physical limits on, for example, the amounts of emissions a factory can produce. It is unclear, however, that regulation is superior to price incentives, such as subsidies or taxes, in this regard. A problem with regulating safety standards or pollution is that it is costly for firms to comply with such regulations. Setting excessively stringent regulations depresses social welfare by raising the costs of doing business and the prices of final products.

A fourth justification for regulation is to improve the distribution of economic opportunities. An example is legislation prohibiting gender or race discrimination in hiring and promotion decisions. Legislation can also be used to attempt to improve the distribution of income, for example by setting an economy-wide minimum wage. Again, the problem with such regulations is that it is difficult to find the balance between effective laws and the costs of compliance incurred by employers.

A final role for regulation is with regard to the use of 'common property' resources, such as the sea and the radio frequency. Such assets cannot be privately owned and, if free access is allowed, will be overexploited. Consider the radio frequency. In Ireland, users of the radio frequency (e.g. radio stations, cellular phone companies) must apply for an operating licence and meet certain requirements. Demand for space on the bandwidth is expected to increase dramatically, with the communications revolution, and hence the allocation of frequencies will be increasingly disputed. In the US, the solution has been to auction off licences, which has raised a substantial amount of revenue for the government.

Much regulation is now conducted at an EU-wide level. An important principle guiding safety and quality standards is reciprocity: if a product meets the requirements in one country, it must be accepted for sale in other member countries. This avoids the difficulty of having to agree on a common set of standards, as exemplified by the EU directives specifying what constitutes a 'banana' and 'chocolate'. However, the Social Charter attempts to impose common regulations in the labour market. This would have the effect of reducing the competitive position of relatively poor countries such as Ireland by limiting the capacity of Irish workers to underbid for projects.

EU competition law provides a common set of anti-monopoly provisions and restricts state aid for local industries. A good example of the latter is the airline industry. In the early 1990s, many state-owned airlines (e.g. Aer Lingus, Air France) were making heavy losses but government subsidies were restricted by EU law to once-off bailouts in order to ensure a level playing field among EU airlines. Another provision of EU competition law is that countries must allow a second provider of telecommunications services, with the result that Telecom Eireann will face increased competition. However, important sectors, such as the automobile industry, were granted exemptions from deregulation, which limits the scope of current EU anti-monopoly policies. Finally, in sectors where local knowledge is important, such as many business services and small-firm loans, EU competition policy may have limited effects as foreign firms may not find it adequately profitable to enter the Irish market.

State-Owned Enterprises
State-owned enterprises play a major role in the Irish economy, with over 100 state-owned enterprises, ranging from Aer Rianta to the ESB, in existence. The historical development of the state-owned commercial sector may be explained by a number of factors. Rather than implement regulation of monopolies (as in the US), European countries tended to favour government ownership of utilities such as electricity production and telecommunications. A second factor was that underdeveloped capital markets prevented private entrepreneurs from building profitable firms in areas such as transportation. It is less clear why extensive public ownership persists, given that many historical obstacles to private enterprise have by now been eliminated.

That is to say, if some combination of public subsidies and regulation can achieve the government's policy objectives, actual government ownership may not be required. In addition, there is widespread sentiment that government ownership may be actually detrimental to performance. As already argued, managers and workers in a state-owned enterprise know that they face a soft budget constraint, in the sense that losses can be covered by the government via taxation or borrowing, and hence have a weak incentive to behave efficiently or control costs. In addition, the government may direct state-owned enterprises to pursue non-commercial objectives, such as providing employment for supporters of the government or locating in disadvantaged regions.[11] While these problems may always be present, regardless of ownership, when the government is the purchaser of the output of these firms, many state-owned enterprises sell directly to the public and hence may act more efficiently under private ownership. Even if privatisation does not occur, there are benefits to depoliticisation of these enterprises, for example by establishing commercial guidelines for the performance of these firms. Commercialisation of many Irish state-owned enterprises occurred in the 1980s. Another benefit to privatisation would be that the proceeds could be applied to reducing the public debt and the level of taxation. Ireland has made some moves towards privatisation in recent years, most notably the Irish Life and Greencore issues, but the process is much less advanced than in many other countries.

Planning and Social Partnership

An important strand of economic theory emphasises the effects of uncertainty and coordination problems across firms and workers as sources of poor economic performance. Uncertainty about future conditions makes investors more reluctant to undertake risky projects. The government can help reduce uncertainty by, at the very least, pre-announcing expenditure and taxation plans. By publishing such a multi-year programme, the government reduces one source of uncertainty for private agents. A multi-year planning approach to public policy can also help foster a longer horizon in decision-making: for example, by making clear the connection between borrowing today and higher taxation in the future. Of course, unanticipated shocks may necessitate adjustment in the government programme but even here uncertainty can be reduced if the government makes it clear in advance how it will behave under different contingencies.

There may also be a role for government in solving coordination problems among firms and workers. If workers are organised into unions, uncoordinated decisions about wage-setting will lead to inefficient outcomes, as no single union has the incentive to moderate wage claims. If unions must come to a collective agreement with employers, they will be forced to internalise the connection between higher wage claims and increased unemployment. A similar analysis indicates that income taxes impose the least distortions on labour markets if unions must coordinate in wage negotiations. Given that the government wants to minimise unemployment and the distortionary costs of taxation, it has an incentive to promote such collective agreements. (Alternatively, it could try to weaken union power sufficiently so that the labour market behaves competitively, which would also deliver an efficient outcome.) In international empirical studies, countries in which wage-setting is either highly centralised or highly decentralised appear to perform better than countries in which individual unions are powerful but do not act cooperatively.[12] A problem is that collective bargaining may politicise the wage-setting process, especially when the government is a significant employer of unionised workers, leading to unrealistic settlements. Another problem is to allow sufficient flexibility that smaller or larger wage increases are possible in particular cases if industry conditions require it. (See also Chapter 8 for a discussion of these issues.)

The Irish experience of such 'corporatist' agreements has been somewhat mixed. There was a series of national wage agreements in the 1970s but these were generally unsuccessful: the centrally-agreed wage increases were regarded by unions as only a lower bound in negotiations with individual firms and the government allowed public sector wages to increase rapidly.[13] In contrast, the 1987 Programme for National Recovery is considered to be a key contributory factor in the economic recovery that began in that year. Agreement on wage moderation and public sector redundancies enhanced the credibility of the government's fiscal adjustment plans and, in turn, the government made concessions on tax reductions and sensitive areas of public expenditure. More recent public sector pay agreements (1991 PESP and 1994 Programme for Competitiveness and Work) have arguably been excessively generous, especially given the continuing high level of unemployment in Ireland.

Cooperation with Other Sovereign Governments

Ireland is a member of a number of international economic organisations, most notably the European Union (EU) and the World Trade Organisation (WTO), as well as a signatory of international agreements on environmental protection. Membership of both the EU and WTO has led to considerable liberalisation of international trade, with zero trade restrictions in many sectors of economic activity. The 1987 Single European Act, the 1993 Maastricht convergence agreement and the 1994 new General Agreement on Tariffs and Trade (GATT) accord have accelerated the pace of international economic policy coordination, even if plans for a single EU currency have been delayed (see Chapter 9). The 1996 Inter-Governmental Conference is expected to make further progress in achieving EU integration.

The driving force behind international policy coordination is the trade-off that internationalisation of many economic activities enhances efficiency but also makes unilateral policy actions ineffective. Governments need to agree on a set of trading rules in order to maximise the gains from international trade in goods and factors. However, international trade also binds together the economies of different countries: a policy decision in country A will also have effects in countries B and C. Chapter 3 describes the benefits to international trade in goods and factors. Since the Second World War, the volume of international trade has grown rapidly, with successive GATT rounds reducing barriers to trade. Members of the EU have liberalised trade rules even further, with the goal of a Single European Market.

Negotiating trade rules is a highly political process: although society as a whole generally gains from freer trade, certain groups may lose, such as firms and workers in protected sectors. A problem is that the benefits are widely diffused (e.g. the benefit to consumers from lower average prices) but costs may be highly concentrated in only a few uncompetitive sectors. Losing groups will fight for exemptions from free trade and beneficiaries must rely on the government to act in the social interest. Although free trade has generally prevailed, important exceptions remain, most notably in the agricultural sector.

In an open economy, the success of the government's stabilisation policy depends on international policy coordination. Unilateral attempts at increasing aggregate demand, such as France's reflation experiment in 1981, are unlikely to be effective in a world with integrated capital and product markets. For example, a fiscal expansion in one country will also stimulate output in other countries, via increased demand for imports. This policy spillover is analytically equivalent to other kinds of externalities and policy coordination will be superior to non-cooperation in these circumstances. However, countries may have different preferences with regard to inflation and unemployment, so that countries may be unable to agree on a common monetary policy. An important problem may arise if EU members coordinate on monetary policy but national fiscal policies remain independently chosen. This could allow an ill-disciplined country (e.g. Italy or Greece) to run yet larger fiscal deficits, in the knowledge that the other member countries would ultimately be forced to bail it out. Moreover, if countries experience different shocks, they may need different policy choices. A notorious example is the collapse of the EMS exchange rate mechanism in 1992. In response to the fiscal costs of reunification, Germany desired a tight monetary policy. Other European countries, in particular the UK, desired a more expansionary monetary policy in the face of ongoing recession. Maintaining a common monetary policy was not possible, given this conflict of objectives. Finally, an increasing problem in EU policy coordination is that the decision-making process in an enlarged EU will be inevitably more complex. The accession of Austria, Finland and Sweden to the EU in 1995 may not be a serious difficulty in this regard because these countries have a similar level of development to other EU member countries. However, this problem would be magnified if the EU further enlarges to include Central and Eastern European countries, given their less advanced level of development. With greater diversity among EU members, the set of policies that will find common agreement is correspondingly reduced.[14] This makes more difficult the negotiation of common EU policies.

EU membership also has consequences for the government's distributional function. A 'competition of rules' may occur, in that countries have to abandon progressive tax systems in order to retain skilled workers. However, it is also the case that closer integration makes the demonstration effect, described earlier in this chapter, all the more powerful in promoting a common social safety net across the EU. Income redistribution also takes on an inter-regional dimension in the EU, with large transfers being made to relatively poor countries (including Ireland). The rationale for these transfers has two dimensions. On the one side, large inter-regional disparities in incomes may be regarded as a barrier to closer political integration among EU countries. On the other side, trade liberalisation within the EU arguably benefits the richer 'core' countries more than the poorer 'peripheral' countries and inter-regional transfers can be interpreted as the pay-off to the peripheral countries for agreeing to a Single European Market. If these transfers are productively invested, moreover, they may allow the recipient countries to compete more effectively in the new trading environment.

Joint efforts to combat environmental destruction are another dimension of international policy coordination. Problems such as the depletion of the ozone layer and destruction of tropical rainforests affect every country in the world, requiring a joint approach to managing the global environment. The global environment can be interpreted as an international public good: no single country has the incentive to practice good behaviour, if other countries behave recklessly. A problem in negotiating international codes of behaviour is that compliance costs are significant for developing countries and that countries in which a rain forest is located, for example, must forego the profits from exploiting such a resource. This calls for substantial international transfers to these countries, which are hard to negotiate. At the EU level, however, it may be possible to foster international cooperation on more local spillovers, such as the joint ecological management of rivers or seas that are shared by different EU members.

4 CONCLUSION

The central theme of this chapter has been that the government is a major agent in the economy. A number of important economic functions, necessary for the efficient working of the economy, can be performed only by the government but it can use an array of different policy instruments in carrying out these functions. The maximisation of social welfare requires that the government chooses the optimal combination of these policy instruments to attain the desired policy objectives.

The analysis in this chapter gives some clues as to the likely evolution of the nature of government intervention in the coming decades. One international trend is a shift from the government as provider to a role in which government offers subsidies to the private provision and consumption of socially desirable goods and services. Another trend is toward ever greater internationalisation of the policymaking process, as trade and financial linkages bind countries closer together. A major potential problem is the difficulty of negotiating common policies across very diverse countries.

Finally, it should be recognised that the performance of the government is an important determinant of international competitiveness. An efficient government enhances the ability of domestic firms to compete in international markets, by reducing the taxation, and other, costs of attaining policy objectives. (In international empirical studies, an efficient government is highly correlated with strong growth performance.[15]) For this reason, and the others discussed in this chapter, the analysis of government intervention in the Irish economy remains a primary task for those interested in maximising Ireland's national welfare.

Endnotes

1 S. Knack and P. Keefer, 'Institutions and Economic Performance' (unpublished paper, American University), February 1994.
2 R. Barro, 'Public Finance in Models of Economic Growth', *Review of Economic Studies,* October 1992.
3 G. Becker, *Human Capital: A Theoretical and Empirical Analysis* (third edition), University of Chicago Press, Chicago 1993.
4 W. Baumol, 'Macroeconomics of Unbalanced Growth: The Anatomy of Urban Crisis', *American Economic Review,* LVII, 1967.
5 J. FitzGerald, 'Babies, Budgets, and the Bathwater: Demographic Change and Public Expenditure in the Medium Term' (unpublished paper, Economic and Social Research Institute), October 1994.
6 A. Alesina and G. Tabellini, 'A Positive Theory of Fiscal Deficits and Government Debt', *Review of Economic Studies,* July 1990.
7 M. Olson, *The Logic of Collective Action: Public Goods and the Theory of Groups,* Harvard University Press, Cambridge MA 1965.
8 J. Lee, *Ireland 1912-85 Politics and Society,* Cambridge University Press, Cambridge MA 1989, p.489.
9 N. Roubini and J. Sachs, 'Political and Economic Determinants of Budget Deficits in the Industrial Democracies', *European Economic Review,* May 1989.
10 A. Annett, 'Elections and Macroeconomic Outcomes in Ireland, 1948-91', *Economic and Social Review,* October 1993.
11 A. Shleifer and R. Vishny, 'Politicians and Firms', *Quarterly Journal of Economics,* November 1994.
12 L. Summers, J. Gruber and R. Vergara, 'Taxation and the Structure of Labor Markets: The Case of Corporatism', *Quarterly Journal of Economics,* May 1993.
13 J. Durkan, 'Social Consensus and Incomes Policy', *Economic and Social Review,* April 1992.
14 A. Alesina and E. Spoloare, 'On The Number and Size of Nations' (NBER Working Paper, no. 5050), Cambridge MA 1995.
15 R. Barro and X. Sala-i-Martin, *Economic Growth,* McGraw-Hill, New York 1995.

CHAPTER 5

Taxation Measures and Policy

Frances Ruane and Francis O'Toole*

1 INTRODUCTION

This chapter profiles and examines in detail the role of taxation in Ireland. The effects of taxation policy permeate across all sectors of the Irish economy and the reader's attention is drawn to the connections between this chapter and other chapters in this book. The previous chapter which describes the role of the government in the economy and the next chapter which overviews fiscal policy are essential reading for an appreciation of the omnipresent nature of the issue of taxation in Ireland. This chapter could also be read in conjunction with Chapter 2 on growth, employment and income distribution, Chapter 8 on employment and unemployment, Chapter 10 on competition policy and Chapter 12 on the manufacturing sector.

There are three separate reasons for the existence of significant levels of taxation in the modern economy. The first, and most important, reason stems from the need to finance the production of goods and services provided by the government. The second role for taxation is to generate funds in order to redistribute income within society. Both of these functions of taxation were discussed at length in Chapter 4. A third reason for some taxes is that they may be designed specifically to alter economic behaviour. A characteristic of such taxes is that they are imposed when there are negative externalities associated with consumption or production, i.e. costs to society from the consumption or production of these goods or services which are not borne by the immediate consumer or producer. Examples of such taxes today are those related to energy consumption, designed to conserve global energy resources and/or to protect the world from undesirably high levels of carbon emissions. The significance of such taxes varies from country to country, but it is not to be expected that these taxes will, on their own, provide adequate finance to meet the fiscal needs of the modern economy. Indeed, a tax designed to reduce consumption or production, if successful, may generate relatively insignificant revenue.

* The authors appreciate John O'Hagan's helpful comments.

Having established the role of taxation in the modern economy, the rest of this chapter attempts a comprehensive survey of positive and normative issues relating to taxation. Section 2 outlines generally accepted criteria for the evaluation of different types of taxes and introduces the relevant taxation terminology. Section 3 contains a positive analysis of the structure of the Irish tax system, contrasting the contribution to revenue of various tax categories in Ireland with the average in the European Union. It also includes a brief description of each of the major taxes in the Irish economy. Section 4 focuses specific attention on some of the most important issues relating to income and consumption taxes in Ireland. Attention is drawn to the interactions between the tax and social welfare systems and the influence of European tax policy on Irish tax policy. Section 5 summarises the core recommendations from recent reports on the Irish tax system and an attempt is made to measure the extent of deviations from these recommendations. Section 6 concludes the chapter by outlining likely future developments in international tax policy and the possible effects on Irish tax policy.

2 PRINCIPLES OF TAXATION

The purpose of this section is to develop criteria by which it will be possible to appraise the relative value of different types of taxes. There is a long-established set of criteria to serve this purpose, namely, Adam Smith's canons of taxation as outlined in *An Inquiry into the Nature and Causes of The Wealth of Nations* (1776).[1] Smith's canons of equity, certainty, convenience of payment and economy of collection are perhaps even more important today as the scale of taxation has increased dramatically in the intervening two centuries. The rest of this section examines these attributes under the headings of equity, efficiency and tax administration.

Equity in the present context is a rather elusive concept. The ability-to-pay principle, which underlies the vast majority of tax systems, relates an individual's tax payment to the individual's ability to pay, which in practice is taken as the individual's level of income. This principle suggests that taxpayers should make similar sacrifices in terms of happiness or utility. Although this principle generally suggests that an individual's tax payment should increase with income, its acceptance does not necessarily demand the adoption of a progressive tax structure. A progressive (regressive) tax structure implies that an individual's average tax rate (tax payment as a proportion of income) would increase (decrease) with income. To focus more explicitly on an individual's relative share of taxation requires the introduction of two further concepts: horizontal equity and vertical equity. Horizontal equity concerns the post-tax positions of individuals in similar pre-tax situations. With income serving as an economically appropriate surrogate for situation, most individuals would subscribe to the view that individuals with similar incomes should face similar tax bills. The vertical equity dimension focuses on the pre-tax and post-tax incomes of individuals in different situations. Those advocating progressive taxation would promote a tax system resulting in the narrowing of income differentials, whereas those advocating regressive taxation would promote one leading to a widening of income differentials. As will be seen in later sections, in practice it is rather difficult to classify certain elements of the tax system as progressive, proportional or regressive.

Efficiency refers to the minimisation of the inevitable distortions which arise in the presence of taxation. A tax imposed on a commodity or factor of production creates a wedge between the buying price and the selling price of the commodity or factor and, as such, results in the distortion of market signals. Efficiency requires that the resulting distortion be as small as possible, subject to meeting the revenue requirement. More specifically, the presence of a tax induces an income effect and a substitution effect. The income effect is related to the reduction in real income or purchasing power caused by the tax and as such is unavoidable; if a tax is to raise revenue for the government it must reduce purchasing power elsewhere in the economy. The substitution effect measures the response to the change in relative prices introduced by the tax. This effect indicates the presence of a loss above and beyond the tax revenue generated, which is accounted for by the income effect; it is sometimes referred to as the excess burden or deadweight loss of the tax. Tax efficiency requires the minimisation of these substitution effects across the economy. If, for example, consumers alter relative purchasing behaviour dramatically in response to a particular commodity tax, this tax is generally regarded as particularly distortionary. In the absence of any particular desire to alter economic behaviour, tax efficiency requires low (high) tax rates to be placed where responses are elastic (inelastic), so that these distortionary effects are minimised.

Tax neutrality refers to a situation where tax rates across a range of commodities are equalised. The concept of tax neutrality is invoked when people speak of a level playing field, suggesting that commodities or factors be taxed equally. Only when elasticities are equivalent will tax efficiency imply tax neutrality, and, in general, tax efficiency will justify different rates of taxation depending on differences in the demand and supply elasticities.

Tax administration is a subject which until recently was largely ignored by economists. In its broad sense, the effective administration of a tax system requires that considerations be given to the following topics: the compliance costs of taxpayers as well as of tax authorities; the effective enforcement of the tax system; and the elimination of uncertainty in the tax code. With respect to the latter issue, Adam Smith's comments seem particularly perceptive:

> Where it is otherwise, every person subject to the tax is put more or less in the power of the tax-gatherer, who can either aggravate the tax upon any obnoxious contributor, or extort, by the terror of such aggravation, some present or perquisite to himself. The uncertainty of taxation encourages the insolence and favours the corruption of an order who are naturally unpopular, even where they are neither insolent nor corrupt. (*An Inquiry into the Nature and Causes of The Wealth of Nations,* Vol.2, Book 5, p.351)

An effective tax system when administered appropriately will be characterised by the lack of scope for widespread tax evasion and tax avoidance. Tax evasion refers to the illegal non-declaration of taxable funds whereas tax avoidance refers to the legal circumvention of the tax system. An environment in which there is a high incidence of tax avoidance and tax evasion fosters disregard for the tax system as happened in Ireland in the late 1970s (see Section 5). More recently, the Irish government has implemented two tax amnesties so as to encourage non-compliant individuals to enter the tax net. Although apparently highly lucrative in terms of extra revenue for the government, many commentators have noted the simultaneous creation of incentives towards the non-declaration of taxable funds, given the possible future repetition of the amnesty.

Although the attributes of equity, efficiency and administrative simplicity have been treated separately so far, the interactions between these goals are fundamental to an understanding of taxation. Economists generally focus on the underlying trade-off between equity and efficiency. Equity, at a general level, requires the equal treatment of similar individuals in terms of income effects combined with some acceptable level of progressivity in the tax system. Efficiency simply requires the minimisation of substitution effects, and consequently the maximisation of income effects, ignoring the relative share-out of income effects. For example, almost all empirical studies show that female labour supply is more responsive than male labour supply to income taxation. Equity considerations dictate the equal taxation of females and males on similar incomes whereas efficiency considerations would dictate the imposition of higher rates of income tax on males.

It is conceivable, however, that economists have overstated the conflicting nature of these goals. Equity and administrative considerations may often work in the same directions since a progressive tax system based on ability to pay as measured by income or expenditure is relatively easy to administer. In the context of the design of optimal tax systems, some trade-offs are inevitable among these goals; however, in the context of the existing Irish tax system, it will be argued in later sections that it is possible to improve simultaneously the equity, efficiency and administrative characteristics of the tax system.

3 STRUCTURE OF IRISH TAXATION

This section begins the examination of the structure of the Irish tax system by noting some general characteristics of taxes and the major sources of Irish tax revenue. The rest of this section looks at each component of the tax system in some detail; the interested reader is referred to annual reviews of the Irish tax system published by the Institute of Taxation, together with annual budget speeches and Finance Acts for comprehensive and up-to-date details on the Irish tax system.

Characteristics of Taxation

Before examining the structure of taxation in the Irish economy, it is useful to note the key elements which determine it. In the first place, a tax may be general or specific; in other words, it may apply to a broad range of activities, or to a subset of activities. For example, a sales tax on all goods and services would be described as a general tax, while a tax on cigarettes would be labelled a specific tax. Similarly a tax on profits would be a general tax, while a manufacturing profits tax would be a specific tax relating to the taxation of profits in the manufacturing sector.

Second, one can distinguish between a tax which is *ad rem,* where the amount of the tax is independent of the monetary value of the good or service, and one which is *ad valorem* where the value depends on the monetary value of the good or service. Examples of the former in Ireland are per-bottle taxes on wine, spirit taxes (based on the alcohol content) and TV licences, while examples of the latter are sales taxes (in Ireland, value-added taxes (VAT)) which depend on the value of the good(s) or services(s) sold, and income taxes, which depend on nominal income levels. A key feature of *ad valorem* taxes is that revenue is automatically indexed to the rate of inflation; hence in a time of inflation, the government has to increase the nominal value of an *ad rem* tax, in order to retain the real value of the revenue raised, while the revenue of an *ad valorem* tax automatically increases.

Third, for any given *ad valorem* tax, there may be a single rate or multiple rates. In the case of a single rate of tax, the marginal tax rate is constant and equal to the average rate, i.e. the tax revenue goes up in constant proportion to the value of the activity being taxed. For example, a proportional tax on income (Y) would be expressed as $T = tY$, where T is the tax revenue and t is the rate at which the tax applies. In the case of multiple rates, there are thresholds at which the marginal tax rate changes, usually increasing as it does so. In this instance the average tax rate is changing, usually rising. The simplest case is the situation where there is a single rate of income tax, but it is not imposed until a certain level of income is reached. Here the equation for the tax may be written as $T = t(Y - R)$, where R (> 0) is the non-taxed component of income. In effect, there are two marginal rates (0 and t), and the average tax rate rises from 0 towards t, as (Y - R) increases. This type of tax is referred to in the public finance literature as a linear progressive tax: the linearity refers to the constant marginal tax rate (above the income level R), while the progressivity refers to the rising average tax rate.

In Ireland, for example, each individual has a range of income (a set of tax allowances) on which no tax is imposed. The individual then confronts the standard rate of income tax which applies over a certain range of income, referred to as the standard rate tax band, beyond which a higher rate of income tax applies. Consequently, even for those on the standard rate of tax in Ireland, the tax system is progressive as the average tax rate is rising.

Tax allowances and tax bands are key concepts in defining the tax base, which is the monetary aggregate to which the tax rates apply. In the case of the income tax, if the allowances are very large, the tax base is reduced and the tax rate required to yield a given tax revenue target increases. In this context, it is important to distinguish between automatic and discretionary allowances, with the former being available to all taxpayers, and the latter being available only to those taxpayers who earn or consume their incomes in particular ways. Automatic allowances are usually intended to facilitate the redistribution of income, allowing the tax system to be progressive even at the standard rate of tax as outlined above. Typically discretionary allowances are introduced to alter behaviour, but they inevitably have effects on income distribution, which often work in the opposite direction to the effects of automatic allowances as will be outlined in the next section.

The issue of the breadth of the tax base arises not just in the case of the income tax but throughout the tax system. Other examples include VAT not applying across all consumption goods, property taxes having a high tax-free threshold and inheritance tax thresholds depending on the relationship between the donor and the donee. In each case the tax base is narrower than it might otherwise be and higher rates of tax, and consequently higher marginal tax rates, are required to generate a particular tax revenue target. In effect, the broader the tax base, the lower the tax rate which is required, and consequentially, because the substitution effect is related to the size of the tax rate, the less distortionary is the tax system.

Sources of Tax Revenue

In the absence of knowledge of the relative importance of different tax categories, discussion in the media or in a particular budgetary context can give a false impression about the significance of any particular tax or proposed tax change.[2] Table 5.1 summarises the major revenue sources in the Irish tax system for 1992, the latest year for which comprehensive and comparable data are available. Similar figures for the European Union average are presented so as to allow for comparison. Total tax revenue in Ireland for 1992 was over IR£10,848 million, so that the sources identified in Table 5.1 account for over 99 per cent of total tax revenue.

Table 5.1

Major Sources of Tax Revenue in Ireland and the European Union, 1992

	Ireland IR£m	Ireland %	(1993)[1] Ireland %	EU %
Taxes on individual income	3,472	32.0	32.2	26.3
Employee social security contributions	590	5.4	5.7	10.6
Taxes on payroll and workforce	143	1.3	1.3	0.4
Employer social security contributions	983	9.1	9.2	15.5
Taxes on goods and services	4,361	40.2	38.6	32.1
value-added taxes	2,179	20.1	19.4	18.0
taxes on specific goods and services	1,962	18.1	17.2	12.4
Corporate taxes	739	6.8	8.2	6.7
Taxes on property	476	4.4	4.2	4.3

Source: OECD, *OECD Revenue Statistics of Member States 1965-1993*, Paris 1994.
[1] Estimates provided by the Revenue Commissioners.

The first item in the table is the taxation of individual income, often referred to as direct personal income tax; the term 'direct' refers to the fact that the tax falls directly onto individuals, and thus it is possible to identify who exactly is paying the tax. This accounted for 32 per cent of total tax revenue in Ireland compared with an EU average of just over 26 per cent. Any small change in the tax rates or tax allowances associated with the income tax system has significant implications for national tax revenues, which explains the emphasis on direct personal income taxation in all discussions of tax systems.

It is common in looking at personal taxation to incorporate employee social security contributions. These contributions can be viewed as a further tax on individuals, since the so-called contributions do not cover the associated social provisions, especially of state pensions. These employee contributions, referred to in Ireland as PRSI (Pay-Related Social Insurance), account for about 5.5 per cent of tax revenue, compared with an EU average of 10.6 per cent. While it is common to combine income tax and employee social security contributions for analytical purposes, it is important to keep in mind that they do not have the same tax base, an issue which is returned to later. In addition to income tax and social security contributions, there are also special levies or payroll taxes which were introduced during the 1980s in Ireland. These levies are identified with specific purposes, namely a health levy and an employment/training levy. Such levies are often referred to as hypothecated taxes, as their revenue is earmarked and does not enter into the general revenue pool. To the extent that social insurance contributions are used for the specified purposes, they also incorporate an element of hypothecation. These taxes, although imposed at very low rates, account for about 1.3 per cent of tax revenue, as they apply to a very broad tax base; the

EU equivalent of such taxes is 0.4 per cent of revenue. Combining these levies with income tax and employee PRSI, 39 per cent of tax revenue comes by way of direct personal taxes on individuals in Ireland, compared with an EU average of 37 per cent.

Before completing the discussion on social security taxes or contributions, it is necessary to comment on the size of employers' contributions in Ireland compared with the EU average. In the EU the average share of revenues arising from employers' contributions is significantly higher than in Ireland, 15.5 per cent compared with 9.1 per cent. To the extent that these taxes are passed on to employees by employers via lower remuneration, these could in principle be added to personal taxes on individuals, in which case taxes on income account for a significantly higher proportion of total revenue in the EU (53 per cent) compared with Ireland (48 per cent).

The other revenue-significant taxes in Ireland are those which fall on the consumption of goods and services. These taxes are typically referred to as indirect taxes. They come under three main headings: value-added taxes, which, as noted above, are *ad valorem* taxes applied to expenditures on goods and services on a proportional basis; excise taxes, which are typically *ad rem* taxes applied to specific goods and services on some measure independent of price; and finally customs and import duties, which have become relatively insignificant for EU member states as membership of the General Agreement on Tariffs and Trade (GATT) and EU membership itself have reduced the domestic revenue implications of taxes imposed on trade. Collectively these taxes account for 40 per cent of Irish tax revenue, compared with an EU average of 32 per cent.

The remaining significant sources of taxation are corporate taxes and taxes on property (somewhat of a misnomer as will be explained below), which account for 8 and 4 per cent of revenue respectively in Ireland and correspondingly 7 and 4 per cent in the EU. A key difference between Ireland and the EU is that the share of revenue accounted for by corporate taxes has been rising (albeit from a very low base) in Ireland over the past decade, while it has generally been falling in other EU countries. Ireland's recent corporate tax history can be explained by the fact that the corporate share of tax had been historically very low, due to the zero-rating of taxation of profits on export sales of the manufacturing sector since the 1950s, and increasing, due to the growth in declared profits in Ireland of multinationals in the manufacturing and internationally-traded services sectors. These issues will be discussed further below.

Income Tax
Broadly speaking, income tax is charged on income accruing to all residents within the state, whether arising within or outside the state, and on income of non-residents generated within the state, to an extent which depends on the double-taxation agreements between Ireland and the home country of the

non-resident. For income-tax purposes, income is taxed according to four different schedules, which in order of importance are: (i) income from an office, employment or pension (Schedule E), which is taxed on a Pay-As-You-Earn (PAYE) basis, with the employer typically deducting tax from gross income on the basis of *ad hominum* certificates from the Revenue Commissioners, and with taxpayers paying out or recouping any outstanding amounts at the end of the tax year (5 April); (ii) profits of trades, professions, etc., rental income, interest income and income from abroad (Schedule D), which includes the incomes of the self-employed; (iii) interest income on certain government and other securities (Schedule C); and (iv) income from distributions received from a resident company (Schedule F), which makes some allowance for tax already paid under the corporate tax system. A continuing source of controversy relates to the definition of income for tax purposes under Schedule D, with some commentators suggesting that Schedule D income is grossly understated, resulting in the underpayment of taxes by those coming under this Schedule compared with those in the PAYE sector. The possibilities for such understatement arise because of the inherent uncertainties regarding the assignment of expenses when premises, transportation, etc. are shared across business and domestic needs.

Taxes are imposed according to a given schedule, which is typically subjected to change in the annual Budget, held in January or February of each year, and introducing changes which usually apply from 6 April of that year. The present system in Ireland, as of 6 April 1995, has two tax rates: a standard rate of 27 per cent and a higher rate of 48 percent. The standard rate applies as soon as the individual's tax-free allowances are used up. The value of the automatic annual allowances (personal allowances) in 1995/96 are IR£2,500 for an individual and IR£5,000 for a married couple, single parent or widow/widower with children. In the case where a married individual is not working in the paid labour market, that individual's full allowance can be transferred to the spouse working in the market. The span of the married couple's standard band is also twice that attaching to the individual (IR£17,800 compared with IR£8,900 in 1995/96). Thus the Irish tax system can be seen as being neutral as between marriage and non-marriage when both individuals are working in the market, but to favour marriage over non-marriage when one individual is not working in the formal labour force.

In addition to the personal allowances, there are allowances which attempt to take account of differences in the social conditions of individuals. These allowances cover contingencies which would affect the taxpayer's ability to pay tax, such as caring for incapacitated children, the presence of dependent relatives, and conditions such as old age and blindness. Furthermore, there are other allowances available which are linked to the way in which income is earned. For example, those paying tax under the PAYE scheme get an additional annual allowance of IR£800 and those paying the higher rate of PRSI (see below for details) receive an extra annual allowance of IR£140. Neither of these allowances, however, is transferable between spouses. In general the self-employed are not eligible for these allowances, but as indicated above they are eligible to apply for deductions in respect of business expenses, including allowances for cars, petrol, business entertainment, etc.

As noted above, there is a set of discretionary allowances which can further reduce the tax unit's tax bill. Perhaps the most important of these are the allowances against tax for contributions to pension funds and superannuation schemes, which are intended to encourage individuals to provide for themselves in retirement. To avail of the tax exemptions, individuals must commit a portion of salary to a pension scheme; the value of the exemption is limited to 15 per cent of earnings. Similar allowances for life insurance premia, however, have been removed in recent budgets, as these were seen to have become tax avoidance mechanisms rather than methods of encouraging individuals to provide for retirement.

Another important discretionary allowance is mortgage interest relief, which is relief against tax on the interest component of mortgage repayments on the individual's primary residence. In 1995/96 the maximum amount of this relief is IR£2,500 for first-time home buyers, and IR£1,900 for other borrowers, with double these allowances being available for married couples. The availability of this relief reflects a stated desire to encourage home ownership in Ireland. The value of these allowances to individuals who can avail of them is considerable, especially when put in the context of the value of the basic allowances. In recent years, to moderate some of the adverse equity effects of the system, wherein the value of the allowances is greater for higher-rate taxpayers, the government has begun the process of standard-rating the allowances so that relief in the future will only be provided at 27 per cent, i.e. the standard rate of tax.

Another important allowance, which relates to health insurance premia, is intended to encourage individuals to provide for unknown health contingencies. All premia to the state health insurance scheme, the Voluntary Health Insurance (VHI), are tax deductible, as are contributions to health benefit schemes. As in the previous case of mortgage interest relief, in the future tax relief for health insurance will only be available at the standard rate of tax.

Other significant discretionary allowances cover business expansion schemes (BES), investment in certain state savings schemes and investments in special long-term savings accounts. In the case of the BES, investments of up to IR£25,000 per annum in qualifying companies are eligible for relief against income tax, as long as the investment is held in place for at least five years. The intention of such schemes is to encourage individuals to invest in unquoted Irish companies, with the significant tax allowances intended to compensate for the higher risks associated with such investments. The allowances for state savings schemes (e.g. post office savings accounts) permit the government to pay a lower interest rate on long-term investments to individuals by allowing preferential tax treatment on the return to savings through these vehicles. The allowances for special long-term savings accounts, which take the form of a preferential tax rate on interest income of 15 per cent compared with the standard rate of 27 per cent, were introduced to reduce the risk of a major capital outflow into foreign savings accounts at the end of 1992 in response to the removal of restraints on capital flows within the European Union.

Pay-Related Social Insurance and Levies

As discussed in relation to Table 5.1 employees are liable for PRSI contributions and health and employment/training levies. The PRSI system is extremely complex, with a variety of rates and conditions applying to different classes of insured individuals. As far as contributions are concerned, it is possible to identify two major groups: Class A1, who are mainly employed persons, and Class S1, who are mainly self-employed persons.[3] The current rate structures for each class are complex and suggestions for rationalisation have been put forward by the Report of the Expert Working Group on the Integration of the Tax and Social Welfare Systems.

Most employees contribute 5.5 per cent of gross income, with a weekly non-cumulative allowance of IR£50 per week, up to an income ceiling of IR£21,500, above which there is no contribution due. At the same time, those with gross incomes above IR£9,250 contribute 1 per cent by way of an employment/training levy and 1.25 per cent by way of a health levy on all income, with no income ceiling. Thus the marginal contribution rate is 5.5 percentage points higher for those at or below the IR£21,500 ceiling compared to those above the ceiling. The corresponding rates for S1 claimants (the self-employed) are 5.0 per cent on gross income up to IR£21,500, with a weekly non-cumulative allowance before tax liability of IR£10 per week. The conditions for the employment/training and health levies are the same as above.

Employer PRSI contributions are quite significant, accounting for over 9 per cent of Irish tax revenues in 1993. The structure of rates is rather complex, reflecting recent changes, some of which were instigated in response to competitive features of the UK social security system. The standard rate of contribution is 12.2 per cent on all incomes up to a ceiling of IR£25,800, after which there is no further contribution due. However, because of the pressure which this tax places on employers in low-wage, labour-intensive sectors (e.g. the clothing sector), the employer rate for incomes at or below IR£12,000 is reduced to 9.0 per cent, with the rate jumping to 12.2 per cent on all income once income rises above the IR£12,000 threshold. Thus while the abatement in the rate below £12,000 reduces the disincentive to create employment in low-wage sectors, the dramatic increase in the tax liability of employers at the threshold level creates complex economic incentives.

Capital Gains Tax

For individuals who invest in shares or other assets, the possibility arises of income being earned in the form of capital gains rather than in the form of dividend income (distributed profits). In Ireland taxes on asset appreciation are only liable at the time of disposal of the asset and only real capital gains are taxed, i.e. the inflation rate is subtracted from the nominal rate of capital gain to compute the real gain. The standard rate of tax is 40 per cent on capital gains over and above an annual exemption of IR£1,000 for an individual and IR£2,000 for a married couple. In the case of special qualifying companies, with an issued share capital of less than IR£25 million and which are unquoted on the stock exchange, a special tax rate of 27 per cent applies. Furthermore, certain Irish government stocks are also exempt from capital gains tax.

The other area in which significant capital gains tax considerations arise is on property. The 40 per cent tax rate applies, except in the case of the sale of an individual's primary residence, which is exempt from capital gains tax, unless its value has been inflated by its redevelopment potential, in which case a development tax applies.

Corporate Income Tax

A key feature of the Irish corporate tax system is its dual tax rate structure. There is a standard rate of 38 per cent and a preferential rate on profits in manufacturing and certain internationally-traded service activities of 10 per cent. In an OECD context, this combination of rates is among the highest and lowest respectively, and the rates apply to a profits tax base which is wide by European standards. In the current tax system, companies are allowed to offset capital costs against corporate income for tax purposes. The amounts allowed are referred to as capital allowances but the levels given may not relate exactly to the actual costs incurred. At present capital allowances are 15 per cent on plant and machinery, 4 per cent on industrial buildings and 15 per cent on hotels, all of which are given on a straight line basis, i.e. an equal proportion of the original capital value is allowed annually. In contrast, motor vehicles have depreciation allowances of 20 per cent, which are applied on a reducing balance.

The rationale for the lower tax rate of 10 per cent in manufacturing is to encourage the expansion of employment, partly by the influx of foreign investment. This rate has been extended to certain qualifying services. The impact of this incentive for Irish companies is less than for foreign companies, because the latter are typically in a position, through transfer pricing, to shift profits from high-tax to low-tax countries (see Chapter 9). While the 10 per cent tax rate encourages profit shifting into Ireland, it discourages a foreign company from engaging in marketing and research and development in Ireland. If these activities are carried out in other countries in which the company is operating, the associated costs can be offset against the higher corporate tax rates prevailing in these countries.

Value-Added Taxes and Excise Duties

Any business in Ireland where the supply of goods has a value in excess of IR£40,000 or the supply of services has a value in excess of IR£20,000 is required to register for VAT. This tax is a highly integrated sales tax, where the tax is levied at each stage of production and distribution and where companies at each stage are required to account for the tax. The development of the Single European Market has meant that non-taxable entities in Ireland are also liable for VAT on goods acquired in other member states, which must be paid to the Irish revenue authorities.

VAT is imposed upon a large range of goods and services in Ireland at four rates: 0 per cent, 2.5 per cent, 12.5 per cent and 21 per cent. The existence of multiple rates could be defended on the grounds that tax efficiency (and equity) need not require tax neutrality. Food, children's clothing and footwear, passenger transport and admission to cultural and sporting events are zero-rated or exempt from VAT.[4] The allocation of goods and services between the two tax bands of 12.5 per cent and 21 per cent appears a somewhat arbitrary procedure. Recent governments have shown a particular interest in switching goods and services produced by labour-intensive sectors into the lower-rate tax band. Examples include garage services and hairdressing. The streamlining of the VAT system which has occurred in recent years has resulted in the introduction into the VAT system of many goods and services previously zero-rated or exempt from VAT. Examples include adult clothing and footwear, legal services and electricity.

Excise duties are imposed across a small range of goods and services in Ireland. The major excisable goods in Ireland in terms of net receipts to the Revenue Commissioners (1993) are hydrocarbon oils (IR£625.5m), alcohol (IR£437m), tobacco products (IR£429.5m) and motor vehicles (IR£204.5m). Approximately 76 per cent of the price of a packet of cigarettes is made up of a combination of VAT and excise duties. Equivalent figures for a litre of leaded petrol, a litre of unleaded petrol, a litre of auto diesel, a pint of beer and a glass of spirits are 65 per cent, 62 per cent, 59 per cent, 37 per cent and 37 per cent respectively. As already outlined above, the main justification given for the imposition of excise duties on specific goods and services is to discourage the consumption and production of goods or services which have detrimental effects on individuals other than the direct consumers or producers of the products in question. It is argued, for example, that alcohol consumption in Ireland imposes significant external costs on the rest of society via an increase in public health costs, an increase in the incidence of intra-family violence as well as other violent and non-violent crimes, and an increase in the number of accidents associated with drunk-driving. It can, however, also be argued from a purely economic perspective that alcohol consumption shortens life-expectancy and consequently lowers public health costs as well as the cost associated with state pension support. Many studies suggest that the revenue yield from excise duties more than compensates the exchequer for the external costs imposed on the exchequer arising from the consumption of the products in question.[5] These cost-benefit analyses should be taken cautiously, however, as '...strictly speaking, a decent person would thus be a person who performs productively to his or her greatest capacity and who passes away on the day of his or her retirement.'[6]

With the implementation of the Single European Market in January 1993, a vehicle registration tax was introduced to replace the existing excise tax on motor vehicles, in such a way as to leave the overall tax revenue from cars unchanged. This tax is essentially an *ad valorem* tax, based on the open market selling price of cars and incorporates the VAT component, and contrasts with the former excise tax which was a specific duty payable by reference to the cubic capacity of the engine.

Taxes on Property
As previously indicated this heading is a misnomer in that the heading encompasses not only recurrent taxes on immovable property (i.e. property taxes) but also a variety of taxes on capital transactions and transfers, such as stamp duty payable on many types of financial transactions, and estate, gift and inheritance taxes. In principle this heading also includes wealth taxes although in the Irish case there has been no tax imposed on wealth *per se* since 1977. Approximately half of the tax yield from this category stems from property taxes.

The most widely discussed property tax in Ireland is the residential property tax, which was introduced in 1983. This tax is chargeable on the market value of residential property in Ireland owned and occupied by a person on 5 April each year and payable by 30 September of the same year. The tax is a rather minor source of revenue for the government, but it carries a disproportionate amount of attention because of its chequered history. Up to 1977 Ireland had a fairly broad based system of property taxes or rates which financed local authorities' expenditure; in that year those attaching to residential property were abolished by the government on the grounds that the basis for the tax, namely, the rateable valuations, were seriously inaccurate. Not only did this result in a significant reduction in revenue, it also removed the underpinnings of local government finance in Ireland, an issue which has come up for serious discussion again in the 1990s. The introduction of the residential property tax, some six years after the abolition of domestic rates, was very controversial, even though the tax was at a very low rate (1.5 per cent), and was only levied on the market value of the property above a significant valuation threshold (IR£94,000 in 1995) where the household income was above a certain threshold (IR£29,500 in 1995). One problem with the tax from an equity viewpoint is that it takes no account of the size of the mortgage outstanding on the house. Attempts to change the tax and introduce a more progressive structure with tiered rates in the 1994 budget failed.

The other significant component in this tax category is revenue from the taxation of capital transfers between individuals, in particular, the capital acquisitions tax and the probate tax. The capital acquisitions tax is a tax levied on the recipient of the transfer of assets belonging to a recently deceased individual whereas the probate tax is a tax levied on the value of the recently deceased individual's estate. The administration of both taxes is supported by the taxation of transfers (gifts) between living individuals, albeit at lower rates. Various rates of capital acquisitions tax apply depending on the value of the assets transferred and the relationship between the donor and donee. For example, a child may receive over IR£175,000 from his or her parent without any tax being imposed. Once this initial threshold is passed inheritances are taxed at marginal rates increasing from 20 per cent to 40 per cent. The probate tax imposes a 2 per cent tax on the value of all estates belonging to a recently deceased individual beyond a threshold of IR£10,000. Transfers between spouses are exempt from this probate tax and for the purposes of this tax, the market value of agricultural land and buildings is reduced by 30 per cent. It is noteworthy that the probate tax, with its lower rate and wider base, raises approximately 30 per cent of the revenue associated with the capital acquisitions tax.

4 ASPECTS OF INCOME AND CONSUMPTION TAXES IN IRELAND

This section develops issues relating to the two most important sources of tax revenue in Ireland: income taxes and consumption taxes. The efficiency, equity and administrative characteristics of each tax category are examined in turn with most emphasis being placed on the first two criteria, i.e. efficiency and equity. As already noted income and consumption taxes are often referred to as direct and indirect taxes respectively, with some analysts suggesting that income tax is less voluntary and more distortionary than consumption tax. It is important to stress that this dichotomy is somewhat artificial. Although the distinction may be true for a particular individual, it is not valid in the aggregate as the government can collect a given amount of tax revenue from consumption taxes by simply raising the tax rates and broadening the tax base to the appropriate extent. Consequently, consumption taxes can have the same distortionary effects on the labour market as income taxes. As will be seen in the next section, the Commission on Taxation in 1984 recommended the introduction of a direct expenditure tax in Ireland which would have further blurred the distinction between the two types of taxes.

In the context of both forms of taxation it is important to distinguish between the formal or legal incidence of a tax and the economic incidence of a tax. Legal incidence refers to who collects and sends the tax revenue to the appropriate authorities whereas economic incidence refers to who bears the incremental cost associated with the imposition of the tax. The determination of who exactly bears the economic incidence of a tax is complex, and, in advance of levying a new tax or altering an existing tax, there is often considerable uncertainty about who will bear such a tax. As an example of the uncertainty associated with the assigning of tax incidence, there has been much discussion in the tax literature about which group faces the economic incidence of the corporation tax: shareholders via a drop in dividends or a decline in the value of shares, final consumers via an increase in the price of goods and services, or employees via a decrease in remuneration. Other illustrative examples of the distinction between formal and legal incidence include the situation where business people send VAT payments to the Revenue Commissioners but it is generally accepted that it is the final consumer who, in effect, pays the VAT via an increase in the price level. It is also clear that a reduction in the size of employers' social security contributions can have benefits for both employers and employees via a reduction in the cost of employing labour and an increase in the nominal wage, respectively.

Income Taxes

It will be remembered from an earlier section that a tax has both income and substitution effects but that the distortionary effect of the tax stems from the substitution effect alone. From the taxpayer's perspective it is the marginal income tax rate which is of prime importance in terms of the decision about whether or not to increase labour supply. Table 5.2 shows the effects of the income tax system on efficiency by focusing on the marginal tax rate confronting taxpayers at different income levels in Ireland over the period 1980 to 1994. All income classifications are with respect to various proportions of average industrial earnings so as to allow a consistent comparison over time. Average (mean) industrial earnings were approximately IR£5,000 in 1980 and IR£13,600 in 1994 although it should be noted that approximately 70 per cent receive less than average (mean) earnings due to the skewed nature of the earnings distribution. It is also assumed that the taxpayer only avails of the standard tax allowances, i.e. the personal allowance, the PAYE and the PRSI allowances of a single individual. In some cases not shown in Table 5.2 a low-income taxpayer, by availing of the income exemption limit, faced a particularly high marginal tax rate of 53.5 per cent in 1994 made up of 48 per cent marginal relief and 5.5 per cent social insurance.

For comparison purposes it should be noted that the number of tax bands and the rates of income tax have fallen considerably over the period in question. In 1980 there were five tax bands (25, 35, 45, 55 and 60 per cent) but by 1994 this number had fallen to two (27 and 48 per cent). Despite these

Table 5.2

Marginal Percentage Rates of Income Tax
for Irish Employees[1]

Income as percentage of average (mean) industrial earnings	1980/81	1987/88	1994/95
50%	29.5	42.75	32.50
80%	39.5	42.75	34.75
100%	39.5	42.75	55.75
150%	45.0	64.50	55.75
200%	55.0	59.00	50.25
500%	60.0	59.00	50.25

[1] The individual exemption limit, personal, PAYE and PRSI allowances are incorporated.

changes, the figures in Table 5.2 indicate that a significant proportion of taxpayers faced a higher marginal tax rate in 1994 than they did in 1980. For example, taxpayers on average industrial earnings had a marginal tax rate of almost 56 per cent in 1994 by comparison with 39.5 per cent in 1980. The main beneficiaries of tax changes in Ireland over the past fifteen years in terms of marginal tax rates have been higher-income taxpayers whose marginal tax rate has fallen from 60 per cent to just over 50 per cent. As will be seen in the next section, this feature of income tax reforms during the 1980s holds across many countries. Equivalent figures for the year 1987 are also included so as to identify an important turning point in Ireland's public finances. As can be seen the marginal tax rate confronting (almost) all taxpayers has fallen significantly since 1987.

Many taxpayers do not have a choice with respect to the number of hours of labour they supply and the distortionary effects on the labour market associated with high marginal tax rates may be overstated. At least some individuals, however, have some control over the decision about whether or not to participate in the labour market. These individuals are particularly interested in the proportion of income that is taken away by income tax. Table 5.3 shows the average tax rates confronting different taxpayers in Ireland. The hypothetical taxpayers once again represent individuals receiving different proportions of average industrial earnings. The figures in Table 5.3 indicate the degree of progressivity within the Irish income tax system and focus attention on equity considerations.

Comparing 1980 to 1994, the Irish income tax system has become less progressive in the intervening time period. Individuals on 50 per cent of the average industrial income have seen their average tax rate increase from 14 per cent to 19 per cent, whereas those on five times the average industrial income have seen their average tax rate fall from 50 per cent to 47 per cent. This decline in the progressivity of the income tax system was a common trend across many countries during the 1980s as will be seen in the next section.

Table 5.3
Average Percentage Rates of Income Tax for Irish Employees[1]

Income as percentage of average (mean) industrial earnings	1980/81	1987/88	1994/95
50%	29.5	42.75	32.50
80%	39.5	42.75	34.75
100%	39.5	42.75	55.75
150%	45.0	64.50	55.75
200%	55.0	59.00	50.25
500%	60.0	59.00	50.25

[1] The individual exemption limit, personal, PAYE and PRSI allowances are incorporated.

Given the substantial decreases in nominal tax rates over the past fifteen years in Ireland, it is striking that many taxpayers appear to be facing a higher, rather than a lower, average tax rate. For taxpayers receiving twice the average industrial earnings, for example, the average tax rate has increased from 37 per cent to 42 per cent. The most obvious source of this feature is the non-indexation of the Irish income tax system. Basic tax allowances have increased by less than inflation and tax band thresholds have also declined in real terms. For example, the personal allowance increased from IR£1,115 in 1980 to IR£2,350 in 1994, an increase of 110 per cent, when prices increased by over 130 per cent. As Irish taxpayers' nominal incomes increased over time, taxpayers have found themselves being pushed into higher tax bands, i.e. bracket creep has occurred. Less obvious but perhaps just as important is the fact that bracket creep would have occurred even if the entire tax system had been indexed in line with inflation. For the tax burden to remain constant over time requires the indexation of the tax system with respect to the growth in nominal income, and not just the inflation component. As Irish taxpayers' real incomes increased over time taxpayers have found themselves being pushed into higher tax bands.

As previously indicated, Tables 5.2 and 5.3 can be misleading in many respects as the figures correspond specifically to a hypothetical individual claiming no extra allowances for 'dependants' and no discretionary tax expenditures. As outlined in Section 3, however, if a married couple is composed of one market-earner and one home-carer, the Irish tax system allows the transferring of the home-carers' major tax allowances to the market-earner. Many other countries do not allow such a significant transfer of allowances between spouses. The assumption that the hypothetical individual avails of no discretionary tax expenditures is particularly misleading as the extent of these expenditures in Ireland is very significant. As outlined above the availability of tax reliefs for mortgage interest payments, pension contributions, private health insurance premia and contributions to business expansion schemes are particularly attractive options for the taxpayer in Ireland.

The initial effect of incorporating these considerations into the above figures would be to decrease the average tax rate across most categories of taxpayers. A second effect would be to reduce the progressivity of the income tax system. It can be shown for the tax year 1989/90, that although high-income earners (defined as above IR£25,000 for 1989) made up a relatively small proportion of taxpayers availing of tax breaks, the extent to which they availed of relief was large. For example, although only 17 per cent of mortgage interest relief claimants were high-income taxpayers, their claims accounted for 24 per cent of the total tax expenditure associated with this relief. Somewhat similar results hold for the relief granted to private medical insurance contributions.[7] Recent movements towards standard-rating some of these reliefs will, however, have a progressive effect on the income tax system.

The above tables also focus exclusively on a PAYE taxpayer coming within the Class A1 PRSI classification, i.e. a taxpayer paying the full rate of 5.5 per cent social insurance. There has been much controversy in Ireland about the relative tax burdens of the PAYE/Class A1 sector, the self-employed sector (including farmers) and employees in the public sector. Part of the justification for the existence of the PAYE allowance was that until recently the self-employed paid tax on a previous, rather than current, year basis. Private sector employees and employers often complain about the relative security of the public sector. As against this argument at least some employees in the private sector appear to be making greater use of fringe benefits, e.g. company cars, preferential loans and various types of share options. Contrary to the impression given by the relative amount of space devoted to the two topics in Ireland, most of the real tax controversy in Ireland centres on the relative share-out of the tax 'burden' rather than on the size of the tax 'burden' itself.

Income Tax and Social Welfare
Although taxation and social welfare may warrant separate administrative units in Ireland, it is not possible to evaluate separately the effects of the social welfare and taxation systems on equity and efficiency. Although a complete analysis of the interactions of these two systems goes well beyond the scope of this chapter, it is possible to allude briefly to some of the more salient issues.[8]

The purpose of the social security safety net is to safeguard the welfare of the least well-off members of society. For the unemployed, this safety net takes the form of unemployment benefit or assistance together with various other benefits such as differential rent, free fuel allowances, butter vouchers, work-seeking expenses, Christmas bonuses and medical cards, which give entitlement to free medical care. For the employed with low incomes, this safety net may take the form of family income supplement (FIS) for those with children together with the possible receipt of other benefits such as differential rent, travel expenses and medical cards. In both cases extra allowances are received for 'dependants'. For example, in 1995 a social welfare recipient receives a weekly adult dependency allowance of IR£37.50 for her or his spouse provided that the spouse earns less than IR£60.00 per week.

Apart from the primary issue of the adequacy or otherwise of these safeguards in terms of eradicating poverty in Irish society, a related issue is the effect of these schemes on the incentives for an individual to take up employment opportunities should they exist.[9] An unemployment trap is said to exist when an individual is as least as well off in financial terms unemployed as employed. The replacement ratio, which measures the proportion of an individual's take-home income replaced by unemployment income, is used to identify the existence or otherwise of an unemployment trap. Many commentators suggest that a replacement ratio of greater than 80 per cent represents serious inefficiencies in the tax and social welfare systems in terms of effects on incentives. A connected issue is the poverty trap which is said to exist when taxpayers face a marginal tax and benefit withdrawal rate (MTBR) of at least 100 per cent. The marginal tax and benefit withdrawal rate encompasses the loss in benefits as well as the increase in tax confronting a tax unit.

Interactions between the tax and social welfare systems in Ireland do lead to the existence of unemployment and poverty traps. Table 5.4, taken from the Interim Report of the Expert Working Group on the Integration of the Tax and Social Welfare Systems, shows the distribution of the actual replacement ratio for various types of families in receipt of unemployment benefit in Dublin in 1989. Although it could be argued that labour supply far exceeds labour demand in Ireland, the potential influence of the tax and transfer system on at least the composition of the unemployed should not be underestimated. In particular, the figures in Table 5.4 suggest that families with children were particularly affected by high replacement ratios. Almost one-fifth of families with three or more children faced replacement ratios in excess of 100 per cent. These high replacement ratios were due in part to the withdrawal of the medical card and allowances for dependent children, which are obviously of particular benefit to large families, when moving from unemployment into employment. The Report suggested that high replacement ratios for individuals are also partly explained by the availability of only relatively low-paid employment opportunities and that females faced particularly high replacement ratios due to a combination of two factors: low-wage part-time employment and the tax treatment of married couples where both individuals work in the market.

It is ironic that the highest tax and benefit withdrawal rates fall on the least well-off, but it is perhaps inevitable given that the system aims to help those in need by taxing those in paid employment. The extent of the problems indicated in Table 5.4 have decreased somewhat in recent years with the introduction of various schemes to ease the transition from unemployment to employment.

Table 5.4

Distribution of Replacement Ratios
for Unemployment Claimants in Dublin, 1989

Replacement ratio x (%)	Single (%)	Married (%)	Married &<3 children (%)	Married &3+ children (%)	All (%)
x ≤ 60	74.3	74.2	62.1	44.1	69.6
60 < x ≤ 70	6.2	6.1	6.2	15.2	6.8
70 < x ≤ 80	6.2	5.3	9.6	8.5	6.9
80 < x ≤ 90	4.3	4.6	5.1	6.8	4.7
90 < x ≤ 100	3.6	3.0	5.1	6.8	4.1
100 ≤ x	5.4	6.8	11.9	18.6	7.9
Sample Size	467	133	177	59	836

Source: Department of Social Welfare, 1989, quoted in *Interim Report of the Expert Working Group on the Integration of the Tax and Social Welfare Systems,* Dublin 1994, Appendix 2.

Further improvements are possible, perhaps by basing family income supplements on net as opposed to gross income, removing the all-or-nothing nature of medical card entitlement and integrating child support into the tax system. A more radical alternative would be to integrate fully the tax and social welfare systems via the introduction of an adequate income scheme whereby every individual is entitled to a level of income which is sufficient to support full participation in society. This adequate income scheme would have to be financed by a (relatively high) tax rate on all income.[10]

Consumption Taxes

Although many countries have experienced a small but significant shift in emphasis away from income taxes and towards consumption taxes, the reverse has occurred in Ireland. There has been an increase in the influence of VAT, similar in magnitude to that experienced by the rest of the EU, but the importance of excise duties in Irish tax revenue has declined sharply in recent years. The percentage of tax revenue accounted for by taxes on specific goods and services in Ireland fell from over 28 per cent in 1980 to just over 17 per cent by 1993. To understand the causes and effects of these changes two issues are examined in the remainder of this section: trends and recent developments in EU policy towards consumption taxes and the impact of consumption taxes on the distribution of post-tax income.

In recent years there has been considerable convergence within the EU with respect to domestic VAT systems. Table 5.5 contains the standard rate of VAT for EU member states for the years 1986 and 1993.

The range of rates was reduced from 0 per cent to 22 per cent in 1986 to 15 per cent to 21 per cent in 1993. It is worth noting that Ireland's standard

Table 5.5
Standard Percentage Rate of VAT in EU Member States, 1986 and 1993

	1986	1993
Belgium	19	19.5
Denmark	22	15
France	18.6	18.6
Germany	14	15
Greece	0	18
Ireland	25	21
Italy	18	19
Luxembourg	12	15
Netherlands	19	18.5
Portugal	16	16
Spain	12	15
United Kingdom	15	17.5

Sources: J. O'Hagan (editor), *The Economy of Ireland: Policy and Performance* (fifth edition), Irish Management Institute, Dublin 1987, and G. Metcalf, 'Value-Added Taxation: A Tax Whose Time Has Come?', *Journal of Economic Perspective*, no.1 1995.

rate was the highest for each year. The figures in Table 5.5, however, are slightly misleading in that many countries have a number of different rates. Ireland has two standard rates of VAT, 12.5 per cent and 21 per cent, and collects the same proportion of its tax revenue from VAT as other EU countries. Most EU member states have been moving towards the EU's harmonisation proposals for VAT. These proposals were drawn up as part of the process of completing the Single Market in 1992. They envisage the existence of a standard rate of VAT of at least 15 per cent, possibly two VAT rates between 5 and 15 per cent and the continued existence of a zero VAT rate on the consumption of certain commodities. At present, the implementation of VAT within the EU is equivalent to a destination-based tax implying that VAT is imposed in the place of consumption rather than production and exports are, in effect, temporarily exempt from VAT. This has the effect of encouraging cross-border shopping by individuals from high tax countries although significant differences in prices inclusive of VAT between countries are required to cover search and transport costs. It is proposed to move to an origin-based VAT system in the EU by 1997, implying that VAT will be imposed in the country of production rather than consumption. If this were to happen, significant discrepancies in VAT rates across the EU would no longer be possible, as arbitrage by business firms would be effective in eliminating any substantial price differences.

The payment of excise duties will, however, remain based on the destination basis within the EU. Although the Commission's draft directive on the harmonisation of excise duty structures or frameworks was not rejected, their proposals for the harmonisation of the rates of excise duties across the EU were rejected by the member states. Compromise proposals which envisage minimum rates of excise duties were accepted. Consequently, the process of harmonising excise duties across the EU will remain dependent on cross-border shopping by individuals. The Commission's proposals for the completion of the Internal Market in the Irish context led to the replacement of excise duties on motor vehicles by a motor vehicle registration tax, as noted in Section 3.

Attempts at measuring the effects of consumption taxes on equity centre on the analysis of household budget survey data. Table 5.6 displays original income, gross income, disposable income and post-tax income for each of the five income quintiles, e.g. the poorest quintile figures are for the poorest 20 per cent of households. Although these figures are for the UK it is unlikely that similar figures for Ireland would show substantially different trends.[11] The figures do not incorporate the effects of benefit-in-kind transfers which may serve to alter the income disparities substantially.

Table 5.6

Effects of Taxes and Benefits on Households[1] by
Income Level in the UK (IR£ per year)

	Poorest Quintile	2nd Quintile	3rd Quintile	4th Quintile	Richest Quintile
Original income	1,530	5,330	12,740	19,930	35,190
plus cash benefits	3,580	3,100	2,040	1,190	670
Gross income	5,110	8,490	14,770	21,120	35,860
less direct taxes	830	1,390	2,770	4,400	7,930
Disposable income	4,280	7,100	12,000	16,720	27,940
less indirect taxes	1,200	1,720	2,630	3,270	4,070
Post-tax income	3,080	5,380	9,370	13,450	23,860

Source: HM Central Statistics Office (1993), quoted in A. Glyn and D. Miliband (editors), *Paying for Inequality: The Economic Cost of Social Injustice,* IPPR/Rivers Oram Press, London 1994, Table 7.1.
[1] Income is measured by disposable income adjusted for family size.

In terms of gross income, the poorest quintile received just over 4 per cent of the richest quintile's income. When cash benefits are incorporated, however, this figure increased to over 14 per cent. Cash benefits include unemployment benefit/assistance, state pensions and child benefit. It is somewhat surprising to note the effect of direct and indirect taxes on the income disparities between rich and poor. The inclusion of the effects of direct taxes only increased the ratio of incomes to just over 15 per cent while the inclusion of the effects of indirect taxes served to decrease the ratio to less than 13 per cent. In effect, the tax system as a whole appeared to increase rather than decrease inequality. One should, however, be cautious before attempting to alter the tax system radically on the basis of Table 5.6, because the above figures, despite their appearance, may fail to estimate truly the progressivity or otherwise of the tax system. It can reasonably be argued that the extent of the inequality in original income is partly due to the existence of the given tax and transfer system. Original income is not necessarily equivalent to income in the absence of a tax system. In particular, the richest quintile have probably reacted to the existence of the tax and transfer system by increasing their income. It could also be argued that the tax system finances very significant redistribution via expenditure on non-cash benefits. Nevertheless, the apparent failure of the direct and indirect tax system to decrease inequality in and of themselves is still noteworthy.

Before drawing this section to a conclusion it is important to address briefly the issue of what relative emphasis should be placed on income taxes and consumption taxes. In terms of efficiency and equity considerations, there is no obvious response to this issue. Given the theoretical equivalence of flat-rate income and consumption taxes (albeit ignoring the important issue of savings), the relative magnitudes of revenue collected from these two taxes may seem irrelevant. For administrative purposes, however, it may be justifiable to rely on a flat-rate VAT and differential rates of excise taxes for revenue-raising purposes and income taxes for redistributive purposes. Utilising both tax bases makes tax evasion and tax avoidance more difficult. The advantage associated with using income rather than consumption taxes for redistributive purposes resides in the relative transparency of the income tax compared with the relatively unknown distributional effects of (indirect) consumption taxes.

5 TAX POLICY AND REFORM

Commission on Taxation
There have been recurrent calls for fundamental tax reform in Ireland since close to 750,000 people participated in protest marches advocating tax reform across the country prior to the 1980 budget. The nominally progressive income tax system was widely perceived to be ineffective in its redistributive role as an abundance of tax expenditures encouraged extensive tax avoidance. The lack of a comprehensive tax administration system also encouraged widespread tax evasion. The tax system could not readily be justified on efficiency, equity or administrative grounds as income taxes, consumption taxes, corporation tax and capital taxes all suffered from the same malaise of high tax rates being imposed on a small tax base. These problems were compounded by the lack of even nominal indexation in an environment of close to 20 per cent inflation. It was against this background that the Commission on Taxation was established in March 1980. The following extract, from its terms of reference, outlines its assignment:

To enquire generally into the present system of taxation and to recommend such change as appears desirable and practicable so as to achieve an equitable incidence of taxation, due attention being paid to the need to encourage development of the national economy and to maintain an adequate revenue yield.

Over the subsequent five years the Commission published five reports which dealt comprehensively with issues relating to the Irish tax system: direct tax; tax incentives; indirect tax; special taxation and tax administration. A list of recommendations was accompanied by a timetable for implementation. The Commission provided a comprehensive and widely-acclaimed blueprint for the implementation of a more equitable and efficient tax system. The Commission's major recommendations have been endorsed by subsequent reports from the National Economic and Social Council (NESC) on the Irish economy and by the Culliton Report on Industrial Policy. Given the widespread support for the Commission on Taxation's major recommendations, the rest of this section attempts to place its proposals into the context of the present tax system in Ireland.

On income tax the Commission chose comprehensive income as the appropriate measure of an individual's income and ability to pay. Under this criterion the measure of an individual's income in a given period is the amount of expenditure possible without altering the individual's net wealth. Income in this sense would include labour income, income from pensions, social welfare income, dividend income, interest income, imputed income from home-ownership, fringe benefits, gifts and inheritances, capital gains and gambling winnings; in fact any increase in net wealth, independent of its source, would constitute an addition to this tax base. The Commission recommended that this comprehensive income base be taxed at a single rate. A rate below the then standard rate of 35 per cent was envisaged with the corresponding reduction in tax revenue to be financed by the elimination of all tax reliefs, apart from a personal tax credit, a married person's tax credit and a head of household tax credit. The distorting influence of inflation on the tax system was recognised by the Commission which called for the full indexation of the tax system.

The Commission also advocated the abolition of social insurance contributions and other payroll taxes, to be replaced by a flat-rate (approximately 5 per cent) social security tax levied on all income with the employer's contributions being based on profits as opposed to payroll. To facilitate the desired level of income redistribution, the Commission proposed the introduction of a direct expenditure tax on the highest-income earners, in addition to the income tax. Such a tax would be levied on income net of newly-registered savings. The Commission recommended a restructuring of the tax treatment of borrowing and saving to facilitate a levelling of the playing field for both. For example, to discourage the use of housing as an investment good, mortgage interest tax relief was to be replaced by a system more directly focused on first-time buyers. After the introduction of a property tax, however, full deductibility of real mortgage interest would be allowed.

With regard to corporation tax the Commission recommended that it should be set at the standard rate of income tax and full imputation allowed, to ensure that the tax system would not influence the organisational form of business activity. The Commission in its Second Report suggested that the perceived need for tax incentives stemmed from the environment of high marginal rates of taxation and recommended an allowance for true economic depreciation only, and the replacement of corporate tax reliefs with direct aid for attracting foreign investment into Ireland, encouragement of market and product development and the short-term protection of infant industries in the traded sector. Debt servicing was not to be allowable against profits to avoid any bias in the choice between equity and debt.

With respect to consumption taxation, the Commission recommended a single rate of VAT on all final purchases. Given a comprehensive base, a VAT rate of 15 per cent was estimated to be revenue neutral, significantly less than the then standard rate of 23 per cent. Continued use of excise taxes on goods such as alcohol, tobacco and motoring were justified along the standard negative externalities grounds, but in setting tax rates due attention was to be paid to the problem of cross-border trade.

The Fourth Report dealt with issues of special taxation including local taxation and the tax treatment of property, natural resources and charities. Major recommendations included a broad-based local property tax, the increased revenue yield to be offset by the abolition of the residential property tax and a general reduction in other taxes, and the possible introduction of an environmental tax. Local service charges were to be implemented where feasible and economic rent accruing from the exploitation of Irish natural resources should be taxed to the greatest possible extent consistent with resource development. The final report dealt with tax administration and recommended a move towards self-assessment to allow the taxpayer take more responsibility for financial affairs, the deduction of tax at source where possible and the granting of extra powers to the Revenue Commissioners in the enforcement of the tax code. The Commission argued that increased compliance with the tax code in terms of less tax evasion and tax avoidance would follow on naturally from the significant simplifications to the overall tax system recommended in earlier reports. The Commission strenuously argued for the adoption of its five reports as an integral package of tax reforms and against selective implementation which would invariably be based on political, rather than economic, considerations. The Commission suggested a time scale of at least three to four years for full implementation of the package of reforms.

Tax Reform in the 1980s

During the 1980s important tax reform legislation was enacted in many countries. Prominent examples include the UK budgets of 1984 and 1988, the US Tax Reform Act of 1986 and the radical restructuring of New Zealand's financial procedures that took place in the period after 1986. Although each reform package was country-specific, the following general features repeated themselves across many countries: a significant decrease in the higher rate(s) of income tax; a move towards a broader income tax base together with lower tax rates; and a shift away from the use of excise taxes and towards the adoption of VAT.

The most significant change that occurred in income tax systems during the 1980s was the reduction in the higher rate(s) of income tax. The UK's top income tax rate, for example, fell from 60 per cent to 40 per cent. Other notable examples included the US, Japan and Sweden where the central government's highest rate of income tax fell from 70 per cent to 31 per cent, 75 per cent to 50 per cent and 50 per cent to 25 per cent respectively. Income from a variety of sources is now subject to tax at rates closer to the rates imposed on labour income with the source of income becoming less important for tax purposes. Capital gains, fringe benefits and dividend income have been at least partially incorporated into the effective definition of income, the inclusion of dividend income is being facilitated by a general movement towards the imputation system of corporation taxation. Canada and Japan provide prominent examples of the shift away from excise duties and towards VAT.

Tax Reform in Ireland

A comprehensive review of the progress made in implementing the Commission on Taxation's recommendations for the Irish tax system can be found elsewhere.[12] The purpose of the present section is to focus attention on the Commission's central recommendations, namely, the adoption of the comprehensive definition of income as the appropriate tax base in Ireland. Tax expenditures represent departures from this comprehensive notion of income and encompass tax exemptions, which exclude certain categories of income from the tax base, and tax allowances, which reduce the tax base by a certain amount. The rich benefit disproportionately due to the 'upside-down' distributional effects of tax expenditures in a progressive tax structure. In an Irish context, for example, a taxpayer in the 48 per cent tax band benefits disproportionately from pension contribution relief compared to a taxpayer in the 27 per cent tax band.

Prior to the formal publication of the Commission on Taxation's First Report it was agreed to publish estimated costs for the major tax expenditures in the annual Statistical Report of the Revenue Commissioners. Costs are based on the revenue foregone concept which allows for no behavioural responses by taxpayers in response to the hypothetical removal of tax expenditures and as such these costs tend to overestimate the expected monetary gain to the exchequer from the removal of a specific tax expenditure. Manufacturing relief, for example, has been very attractive to foreign firms and it seems naive to suggest, as the revenue foregone method does, that foreign direct investment has not been responsive to these tax reliefs and would not be responsive to their removal. Notwithstanding this criticism, however, Table 5.7 contains the revenue foregone estimates for the major discretionary tax expenditures in Ireland for 1980/81, the year of the 'tax revolt', and 1991/92, the most recent year for which comprehensive data are available.

Table 5.7

Major Discretionary Tax Expenditures (IR£m)
in Ireland, 1980/81 and 1991/92

	1980/81	1991/92
Income Tax		
Medical insurance premiums	6.0	51.9
Employees' pension contributions	10.0	57.0
Self-employed retirement premiums	10.0	27.9
Superannuation income	30.0	216.0
Mortgage interest	36.0	181.4
Interest on Post Office savings	1.2	23.9
Business expansion scheme	0.9[1]	31.3
Corporation Tax		
Manufacturing relief (10 per cent tax rate)	40.0[2]	748.9
Capital allowances	99.0	351.0
Section 84 loans	76.5[3]	131.0

Source: Statistical Reports of the Revenue Commissioners, various years.
[1]1984/85. [2]1982/83. [3]1985/86.

Given that inflation between 1980 and 1991 was approximately 120 per cent the figures in Table 5.7 clearly indicate that the real value of discretionary tax expenditures have increased substantially over the time period in question. For example, the value of the tax relief associated with medical insurance premiums (e.g. VHI premiums) increased by over 750 per cent during the same time period. The total estimated value of discretionary tax expenditures in Ireland as a percentage of GNP increased from 4.3 per cent in 1980 to 11.2 per cent in 1989. Subsequently the ratio declined to a value of 9.1 per cent in 1990.[13] The progressivity of the tax system was undermined by increasing the value of discretionary tax expenditures and decreasing the value of automatic tax expenditures as the total estimated value of automatic tax expenditures in Ireland as a percentage of GNP decreased from 8.6 per cent in 1980 to 7.0 per cent in

1989. Tax revenue as a percentage of GNP, however, increased over the decade implying an increase in effective tax rates for individuals unfortunate enough not to have received the benefit of discretionary tax expenditures. These details are consistent with the figures in Table 5.3 which showed an increase in the average tax rates confronting many taxpayers in Ireland.

6 FURTHER ISSUES IN TAXATION

This chapter has given a snapshot of current taxation in Ireland. It has also tried to give some background as to how the tax system has developed, in the context of internal and external pressures for tax reform. However, tax systems do not stay constant and in completing an overview of current tax policy it is important to reflect on how things might change in the years ahead.

One feature of tax systems is that they can no longer be country-specific. In effect, the evolution of tax systems in any one country will occur in the context of developments in related economies. These relationships, which arise primarily through trade in goods, services and factors of production (capital and labour), are both direct (to the countries with which Ireland trades), and indirect (to third countries with which Ireland does not trade directly but with which it competes in other markets). It has long since been recognised, and indeed it is part of the development of the GATT, that countries' trade taxes will inevitably be driven to similar patterns. However, it has only been relatively recently recognised that with the increased openness of world economies many other (non-trade) taxes are under pressure to follow patterns established elsewhere.

The evolution of increasingly similar patterns of taxes is being promoted through formal tax harmonisation. While the EU has not set particular rates which countries must adopt, it has defined ranges into which tax rates are expected to fall. These are defined quite precisely in the context of VAT as outlined previously, and a detailed proposal is to be found for corporate tax in the Ruding Committee Report.[14] Another major factor supporting the development of similar taxation patterns is tax competition, whereby countries view and evaluate their tax systems with reference to those of their competitors, and because of such pressures, they are constrained in the extent to which they can operate independent tax policies. Thus while the EU might set a broad range for certain taxes, tax competition may well lead competing countries to converge on virtually identical rates within that range. In the case where there are no such ranges recommended, tax competition operates in two ways; firstly, cross-country comparisons are made by interest groups, who lobby governments when relevant tax rates in competing countries are lower. This puts pressure on a tax-by-tax basis for tax reductions, with no similar pressure for tax increases whenever taxes are found to be below competitor levels. Second, to entice mobile investments countries compete by reducing tax rates or narrowing the tax base to increase their attractiveness as a location for such investment. The growth in tax competition, which is ever more likely with the pressure to attract mobile investment into the EU in the face of increasing competition from Eastern European sources, will affect the overall ability of governments to raise revenue.

In the Irish context, the pressure of EU-harmonised VAT rates has been reinforced by the need to compete in retail markets with Northern Ireland, particularly since the establishment of the Single European Market, which allows any volume of cross-border shopping for personal consumption. In the case of corporate tax rates, the period of Ireland's preferential tax rate of 10 per cent for manufacturing comes to an end in 2010. Whatever the policy put in place in 2010, it will have to be approved by the European Commission and there will be pressure to reduce or even remove the disparity between the preferential rate and the standard rate, currently 38 per cent. Furthermore, it is likely that the Commission will identify both the base and the rates in its future deliberations, since both are required to determine the effects of the tax. The position of the International Financial Services Centre in 2005 is such that the European Commission will be under pressure from other EU member states not to countenance the continuance of any significant preferential tax rate.

It is inevitable that the pressure for similar rates, through formal harmonisation or tax competition, would occur initially on mobile items, i.e. VAT on goods and taxes on capital. Will the pressure stop there? Inevitably there will be pressures from Irish firms to have relevant tax rates matched to UK rates, where these are lower than Irish rates. This pressure is already evident in the case of employers' PRSI and with the lowering of top marginal tax rates on income in the UK. Clearly if the pressure on income taxes becomes considerable, given the VAT and capital tax constraints, tax revenue potential in Ireland is going to be limited, as the range of items and activities which can legally avoid tax increases. In this context, there is every reason to believe that there will be increasing pressures for broad-based property taxation. Whether this will happen depends on both political will and the cost of collecting such a tax.

Strictly speaking, even in a globalised economy it is not necessary to have similar taxation and, given the difference across countries, such similarities may not be appropriate. Countries differ in many respects, so why should their tax systems be identical? To achieve tax diversity, which is something to which Ireland has traditionally aspired, requires tax coordination covering the whole system. Pairwise comparisons of individual taxes can be most misleading in determining whether or not competition is being impeded. For example, while Irish PRSI rates may be less favourable than UK rates, Irish corporate tax rates are generally lower, so that from the point of view of an individual Irish firm the overall taxation effect may be more favourable than for a UK firm in the same sector.

In addition to the pressures imposed by the increasing internationalisation of transactions, there are effects generated by developments in technology, which have reduced the administrative costs of certain taxes, and by the increased use of litigation in tax matters, which has increased the cost of certain taxes. Kay concludes that, as a result of these two effects, 'it is attractive to rely on taxes which might have previously been excluded because of their extensive requirements for the maintenance of records'.[15] Kay attributes the increased significance in revenue terms, noted in Section 5.3 above, of VAT, social security and income tax to the reduced costs of collecting these taxes; for example, low-cost record keeping has made it possible to extend VAT coverage to very small units. Similarly, he attributes the declining share of taxation of capital and capital income to the increased costs of administering such taxes, because these involve high administration costs and the exercise of judgement, which can be open to dispute. Thus, if Kay's analysis is correct, the pressure for taxation on those items which are immobile, e.g. a broad-based property tax as noted above may be partially offset by the likely cost of realising revenue from these sources.

Allowing for the fact that the efficiency of the Irish revenue authorities has increased dramatically as a result of the application of new technology, what are the implications of this for Ireland? It suggests that the recent trend towards an increasing yield from capital income will not continue and that the revenue potential of a broad-based property tax may be more limited than often thought. The impact of this is that the primary source of increasing tax revenue is likely to be via existing taxes: VAT, income tax and PRSI. For countries, like Ireland, with significant commitments to public expenditure, the constraints on revenue raising over the next decades may be much greater than in the past two decades. The only source of new taxation is likely to be through environmental taxes, but these are likely to be destined for European, rather than Irish, coffers.

Endnotes

1 The edition referred to in the text was published by the University of Chicago Press in 1976.
2 Many tax changes which involve a great deal of discussion often raise a relatively small proportion of the country's tax revenue. It could be argued, however, that such taxes may have serious allocative effects despite their limited revenue implications. A possible example of the latter would be wealth taxes.
3 The vast majority of public sector employees belong to neither of these classes. They pay a particularly low rate of PRSI but are entitled to very few benefits. Newly-employed public sector employees are, however, in Class A1.
4 Traders carrying on exempted activities cannot register for VAT. Traders carrying on zero-rated activities can register for VAT and consequently are entitled to reclaim VAT already paid at an earlier stage in the production process.

5 For a comprehensive review of the literature on the external effects of alcohol consumption, see A. Reilly, 'Issues in Excise Taxation: A Case Study of Alcohol Taxes' (unpublished M.Litt Dissertation, University of Dublin), February 1995.

6 E. Osterberg, as quoted in Reilly, *op. cit.,* p.66.

7 For further details see F. O'Toole, and F. Ruane, 'Taxation of High-Income Earners in Ireland: The Present Situation', in F. Ruane (editor), *Taxation of High Earners,* Proceedings of the Eighth Annual Conference of the Foundation for Fiscal Studies, Dublin 1994.

8 For a review of the efficiency and effectiveness of the tax and transfer systems in Ireland with regard to the reduction of poverty, see B. Nolan and T. Callan (editors), *Poverty and Policy in Ireland,* Gill and Macmillan, Dublin 1994. *The Report of the Expert Working Group on the Integration of the Tax and Social Welfare Systems,* 1995, also provides an excellent review of the interactions between the two systems.

9 See T. Callan and B. Nolan, 'The Role of the Tax and Social Welfare Systems', and T. Callan and C.J. O'Neill 'Reform of Tax and Transfer Policy', Chapters 15 and 16, respectively, of Nolan and Callan, *op. cit.,* 1994.

10 For a review of the issues surrounding the implementation of an adequate income scheme in Ireland, see B. Reynolds, and S. Healy, *Towards An Adequate Income For All,* Conference of Religious of Ireland, Dublin 1994.

11 For distribution statistics based on the 1980 Household Budget Survey in Ireland, see D. Murphy, 'The Impact of State Benefits on Irish Household Incomes', *Journal of the Statistical and Social Inquiry Society of Ireland,* 1983/84.

12 See F. O'Toole, Tax Reform in Ireland Since the Commission on Taxation', *Journal of the Social and Statistical Society of Ireland,* 1993/94.

13 For more details, see F. O'Toole, 'Discretionary Tax Expenditures and Tax Reform in Ireland' in S. Cantillon *et al* (editors), *Economic Perspectives for the Medium Term,* Economic and Social Research Institute, Dublin, 1994.

14 See *Conclusions and Recommendations of the Committee of Independent Experts on Company Taxation,* Commission of the European Communities, Brussels 1992.

15 For more details, see J. Kay, 'Tax Reform: A Perspective Longer Than the Life of One Parliament', in F. Ruane (editor), *The Irish Dilemma: How to Achieve Fiscal Reform,* Proceedings of the Ninth Annual Conference of the Foundation for Fiscal Studies, Dublin 1994.

CHAPTER 6

Fiscal, Monetary and Exchange Rate Policy

Anthony Leddin and Jim O'Leary

1 INTRODUCTION

The principal objective of this chapter is to provide an overview of fiscal, monetary and exchange rate policy in Ireland. Section 2 discusses the role of fiscal policy from 1973 to 1995. Issues of particular concern include the effectiveness of fiscal policy in achieving growth and employment objectives, the factors underlying the rise in Ireland's national debt, the burden of that debt and the conditions under which the debt can be reduced in the future. Section 3 discusses the development of central banking in Ireland from the early nineteenth century to the present day. Section 4 discusses monetary policy and in particular the Central Bank's interest rate and credit policies. Section 5 examines exchange rate policy, the experience in the EMS and the policy implications arising from the currency crisis of 1992/93. Finally, Section 6 discusses certain issues relating to the proposal to create a monetary union in Europe.

2 FISCAL POLICY

Introduction

Governments spend money across a wide range of areas including the provision of education and health services, the maintenance of a system of justice and national defence, the construction of roads and public buildings and the payment of social welfare to people who are deemed to be in need of income maintenance. Expenditure by government is classified as either current or capital. Current items include the wages and salaries paid to public servants and transfer payments made to social welfare recipients. The capital budget covers investment in the building of schools and hospitals, and the construction of roads, airports and sewage facilities.

Government spending, like the spending of private sector agents, has to be financed. The bulk of this is raised through taxation. Again, just as there is a myriad of schemes under which public funds are disbursed, there is a large number of different taxes on personal income, corporate profits, consumption, capital gains and so on (see Chapter 5). However, it is typically the case that what governments raise in tax and other forms of revenue is insufficient to match their expenditure. The balance – the government's borrowing requirement – has to be met by raising money through the creation of debt.

Given their scale, it is not surprising that the activities of government raise a great many analytical issues of interest to economists and to the public at large. The most basic of these relate to the extent of government intervention in the economy, since this defines the overall level of government spending (and taxation). In this respect the most extreme proponents of free enterprise challenge the status quo with some very radical questions indeed. Why not leave education and health entirely in the hands of the private sector? Why not have private armies and security firms look after the functions of defence and the protection of private property? Why should governments concern themselves at all with the welfare of those on low incomes?

Ultimately such questions can only be resolved through the political process. In broad terms electorates signal their preferences about the extent of government intervention by their voting behaviour. The preferences that are expressed are not, of course, devoid of economic implications. The electorate having decided, for example, that the living standards of the poor should be protected, it is up to government to put together the nuts and bolts of a system of income maintenance. The manner in which that system operates can have profound consequences for incentives, depending on how social welfare payments relate to income from employment. Moreover, the way in which the social welfare system (and public spending generally) is financed can have profound implications for the operation of the economic system as a whole. A given level of tax revenues can be raised in ways that are more or less damaging to economic efficiency depending on the composition of revenues as between income and expenditure taxes, and the structure of marginal rates of income tax.

All the issues touched on above are of considerable interest in themselves and have spawned different branches of enquiry within the economics profession. They have also been associated with the emergence of new policy preoccupations on the part of governments worldwide over the past twenty years or so. For example, the policy agenda of Mrs Thatcher's Conservative administrations of the 1980s was based on a radical questioning of the state's role in the economy, and the pursuit of that agenda resulted in government intervention being significantly scaled down in the UK.

The Place of Fiscal Policy
There are two profoundly different views of what fiscal policy is all about.

One school of thought, which for convenience we will call the neoclassical school, attaches a low value to fiscal policy as an independent instrument of macroeconomic management. The neoclassical view is that the level of government spending should be set with exclusive reference to considerations of economic efficiency, and independently of the levels of output, employment or prices. As far as taxes are concerned, the neoclassical position is that taxation should be set at a level that permits the government to finance the efficiency-maximising level of public spending while maintaining non-inflationary growth in the money supply.

In the classical model the role of fiscal policy is based on the premise that unregulated market economies tend to operate in the vicinity of full employment, except for short periods during which transitory unemployment may arise because of external shocks to the system. To the extent that unemployment persists, its source is to be sought in market rigidities caused, for example, by the interaction of the tax and social welfare systems.

The other view of fiscal policy comes from the Keynesian school. Keynesians look to fiscal policy as an active instrument of demand management and hold that modern economies are inherently unstable and private sector demand has an inherent tendency to fall short of the level required to maintain full employment. When output is below the full employment level, the Keynesian policy prescription is to adopt an expansionary fiscal policy by cutting taxes and/or raising government spending. Conversely, in circumstances where output is above its full employment level, the appropriate response is to raise taxes or cut spending. In a Keynesian world therefore, fiscal policy is ascribed the role of stabilising output around its trend growth path by manipulating the balance between government spending and taxation. In contrast to its neoclassical counterpart, the Keynesian model of fiscal policy has little to say about the *levels* or *composition* of taxation or spending.

The Keynesian view of the world held sway in the 1950s and 1960s. Throughout this period western economies managed to combine steady growth rates with moderate rates of inflation. That they did so was put down to the willingness of governments to adopt active fiscal policies, restraining demand when inflation threatened to accelerate and boosting demand when output fell below its full employment level. The thinking which underpinned this approach to fiscal policy was nicely complemented by the 'discovery' in 1958 of the Phillips Curve which suggested the existence of a stable inverse relationship between the inflation rate and unemployment.

The intellectual basis for 'fiscal activism' was dealt a severe blow in the 1970s. The aftermath of the two oil price shocks of 1973 and 1979 demonstrated that high and rising inflation could coexist with high and rising levels of unemployment, contrary to the relationship suggested by the Phillips Curve. In the circumstances it was not surprising that economists and policymakers sought alternative theories.

The renewed interest in monetarism and in classical economic thought that characterised the 1970s and 1980s can be traced to the oil price shocks. Governments' initial reaction to the first of these shocks was such that monetary aggregates expanded very rapidly. The conjunction of rapid money supply growth and accelerating inflation which followed conferred a fresh relevance on the quantity theory of money and the empirical evidence thrown up by the 1970s tended to favour the monetarist interpretation of inflation.

The 1970s also contained the seeds of the jettisoning of fiscal activism. Not alone had the simple Phillips Curve relationship broken down, but in the aftermath of the first oil price shock government deficits rose strongly. This resulted in the rapid growth of government debt and debt-service costs. The proportion of public spending accounted for by debt service also increased, and this constrained the ability of governments to engage in expansionary fiscal policies.

Another strand of thought which engendered scepticism about the validity of Keynesian prescriptions in the 1970s was the theory of the small open economy. Traditionally the focus of macroeconomic theory was on large economies in which international trade played a modest role, reflecting economists' preoccupation with the bigger economies such as the US and also the fact that when macroeconomic theory was in its infancy, barriers to trade were such that in all economies international trade was much less significant than it is now. In the 1970s, however, the small open economy became recognised as a valid and separate entity to which conventional thinking was inappropriate.

The significance of 'smallness' and 'openness' in the design of fiscal policy is captured by the following two observations. First, in a small open economy with unhindered access to world markets the fundamental Keynesian assumption that output is constrained by demand is difficult to sustain. For such an economy, a relatively small increase in its share of world trade would result in a large increase in output. Second, in such an economy the impact of expansionary fiscal policy is likely to be dissipated by leakages through imports to a significantly greater extent than in larger, relatively closed economies.

It would be unfair to conclude that the neoclassical view has now entirely supplanted its Keynesian counterpart or that fiscal policy in the world's major economies has become wholly shaped by neoclassical thinking. There is much in contemporary economic experience that is at odds with a world view based on the proposition that unregulated market economies operate in the vicinity of full employment. The pervasive incidence of high unemployment throughout the industrialised world is an obvious counterpoint. However, the current policy agenda in most western countries owes a good deal to the influence of neoclassical and supply-side theories, and fiscal policy as practised today is far removed from the pre-eminent demand management role it enjoyed in the 1950s and 1960s.

Measuring the Policy Stance

Discussions of fiscal policy are replete with references to the policy 'stance'. What is in question here is whether fiscal policy is expansionary or contractionary.

Before attempting to measure the stance of policy one must be clear about what it is one intends to base the measure on. In the Keynesian scheme of things the focus is on changes in the government's deficit (or surplus). In Ireland, data on government spending and receipts are published in both budgetary and national accounts format. In what follows we use the budgetary format since this is the one that is at the same time the less complicated and the more widely understood.

The narrowest definition of the budget deficit in the Irish case is the *current budget deficit* (CBD). This is the difference between government current spending and current receipts (tax and non-tax). A wider measure is the *exchequer borrowing requirement* (EBR) which also includes exchequer borrowing for capital purposes, or the shortfall between capital receipts and capital spending of the exchequer. The most comprehensive deficit measure is the *public sector borrowing requirement* (PSBR) which includes the borrowing of the local authorities and all the semi-state bodies. Another measure, which has gained currency since the ratification of the Maastricht Treaty, is the *general government deficit* (GGD) which lies between the EBR and PSBR, including as it does the borrowing of the local authorities and the non-commercial semi-state bodies but excluding the commercial semi-state bodies.

It used to be the case in Ireland that discussion of fiscal policy was couched primarily in terms of the current budget deficit. A strong distinction was drawn between the current and capital budgets on the grounds that borrowing to fund a current deficit was unsustainable whereas borrowing for capital purposes was not since capital spending produces a rate of return. Gradually it came to be recognised that this distinction, however valid in theory, was predicated on a rather naive view of the practice of public investment. In many cases state investment projects were embarked upon without proper investment appraisal and, when completed, yielded a rate of return below that required to service the debt contracted to finance them. In such circumstances a meaningful distinction between current and capital spending was difficult to operationalise.

In recent years the principal focus has been on the EBR. This reflects not only the difficulties that arise when trying to differentiate between the current and capital budgets, but also the fact that since 1987 the overriding objective of fiscal policy has been to reduce the ratio of government debt to GNP. The growth of government debt is the result not only of government current budget deficits but also of exchequer borrowing for capital purposes. When the government deficit is referred to throughout the rest of this section, the EBR is implied, although we shall also have reason to refer to the general government deficit (GGD) in the context of the Maastricht Treaty.

At the simplest level of abstraction, fiscal policy may be characterised as expansionary when the government deficit is increasing (or the surplus is falling) and contractionary when the deficit is falling (the surplus is rising). However, this characterisation is rather too simple to be of much value. In the first instance it is necessary to recognise that changes in the deficit can arise from two very different sets of influences: (i) deliberate decisions by government to change expenditure allocations or tax rates, and (ii) changes in the level of economic activity that produce consequential changes in spending and/or tax revenues. The first set of changes are *discretionary;* the second are called *automatic stabilisers.* It is only the first set that can validly be regarded as constituting a shift in policy. Changes of the second type are endogenous and should be excluded from any attempt to measure shifts in the policy stance.

Automatic stabilisers include spending on unemployment compensation and taxes on income and expenditure. Without any changes in policy, the former will tend to rise in periods of weak economic activity while the latter will be depressed in similar circumstances. Consequently, when the economy is slowing down the budget deficit will tend to rise, all other things equal.

If the effects of automatic stabilisers are removed from the budgetary arithmetic the result is the 'cyclically-adjusted' or 'structural' budget deficit. Several methods of deriving such estimates have been proposed. Basically, they all involve the calculation of government spending and revenues at the full employment level of economic activity. Such calculations have not become routinely available, although the OECD have produced estimates for Ireland.

Deficits and the Level of Output
In the simple Keynesian framework, expounded in many introductory textbooks, the effects of fiscal policy are modelled in terms of the economy's responsiveness to changes in aggregate demand. It is assumed that output in the economy is constrained by a deficiency in aggregate demand rather than by cost or supply-side factors. In this scheme of things an autonomous increase in consumer spending or in investment, caused by higher government spending and/or a reduction in taxation, increases the equilibrium level of output by a multiplier of the initial impulse.

In its simplest guise the multiplier is equal to (1/MPS) where MPS is the marginal propensity to save. More realistic formulations reflect the fact that the multiplier is a function of leakages not only through savings but also through taxation and imports. In economies where the marginal propensities to save and import are small and the marginal tax rate is also low, the multiplier may assume a value in the range 2.5 to 4, implying that expansionary fiscal policy imparts a considerable boost to output. Estimates for the US economy, for example, have produced figures in this range.

In Ireland, by contrast, where the marginal propensity to import is extremely high and both the savings rate and the marginal tax rate are also high, the multiplier is a good deal lower, and is unlikely to be much greater than 1. This implies that an injection of government spending raises output by no more than the amount of the initial increment of spending. However, that would not be an insignificant feat, and a multiplier of 1 should not be confused with a multiplier of zero. Indeed, the question arises: if an increase in government spending has the capacity to raise national output by an equivalent amount, why not increase government spending continuously and run budget deficits indefinitely?

There are several important objections to the policy prescription contained in this question. First, if the multiplier is as small as suggested by available estimates for Ireland, an expansionary fiscal policy has an inherent tendency to increase the share of government spending, and hence taxation, in GNP. But taxes involve efficiency losses because of the way in which they distort the responses of economic agents, and their efficiency or deadweight losses increase with the size of the tax burden. These adverse longer-term supply-side consequences of expansionary fiscal policy received little attention from the earlier advocates of Keynesian policies.

Second, it is important to remember that the Keynesian approach to fiscal policy is predicated on the assumption that the economy is demand- rather than supply-constrained. However, in a small open economy (SOE) with free access to international markets, the assumption that output is constrained by a deficiency in aggregate demand is hard to defend. After all, a relatively small increase in such an economy's share of world trade would produce a large increase in domestic output. Viewed from the SOE perspective, it would seem more logical to look for the constraints on output in the supply side of the economy, including the domestic cost structure. Pursuing expansionary fiscal policies in such an economy is more likely to result in a rise in imports and inflationary pressures than an increase in output. Indeed, in these circumstances, expansionary fiscal policy, by putting upward pressure on costs, runs the risk of exacerbating the very supply-side constraints inhibiting the economy's growth in the first place.

Third, it must be emphasised that Keynesians see fiscal policy as an instrument of *short-term* demand management. Government deficits are to be increased during intervals of aggregate demand deficiency but not maintained at their increased levels, or raised to even higher levels, throughout the cycle. The maintenance of such deficits and the resultant high and rising level of indebtedness in themselves create a negative climate for growth.

A commonly-heard proposition is that a high level of government borrowing results in upward pressure on interest rates through its impact on the balance between the supply of and the demand for loanable funds. This proposition has a seductive intuitive appeal about it but in reality the matter is not that simple. It is true that, all other things equal, an increase in government borrowing raises the demand for loanable funds relative to their supply, but as in so many other areas of economic enquiry, all other things are unlikely to be equal. For example, the Ricardian Equivalence Theorem hypothesises that the private sector anticipates the burden of future taxation implicit in increased government borrowing and increases its savings in order to provide for this. If this theorem is correct, an increase in government borrowing will be matched by an increase in household or corporate savings which will be available to finance it.

Over time, however, budget deficits can lead to higher interest rates and the possible 'crowding-out' of investment. There are at least two reasons why this might occur. First, there is what might be termed a 'portfolio effect'. As high levels of borrowing persist and the outstanding volume of government debt increases, the share of government debt in the portfolios of private investors will rise. As the asset composition of such portfolios changes, higher interest rates on government bonds may be required to induce the private sector to accommodate the higher weighting accounted for by government debt.

Second, there may be a 'credit risk' effect. As government debt increases, investors may fear that the authorities will be tempted to reduce the real burden of the debt by, for example, allowing the currency to depreciate. But what to the government is a process that reduces the real burden of its obligations, is to private investors a process that reduces the real value of their assets. Investors will seek compensation for this risk by way of higher interest rates. Moreover, if debt is being accumulated at an unsustainable rate by government, it may give rise to the fear that the authorities lack the economic and/or political resources to take the necessary corrective measures. This in turn may generate fears that the government will default on its obligations. Again, protection against this risk will require that interest rates on the debt be raised.

Fiscal Policy in Ireland 1973-86
Prior to the 1970s current budget deficits were not a feature of Irish fiscal policy, and government borrowing was planned for the purpose of financing capital spending only. In the aftermath of the first oil crisis in 1973, however, a current budget deficit was introduced as a means of offsetting the perceived deflationary effects of higher oil prices, i.e. on traditional Keynesian demand management grounds. However, deficits that are rationalised in terms of demand stabilisation should subsequently disappear. In the Irish case this did not happen. Instead the current budget deficit remained on an unrelenting upward trend until the early 1980s when it reached 8 per cent of GNP.

Table 6.1 tracks the evolution of public sector borrowing over the period since 1977. Four sub-periods can be identified: (i) 1977-82 when borrowing increased sharply; (ii) 1983-86 when borrowing stabilised at a very high level; (iii) 1987-89 when a sharp reduction in borrowing was achieved, and (iv) 1990 to date which has seen the deficit stabilised at a low level.

From 1973 through 1986 there was no coherent or consistent fiscal policy. The fact that a large and growing current budget deficit characterised this period indicates that the original declared purpose of running such a deficit became redundant. In the years 1977 through 1979, for example, the economy grew rapidly and would have done so without any fiscal stimulus and the increase in borrowing that occurred over this period is more than fully explained by an increase in the 'structural' deficit, that is, by conscious policy changes.

Table 6.1

The Public Sector Borrowing Requirement (PSBR)
and its Components as a Percentage of GNP, 1977-95

	Current budget deficit	Exchequer borrowing for capital purposes	Exchequer borrowing requirement	PSBR
1977	3.6	6.1	9.7	12.5
1978	6.1	6.3	12.4	14.9
1979	6.8	6.4	13.2	16.1
1980	6.0	7.4	13.4	17.2
1981	7.3	8.4	15.7	20.1
1982	7.9	7.6	15.5	19.6
1983	7.9	5.6	13.5	16.6
1984	7.0	5.3	12.2	15.9
1985	7.7	4.4	12.1	14.7
1986	7.9	4.2	12.1	14.2
1987	6.2	3.2	9.4	10.8
1988	1.6	1.5	3.1	3.8
1989	1.2	1.0	2.2	3.0
1990	0.6	1.3	1.9	2.8
1991	1.2	0.8	2.0	3.2
1992	1.7	1.0	2.7	3.2
1993	1.3	1.1	2.4	3.0
1994	0.0	2.2	2.2	2.5
1995[1]	0.9	1.5	2.4	3.0

Source: Department of Finance.
[1] Post-budget forecast.

By the early 1980s it was evident that government borrowing had become excessive and the 1983-86 period witnessed the first attempts to address this problem. But just as the absence of a coherent fiscal policy in the previous decade lay behind the emergence of the problem in the first instance, so it was that the absence of coherent policies in the years 1983 through 1986 limited the success of attempts to redress the situation.

First, it should be noted that the small reduction in exchequer borrowing achieved over this period was entirely due to a decline in borrowing for capital purposes. This was due not so much to conscious policy decisions as to the completion of a number of large projects that had previously boosted capital spending (the upgrading of the telephone network, the Cork-Dublin gas pipeline, the ESB power installation at Moneypoint, and the DART).

Second, what restraints were placed on the growth in the current budget deficit came as much from increases in taxation as from spending controls. Tax receipts rose from 32.3 per cent of GNP in 1982 to 34.4 per cent four years later (see Table 6.2).

Table 6.2

Government Current Spending and Revenue as a
Percentage of GNP, 1980-95

	Spending	Revenue	
		tax	total
1980	40.8	28.9	34.8
1981	43.6	30.3	36.3
1982	46.9	32.3	39.1
1983	46.2	34.1	38.3
1984	46.9	35.6	39.9
1985	45.8	33.6	38.1
1986	45.8	34.4	37.9
1987	43.9	34.2	37.7
1988	40.0	35.7	38.5
1989	36.2	33.6	35.0
1990	35.1	33.0	34.5
1991	35.8	33.0	34.7
1992	36.7	33.4	35.1
1993	36.8	34.0	35.5
1994	36.1	34.9	36.1
1995[1]	35.3	33.4	34.4

Source: Department of Finance.
Notes: The revenue data include once-off receipts under the Tax Amnesties of 1988 and 1994.
[1] Post-budget forecast.

By the end of 1986 the Irish public finances were in a state that offended against the basic tenets of the Keynesian and neoclassical schools alike. The size of the borrowing requirement could not be justified on demand management grounds. Nor could its evolution over the previous decade or so. From a neoclassical perspective there were several aspects of the situation that were of great concern: the high level of public spending could scarcely be defended with reference to efficiency criteria, likewise the level and structure of taxation.

Fiscal Policy Since 1987
The aspect of fiscal policy that eventually galvanised policymakers into firm corrective action was the extent of government indebtedness. Between 1977 and 1986 the absolute quantity of debt outstanding increased more than fivefold from IR£4.2 billion to IR£21.6 billion. As a proportion of GNP the debt increased from 75 per cent in 1977 to almost 122 per cent in 1986, by which stage it had become the highest in the OECD area. Debt-service costs

burgeoned. Interest payments on the debt amounted to the equivalent of 5 per cent of GNP in 1977; by 1985 the proportion was 11 per cent.

A NESC Report, *A Strategy for Development 1986-1990,* published in November 1986, argued that the stabilisation of the debt/GNP ratio and its subsequent reduction should become the overriding objective of fiscal policy. That report, which provided the foundations for the economic strategy of the government elected the following year, outlined the conditions required for the debt/GNP ratio to be brought under control.

Table 6.3

The National Debt and Interest Payments, 1977-95

	National debt		Interest payments	
	IR£m	% of GNP	IR£m	% of GNP
1977	4,229	75.2	279	5.0
1978	5,167	78.6	361	5.5
1979	6,540	85.0	450	5.8
1980	7,896	87.0	583	6.4
1981	10,195	93.2	796	7.3
1982	11,669	92.9	1,143	9.1
1983	14,392	104.8	1,330	9.7
1984	16,821	112.8	1,566	10.5
1985	18,502	111.4	1,827	11.0
1986	21,611	122.2	1,818	10.3
1987	23,694	125.0	1,935	10.2
1988	24,611	123.1	1,962	9.8
1989	24,828	112.0	1,956	8.8
1990	25,083	104.7	2,107	8.8
1991	25,391	100.3	2,147	8.5
1992	26,344	98.7	2,096	7.9
1993	28,358	99.3	2,159	7.6
1994	29,300	94.5	2,004	6.5
1995[1]	30,000	89.5	2,143	6.4

Source: Department of Finance.
[1] Author's forecast.

These conditions are best understood with reference to four magnitudes: (i) the growth rate of nominal GNP; (ii) the nominal interest rate; (iii) the national debt/GNP ratio itself, and (iv) the government's primary budget balance, which is simply the exchequer borrowing requirement exclusive of interest payment. It can be demonstrated that, with some simplification, the following relationship holds:

(1) $$\Delta d = b + (i - r) d$$

This equation states that the change in the debt/GNP ratio (Δd) depends on the primary budget deficit as a proportion of GNP (b), the initial debt/GNP ratio (d), and the gap between the nominal interest rate (i), and the rate of growth in nominal GNP (r). In order for the debt/GNP ratio to stabilise, i.e. for Δd to equal zero, the expression on the right hand side of the above equation must also equal zero. In other words the following condition must hold:

(2) $(i - r) d = - b$

Note that the minus sign indicates a primary budget surplus. What this condition means is that either the government's primary budget be in surplus, or the nominal growth rate in GNP exceed the nominal interest rate. In the event that the GNP growth rate is less than the interest rate, a primary budget surplus must be run in order to prevent the debt/GNP ratio from rising. The size of the primary surplus required to achieve this will depend on the gap between the growth rate and the interest rate and on the initial debt/GNP ratio. For example, an interest rate of 8.5 per cent and a nominal GNP growth rate of 6 per cent would require a primary surplus amounting to 3 per cent of GNP in order to stabilise the debt/GNP ratio at 1.20 or 120 per cent.

This simple algebra provides a useful framework for analysing the evolution of the Irish public finances since 1983. The period 1983 through 1986 was characterised by a primary budget deficit. That this occurred in circumstances where the interest rate faced by the government exceeded the growth rate of GNP meant that the debt/GNP ratio continued to increase. Note that for most of the subsequent period 1987 to 1993 the interest rate has continued to exceed the growth rate, but the primary budget balance swung sharply into surplus and by 1988 that surplus was sufficiently large to produce a decline in the debt/GNP ratio.

The main reason for this turnaround was policy action by the government in the 1987-89 period, including cuts in government spending (observe the behaviour of current spending as a proportion of GNP in Table 6.2) and a widening of the tax base through, for example, a highly successful tax amnesty in 1988. Moreover, exchequer borrowing for capital purposes was considerably reduced: in 1986 the capital deficit amount to the equivalent of 4.2 per cent of GNP while three years later this proportion had fallen to just 1 per cent (see Table 6.1).

Since the mid-1980s the restoration of order to the public finances has also been helped by the behaviour of interest rates as Table 6.4 illustrates. The nominal interest rate on exchequer debt reached 9.9 per cent in 1985 and averaged 9.2 per cent over the 1983-86 period. Since then it has been on a downward trajectory and had fallen to about 7 per cent by 1994-95. Taken together with the trend in outstanding debt, this resulted in a sustained and appreciable decline in interest payments relative to GNP, from 11 per cent in 1985 to an expected 6.4 per cent in 1995 (see Table 6.3).

Table 6.4

Factors Governing Sustainability of Public Finances

	Nominal GNP growth (%)	Nominal interest rate	Primary deficit (% of GNP)
1983	9.3	9.2	3.8
1984	8.6	9.3	1.8
1985	7.3	9.9	1.1
1986	6.5	8.4	1.8
1987	7.2	8.2	-0.8
1988	5.4	8.0	-6.7
1989	10.8	7.9	-6.7
1990	8.1	8.4	-6.9
1991	5.7	8.5	-6.5
1992	5.4	8.0	-5.2
1993	7.0	7.6	-5.1
1994	8.4	6.8	-4.3
1995[1]	8.4	7.1	-4.0

Source: Department of Finance.

[1] Post-budget forecast; minus sign indicates primary budget surplus.

The achievement of a substantial primary budget surplus and the resultant fall in the debt/GNP ratio on the one hand, and the decline in interest rates on the other, should not be regarded as independent events. As the earlier discussion suggests, they are inextricably linked. As the state of the Irish public finances have improved so has financial market confidence in government policies and investors have required a diminishing risk premium to invest in Irish government bonds and indeed, in Irish pound assets generally.

The Maastricht Treaty and Fiscal Policy in the Years Ahead
As in many other areas of economic policy (e.g. agriculture, competition) fiscal policy in Ireland has increasingly become subject to EU influence in recent years. At a micro level, indirect taxation, for example, is now subject to EU harmonisation requirements. At a macro level, budgetary policy must now be designed with reference to parameters laid down in the Treaty on European Union. The Treaty was signed in Maastricht in February 1992, and came into effect in November 1993.

One of the articles of the Maastricht Treaty stipulates that member states shall avoid excessive government deficits and the Treaty specifies procedures for ensuring that this requirement is honoured. A Protocol appended to the Treaty sets out the relevant reference values in respect of government deficits and debt, often referred to as the Maastricht convergence criteria. The reference values are 3 per cent of GDP for the government deficit and 60 per cent for the ratio of government debt to GDP. At the risk of oversimplification, the position is that member states will not qualify for membership of European Monetary Union (EMU) unless these two criteria are met.

Whatever their shortcomings, the deficit and debt reference values have come to dominate the setting for Irish fiscal policy in recent years and each of the last three budgets has cited the Maastricht criteria as the principal parameters guiding the government's budgetary targets. This situation may be viewed as a source of both strength and weakness: strength in so far as the continued adherence to a set of well-defined, externally-imposed constraints removes the risk of the public finances spiralling out of control as happened in the late 1970s and early 1980s; weakness in so far as the Maastricht reference values may induce a satisficing approach to fiscal policy, may cause the policy stance to be inappropriate in demand management terms, and may deflect attention away from the *levels* of government spending and taxation, as distinct from the balance between them. These weaknesses are well illustrated by the conduct of Irish fiscal policy in recent years, especially since 1990.

As Table 6.1 indicates, the EBR was reduced sharply between 1986 and 1990, falling over this period from over 12 per cent to less than 2 per cent of GNP. At the same time, the current budget deficit was virtually eliminated – by 1990 it had fallen to just 0.6 per cent of GNP compared with 8 per cent of GNP four years earlier – and the primary budget surplus was raised to almost 7 per cent of GNP (see Table 6.4). Since 1990, this momentum has been lost. In each of the succeeding five years the primary surplus has *declined,* and by 1995 had contracted to 4 per cent of GNP, while the EBR has edged up slightly and, in the context of a shrinking primary surplus, would have increased significantly were it not for a declining burden of interest payments.

That the primary surplus has fallen since 1990 (and the EBR has risen, albeit marginally) cannot be ascribed to cyclical factors because the economy has not been growing at a rate below trend over this period. In the years 1990 through 1995 the average annual volume growth in GNP was about 4.5 per cent, broadly in line with its longer-term average. Accordingly, the behaviour of the budgetary aggregates in recent years can be interpreted as evidence of a loosening of the overall fiscal stance or as evidence of satisficing behaviour by government.

This satisficing behaviour was particularly evident in the 1995 budget which set an EBR target of 2.4 per cent of GNP, up slightly on the 1994 outturn, despite the prospect of a robust growth rate in the economy. (The official forecast at budget time was a GNP growth rate of 5.25 per cent in volume terms, a rate significantly above trend). The budget target for 1995 seemed to be based on the thinking that once the relevant Maastricht reference value was comfortably undershot nothing else mattered much, including the consideration that a lower target than the 1994 outturn would have been warranted on Keynesian demand management grounds.

Moreover, since the Maastricht Treaty is silent on the question of the shares of government spending and revenues in GNP, an approach to fiscal policy which takes the Treaty as the primary point of reference downplays classical concerns about economic efficiency. In the Irish context it is again worth noting what has happened on this front since 1990. In the first instance current spending has tended to rise again relative to GNP, which means that spending has grown very rapidly in real terms. Second, exceptional tax buoyancy has meant that taxation revenue has also drifted upwards as a proportion of GNP.

Table 6.5

General Government Deficits and Debt as a Percentage of GNP

	Deficit 1995	Debt 1994	1996(f)
Belgium	4.7	140.1	136.0
Denmark	3.0	78.0	78.2
Germany	2.4	51.0	58.9
Greece	13.3	121.3	128.0
Spain	6.0	63.5	66.1
France	4.9	50.4	55.6
Ireland	*2.4*	*89.0*	*79.1*
Italy	8.6	123.7	128.6
Luxembourg	-1.6	9.2	9.9
Netherlands	3.5	78.8	78.0
Portugal	5.8	70.4	72.3
UK	4.6	50.4	53.1
EU 12	4.7	69.0	73.5

Source: European Economy, Supplement A, Nov/Dec 1994.
Note: minus sign denotes surplus.

Despite the evidence of a softer line on the public finances since 1990, the debt/GNP ratio has continued to fall as the primary budget surplus has either been (i) large enough to compensate for a GNP growth rate lower than the interest rate (1991 through 1993), or, (ii) has been accompanied by a situation where GNP growth has *exceeded* the interest rate (1994 and 1995). But the laxity of recent years would, if continued, produce a renewed increase in the debt/GNP ratio if GNP growth were to decelerate sharply and/or interest rates were to rise sharply. In other words the Irish public finances may currently be benefiting from a virtuous circle of sorts, based on the combination of a primary budget surplus, low interest rates and robust economic growth, but that virtuous circle is by no means unbreakable.

Still, it must be acknowledged that the public finances are currently in better shape in Ireland than in most of the other EU member states as Table 6.5 illustrates. Excluding Luxembourg the Irish government's deficit will be the lowest in the EU in 1995, a position that it also obtained in each of the years 1992 through 1994. As far as the debt/GDP ratio is concerned, the Irish ratio at end-1994, at 89 per cent, was still well above the EU average, but it is expected that the two positions will converge in the coming years. European Commission forecasts envisage the Irish ratio falling to 79 per cent by end-1996 at which point it will be no more than 5-6 per cent above the average for the EU as a whole.

3 THE CENTRAL BANK OF IRELAND:
ORIGINS AND DEVELOPMENT

The forerunner of the Central Bank of Ireland was the Bank of Ireland (now a commercial bank) which was established by the Irish Parliament in 1783. In the early years of the nineteenth century the Bank of Ireland performed duties normally attributable to a central bank. For example, it managed the government's account, it issued currency and it acted as a lender of last resort to other banks.

The Bank of Ireland, however, was never likely to evolve into a central bank. Following the Act of Union on 1 January 1801 and the amalgamation of the Irish and British currencies in 1826, the Bank of England assumed an increased responsibility for banking and promoted the use of sterling as the medium of exchange in Ireland. This diminished the need for the Bank of Ireland to develop its central bank activities. Simultaneously, other forces were operating to increase the commercial activities of the Bank of Ireland. For example, the emergence of the joint stock banks in the 1820s and the passage of the Bankers (Ireland) Act of 1845, led to an increase in bank competition and the Bank of Ireland evolved within this environment. By the time the country achieved political independence from Britain in 1922 the Bank of Ireland's commercial interests and its central banking obligations could not be easily reconciled.

In the years immediately following Independence in 1922 there was little change in the Irish monetary environment. It was not until the passage of the Coinage Act 1926 that the Irish Minister of Finance possessed the legislative authority to issue coinage. The first new coins (silver and copper and designed by a committee under the chairmanship of W. B. Yeats) were put into circulation on 12 December 1928. The new coins were quickly adopted by the general public and in the words of Yeats became 'the silent ambassadors of good taste'. This distinctive coinage remained in circulation until February 1971 when new decimal currency was introduced.[1]

On 8 March 1926 the Irish government appointed a Commission of Inquiry into Banking and the Note Issue. This Commission subsequently became known as the 'Parker-Willis Commission' after its chairman Professor Henry Parker Willis (1874-1937) of Columbia University and a former Secretary of the US Federal Reserve Board. Its function was to determine what changes were necessary or desirable in the law relating to banking and the note issue. The Commission presented its final (Majority) report on 21 January 1927. It recommended the issue of a new Irish currency (known as the Saorstát pound but renamed the Irish pound in 1937) which was to be maintained on a one-to-one, no margins, exchange rate with sterling. This rigid exchange rate policy was a reflection of the importance of Irish trade with the UK (approximately 95 per cent in the 1920s). To ensure public confidence, the Irish currency was to be backed 100 per cent by sterling reserves. The establishment of a Central Bank was 'not to be recommended as an immediate expedient'. Instead a Currency Commission (located in Foster Place in central Dublin) was to be established to supervise the issue the new currency.

The Currency Act 1927, passed by the Dáil on 20 August 1927, provided the legislation necessary to implement the Commission's proposals and the first of the new legal tender notes were issued on 10 September 1928.

In September 1931 Britain left the gold standard and sterling was devalued by 25 per cent on foreign exchanges. This enabled the new Fianna Fáil government to set up a second inquiry into money and banking. In November 1934 the government appointed a Commission of Inquiry into Banking, Currency and Credit which was chaired by Joseph Brennan and included the economist Per Jacobssen who subsequently became President of the International Monetary Fund. It is generally held that the Majority Report of the Commission published in August 1938 recommended that the Banking Commission be replaced by a Central Bank. However, Ó Gráda disputes this view by pointing out that the Committee '... in the end proposed that the Currency Commission be granted limited powers to engage in open market operations, and recommended an unspecified name change to reflect this central banking feature.' He argues that the government ignored the Report and that the Central Bank Act 1942 was a compromise between the government's ministers, on one side, and Brennan, on the other. [2]

The Central Bank Act 1942 led to the creation, on 1 February 1943, of the Central Bank of Ireland. The primary responsibility of the new Central Bank was to protect the 'integrity of the currency' and to this end the Central Bank could attempt to control credit in the economy and rediscount government stock. However, the powers of the new Central Bank were severely limited. The Central Bank did not, for example, have the power to set reserve requirements for commercial banks. The commercial banks continued to keep their reserves in the London money markets and were independent of the Central Bank for their liquidity requirements. Also the Bank of Ireland continued to manage the government's account. Joseph Brennan became the first Chairman of the Central Bank of Ireland. He resigned in March 1953 following a dispute with the government over economic and financial policy.

In the late 1960s it became clear that, due to the structural changes taking place in the banking industry, the Central Bank Act 1942 would have to be amended. (There was a previous, if minor, amendment in March 1964.) The Irish banking industry had grown rapidly and competition between the banks had intensified (largely due to the setting up in Ireland of subsidiaries of foreign banks). Also a number of mergers took place leading to the formation of the Bank of Ireland and Allied Irish Bank groups. The Central Bank had little supervisory control over the new arrivals and it was argued that additional legislative powers would be required if the Bank was to fulfil successfully its statutory duties in the future.

In September 1971, the Central Bank Act 1971 came into operation. This Act was based on proposals issued by the Central Bank in 1966 and had the effect of considerably increasing the powers of the Central Bank. Some of the main changes included the transfer of the commercial banks' reserves from the London money markets to the Central Bank. The Central Bank became the licensing and supervision authority for commercial banks and could set minimum reserve requirements. The government's account was transferred from the Bank of Ireland to the Central Bank. Also Section 4 of the Currency Act 1927 was repealed. This enabled the government to change the exchange rate of the Irish pound if it was considered desirable.

In 1989 a number of bills were passed which further extended the supervisory powers of the Central Bank. First, the Central Bank Act 1989 brought money brokers, financial futures traders and companies operating out of the new International Financial Services Centre (IFSC) in Dublin under the supervision of the Central Bank. In addition, a deposit protection account was established to protect small depositors and the Central Bank's statutory powers were extended to control bank charges. Also the Act gave power to the Minister for Finance to change the exchange rate or the existing arrangements for the Irish pound. The Building Society Act 1989, the Trustee Savings Bank (TSB) Act 1989, the ACC Bank Act 1992 and the ICC Bank Act 1992 brought the building societies, the TSB banks, the ACC and ICC banks under the supervisory control of the Central Bank.

In the future, the role and powers of the Central Bank of Ireland are likely to diminish rather than increase. The reason is that the Maastricht Treaty 1993 created a European Monetary Institute (EMI) which is intended to evolve into a European Central Bank. This new European Central Bank will replace existing national Central Banks and will have responsibility for monetary and exchange rate policy and for maintaining price stability in the EU. It is not, as yet, entirely clear what role national Central Banks will play within the European Central Bank but the expectation must be that the powers of Ireland's Central Bank will be significantly eroded.

4 MONETARY POLICY

Credit Guidelines
Before discussing the conduct of monetary policy in Ireland, one essential point should be emphasised from the outset. Under *fixed* exchange rates and perfect capital mobility, it is not possible for the Central Bank to control the

domestic money supply or interest rates. The reason is that differences between domestic and foreign interest rates will provoke offsetting capital flows and the money supply will quickly revert back to its initial level. For example, suppose the Central Bank decides to increase the money supply and reduce interest rates in order to, say, stimulate investment or boost consumer expenditure. Relatively low domestic interest rates will provoke a capital outflow until such time as both the money supply and the interest rate return to their original levels. This happens very quickly and interest rates do not remain low long enough to have any effect on investment, consumption or aggregate demand.

Conversely, suppose the Central Bank decides to decrease the money supply and increase interest rates in order to, say, reduce inflation. Relatively high interest rates in Ireland will lead to a capital inflow and again the domestic interest rate will revert back to its original level. Under a fixed exchange rate system and perfect capital mobility, there is little or no scope for an independent monetary policy. In these circumstance the best the Central Bank can do is to influence the *composition* of the money supply so as to achieve an external reserves target. This type of policy is discussed later in this section. This conclusion about the ineffectiveness of monetary policy does not, however, hold if exchange rates are *flexible*. If the exchange rate is allowed to float, monetary policy can be effective (at least in the short run) in influencing aggregate demand.

The Central Bank of Ireland first began to pursue an active monetary policy in May 1965 when credit guidelines were issued to regulate the growth in bank credit. Credit guidelines simply dictate how much money the banks can lend over a specific period of time. In the early years the guidelines were not enforced but later on penalties were introduced to ensure that the banks complied with the credit stipulations.

The theoretical foundation underlying the credit guidelines were outlined by the Central Bank's economist Josef Oslizlok.[3] The format was as follows: the guidelines were intended to control credit and, in this way, influence the rate of growth of the domestic money supply. Hence, contrary to the point made above, the objective of monetary policy in the early years was to regulate the money supply. It was then hoped that control of the money supply would, via the quantity theory of money, enable the Central Bank to influence nominal GNP. The quantity theory of money states that the money supply multiplied by the velocity of circulation of money is identically equal to nominal GNP. If velocity is constant, changes in the money supply must lead to changes in nominal GNP. (Economists of a Keynesian persuasion would, however, deny this. They would argue that the causation is the other way around.)

It was hoped that the price or inflation component of nominal GNP would be most affected by the changes in the money supply. If this was the case, the credit guidelines could be used to curtail inflation in the economy.

Moreover, changes in nominal GNP, via the marginal propensity to import, should affect imports into the economy. Hence, a restrictive credit policy could have the dual effect of curtailing inflation and simultaneously restricting imports.

This quantity theory approach was used by the Central Bank up to 1972 when credit guidelines were abandoned on the grounds that they stifled competition between the banks. Instead, the Central Bank used changes in the reserve requirements as a means of controlling the money supply. However, between 1973 and 1978 the reserve ratios remained unchanged. Hence, it cannot be said that the Central Bank pursued an active monetary policy during these years.

In 1978 a number of significant changes took place in the conduct of Irish monetary policy. Contrary to what had gone before, it was now acknowledged by the Central Bank that, under a fixed exchange rate, it was not possible to control the domestic money supply. Credit guidelines were reintroduced but this time the underlying theory was the monetary approach to the balance of payments (MAB). MAB theory is based on the identity that the money supply equals domestic credit plus the external reserves. This identity can be derived from the consolidated balance sheet of the banking system.

In its simplest form, MAB theory states that the money supply is determined by the demand for money. If the demand for money should increase by, say, 20 per cent over the year, then the money supply will increase by 20 per cent. In other words, the money supply is demand-led and is, in effect, exogenous.

What the Central Bank can do in these circumstance is to influence the *composition* of the money supply between its components of domestic credit and the external reserves. For example, suppose the money supply was predicted to rise by 20 per cent over the forthcoming year. The Central Bank could impose a credit guideline on domestic credit restricting its growth to, say, 15 per cent. Given an increase of 20 per cent in the money supply, this must mean that the external reserves would increase by 5 per cent. Alternatively, if the objective was to increase the external reserves by, say, 2 per cent, a credit guideline of 18 per cent would be appropriate. In this way, the Central Bank can use credit guidelines to achieve an external reserves target.

An examination of the underlying data suggests that the credit guidelines had little success in achieving an external reserves target. It seems that one of the main problems was accurately predicting the demand for money and therefore the money supply. Also the Central Bank experienced considerable difficulties obtaining the commercial banks adherence to the stipulations. In 1983, as the economy moved into recession, the demand for credit fell significantly and the credit guidelines became redundant. If there is little or no demand for credit, there is no point in imposing credit restrictions on banks and consequentially there is very limited scope to achieve an external reserve target. As a result, the Central Bank abandoned its credit policy and credit guidelines have not, as yet, been reintroduced.[4]

Interest Rate Policy

Given that interest rates cannot be controlled when the exchange rate is fixed, the Central Bank has pursued since 1978 an interest rate policy which is intended to smooth temporary and predictable fluctuations in domestic interest rates. It was argued that unnecessary or temporary variations in interest rates had a harmful effect on investment decisions. If this volatility could be reduced then it would be of benefit to the economy.

This policy hinges very much around the primary reserve ratio which dictates what percentage of current and deposit accounts the banks must keep in reserve. If the primary reserve is, say, 10 per cent then the banks must keep 10 pence in reserve for every IR£1 in deposit accounts. This is a minimum reserve requirement and the banks can keep excess reserves if they wish. However, the banks are unlikely to do so as profits can be increased if the excess reserves are lent out or deposited on the inter-bank market.

The inter-bank market is a market where banks either lend to or borrow from each other. The supply and demand forces on this market determine an inter-bank interest rate and this rate, in turn, determines all other interest rates (the associated banks', the non-associated banks' and the building society rates) in the system. The important point is that the supply and demand forces on the inter-bank market are in very large part determined by the banks' reserve position. For example, suppose that a bank has a deficiency in reserves in relation to the primary reserve ratio. That bank would attempt to borrow funds in the inter-bank market and that increase in demand would push up inter-bank interest rates. Conversely, if a bank had excess reserves in relation to the primary reserve ratio, the bank would deposit the funds on the inter-bank market. That increase in supply would lead to lower interest rates.

Over the course of the year, there will be predictable, seasonal fluctuations in the commercial bank reserves and, given the banks' dependence on the inter-bank market, this will lead to predictable fluctuations in inter-bank interest rates and therefore in all other rates in the economy. The Central Bank's interest rate policy essentially breaks this link between shortages and surpluses in bank reserves on the one hand and the inter-bank market on the other by providing or withdrawing funds from the system. The Central Bank does this by providing a credit facility for the banks or by changing the primary reserve requirement.

For example, suppose a bank was short of reserves but instead of borrowing in the inter-bank market borrowed from the Central Bank. Inter-bank interest rates would remain unchanged. Similarly, suppose that there is an excess of funds in the market. The Central Bank could 'mop up' this excess liquidity by increasing the primary reserve ratio. While the process is somewhat more complex than this in practice the policy basically involves the Central Bank withdrawing or injecting liquidity into the system in order to avoid unnecessary changes in domestic interest rates. The reduction in interest rate volatility, in turn, should reduce uncertainty and thereby encourage investment in the economy.

There can, however, be problems with this type of interest rate policy. For example, it is not always clear when a change in interest rates is temporary or permanent. In 1979, the Central Bank consistently provided funds to the market over a period of nearly nine months. This resulted in associated bank debt to the Central Bank of IR£350 million. The Central Bank subsequently lowered the reserve requirements and this enabled the associated banks to repay the debt. In this particular case, the policy was more akin to the Central Bank deliberately using up its external reserves in order to keep interest rates below their true market level. Clearly, this type of policy could prove very expensive if maintained for any length of time.

The Central Bank continues to provide (and withdraw funds) to the market but only on a short-term basis. The policy now appears to be that interest rates are allowed to vary in order to maintain an adequate level of external reserves. The external reserves, in turn, are used to ensure the stability of the exchange rate in the European Monetary System. If there is an outflow of funds for whatever reason, the Central Bank allows inter-bank interest rates to rise and this stems the outflow. Similarly, if there is an inflow of funds, the Bank allows interest rates to fall. This type of policy is much more in keeping with the view that there is little or no scope for an independent monetary policy when the exchange rate is fixed.

5 EXCHANGE RATE POLICY AND THE DECISION TO JOIN THE EUROPEAN MONETARY SYSTEM

As mentioned, the Irish and the British currencies were amalgamated in 1826. That situation prevailed until 1928 when the new Irish pound was introduced. From 1928 to 1979 the sterling/Irish pound exchange rate was maintained on a one-for-one, no margins, basis. Hence, for a period of 153 years, Ireland was in a monetary union with Britain.

The theory of purchasing power parity (PPP) predicts that, given the small size of the Irish economy relative to the UK, the Irish price level (or the inflation rate) would, in large part, be determined by the UK price level for as long as the fixed exchange rate was maintained. This conclusion is based on the argument that if there is a fixed exchange rate between two currencies, and there are no impediments to trade, then prices in those two countries cannot diverge very much. If prices are not the same, arbitrage profits are available and transactors in the pursuit of such profits should force a convergence of prices.

Up to 1979, and with the exception of the certain years during the Second World War, PPP theory seemed to provide a reasonable explanation for the determination of Irish inflation. For example, between 1964 to 1978 the average differential between Irish and UK inflation (based on consumer prices) was only 0.3 per cent. Once transport costs and taxation were allowed for, there appeared to be little or no difference between inflation rates in the two countries. The generally accepted view in the late 1970s, therefore, was that as long as the fixed exchange rate with sterling was maintained, the Irish economy would inherit the UK inflation rate. (As mentioned above, this represented a change of mind on the part of the Central Bank. Earlier the Central Bank was of the view that domestic forces, such as wages, were an important determinant of Irish inflation.)

This arrangement did not provoke much debate until the 1970s when it was observed that UK inflation (and therefore Irish inflation) was consistently well above the West German inflation rate. Over the period 1964 to 1978, Irish inflation exceeded German inflation by an average 5.7 percentage points. In turn, the relatively higher UK inflation was reflected in a depreciation of sterling (and, of course, the Irish pound) from DM11.0/IR£1 in 1964 to DM3.7/IR£1 in 1978. Compared to Germany, the UK and Ireland were experiencing a situation of rapid inflation and a depreciating exchange rate.

There appeared to be no realistic alternative to the sterling link until the late 1970s when the opportunity to join the European Monetary System (EMS) presented itself. Even after it became clear in late 1978 that the UK would not participate in the new system, it was believed that if the Irish exchange rate was tied to the German currency in the EMS then, in line with PPP theory, the Irish inflation rate would converge to the lower German inflation rate. The EMS presented the Irish authorities with an opportunity to break from the inflation/depreciation spiral under the sterling link to a situation of low inflation and a stable exchange rate under the DM link. Other considerations included making a commitment to a major EU initiative and the possibility of obtaining a transfer of resources from the EU budget. Concern was, however, expressed that for the first time in over 150 years there would be two currencies on the island.

It should be noted that there is an important political dimension to formulating exchange rate policy. As mentioned earlier, it is the Minister for Finance who decides exchange rate policy and the Central Bank's function is to implement that policy.

The EMS, which started on the 13 March 1979, is a system of quasi-fixed exchange rates. At the heart of the system is the exchange rate mechanism (ERM). Each currency was given a central exchange rate against the European Currency Unit (ECU). (The ECU is a weighted basket of currencies.) Exchange rates are then allowed to float up to a ceiling or down to the floor of a band. Most countries opted for a narrow band of ± 2.25 per cent while some countries, such as Italy, chose a ± 6 per cent band. When an exchange rate is about to break out of the band Central Banks intervene by buying or selling currency in order to push rates back into the band. At the start of the system each country contributed 20 per cent of its external reserves to a new European Monetary Cooperation Fund (EMCF). The EMCF used these reserves to provide funds to countries experiencing balance of payments difficulties.

Real Exchange Rate
Before proceeding it is important to explain briefly what is meant by the real exchange rate. In an international setting, there are three dimensions to price competitiveness. The price charged by the domestic firm, the nominal exchange rate and the price charged by the foreign competitor. The real exchange rate index is a statistic which summarises movements in these three variables. The index may be written as:

$$(P_{IRL} \times E)P_F = 100$$

where P_{IRL} and P_F is the Irish and 'foreign' price level respectively and E is the nominal exchange rate expressed as the foreign currency per unit of domestic currency (for example, Stg£/IR£).

This index is set equal to 100 in an arbitrary chosen base year. This is not to suggest that domestic and foreign prices were exactly equal or perfectly competitive in the base year. Rather the idea is simply to monitor movements in price competitiveness from the base year. An increase in the index indicates a loss in price competitiveness and an overvalued exchange rate. This would occur, *ceteris paribus*, if the domestic price increased relative to the foreign price or if the exchange rate appreciated on the foreign exchange market or some combination.

Conversely, a decrease in the index indicates a gain in price competitiveness and an undervalued exchange rate. This would occur if the domestic price fell relative to the foreign price or if the exchange rate depreciated or some combination of both factors.

Price competitiveness is important as it is a key factor underlying a country's economic performance. Firms which succeed in improving competitiveness should capture a greater share of both domestic and foreign markets and, in this way, contribute to increasing the nations output and income and reducing unemployment. Conversely, *ceteris paribus*, a loss of price competitiveness will result in a loss of market share and lower output and employment.

A broader definition of the concept of price competitiveness is the *real trade-weighted exchange rate index* (sometimes referred to as the real effective exchange rate index). This index is derived by first calculating the real exchange rate between Ireland and each its main trading partners. An average index is then calculated by giving each country a weight according to its importance in Irish trade. The UK would have the largest weight followed by Germany, the US and France. The countries with the lowest weight are Japan and Denmark.

Aspects of the Irish Experience in.the EMS
The White Paper on EMS membership published in December 1978 anticipated that the adjustment of the Irish economy from the sterling link to the EMS regime would entail an overvaluation of the Irish pound in the short run. Due to traditional links with the UK, the need to fulfil existing contracts and delays in obtaining information on German inflation, the Irish inflation rate was likely to continue mirroring the relatively high UK inflation in the short run. With the nominal exchange rate fixed in the exchange rate mechanism (ERM) of the EMS, the result would be an overvalued real exchange rate. In terms of the real exchange rate index formula, P_{IRL} would rise relative to P_G (the German price is substituted for the 'foreign' price in the denominator) while the nominal exchange rate would remain constant. The result would be an increase in the index, an overvalued exchange rate and a loss of price competitiveness.

The important question is how long the Irish pound would remain overvalued? If the EMS policy was seen as credible by trade unions and employer organisations, firms and workers would take German inflation rather than UK inflation as their guide in setting domestic prices and wages. In this case, Irish inflation and wage demands would quickly converge to the German inflation rate. The overvalued exchange rate would be short-lived and the costs of the adjustment process, as measured in terms of lost output and employment, would be relatively small. The EMS policy could be said to have conferred a 'disinflation bonus' on the Irish economy. That is, the economy has switched from a high-inflation path to a low-inflation path at a low cost.

On the other hand, if the EMS policy was not seen as credible by workers or firms either because of an inconsistent (expansionary) fiscal policy or because the Central Bank failed to communicate the new policy to all relevant parties, then price and wage inflation might be slow to adjust to the German rates. In this case, the overvalued exchange rate would drive the economy into recession and unemployment would increase. The recession, in turn, would eventually force price and wage inflation downwards and convergence would eventually take place. As this convergence process would be long-lived, the costs of adjustment in terms of lost output and employment would be high.

Figure 6.1 shows the real effective (trade-weighted) exchange rate for the Irish pound (calculated using consumer prices) over the period 1979 to 1995. Also included is the real Deutsche mark exchange rate. The real effective exchange rate appreciated by 21 per cent in the period to 1986. Against the Deutsche mark the real appreciation was 44 per cent. The failure of the real exchange rate to revert quickly to its 1979 level indicates that the adjustment process was prolonged. This, in turn, suggests that the cost of adjustment was high.

Figure 6.1

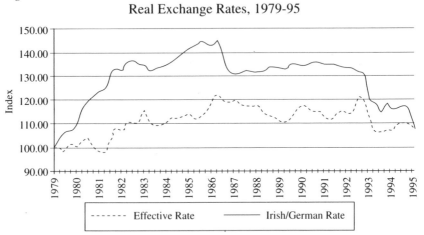

Real Exchange Rates, 1979-95

There is empirical evidence which indicates that this overvaluation of the real exchange rate is an important determinant of the rise in Irish unemployment.[5] Despite substantial emigration, Ireland's unemployment rate increased from 7.1 per cent in 1979 to 17.4 per cent in 1986. Of course, not all of the increase in unemployment can be attributed to an overvalued exchange rate. The downturn in the world, and in particular the UK, economy in the early 1980s, the increase in oil prices in 1979, the rise in taxation and the effect of this on the incentive to work and the creation of poverty traps are all potentially important factors underlying the rise in Irish unemployment. (A more complete analysis of the unemployment problem in given in Chapter 8.) However, the adjustment of the Irish economy to the new EMS regime clearly took much longer than envisaged by the authorities at the time of entry in 1979.

Currency Crisis 1992-93

As can be seen from Figure 6.1 the real exchange rate of the Irish pound against the Deutsche mark stabilised from 1987 to 1992. There were no realignments of exchange rates within the ERM during this time. This stable real exchange rate reflected the fact that Irish inflation had finally converged to the German rate. At last, Ireland was reaping the benefits of EMS membership as relatively low inflation was combined with a stable exchange rate *vis-à-vis* the EMS countries. Moreover, the UK joined the ERM in October 1990. Hence, with the exception of the US, all of Ireland's main trading partners were members of the EMS.

The calm waters were abruptly disturbed in September 1992 when the pound sterling and the Italian lira were forced to withdraw from the ERM. The main underlying reasons for this withdrawal were the 'No' vote in the Danish referendum in June 1992 (which undermined confidence and created uncertainty) and German unification. In July 1990, East and West Germany were united in an economic, monetary and social union. In October 1990, the economic union was made irreversible by political union. However, the economically-weak East German economy required substantial transfers from the economically-strong West (over IR£200 billion by 1994). To pay for this, the German government chose to borrow rather than raise taxes and this had the effect of increasing German interest rates. Alternatively, the Bundesbank could have printed money to finance unification and thereby prevented the rise in interest rates. The Bundesbank was, however, concerned about inflation and kept a tight control on the money supply. As the demand for money increased and the money supply was kept relatively constant, the inevitable result was higher interest rates.

Because exchange rates were fixed in the ERM, the increase in German interest rates was transmitted to all other EMS countries. However, the UK economy was in recession in 1990 and what was required was lower, not higher, interest rates. Speculators soon realised that if the UK economy was to move out of recession, the pound sterling would have to be devalued in an ERM realignment. But as long as sterling remained tied to the Deutsche mark, interest rates could not fall at least in the immediate future. The speculators chose to bet on devaluation and an end to the recession. Following intense speculative pressure the Bank of England decided to withdraw sterling from the ERM on Wednesday, 13 September 1992. Sterling subsequently fell by 15 per cent on the foreign exchange market.

This devaluation of sterling created immense difficulties for the Irish economy. At an exchange rate of Stg£1.09/IR£1 it was obvious that the Irish pound was overvalued relative to sterling. Sectors such as clothing, footwear and forestry, were now uncompetitive and a loss of output and a rise in unemployment were inevitable. The devaluation of sterling exposed once again the dilemma inherent in Irish exchange rate policy; it is not possible to target simultaneously two separate (and mostly divergent) currencies such as the Deutsche mark and sterling. As happened in March 1983 and August 1986, once sterling weakens on the foreign exchanges, the Irish authorities are forced to devalue the Irish pound to restore competitiveness. The commitment to the ERM must be put aside until sterling again stabilises.

On this occasion, however, the Irish government decided not to devalue. It was argue that the pound was not overvalued; that speculators could not be allowed to destroy the ERM; that it was desirable to break our dependence on the UK; and that devaluation was ineffective and would only confer a short-run competitive gain on the economy. The *Irish Times* in an editorial stated; 'that it was the duty of a sovereign government to defend its currency as it would its national territory'.[6] The trade unions spoke of 'sabotage' and pointed to the 'unpatriotic behaviour of speculators'.

It is estimated that the Central Bank spent IR£5,000 million in foreign currency intervening in the foreign exchange market in order to maintain the value of the pound.[7] That is, the Central Bank used its external reserves to purchase Irish pounds. This artificial demand for the Irish pound kept its price (the exchange rate) in the ERM. However, on 31 January 1993, following another bout of sterling weakness and the prospect of American banks taking positions against the Irish pound, the government relinquished and the pound was devalued by 10 per cent. This devaluation restored confidence to the markets, money began to flow back into the economy and domestic interest rates declined. The competitive position against the UK economy had been restored and a competitive gain had been achieved against the other European countries.

German unification again created tensions on the foreign exchanges in the summer of 1993 as speculators bet on a devaluation of the French franc, the Belgian franc and the Danish krone. After considerable intervention by European Central Banks, it was decided to abandon the ERM's ± 2.25 per cent band and move to a wider ±15 per cent band. This all but heralded the end of the ERM and put in doubt the plans to create a monetary union in Europe. It should be noted however that to date countries have not taken advantage of the wider bands but have instead strived to keep exchange rates within the old narrow bands. For example, there has been very little change in the Deutsche mark/French franc exchange rate since 1986. Central Banks hope that as the difficulties associated with German unification are resolved, countries can revert to the narrow bands and recommence the path to EMU.

Lessons from the Currency Crisis

The currency crisis raises a number of important issues for the Irish economy. First, the inconsistencies in our exchange rate policy were again exposed. The Irish pound can remain in the ERM only for as long as sterling remains stable on the foreign exchanges. Once sterling weakens, the Irish pound comes under speculative attack. The pressing challenge facing economists is to formulate an exchange rate policy that achieves the dual objective of targeting both the Deutsche mark and sterling.[8]

Second, at least up to the time of the currency crisis, the prevalent view among Irish economists was that the competitive gain resulting from a devaluation was short-lived. That is, the devaluation of the nominal exchange rate leads to an increase in import prices which, in turn, pushes up the overall consumer price index. As the devaluation is offset by an increase in domestic prices, the real exchange rate remains unchanged. This is supposed to happen quickly and, as a result, there is no long-lasting competitive gain. One Central Bank economist estimated that the adjustment would take as little as three months. However, as can be seen from the real Deutsche mark exchange rate in Figure 6.1, this is not the case. The real exchange rate never reverted back to its original level following the 1986 devaluation. Similarly (at the time of writing) it is two-and-a-half years since the 1993 devaluation and the real exchange rate shows no sign of reverting back to its previous level. It therefore seems likely that movements in the nominal exchange rate can affect real output and employment. This makes it all the more imperative to find a realistic and workable exchange rate policy.

Third, and most important, rigidities in the labour market, such as wage agreements like the Programme for Economic and Social Progress (PESP), are inconsistent with a fixed exchange rate policy. If the exchange rate is fixed, wages must be flexible so that the economy can adjust to shocks. The appreciation of the Irish pound during the currency crisis should have led to a fall in the domestic price level. (Imported goods become cheaper.) The decrease in prices, in turn, implies an increase in the real wage rate (W/P). In the labour market, workers should therefore accept a decrease in the nominal wage so as to restore the original real wage. It is the increase in the real wage that is reducing output and increasing unemployment. If the trade unions had accepted a lower nominal wage the devaluation of the Irish pound could have been adverted. However, neither the government nor the trade unions were willing to renegotiate the national understanding on wages (PESP agreement) and this meant that devaluation was inevitable. National wage agreements such as the PESP or the current Programme for Competitiveness and Work 1994-96 are inconsistent with a fixed exchange rate policy.

There is an important caveat to the above analysis. It is essential that the exchange rate appreciation does lead to lower domestic prices. During the currency crisis firms seemed to be very reluctant to pass on the reduction in import prices and instead engaged in profit-taking.

Currency Crisis 1995
A second currency crisis emerged in March 1995. Political and economic instability in Mexico led to a 45 per cent devaluation of the peso. The US intervened heavily in the foreign exchange markets to support the peso and this seems to have provoked a capital flight from dollars into Deutsche marks. Because of the strong trading links between the US and the UK, dollar depreciation was reflected in a fall in sterling. The Central Bank's reaction to this currency crisis represented a fundamental change in Irish exchange rate policy. The old EMS policy was based on fixing the Irish pound to the DM within a very narrow band in the hope that Irish inflation would converge to the German rate. On this occasion the Central

Bank took advantage of the $\pm$ 15 per cent EMS bands and the Irish pound was allowed to devalue against the DM. This depreciation against the DM prevented an excessive appreciation against sterling and curtailed the rise in domestic interest rates.

The greater the divergence between sterling and the DM, the more difficult the balancing act becomes. Adopting a middle-of-the-road approach could see the Irish pound moving above parity against sterling and, simultaneously, moving down against the DM towards the bottom of the EMS band. Herein lies the policy dilemma facing the Minister for Finance. Which of these two opposing movements involves the greatest cost? Should we lean towards maintaining sterling parity or alternatively the DM link? Of course if the sterling/DM exchange rate remains stable the problem does not arise.

The disadvantage in having a sterling/Irish pound exchange rate above parity is obvious. Our competitive position against our main trading partner is eroded with the inevitable result of lower growth and higher unemployment.

On the other hand, there are two possible reasons why the Minister does not want the pound to fall against the DM. First, there is the continuing belief that a DM link will ensure relatively low inflation rates in Ireland. Second, there is concern that depreciation against the DM will make it more difficult for Ireland to qualify for a single currency EMU if and when it commences.

6 EUROPEAN MONETARY UNION

The broad objectives of European Monetary Union (EMU) were outlined in the Delors committee report which was published in April 1989.[9] This document was subsequently superseded by the Maastricht Treaty 1993. In line with the Delors Report, the main recommendation in the Maastricht Treaty is that EMU be achieved in three stages.

Stage 1 commenced July 1990. A number of measures were introduced to create both an economic and a monetary union in Europe. On the *economic* front, it was proposed to allow the free movement of persons, goods, services and capital (the four freedoms) between member states. This means that all cross-border restrictions and any other obstruction to the free movement of persons, goods, services and capital be removed (see Chapter 9). Second, policies were introduced to promote competition and strengthen market structures in a large number of areas within the EU. The overall effect will be to increase competition in all markets substantially. To this end, the Commission also proposed structural and regional development within the EU. This is particularly important for Ireland as substantial improvements in roads, telecommunications and both sea and air ports are necessary if Ireland is to compete successfully in EMU.

With regard to *monetary* union, the objective during Stage 1 was to create a single financial area in Europe. Capital transactions were to be fully liberalised and banking and other financial markets were to be completely integrated. All twelve countries in the EU were to adhere to the narrow exchange rate mechanism (ERM) of the EMS. Also there was to be enhanced policy coordination between member states. This is a vital aspect to the EMU proposal, as previous experience with international monetary systems, such as the Bretton Woods and 'Snake' system, and indeed the currency crisis of 1992/93 have demonstrated. If a fixed exchange rate system is to be successful, countries participating in the system must pursue similar fiscal and monetary policies. If one country implements an expansionary fiscal or monetary policy relative to the other countries, the result will be a balance of payments deficit in the expanding country. The balance of payments deficit will, in turn, put downward pressure on the exchange rate and eventually force a realignment of exchange rates. If there is no convergence of fiscal and monetary policy between participating countries, the fixed exchange rate system has little chance of success.

To a large extent the proposals in Stage 1 were facilitated by two pieces of legislation which pre-date the Delors Report. The Single European Act 1987 went some considerable way towards achieving an economic union by attempting to create a Single European Market. The directive by the Council of Economic Ministers in June 1988 to liberalise capital movements by July 1990 (Greece, Ireland, Spain and Portugal were allowed until the end of 1992) attempted to create a single financial area which is the main component of a monetary union.

Stage 2 started on the 1st January 1994. This is largely an institutional stage in which a European Monetary Institute (EMI) is established. The EMI, which is located in Frankfurt, has very limited powers. It is intended that the EMI uses Stage 2 to 'learn the ropes' of functioning like a European Central Bank. If and when Stage 3 starts, the EMI will evolve into a fully-fledged European Central Bank.

Provided a majority of countries satisfy certain criteria, Stage 3 is expected to start on January 1997. The criteria states that interest and inflation rates must be within 1.5 per cent of the three lowest in the Community and that annual budget deficits and public debt are within 3 per cent and 60 per cent of GDP respectively. Countries must also have adhered to the narrow band of the ERM for at least two years. This final stage would entail exchange rates being irrevocably fixed and the introduction of a common currency (probably the ECU). Monetary policy would be controlled by the European Central Bank and some form of federal authority would coordinate national fiscal policies. Also governments will not be allowed to resort to monetary financing (borrowing from the Central Bank or commercial banks) to finance annual budget deficits. Taking all the main proposals under each of the stages together, the end result would be a United States of Europe in which there would be a single currency, a European Central Bank and complete freedom of movement for people, goods, services and capital. If a majority of countries do not meet the Maastricht criteria, then an automatic process will get underway to introduce a single currency by January 1999 at the latest. Hence, by signing the Maastricht Treaty, EU governments have agreed to introduce a single currency in Europe by the end of the century.

It is interesting to note that, at this point in time, it is unclear what number of countries constitutes a majority. Both Britain and Denmark have Treaty opt-out clauses. In 1994 Austria, Finland and Sweden voted 'yes' in referenda on accession to the EU. (Norway, Iceland and Switzerland have decided not to join the EU.) Also an inter-governmental conference in 1996 will finalise proposals for six Eastern Europe countries – Poland, Czech Republic, Slovakia, Bulgaria, Hungary and Romania – to join the EU by the year 2000. Given the enlargement of the EU there is some debate on what legally constitutes a majority.

A central issue relating to the creation of EMU is that there is a convergence between member states in inflation rates, balance of payments and government budget deficits. At the present time there are different views on how convergence might be achieved. One view is that member states should proceed with EMU and that this would force member states to implement policies which would hasten convergence. Another view is that member states should first converge and only then should EMU be considered. The current lack of convergence between certain member states (for example, Greece and Germany) has led to a proposal for a two-speed path to EMU. Under this plan, countries which have converged would proceed to EMU and the remaining countries could join at a later stage.

At the present time, the Irish inflation rate has converged to the German rate and both Irish fiscal and monetary policies are in line with the policies being adopted in Germany and the Benelux countries. Ireland's main difficulty relates to the debt/GNP ratio which in 1994 stood at 89 per cent (see Table 6.5); well above the Maastricht criteria. The government has, however, made it clear on numerous occasions that if a two-speed system is introduced Ireland will press to be among the front runners.

Costs and Benefits of EMU

EMU is an evolving process which will provoke unpredictable changes in both policy and how people and firms react to policy and, as such, it is virtually impossible at this stage to quantify with any degree of exactness what will be the overall costs and benefits. Also the costs and benefits depend very much on whether or not the UK participates in the system. It is possible to have an EMU with (i) both Ireland and the UK in, (ii) Ireland in, UK not in, (iii) Ireland and the UK not in, and (iv) Ireland not in, UK in. Furthermore there is the question of the costs and benefits of *not* participating in EMU. Staying out could have serious implications for long-run economic development. Despite these uncertainties it is still possible to identify some of the possible consequences of EMU membership. In general, there seems to be agreement that Europe as a whole will benefit from EMU. The contentious issue is how those gains will be distributed between the member states.

Europe will gain from EMU for three basic reasons. First, a single currency entails a considerable reduction in currency-related transaction costs. Importers and exporters will no longer need to convert currencies and will therefore avoid the bank charges involved. (The banks, however, will lose out on this score.) Second, under a monetary union, exchange rate risk will be eliminated and this will reduce uncertainty and thereby promote trade within the EU. Third, a single currency will highlight price differentials within the EU and this, in conjunction with the Single Market proposals, should encourage greater competition. Taking these three points together, markets in the EU will become more efficient and this should lead to an increase in European output.

Furthermore, over time, the risk-adjusted rate of interest will decline and this will encourage greater investment in new plant and machinery. This increase in investment will, in turn, facilitate a movement to a higher long-run growth path within the Union and higher employment.

The main cost of EMU will be a loss of sovereignty for each of the member states. In particular, member states cannot use the exchange rate as a policy instrument and will not be able to control domestic money supplies. If, for example, a country suffers a loss of competitiveness either through an excessive increase in wages, a fall in productivity or rising export prices, devaluation will not be available as a means or restoring competitiveness. In the case of the large countries like France and Germany, the loss of the exchange rate as a policy instrument represents a substantial loss of independence. In Ireland, it is debatable whether the loss of the exchange rate as a policy instrument is important or not. Some economists argue that devaluation cannot be used to increase real output because import prices quickly increase to erode the competitive gain. However, as shown in Figure 1, this view is not supported by the experience with the 1986 or 1993 devaluations. Hence, the loss of the exchange rate as a policy instrument might be much more costly that heretofore realised.

In the past investors have demanded a risk premium on investments in Ireland to compensate for the possibility of devaluation. As a result, Irish interest rates have usually been higher than similar rates in Germany. With a single currency, however, there is no prospect of devaluation and therefore the risk premium must disappear. Irish interest rates will fall to the Germany level. Lower interest rates, in turn, should encourage investment in Ireland and also lead to a lower debt service on the national debt. Given a debt service of IR£2,168 million in 1994 this is an important consideration.

A major concern relates to the impact on Irish trade. Most of the points raised here will happen as a consequence of the Single Market and are not depended on the creation of EMU. The removal of trade barriers will facilitate an increase in exports. But imports will also rise so the effect on the trade balance is ambiguous. Some economists are more pessimistic. They point to Ireland's entry into the EEC in 1973 and the adverse effect this had on Irish trade. A very important consideration is the impact of greater competition in the EU on Irish trade share. The Single Market should allow for greater economies of scale. In order to take advantage of these economies of scale, and the associated reduction in costs and higher profits, firms must increase their size by expansion or by engaging in mergers and takeovers. The fear is that the newly-enlarged firms will locate in the centre of the EU and not in the peripheral regions. If after all a firms main market is in Dublin why would they locate their plant in Letterkenny? By locating near or in the main market, firms avoid the high cost of transporting both raw materials and, more importantly, the finished product. These costs are, of course, exacerbated by poor infrastructure in the regions. Furthermore, the supply of raw materials, the research and development and specialised labour all tend to be more readily available in the centre.

If firms on the periphery cannot achieve the same efficiencies, they lose competitiveness and either go out of business or are taken over by the larger firms located in the centre. If Irish firms should go out of business the likely result is a reduction in exports and an increase in imports. As aggregate demand falls, both output and national income will decrease and unemployment will rise. The increase in unemployment will lead to an enlarged government deficit as less monies will be collected in tax revenue and expenditure on social welfare will rise. In sum, a loss of competitiveness could have a disastrous effect on a number of key macroeconomic variables.

The European Commission in its report, 'One Market, One Money', unconvincingly argues that EMU, via lower non-tariff or tariff barriers, will reduce transport costs which will give producers in the regions easier access to the main markets in the centre.[10] It therefore concludes that EMU will result in a disproportionate amount of the efficiency gains going to the regions. However, as a former Governor of the Central Bank of Ireland pointed out, this view is incomplete in that it only looks at one side of the argument. Easier access to the regions may simply expose the peripheral producer to greater competition from the large scale firms in the centre and lead to widespread closures. The Governor is unambiguous on this point:

> I do not accept the rather complacent views of the Commission on the likely effects on peripheral regions. It seems to me self-evident that the economies of scale in production ... must work in favour of the further development of the central regions. The effects of other factors such as transport costs ... and other

linguistic, cultural and habitual barriers ... will all tend to work in the same direction..[11]

An important objective of EMU is that the living standards in the poorer member states converge to the EU average. But what are the mechanisms that will facilitate this 'catching-up'? Since 1975, Portugal and Ireland have narrowed the gap albeit very marginally. Spain and Greece, on the other hand, have fallen further behind. The various EU budgets amount to only 1 per cent of Europe's GDP. This is very small compared to countries like the US or Canada. Hence, convergence is not going to come about through a transfer of resources. Moreover, transfers from the EU budgets are linked to specific projects such as improving roads, etc. This means that there is no *automatic* transfer to a region that experiences an increase in unemployment. If the EU budget were operated along the lines of a normal government budget, the disadvantaged region would receive injections in the form of social welfare and pay less in tax and this would help alleviate the problem.

There is an obvious danger of slipping further behind. Ireland has a large *foreign* debt and the interest payments (IR£1,126 million in 1992) represent an important leakage from the economy. Also the high unemployment, poor infrastructure and constraints on fiscal and monetary policy all act as impediments to the convergence process. It seems likely that if a cohesion of living standards is to take place it will depend very much on our own efforts and not through any EU policy.

Another issue, mentioned earlier in the discussion on the currency crisis, relates to how the economy will adjust to shocks in EMU. This issue is of major concern whether or not the UK participates in EMU. The problem is that if prices and wages are inflexible, or are unresponsive to the forces of supply and demand, then adjustment to shocks will involve a long and protracted process. The economy may have to endure severe recession and high unemployment before prices and wages adjust and the economy moves back to full employment GNP. Because the Irish economy, and the labour market in particular, is regarded as being generally inflexible this is a very important consideration. As such, entry into EMU could have very serious consequences for the Irish economy. The situation will be further exasperated if the UK declines to join in EMU.

Providing Stage 3 of the Maastricht Treaty does go ahead and Ireland meets the membership criteria, there seems to be little doubt that Ireland will participate in EMU. Ireland has already paid a substantial deposit in the form of the costs of adjusting to the EMS regime. Also there is the important consideration that the costs of not participating in EMU are likely to be greater than if Ireland does join. If, for example, the EU should adopt projectionist policies and become 'Fortress Europe', Ireland outside the union will not have access to some of its main markets. This would, of course, have a detrimental effect on the long-term development of the economy. One way or the other, the increase in competition in Europe will require significant changes in the Irish economy. The important questions relate to how industry can best react to the new environment so as to minimise the costs and maximise the benefits.

7 CONCLUSION

The effectiveness of fiscal policy to achieve growth and employment in a small open economy with high savings, tax and import leakages is questionable. In addition, there is the added consideration that fiscal policy may 'crowd out' private sector investment. This conclusion would appear to be borne out by the Irish experience. Between 1972 and 1987 fiscal policy in Ireland led to a significant increase in the national debt without having the desired effect on growth and employment in the economy. Despite substantial increases in taxation, the size and the burden of the debt increased to such an extent that in the 1980s restoring order to the public finances was more important than implementing policies to promote growth or reduce unemployment.

During the 1987-89 period, the government achieved a turnaround in these trends and order was restored to the public finances. Over the last few years the Maastricht criteria for EMU entry have come to dominate the government's budgetary targets.

Under fixed exchange rates and perfect capital mobility, it is not possible to control the money supply so as to achieve growth and employment objectives. Any deviation of the domestic interest rate from 'world' rates will lead to offsetting capital flows. In this context the Central Bank of Ireland pursues an interest rate policy. The discussion in this chapter highlighted the limitations of such a policy and raised doubts about using interest rates to support the Irish pound in the EMS.

The discussion of Ireland's experience in the EMS pointed out that the benefit of low inflation and exchange rate stability associated with membership come at a high price. Throughout the 1980s, the real exchange rate was overvalued and this eroded price competitiveness and aggravated the unemployment problem. Following the currency crisis of 1993 and 1995, it was argued that the EMS policy has now been changed to one of allowing the pound to depreciate against the Deutsche mark so as to prevent a loss of competitiveness against sterling.

Despite the slow decline in the debt/GNP ratio, the main political parties are adamant that Ireland will participate in a monetary union in Europe if and when it starts towards the end of the century. EMU will undoubtedly increase competition in Europe and this will lead to changes in the structure of industry and commerce in Ireland. The effects will be similar to those experienced following the ending of protectionist policies in the 1960s. A major concern is how the Irish economy will adjust to economic shocks in

EMU. Because of inflexible wages and prices, an adverse economic shock could result in a costly, protracted recession.

One of the main objectives of EMU is that the smaller, less well-off, countries in the EU do better than the European average in order to standardise income levels in the EU. However, if the countries on the periphery cannot withstand the greater competition which EMU entails, it seems likely that the rich countries will benefit disproportionately from EMU and the small countries or regions on the periphery will lose out. In this context is vital to identify the forces that will bring about a convergence of living standards within the EU.

The next ten years are likely to see major changes in Europe and the world economy (see Chapter 9). The enlargement of the EU, the move to market economies in Eastern Europe and the former Soviet Union, German unification, the uncertainty regarding UK participation in EMU, the completion of the GATT Agreement are some of the developments that will lead to a whole new global economic environment and present challenging new economic problems. Ireland as part of the EU will be to the forefront of these new developments.

Endnotes

1 For a detailed discussion of early money and banking in Ireland see P. McGowan, *Money and Banking in Ireland: Origins, Development and Future,* Institute of Public Administration, Dublin 1990.

2 C. Ó Gráda, *Ireland 1780-1939: A New Economic History,* Oxford University Press, Oxford 1994, pp.431-432.

3 See J. Oslizlok, 'Towards a Monetary Analysis of Aggregate Demand', Central Bank of Ireland, *Quarterly Bulletin,* November 1967.

4 For an extended discussion of the Central Bank's credit, interest and exchange rate policies see A. Leddin and B.M. Walsh, *The Macroeconomy of Ireland* (third edition), Gill and Macmillan, Dublin 1995.

5 A. Leddin, 'An Analysis of the Irish Unemployment Problem in the Context of EMS Membership' (Paper presented to the Department of Economics, University College, Cork), January 1991.

6 *Irish Times,* 9 January 1993.

7 P. Honohan, 'Costing the Delay in Devaluing, 1992-93', *Irish Banking Review,* Spring 1994.

8 See P. Honohan, *An Examination of Irish Currency Policy,* Economic and Social Research Institute, Dublin 1993. One option, not discussed by Honohan, is that the government pursue a real exchange rate target. See A. Leddin, 'Flaws of a Flexible Exchange Rate Policy', *Irish Times,* 12 August 1993.

9 European Community, *Report on Economic and Monetary Union in the European Community,* Office of the Official Publications of the European Communities, Brussels 1989.

10 European Commission, 'One Market, One Money', *European Economy,* No. 44, Commission of the European Communities, Brussels, October, 1990.

11 M. Doyle, 'Implications of Economic and Monetary Union for Ireland' (address to the Irish Council of the European Movement), Galway, April 1991.

PART III

PERFORMANCE AND POLICY ISSUES AT A NATIONAL LEVEL

CHAPTER 7

Economic Growth: Performance and Explanations

Cormac Ó Gráda and Kevin O'Rourke

1 INTRODUCTION

Why are some countries rich and other countries poor? This is the single most important question in economics. When aid agencies ask us to reflect on third world poverty, the question is often posed as: why are they poor? But a historical perspective makes it clear that poverty has been the lot of the vast majority of mankind over the vast majority of the course of history. In fact, the real puzzle is: why are we in the West so rich? In 1400, Western European GDP per capita stood at $430 (in 1985 prices), while China's amounted to $500. By 1950, Western European output per capita had grown to $4,902, while the figure for China had actually declined slightly, to $454; the figures for Western Europe and China in 1989 were $14,413 and $2,361 respectively.[1]

Why did the West grow so rapidly over the last 500 years, while much of the rest of the world stagnated? And why have several countries, especially in East Asia, grown so fast over the last half-century? If we can understand these growth experiences, and identify the forces which made them possible, we will be a lot closer to understanding what it is that poor countries today must do if they are to escape from poverty. More modestly, we will be better able to judge Ireland's growth performance since World War II, and think about ways in which that performance may be improved. The first necessary step in making intellectual headway on these questions is to explore briefly the theory of economic growth.

2 THE SOURCES OF ECONOMIC GROWTH

Aggregate Production Functions
In order to understand how economies grow over time, it is useful to

simplify greatly at the start. Imagine the simplest type of economy: one which produces only one good. Imagine that this good is produced using only three factors of production: labour (L), physical capital (K) and human capital (H). Output can be related to inputs via an aggregate production function:

(1)
$$Q = Af(L, K, H)$$

where Q is aggregate output, and A is a constant. Equation (1) simply relates a country's output, or Gross Domestic Product (GDP), to its endowments of labour, capital, and human capital.

If A increases, the same inputs yield a greater level of output. Economic theorists thus tend to think of A as being an index of technology, and of increases in A as representing technological progress. In fact, while technological progress will indeed increase A, there are other reasons in practice why A may increase or decline. Anything which reduces distortions and improves resource allocation will increase A: increases in competition, for example, or a move to free trade, or the elimination of distortionary taxes and subsidies. Cutting back a bloated public sector may spur economic growth by reducing taxation and the public debt. In general, beneficial microeconomic policies increase A and harmful microeconomic policies reduce A. A can also be influenced by factors that might seem non-economic. Economic historians have stressed that institutional change – the development of markets, the rule of law, and private property, for example – can have a profound impact on the overall productivity of societies, as can the level of political stability (see Chapter 1).

Imagine for the sake of simplicity that the production function in (1) embodies constant returns to scale. This implies that if you multiply all inputs by a constant, λ, output is also increased by a factor λ. We have:

(2)
$$\lambda Q = Af(\lambda L, \lambda K, \lambda H)$$

where λ is any positive number. In particular, λ could be equal to 1/L. Equation (2) now implies:

(3)
$$Q/L = Af(1, K/L, H/L)$$

This equation says that output per capita is a function of the capital/labour ratio, and the human capital/labour ratio, only. The equation can thus be simplified:

(4)
$$Q/L = AF(K/L, H/L)$$

where $F(K/L, H/L) = f(1, K/L, H/L)$.

Equation (4) is the single most important equation in growth theory. It says that output per capita can only be increased through three means: an increase in the amount of physical capital per worker; an increase in the amount of human capital per worker; and an increase in A.[2] In the long run, economic growth takes place through the accumulation of physical capital, through the accumulation of human capital, and through improvements in resource allocation and technology, perhaps associated with institutional progress. This in turn implies that the sources of economic growth are to be found in: (i) the level of savings and investment, which determines the rate at which capital is accumulated; (ii) education and training, which determine the rate at which human capital is accumulated; (iii) invention (the discovery of new technology) and innovation (the implementation of new technology); (iv) microeconomic policies which improve resource allocation; (v) political and institutional developments. These five sources of growth will now be examined in greater detail.

Capital Accumulation: The Solow Model
The simplest possible growth model, due to another American Nobel laureate in economics, Robert Solow, focuses on capital accumulation. To keep the discussion clear, the model ignores the role of human capital, and assumes that output is produced with capital and labour only. To keep things really simple, let the labour supply be fixed, and equal to one. Equation (4) then simplifies to:

$$(5) \qquad Q/L = Q = AF(K) = Af(1, K)$$

In this simple model, GDP per capita depends only on technology and the capital/labour ratio (or capital stock, since $L = 1$). Increasing the capital stock increases output, and hence output per capita. However, the law of diminishing returns implies that as you combine more and more capital with a given amount (i.e. one unit) of labour, the marginal contribution of successive units of capital diminishes: the marginal product of capital declines as accumulation takes place.

The relationship between output and the capital stock is shown in Figure 7.1, which graphs the relationship given in equation (5). The curve OA is positively sloped, but gets flatter as we move to the right; this reflects the diminishing returns to capital mentioned above.

Assume that in any given period, a constant proportion δ (5 per cent, say) of the capital stock disappears as a result of wear and tear, or depreciation. OB shows the relationship between the total amount of depreciation, δK, in a year, and the capital stock, K, in that year. The relationship is clearly linear, as shown.

Further assume that in any year, a constant fraction, s, of GDP is saved and invested. This implies that gross investment can be given by $sQ =$

sAF(K); OC graphs this relationship. Net investment, i.e. gross investment minus depreciation, is however a more interesting concept than gross investment, since it is net investment which determines the rate at which a country's capital stock increases. In the diagram, net investment is simply the vertical distance between OC and OB. To the left of K*, net investment is positive, while to the right of K*, net investment is negative.

These three curves together tell a simple but important story: growth based on capital accumulation alone eventually fizzles out. Say an economy starts out poor, with a low initial capital stock. It is clear from the diagram that gross investment exceeds depreciation, and net investment is positive; the capital stock will thus increase, and the economy will move to the right along the production function OA. Output expands, and the economy grows. However, while successive units of capital involve a constant cost (in that they depreciate at a fixed rate, δ) they yield a diminishing return (in that the marginal product of capital is declining). As the capital stock increases, output, and hence savings and investment, grows at a slower and slower pace. Eventually, the marginal return no longer covers the marginal cost; if the capital stock were to expand beyond K*, where OB intersects OC, depreciation would exceed gross investment, and the capital stock would actually decline. K* is thus the long-run equilibrium level of the capital stock; Q* is the corresponding long-run level of output.

Figure 7.1

The Solow Growth Model

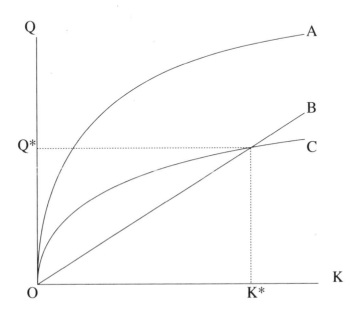

The Solow model implies that increasing the share of GDP which is saved and invested increases the long-run level of income. When s is increased, OC shifts up, which implies a new long-run equilibrium (where it intersects OB) to the right of Q*. However, an increase in s does not increase the long-run growth rate of the economy; which in this simple model is zero (unless A is increasing over time).

The simple Solow model thus suggests that while capital accumulation may enable countries to grow in the short run, on its own it is not a source of infinite growth. If growth were based on accumulation alone, countries could not achieve GDP levels higher than Q*; growth would come to an end eventually. The logic implies that long-run economic growth must therefore be due to increases in A (i.e. to improvements in technology or resource allocation).[3]

The Solow model also implies that, other things being equal, poor countries should grow more rapidly than rich countries. There are two key determinants of economic growth in the Solow model, apart from increases in A. First, there is net investment per capita, which determines the rate at which the capital stock increases. This is higher the further to the left you are in Figure 7.1. Second, there is the additional output which extra capital gives rise to: this is also higher in poor countries, where the marginal product of capital is higher. For both of these reasons, growth should be higher in capital-scarce poor countries than in capital-abundant rich countries (for a given rate of saving). Moreover, poorer countries may be able to import new technology already developed in rich countries. By catching up technologically, poor countries thus experience a more rapid growth in A than do rich countries. For all these reasons, the Solow model predicts that followers should catch up with leaders in the long run. In the limit, if A and s were the same in all countries, they would all end up with an output per capita equal to Q*; poor countries would eventually catch up completely with rich countries. More generally, poor countries will grow faster than rich countries, conditional on the savings rate. The Solow model thus implies that over time, the dispersion of income levels should decline: convergence should be a feature of the international economy.

The basic Solow model would have to be considerably modified in order to be applicable to a small open economy (SOE) like Ireland. The crucial variable in the model as presented above is the capital stock; more generally, it is the capital/labour ratio. In a closed economy, the capital stock depends on domestic savings, which equal gross domestic investment. The higher are savings, the higher is investment. This identity does not hold in Ireland; foreigners may invest their savings in the Irish economy (i.e. the economy may experience capital inflows); or Irish savers may buy foreign assets, rather than invest domestically (i.e. the economy may experience capital outflows). International capital flows are thus crucial in Ireland. If Irish investment opportunities are good by international standards, there will be capital inflows; otherwise, there will be capital outflows. The profitability of investment opportunities in an open economy such as Ireland is thus the single most important determinant of investment there. In turn, key determinants of Irish profitability include the price and quality of our workforce and infrastructure, and our legal and tax systems.

Furthermore, the capital/labour ratio depends not only on the capital stock, but on the size of the labour force, and in Ireland the latter is influenced by international migration. Emigration, by reducing L, can increase K/L, and thus increase output per capita in precisely the same way as capital investments. Indeed, emigration since the Famine has probably increased Irish living standards significantly, compared to what they would have been in its absence (see Chapter 1).

The standard Solow model treats labour and capital symmetrically, which is why a reduction in labour supply can have the same impact on K/L, and thus on output per capita, as an increase in the capital stock. This suggests an interesting question to pose of the Irish experience from the 1850s to the 1950s. As a poor country, our wages were relatively low. This might have attracted large capital inflows; instead, large numbers emigrated. If the Solow model is to be believed, the net impact on average living standards was the same; but why is it that labour flowed out of the country, when capital might have flowed in?

Human Capital and Education

Education and training increase the endowment of human capital per worker. They thus make workers more productive, and increase living standards. Equation (4) treats human capital and physical capital as essentially similar: thus, investment in education increases GDP per capita in the same way as investment in manufacturing, say. If that is the end of the story, then the Solow model can be used to investigate the impact of human capital accumulation on growth. In particular, the basic conclusion of the previous analysis carries over: growth based on the accumulation of human capital alone ultimately fizzles out, due to diminishing returns.

In fact, it has been found that the Solow model does a lot better in explaining the real world when human capital is included in the model (as in equation (4)), than when it is omitted (as in equation (5)).[4] For example, the Solow model tends to explain international income differences as being due to different capital/labour ratios, which are in turn due to different savings and investment rates. Physical capital investment rates do not differ sufficiently between countries to explain the huge income differences which exist today; but the level of education varies enormously across the world. Investment rates in all capital (both physical and human) vary enough internationally to explain much of the huge gulf between rich and poor nations.

Similarly, we saw earlier that the Solow model predicts convergence: for a given savings rate, poor countries should grow faster than rich countries.

This crude prediction is not verified for the world as a whole. However, an important reason for this is that poor countries, which do indeed have low physical capital/labour ratios (which is good for growth) also tend to have uneducated populations (which is bad for growth). The net result is that poverty and growth are not well-correlated. However, empirical economists have found that, for a given level of human capital per worker, poor countries tend to grow more rapidly than rich countries, as the theory predicts. The data do show conditional convergence, i.e. there is convergence once differences in education have been statistically controlled for.

This finding suggests that education and training are immensely important for poor countries. If a poor country has an educated, relatively skilled labour force, then it has a good chance of outpacing rich countries. In the absence of such human capital advantages, however, it will be left further behind.

One reason why education may be important in explaining a poor country's ability to catch up with the rest of the world was stated in a famous article by an economic historian, Richard Easterlin:

> Explanation of the limited spread of modern economic growth turns into a question of identifying the factors that have constrained the dissemination of a new type of technology – that of modern technology... If one's concern is to explain why some nations were rapid learners and others slow, it seems only reasonable to ask what sort of differences there were in the educational systems that prepared their populations for acquiring new knowledges.[5]

Could it be that better-educated countries are better able to absorb new technology? It has been argued, for example, that in the late nineteenth century, well-educated Scandinavia adopted new farming techniques, including cooperation, which greatly improved living standards, while largely illiterate Iberia stagnated. The thesis is certainly plausible, although difficult to test.

A key issue for an SOE such as Ireland is obviously the extent to which human capital is internationally mobile. In particular, if it is predominantly unskilled workers who emigrate, then emigration will increase the average human capital of those staying behind. On the other hand, if it is the most skilled who emigrate (the 'brain drain' scenario), then emigration leaves behind a population that is less educated and skilled than before. The question of whether emigration is selective in terms of education is thus of great interest to policymakers.

Technological Change and the Importance of Institutions
The Solow model suggests that long-run economic growth is ultimately based on technological and institutional progress. Economic historians have

spent a lot of time examining the sources of economic growth, and have typically found that increases in A in equation (4) above explain a large proportion of the total growth observed in different countries at different times. It would seem, therefore, that understanding why some societies are able to innovate, and others are not, is crucial for understanding long-run growth.

Unfortunately, understanding technological change is a lot less easy than understanding the level of investment, say, in an economy. Presumably invention is positively related to research and development (R&D) expenditures. Such expenditures, in turn, will vary according to their expected profitability, which depends among other things on: the level of competition firms are facing; government taxes and incentives; the supply of well-trained scientists and technicians; and the educational system and university infrastructure. Moreover, since R&D expenditures are a form of investment, they are influenced by factors affecting all forms of investment: for example, the tax code, interest rates, and the level of uncertainty about the future.

Unfortunately, some of these factors have theoretically ambiguous effects on R&D. For example, increasing the level of competition in a market might increase R&D (because firms need to innovate in order to survive); or it might reduce R&D (because there are fewer profits available to fund it, or because any profits the R&D might give rise to would be instantly competed away). Casual inspection of the evidence suggests that in countries where firms face a lot of domestic competition (Japan, for example), there is more invention, and certainly more innovation, than in countries with cosseted 'national champions' (France before 1992, say); but these issues have still not been fully sorted out by economists.

From the perspective of an SOE like Ireland, many if not most of the inventions that are relevant to us will probably take place elsewhere; it is whether or not we adopt these inventions that is crucial. There are many possible reasons why some SOEs are better at adapting foreign technology than others. First, we have already seen that education may aid the diffusion of new technology, and that there is empirical evidence that education does indeed help countries grow faster. Second, in a small open economy a highly-educated labour force may entice multinational corporations. Since multinationals can play an important role in the international diffusion of technology, increasing an SOE's attractiveness as a location for direct foreign investment may therefore increase domestic innovation. Third, increased participation in the world economy through trade increases innovation, by exposing firms to new ideas, products, and competition.

Fourth, and perhaps most importantly, when seeking to explain the level of innovation, as distinct from invention, it is important to recognise that innovation is not only an economic issue: it is also an inherently political one. This is because, while innovation makes society as a whole better off, it can create losers as well as winners. For example, automating a telephone exchange may improve crucial telecommunications links for everyone; but it will also involve laying off workers. Such considerations suggest that political and institutional factors may be very important in determining long-run economic performance: some countries may have political institutions which are more protective of the status quo, and less conducive to growth, than others. (For a more detailed discussion of these issues, see Chapter 12).

A key issue which arises when considering different countries' economic institutions is the extent to which they promote or hinder rent-seeking behaviour. Such behaviour involves firms lobbying government for preferential treatment: special subsidies, for example, or protection from domestic or international competition. Rent-seeking can lower a country's growth for several reasons. First, it can directly hinder innovation (in the case where potential losers lobby successfully to get the innovation blocked). Second, rent-seeking involves a waste of resources. Such behaviour can benefit an individual firm, but only by making others worse off: it does not benefit society as a whole. The resources devoted to such lobbying would thus be better employed, from society's point of view, in alternative activities. In a country like Ireland, where entrepreneurship may have been a scarce resource at various points in time, the diversion of that resource to 'grantepreneurship' could be particularly harmful.

In Section 3 we will explore ways in which Irish institutions may have acted as barriers to growth over the past fifty years.

'New Growth Theory'
The traditional growth analysis examined above has several strong implications. First, while accumulation of human or physical capital will generate growth while an economy adjusts to its long-run equilibrium, long-run equilibrium growth will ultimately depend on increases in A, due for example to technological progress. Second, increased investment in physical capital, or indeed human capital (i.e. education) will increase a country's income level, but not its long-run growth rate.

Both of these implications follow from the assumption that there are diminishing returns to capital, which give rise to the shape of OA in Figure 7.1. Recent theory has suggested that there may in fact be constant or even increasing returns to investments in physical and/or human capital.[6] For example, new technology is embodied in specific investments: thus, increases in the capital stock might be associated with increases in A in the aggregate production function. If one firm's investment in new technology boosts other firms' productivity through some 'spillover' effect, the beneficial consequences of investment will be even greater. Countries with higher capital stocks would in such cases be much more productive than poor countries; so much more productive, in fact, that marginal returns to capital would be higher than in countries with low capital stocks.

The implications of this can be seen by envisaging the slope of OA increasing with the level of K, rather than declining. The slope of OC is thus also increasing. This has four key implications. First, net investment (per capita) increases continuously, as capital is accumulated; and the extra capital this gives rise to is increasingly productive. Growth based on accumulation alone can thus go on for ever, rather than fizzling out, as before. Second, increasing the savings rate, s, which shifts OC upwards, increases the level of net investment for any initial K/L, and thus boosts the long-run growth rate. *Growth rates,* as well as income *levels,* should thus be positively related to savings and investment rates. Third, a once-off increase in A, due for example to beneficial microeconomic policies, will also boost a country's long-run growth rate; in the Solow model, there would have been a once-off static gain as OA shifted upwards, followed by a 'medium-run growth bonus',[7] as the economy adjusted to a new long-run equilibrium, but no change in the long-run growth rate itself. Fourth, in this scenario convergence is no longer inevitable: rich countries with high capital stocks may well grow more rapidly than poor, capital-scarce, countries.

International Integration and Growth in Poor Countries
Simple economic logic suggests that economic integration with the outside world should be good for poor countries. Poor countries have low wages; integration should lead to capital inflows (and possibly labour outflows), both of which increase the capital/labour ratio and living standards (as argued earlier). Furthermore, low-wage economies should be good at producing labour-intensive products cheaply. As trade expands, they should be able to specialise in labour-intensive production, which leads to an increase in the demand for unskilled labour, and hence to an increase in unskilled wages. Finally, as already mentioned, poor countries tend to be technologically backward. Increasing international integration should speed up technological progress in poor countries, both directly (as a result of multinationals introducing new technologies) and indirectly (as exposing domestic firms to international competition makes them more innovative).

In the context of simple growth models, economic integration with the rest of the world should improve resource allocation. This corresponds to an increase in A in the aggregate production function. This will either lead to a once-off increase in income (in the context of the Solow model) or an increase in long-run growth rates (in the context of the very simple new growth model sketched out above). Moreover, if integration increases the rate of innovation, as a result of direct foreign investment, competition, or information flows, A will increase at a faster rate than under autarky. This will clearly increase long-run growth rates.

These simple arguments predict that EU membership should have boosted growth in poor European countries like Ireland. However, a more recent stream of literature (partly deriving from the new growth theory) predicts precisely the opposite, and it is to these arguments that we now turn.

Economic Geography and Peripherality

Ireland is a geographically peripheral country. Despite the enormous economic success of equally peripheral economies, Japan and Iceland for example, it has often been argued that Ireland's location has served as a barrier to growth. In recent years, mainstream economic theory has begun to examine how economic activity is distributed across different locations; this 'new economic geography' suggests that international economic integration can harm as well as help peripheral economies.[8]

External economies of scale are a key concept in economic geography. Standard economies of scale imply that when a firm expands, its own average costs fall; external economies imply that one firm's expansion improves all firms' productivity, in a given region and industry. Thus, an industry is said to experience external economies of scale if all firms in the industry can produce more efficiently when the industry as a whole expands.

If an industry experiences external economies of scale, there are several theoretical implications. In particular, when two economies start trading with each other, it is possible that the industry will end up being entirely located in one or other of the two countries; the industry which was bigger initially will have cost advantages over the smaller industry, enabling it to grow further at the expense of its rival, thus increasing its cost advantage further, and so on. The argument is thus made that EU integration might deprive small peripheral economies like Ireland of industries enjoying significant external scale economies.

A more sophisticated argument which has been developed recently emphasises transport costs, which are obviously a key factor for peripheral economies.[9] Transport costs help to segment markets: they give firms an incentive to locate close to larger markets. This incentive works against small peripheral economies. On the other hand, poorer economies have lower wage costs, which gives firms an incentive to locate there.

If transport costs are zero, firms will find it optimal to locate in the low-wage periphery, and export to large core markets: a lot of economic activity will be located in the periphery. If transport costs are so high, on the other hand, that transporting goods between markets is unaffordable, then core markets will be served by core industries, and peripheral markets will be served from the periphery: some activity, at least, will be located in the periphery. Finally, intermediate levels of transport costs may be sufficiently low that small peripheral markets can be serviced by the core; but high enough that it would not be profitable to export huge quantities of goods from the low-wage periphery to large core markets. The analysis suggests that, starting from a situation where international goods markets are very disintegrated, increasing market integration may first lead to peripheral production declining; but that beyond a certain point, further integration will lead to peripheral production expanding again. If the Irish market was very isolated from the world market in 1958, or 1973, then trade liberalisation could have hurt Irish industry, rather than helped it.

In the context of simple growth theory, this economic geography argument is suggesting that economic integration with the outside world may reduce A in the aggregate production function, rather than increase it: it all depends on the specific circumstances. In turn, if moving towards free trade reduces A, then that will lead to a once-off fall in income (in the context of the Solow model), or a permanent fall in growth rates (in the context of the very simple new growth model presented earlier).

Finally, there are various theoretical arguments that have been made suggesting that poor economies will become less technologically dynamic as a result of international economic integration. These arguments suggest that economic integration will directly reduce growth rates, by reducing the rate at which A increases. First, it is claimed that they will not be able to compete with core countries in R&D-intensive activities; thus integration may lead to such activities, and all the beneficial spillovers associated with them, being located in the core. Second, as mentioned in the previous section, economic integration may increase unskilled wages in poor countries; this will lower the gap between skilled and unskilled wages, which may reduce the incentive peripheral workers have to acquire further education or skills. Third, it may be that trade forces peripheral countries to specialise in goods with few prospects for technological progress, while core countries specialise in more technologically progressive goods – for example, during the early Industrial Revolution Ireland specialised in linen, which turned out to be difficult to mechanise, while Britain specialised in easily-mechanised cotton.

Theory is thus agnostic on whether economic integration with the outside world boosts or reduces peripheral growth rates. This is to be expected: theoretical results always depend on the assumptions built into the models in question. Theory alone cannot therefore be a guide to policy: economists must examine the empirical evidence before reaching policy conclusions. Sections 2 and 3 will therefore ask which theories are more relevant empirically in understanding recent Irish history.

Some Key Empirical Findings
There has been a lot of empirical work recently which has explored differences in economic growth rates across countries. Some of the findings support traditional growth theory, while others support the new growth theory. In particular:
(i)   Long-run growth rates seem to be positively related to investment in physical and human capital. Old growth theory predicts that investment (as measured by the savings rate in the Solow model) and growth are correlated only as the economy converges to the long-run equilibrium; new growth

theory suggests that higher investment implies higher growth even in the long run.

(ii) As mentioned earlier, poor countries grow more rapidly than rich countries, provided they have an adequate human capital endowment: this is compatible with traditional theory.

(iii) Outward-oriented countries (in South-East Asia, for example) have grown more rapidly than inward-oriented countries (such as those of Latin America).

In Section 3 we will examine Ireland's growth performance since 1950, establishing how well it has done. In Section 4, we will see to what extent Ireland's growth performance can be explained by the various theories outlined above.

3 IRISH PERFORMANCE SINCE 1950

Introduction

The Irish economy that emerged out of the semi-autarky of the Emergency (1939-45) had escaped the ravages of war, but it had been badly bruised by the shortage of raw materials such as fertilisers and oil and of capital goods. A half-decade or so of recovery, spurred on by the European Recovery Programme (or Marshall Plan), was followed by a decade of stagnation (see Chapter 1). In the late 1950s the economy remained highly protectionist, and largely dependent on an inefficient farming sector for exports and employment. A switch to more outward-looking policies in the 1960s (reduced protection, and tax reliefs and grants aimed at attracting foreign industry) seemed to work, and the pervasive gloom about Irish economic prospects gave way to growth and optimism. For the first time since the Famine there was a period of sustained population and employment growth, accompanied by significant structural change. Agriculture, which accounted for nearly one job in two in the 1940s, accounted for only one in four in 1971. The good times did not last, however, and the 'gloom and doom' of the late 1970s and early 1980s matched that of the bleak 1950s. Since the late 1980s the economy has been growing steadily again.

There is a widespread perception, not least in Ireland, that independent Ireland 'blew it'. Two recently published and influential books have made the point forcefully.[10] Using Cullen's tentative estimate of Irish national income per capita in 1911 they have argued that while Ireland was a respectably wealthy country on the eve of World War I, its subsequent growth experience was disastrous, with the result that it slipped dramatically down the European income league.

Kennedy *et al* make their point largely with reference to growth rates in the UK. Over the period 1926-85, GNP grew at the same rate, 2.1 per cent per annum, in both countries, while per capita product grew at 1.8 per cent per annum in Ireland, and 1.7 per cent per annum in the UK. They then point out that this performance is unsatisfactory, for two reasons. First, per capita incomes in Ireland were lower than in the UK over this period, so Ireland should have been catching up rather than merely keeping pace with the UK (see later). Second, British growth rates were low by European standards, and so keeping pace with Britain ensured long-run decline with respect to the Continent.[11]

Lee is even more pessimistic. 'Ireland recorded the slowest growth of per capita income between 1910 and 1970 of any European country except the United Kingdom... Ireland slid from being a reasonably representative Western European economy, in terms of income per head, at the time of Independence, to a position far below the Western European average in 1970'. Moreover, since the modest rise in Irish living standards occurred at the expense of considerable population loss, 'a wide gap opened between developments at the individual and the national levels... No other European country, east or west, north or south, for which remotely reliable evidence exists, has recorded so slow a rate of growth of national income in the twentieth century'.[12] Lee's views, though, as pointed out in Chapter 1, may be considered somewhat overpessimistic.

There are several difficulties which arise when comparing the growth performances of different countries. Do you use GDP or GNP statistics, for example? An output measure such as GDP per worker is relevant when comparing productivity across countries; an income measure such as Gross National Product (GNP) per capita would be more relevant for living standards. Gross National Disposable Income (GNDI), which includes foreign transfers, is the measure most directly linked to living standards, but is not particularly relevant when assessing a country's economic performance. The three measures are related to each other as follows:

GNDI = GNP + Net transfer payments from abroad (NTP)
      = GDP + Net factor payments from abroad (NFI) + NTP

The most readily available data are GDP per capita statistics, and we use those here; but as we shall see, the differences matter a lot for Ireland. (See Table 1.6 for some data on this.)

A second issue arises when trying to convert national GDP figures, which are measured in national currencies, into a common denominator. The most obvious solution, using nominal exchange rates to convert GDP data, can be seriously misleading. 100 Swiss francs, for example, can buy a lot less in Switzerland than the equivalent amount of drachmas could buy in Greece. Thus, converting GDP data using market exchange rates will make rich countries look richer than they are, and poor countries look poorer than they actually are.

Economists have thus developed a method for comparing GDP statistics, known as purchasing-power-parity(PPP)-adjustment, which corrects for differences in national price levels, as well as for nominal exchange rates. In this section we compare Ireland's performance to that of other European economies over the period 1950-94, using the most recent PPP-adjusted GDP statistics produced by the OECD.

Comparing Raw Growth Rates
Table 7.1 gives average growth rates in GDP per capita for Ireland, the UK, and the rest of Europe.[13] The entire period is split into four phases, which economic historians often distinguish from each other: the 1950s (when Europe was still recovering from the economic dislocation associated with the war); the 'Golden Age' of 1960-73, when European growth reached unprecedented levels; 1973-88, when Europe had to cope with the oil crises of the 1970s, and the unemployment of the 1980s; and the recent past (1988-94). Over the period as a whole, Ireland grew at about the same rate as the rest of Europe (2.9 per cent per annum), but significantly faster than the UK (2.0 per cent per annum). Focusing on the UK comparison thus makes Ireland look successful; but in a broader context, our performance has been unimpressive. (See also Table 1.4 for interesting longer-term data on this issue.)

Table 7.1
Average Annual Growth Rates, GDP per capita, 1950-94

Period	Ireland	UK	Europe
1950-60	2.2	2.3	3.7
1960-73	3.7	2.6	4.2
1973-88	2.1	1.9	1.9
1988-94	4.7	0.4	1.0
1950-94	2.9	2.0	2.9

Source: Derived from OECD National Accounts (unpublished worksheets kindly supplied by Angus Maddison).

Given that we are a relatively poor nation, we should have been growing more rapidly than Europe as a whole. There are several reasons for this. First, there is the logic of the Solow model: the marginal product of capital should be higher in poorer countries, and therefore lead to more investment. Second, there is the simple logic of international trade models, separate from any growth theory: poorer countries should experience capital inflows and labour outflows, which boost the capital/labour ratio; they should see their wage rates increasing, as a result of commodity trade; and they should be able to 'catch up', by importing best-practice technology from abroad. Third, and most importantly, we will see that the empirical evidence clearly shows that convergence has been a feature of the post-war European experience:

despite the gloomier predictions of the new growth theory, and economic geography theory, poorer European countries grew more rapidly than rich countries. In 1950, Italy, Spain, Greece and Portugal, all peripheral economies, were poorer than Ireland, Italy only marginally so. Between 1950 and 1994, Italy's average growth rate was 3.6 per cent per annum; and Greece, Portugal and Spain all achieved growth rates of 3.8 per cent per annum. The fact that Ireland did not grow as rapidly as other peripheral European economies, or more rapidly than the European average, represents a significant economic failure.

In the 1950s, Ireland's relative performance was disastrous; poorer than that of the UK as well as the European average. Things improved significantly in the Golden Age, when Ireland easily outperformed the UK; but even then, Ireland was not doing as well as the rest of Europe. In relative terms, then, the 1960s were not such a success story for Ireland as some accounts might suggest. Growth everywhere fell after 1973, but Ireland's growth rate exceeded (slightly) that of both the UK and the rest of Europe. Finally, Ireland's growth since 1988 has been spectacularly high, as measured by official per capita GDP statistics.

Comparing Growth Rates in the Light of Convergence
With the exception of the last six years, Ireland's growth has been unexceptional. Moreover, Table 7.1, by focusing on average growth rates, conceals important information which makes Ireland's relative performance look worse. In 1950 Irish GDP per capita was 49 per cent lower than in the UK, and 25 per cent lower than in Western Europe. As mentioned earlier, convergence has in fact been a feature of the OECD as a whole: Ireland should therefore have grown more rapidly than Western Europe as a whole. That it did not, until the post-1988 period, makes Ireland an important outlier.

This outlier status appears most clearly when one examines the relationship between GDP per capita growth rates and initial GDP per capita levels. Several things emerge at once from this analysis.

First, initially poor countries have on average grown more rapidly than initially rich countries: the post-war period has seen a convergence in living standards across Europe (see Table 1.4). Second, Ireland is a clear outlier over the period 1950-88, having a much lower growth rate than its initial income would suggest. Third, and importantly, the figures make it clear how fragile judgements on a country's relative performance can be. Data indicate that over the period 1950-88 Ireland was an under-achiever. However, strong growth over just six years was enough to make Ireland's performance between 1950 and 1994 look a lot more respectable, if not entirely satisfactory.

There has, moreover, been enormous controversy about the quality of official GDP statistics in recent years, with the claim being made that they are artificially inflated. There have been important revisions made to the national accounts in recent years, and such revisions could be made again in the future, leading to yet another assessment of our relative historical performance.

It is worth taking some time to examine the claim that Ireland's growth in the last few years has been overstated by official statisticians. The argument has to do with the stated profits of multinational companies. Such profits enter into Ireland's GDP (although, if repatriated, not its GNP), and there are suspicions that multinationals artificially boost these profits through 'transfer pricing'.[14] In some cases recorded profits have been quite dramatic; an extreme case is provided by the screening equipment company, Powerscreen, which in the year ending 1990-91 reported pre-tax profits of £5.8 million on a turnover of £6 million. In recent years flows of repatriated profits have been huge, absorbing about one-quarter of the output of the entire manufacturing sector in the early 1990s (see also Chapter 9).

The evidence for 'transfer pricing' can, by definition, be only circumstantial, but it is convincing enough. First, the enormous drop in the share of wages and salaries in net output of the industrial sector as a whole – from 50-60 per cent in the 1950s and 1960s to 40-45 per cent in the 1970s and less than thirty per cent today – can hardly be explained by technological change or composition effects. Comparing the shares of wages and salaries in a few selected industries in Ireland and in the UK is also illuminating. It is hard to believe that the labour intensity of production in Ireland is really as much lower than in Britain as implied there. However, the figures become understandable if it is the case that output (Q) is artificially inflated, thus reducing labour's share of output (W/Q) for a given wage bill (W).

In addition, the ratio of GNP to GDP in Ireland has declined over the last twenty years, from almost 100 per cent in the early 1970s to 88 per cent in 1994. The repatriation of profits promises a further widening in the gap between GDP and GNP in 1995. This is partly due to increasing flows of repatriated profits, partly due to the consequences of the enormous borrowing of the late 1970s and early 1980s. Irish performance would thus look a lot worse if GNP were the focus.

Fourth, one result of Ireland's relatively slow growth was that between 1950 and 1973, it was overtaken by Italy, Spain, Portugal and Greece in terms of GDP per capita. It was still behind these other peripheral economies in 1988, although our recent growth spurt means that our official GDP per capita was higher than all but Italy's in 1994.

To summarise: Ireland's performance was relatively poor between 1950 and 1988, although official statistics show a spectacular performance since 1988. Irish GNP growth has been lower than Irish GDP growth; Ireland's GDP performance was particularly disappointing in the 1950s, and to a certain extent the 1960s; Ireland's GNP performance was poor between 1973 and 1988. What can explain the poor performance experienced over most of this period? What can explain the turnaround which official statistics suggest has taken place since 1988? It is to these questions that the chapter now turns.

4 ANALYSING IRISH PERFORMANCE

Investment: Quantity and Quality

As seen above, traditional growth theory places much emphasis on investment, even though steady state growth is not affected by it; while the new growth literature attributes both level and growth effects to investment. The empirical literature has tended to find a significant positive relationship between investment shares and growth. Moreover, investment is itself an endogenous variable related to, among other things, initial income levels. Traditional growth models suggest that in poorer countries returns to capital, and hence investment shares, should be higher than in rich countries. The American economist Robert Barro found this to be so, once initial levels of human capital had been controlled for.

Theory and international experience thus suggest that Ireland should have had very high investment shares during our period; if it did not, this might help explain its failure to grow faster than the rest of Europe. Irish policy makers were traditionally concerned about a lack of investment in the Irish economy. The 1958 White Paper (1958, p.35) highlighted 'the insufficiency of our current savings as a basis for national capital formation on the scale which would be necessary to enable us even to follow at some distance the rising standards in the rest of Europe'. (Of course, an SOE can import capital, leading to investment rates greater than savings rates; but capital was not as mobile internationally in the 1950s as it has subsequently become.) Were these official fears justified?

Table 7.2

Gross Investment (Per Cent of GDP), 1960-90

Period	Ireland	UK	EU 12
1960-69	19.5	18.1	22.8
1970-79	25.0	19.2	22.8
1980-90	21.6	17.5	20.1

Source: European Economy, December 1991, Table 20.

Table 7.2, using EU data, gives investment shares for Ireland, the UK and the 12 present EU members since 1960. Irish investment rates were consistently above UK levels, but only exceeded average EU levels after 1970. Moreover, these data understate the extent to which Ireland was underinvesting prior to 1970. Ireland was a poor county: theory and cross-country evidence suggest that, for that reason, it should have been investing more than other EU members, who were on average richer. Table 7.3 therefore attempts to capture Ireland's investment performance in the light of its relative backwardness. It compares the Irish investment level in a particular year, not with average EU investment in that year, but with a 'European norm' corresponding to Ireland's GDP per capita in that year. For example, Ireland's investment in 1950 is compared with investment in other European countries with GDP per capita levels equal to that of Ireland in 1950: Greece (in 1964), Italy (in 1950), Portugal (in 1968), and Spain (in 1956). The table suggests that Ireland was substantially underinvesting during much of the period, including (interestingly) 1988, the eve of its apparent growth spurt.

Table 7.3

Gross Investment (Per Cent of GDP), 1950-88,
Relative to European Norm

Year	Ireland	European norm (n)[1]
1950	17.3	22.3 (4)
1960	16.4	22.0 (7)
1970	22.7	22.3 (15)
1980	28.2	24.0 (14)
1988	16.2	24.0 (14)

Source: OECD, *National Accounts 1950-1979, Volume 1,* Paris 1981, and OECD, *National Accounts 1960-1989,* Paris 1991.
[1] Number of countries defining the European norm (n) in parentheses.

Furthermore, it may be that the quality of Irish investment was poor and its composition wrong. Table 7.4 summarises trends in the share of gross investment by use. The share of agricultural machinery in total investment has dropped steadily since the 1950s, while that of 'other machinery' has risen steadily, from one-fifth of the total in the 1950s to over one-third today. But the consistently high proportion spent on transport equipment is the most noteworthy feature of Table 7.4. Was this 'unproductive' investment, or was communications a relatively important industry in Ireland for geographical or other reasons? The output of the Irish transport and communications sector – about six per cent of GDP, proportionately no greater in Ireland than in other European countries in the period under review – casts doubt on the last explanation. A more plausible explanation for the high share of transport may be the loss-making capital grants to concerns such as the national air, rail, and sea carriers. Dividing the output of the transport sector by the sum invested in it in a selection of European economies indicates that the return on investment in transport equipment was lower in Ireland than in any of the other European economies examined.

Table 7.4

Investment by Use (Per Cent), 1953-90

Period	A	B	C	D	E	F
1953-59	17.1	5.6	37.0	14.1	5.5	20.6
1960-69	15.9	4.3	33.5	14.4	4.8	27.1
1970-79	22.9	2.1	26.8	12.4	4.5	31.3
1980-90	22.4	3.7	24.2	14.0	2.5	33.2

Source: C. Ó Gráda and K. O'Rourke, 'Irish Economic Growth 1945-1988', in N. Crafts and G. Toniolo (editors), *Economic Growth in Postwar Europe,* Cambridge University Press, Cambridge 1995.
A = dwellings; B = roads; C = other buildings; D = transport equipment; E = agricultural machinery; F = other machinery.

It is also sometimes alleged that too much Irish capital formation has been in the form of public sector investment. The argument is that the public sector feels less pressure to allocate funds to the most profitable uses. Defining public capital formation as public capital expenditure minus redemption of securities and payments to the rest of the world (usually a small item), the public share in total gross fixed capital formation in Ireland has indeed been high, usually ranging between thirty and forty per cent between the 1950s and the 1980s, and falling below twenty per cent only in 1990 and 1991. Eurostat provides a comparative perspective: it suggests that the public share in gross fixed capital formation was not particularly high in Ireland in 1970, but that by the mid-1980s it was highest in the EU.

In summary, Ireland's investment rate was consistently lower than investment rates in other countries at a similar stage of development. Moreover, such investment as did take place was not necessarily allocated appropriately. These facts can clearly help explain Ireland's relatively slow growth. In the Solow model, low investment implies slow growth during the transition to long-run equilibrium; in new growth models, low investment implies growth rates that are permanently lower than they would otherwise be.

Education and Training

Surprisingly, Ireland does quite well in international comparisons of educational expenditure and output. Irish expenditure on education has been both high and rising (from 3.1 per cent of GNP in 1962 to 6.4 per cent in 1989). This is reflected in Ireland's relatively high rate of school attendance in a recent study by Mankiw, Roemer, and Weil, where Ireland ranks seventh out of 121 countries.[15]

Decline in the quality of education is unlikely: analyses of the contribution of education (measured by years of schooling) to earnings in 1972 and 1987 imply no decline in the interim, and the marginal returns to higher education are at least as high in Ireland as in other countries offering comparable data. Nor is the frequently alleged bias against technical and science-oriented subjects in the Irish educational system supported by the facts.[16] It seems difficult, then, to argue that Ireland's poor performance before 1988 was due to a lack of investment in education.

Emigration

Ireland has been an outlier as regards emigration over the last 150 years. While emigration is clearly a response to poor economic performance, it can increase the living standards of those remaining, by increasing capital/labour ratios. None the less, there are those who argue that emigration is partly to blame for Ireland's poor performance. Since most emigrants leave at an age when they switch from being net consumers to net producers, sending countries like Ireland bear the 'life cycle' burden of producing workers who spend their productive years elsewhere. Sending countries may also suffer from a 'brain drain', when emigration reduces the national human capital/labour ratio. If emigrants are better educated than the population at large, emigration will reduce the growth of income per capita in the sending country. On the other hand, emigration of unskilled workers should improve the lot of those unskilled workers remaining behind.

Irish emigration, like all emigration, is selective as far as age is concerned. The migrants tend to be young and single, maximising the gain from moving. However, the proportion of teenagers is less today than it was in the 1950s. Women have been as likely to leave as men. For reasons still not quite understood, they have tended to leave at a younger age than the men; in 1987-93, 60.6 per cent were in the 15-24 age bracket compared to a figure of 52.7 per cent for men. The destinations have changed over time. The UK has been the dominant destination since the 1920s, but its share slipped in the 1980s: in 1987-93, only three in five went to the UK, and over one in four to the US.

Trends in net emigration rates by province have converged in recent decades. The convergence reflects the gradual convergence in living standards between rich and poor provinces. Until recently, higher emigration rates from Connaught and Ulster reflected their greater poverty; the emigration in turn narrowed the gap in living standards between poor and rich provinces.

The notion that Ireland has lost its best and brightest through emigration is a long-standing one. The sociologist Richard Lynn likened the impact of the outflow to 'what would occur if the best specimens of a herd of cattle were continually exported and the herd replenished by breeding from the inferior stock that remained'. Yet between the 1930s and 1970s at least, emigration 'improved' Ireland's occupational distribution, by targeting disproportionate numbers of domestic servants and young men from small farming and farm labouring backgrounds. If the 'brain drain' argument applies at all, it applies only to the period after 1980.

For the 1980s and 1990s, the evidence as to the skill composition of emigrants is mixed, although the educational standards of emigrants have clearly been higher in recent decades. True, the evidence of a four-thousand sample survey of young people emigrating during the 1980s carried out by the Irish Episcopal Commission on Emigrants in 1991-92 suggests that one-third of them had left without finishing secondary schooling, just over half had second-level qualifications, and less than one-tenth had higher-level qualifications. On the other hand, surveys carried out by the Higher Education Authority in the 1980s show a substantial share of university graduates leaving. The proportion was quite variable, peaking at 26.1 per cent in 1988 and declining thereafter to 14-15 per cent in 1992 and 1993. Further analysis of graduates of five different Irish universities showed that 40-50 per cent of those who had graduated in 1983, 1984, or 1986 had been abroad or were still abroad at the beginning of 1990.

Others propose a more Boserupian theory of the long-run damage inflicted by emigration, arguing that it removed 'pressures to reform a conservative and conformist social structure, the institutions of which were ill-adapted to innovation'.[17] However plausible, this hypothesis is extremely difficult to test.

Trade Policy

We saw in Section 2 that microeconomic policies which change the value of A in the aggregate production function can have effects on the level of GDP (in the context of the Solow model) or on the long-run growth of GDP (in the context of new growth theory). Moreover, such policies can more directly influence long-run growth, by increasing or reducing the innovativeness of the economy. More open economies tend to be more technologically progressive than closed economies: trade policy can thus be an important determinant of long-run growth.

The policy of protection brought in by de Valera in the early 1930s (see Chapter 1) was not unique, and may have been a sensible response to the circumstances of the time. Ireland was however slow to jump on the GATT bandwagon, only significantly liberalising towards the mid-1960s with the Anglo-Irish Free Trade Agreement (AIFTA). It thus seems reasonable to enquire whether Ireland's failure to ride the post-war boom was due to its mistaken adherence to trade policies that had outlived their usefulness.

How did protection affect the Irish economy? It certainly made it a lot more inward-looking. The resulting industrial structure – a large number of widely dispersed small firms and a low degree of horizontal integration – reflected both the power of local pressure groups and the small size of the local market. The following passage on the 1930s will give a flavour of the distortions involved:

J.H. Woodington was refused permission to build a tannery adjacent to his Drogheda shoe plant or in an adjoining town. He was informed that the minister preferred a town that did not have an industry and was dispatched to Mountmellick following local representations, despite the lack of a suitable site. When he turned his attentions to Portlaoise because of an offer of local capital, officials proposed Tralee, 'where all the capital necessary would be available'.[18]

Few other sizeable towns in Ireland are as far from Drogheda as Tralee!

Such a structure was unlikely to support the innovation necessary for sustained economic growth. It was also bound to deprive Irish industry of precisely the sorts of external economies of scale (skilled local labour forces, for example) that have been used to justify industrial protection. Why then did Ireland take so long to liberalise?

Although the protectionist policies pursued by successive administrations since the early 1930s always had their critics, evidence of the damage caused was elusive before the 1950s. The tariffs imposed in the early 1930s initially produced a sharp rise in industrial employment. Admittedly, it did not take capital long to absorb the sheltered home market, and industrial employment had already peaked before 1939. However, the message that import substitution could not have produced sustained economic growth was blurred by the enforced autarky of 1939-45, and the post-war recovery produced the illusion that protectionism was doing no harm. 1946 to 1951 was the first five-year period since the Famine to experience population growth. Industrial employment rose considerably, industrial profits rose, and the rate of economic growth was respectable by European standards. It was only when the rest of Europe left the Irish economy standing in the 1950s that the bankruptcy of the old policies became clear to policymakers.

Policymakers and most opinion-makers in the early 1950s took protection for granted. The Commission on Emigration (1956) defended tariffs by noting that without them 'it would be difficult to conceive of industry on any wide scale maintaining itself or developing further' and insisted that future commitments to international agreements should not compromise 'our freedom to develop our industries as we think fit'. To those economists who continued to support free trade, in the mid-1950s it was still 'an unlikely Utopia'. Even Whitaker's landmark Economic Development (1958), the government report which paved the way for the new economic policies of the 1960s, was circumspect about the issue. Noting that 'the coming of free trade in Europe in one form or another must be faced in due course' (p.190), its main emphasis was on the need to allow in foreign capital rather than on abolishing tariffs. Indeed, the new Industrial Development Authority, established to attract direct foreign investment, sanctioned some tariff increases in its early years, and neither the Central Bank nor the Department of Finance proposed freer trade as a panacea in the early 1950s. Policymakers emphasised instead the need for state mobilisation of investment funds and demand management. It took time for the argument for freer trade to sink in. Still, Córas Tráchtála (the state export-promotion agency) was founded in 1952, and export tax reliefs date from 1956.

It seems likely that slow growth during the 1950s was at least in part due to the continuation of protection. Conversely, free trade since 1960 appears to have helped boost Irish growth (see Table 7.1). On the other hand, Ireland continued to underperform relative to Europe. Perhaps this was because free trade did not mean an end to government distortions. For example, as Lee notes, it was surely no accident that the new tax incentives and grants introduced to attract foreign investment in export-oriented industries were geared to complement, rather than substitute for, existing inward-looking Irish-owned industries. To this extent the Irish campaign to attract foreign investment was constrained from the start by the protectionist legacy.

What were the consequences of trade liberalisation for previously protected sectors? Penetration of the domestic market by imports was significant in apparel and clothing, soap and detergents, footwear, carpets, and leather handbags. On accession to the EEC, domestic producers were still holding their own in several sectors (notably vehicle assembly) which would suffer during the 1970s and 1980s. For example, of the network of shoemaking factories opened under protection only Dubarry in Ballinasloe was left in 1994.

Industrial Policy

Irish industrial policy changed radically in the early 1960s. The policy of relying on tariffs to protect domestic producers and on the Control of Manufactures Acts to keep Irish industry in Irish hands was abandoned (see Chapter 1). Since then, foreign investment in Irish industry has been the cornerstone of government policy. New companies such as Potez Aerospace (French-owned with a plant in Baldonnel) and Verolme (Dutch-owned, operating a shipyard in Cork) received large grants amid great publicity. The remarkable structural transformation of the economy between the late 1950s and the early 1970s may be largely attributed to their arrival. By 1973 overseas firms accounted for almost one-third of all employment in manufacturing. Even in the less propitious climate of post-1973 the number of foreign-owned firms continued to grow. By 1983 there were almost a thousand of them, with a labour force of 87,600, while employment in Irish-owned concerns continued to drop. In the 1980s the newer (foreign) industrial concerns, concentrated in a few sectors, seemed to perform better than the old (indigenous) companies. If industry is divided into 'modern' (pharmaceuticals, engineering, and a category called 'other foods') and 'traditional' (the rest), it can be shown that the two have differed markedly in terms of performance. During the 1980s 'modern' – largely foreign-owned –

industry trebled its output, while 'traditional' industry barely held its own (see Chapter 12).

However, critics have pointed to flaws in government policy attracting foreign capital and in the kind of industry attracted (see Chapter 12). The IDA offered foreign investors the wrong kind of incentive package. Instead of subsidising labour and employment, they subsidised capital. The tax benefits prompted firms to engage in transfer pricing, and virtually ruled out production for the home market. Moreover, the IDA had a penchant for picking products far advanced in their product cycle, where competition from less developed countries would soon prove serious or fatal.

When the government first started attracting multinationals, the results were deemed a great success; output, exports and employment grew. Yet today, despite massive outlays, Irish manufacturing employs fewer people than in the 1960s. The message that manufacturing's job-creating potential is weak is finally sinking in. Indeed, the IDA has taken to comparing the modest losses in manufacturing employment in Ireland – for which it claims credit – to the huge losses elsewhere in Europe in the 1970s and 1980s (e.g. 38.2 per cent in the U.K., 18 per cent in Norway, 17.4 per cent in Denmark, 16.9 per cent in France). The logic of Ireland's quest for manufacturing jobs is however unclear. Is this really where Ireland's comparative advantage lies? If it lies elsewhere, then promoting industry at the expense of other sectors of the economy misallocates resources, reduces the value of A in the aggregate production function, and lowers the level (and possibly the growth rate) of GDP.

Since the 1960s policy has shifted from an anti-export to a pro-export bias. In effect one form of distortion (capital subsidies, tax relief on exports) replaced another (protection). The new regime represented protection by another name. Certainly, many high-profile companies would not have chosen Ireland as a base but for its uniquely generous combination of grants and tax reliefs. The shift to 'free trade' in Ireland was matched by a big increase in non-tariff distortions in the form of a huge rise in aids to industry. One indication of its effect is provided by the ratio of IDA grants to net industrial output. They dropped from 4.4 per cent in 1976-83 to 1.9 per cent in 1984-90. However, this represents only a small part of total state aid to the sector. EU calculations put this at 6.4 per cent of GDP in 1986-88 and 4.9 per cent in 1988-90. Tax deductions, due in large part to the imputed value of the special 10 per cent corporation tax applied to manufacturing, account for half of this aid. In the mid-1980s 3 per cent of GNP was being spent on promoting industrial development, equalling about one-eighth of industrial value added. The effect of the above is that investors receiving the maximum cash grant are being protected with the equivalent of a 24 per cent tariff.

Such government distortions could clearly lead to a similar misallocation of capital (and labour) as would outright protection, lowering the level of A in equation (1). Moreover, industrial policy might have more direct effects on growth, by lowering the growth rate of A. Direct government subsidies might be even more 'capturable' by interest groups than across-the-board protection; rent-seeking might be as much more of a problem; the result might be an allocation of management resources towards 'grantepreneurship', and away from innovation.

Macroeconomic Policy

Irish macroeconomic policy has tended to follow, with a lag, the fashions practised elsewhere in Western Europe since 1945. This makes it difficult to blame our poor performance on particularly inappropriate macroeconomic policies. Thus Keynesian deficit spending was introduced in the early 1950s, a little later than elsewhere, and a timorous version of economic planning along French lines in the late 1950s. As in other countries, the reaction to the first oil crisis of the early 1970s was to engage in public borrowing on a large scale. 1979 brought membership of the European Monetary System for Ireland along with most other EU members, implying a break with sterling for the first time since 1826. In recent years, the focus has been more on supply-side measures to relieve Ireland's serious unemployment problem, again in line with developments in Britain, the US, and Europe. In all cases Irish policymakers were applying lessons already learned elsewhere. When, then, did Irish exceptionalism in fiscal policy affect its comparative growth performance? No rigorous analysis can be provided here, but a comparative look suggests that the damage inflicted by public spending on both taxation and the public sector borrowing requirement in the late 1970s was particularly severe in Ireland (see Chapters 5 and 6). The evidence suggests that since the 1970s at least Ireland's public sector has been 'large' by European standards. If macroeconomic policy can be blamed at all for Ireland's poor comparative performance, it is the excessive spending of the late 1970s that emerges as the culprit (see Chapter 6). Otherwise, the important policy failures were predominantly microeconomic in nature.

Ireland and the New Economic Geography

The Irish experience fails to support those arguments which suggest that increasing international integration reduces peripheral R&D, education, or innovation. Since 1973 R&D expenditure in Ireland has increased dramatically; the returns to education as measured by skill differentials have remained steady, and the workforce has become more educated; the share of increasing returns to scale industries in total industrial employment has risen; and high-tech employment has expanded. These trends are largely explained by the importance of multinationals in the Irish economy, an institutional feature ignored by simple economic geography models. Comparing Ireland's relative macro-performance before and after 1973, it is certainly clear that EU membership did not hurt Ireland in relative terms. The simple theoretical intuition that increased integration with the world economy is good for small, poor, countries seems to do better when confronted with the Irish evidence than the more esoteric predictions of recent theory (see Section 2).

Political Economy and Rent-Seeking

In Section 2 we saw that rent-seeking behaviour can block innovation and waste scarce resources. The implication is that political institutions can matter for a country's growth performance. To what extent have Irish institutions helped or hindered growth?

The rent-seeking approach associated with Mancur Olson seems to offer a good framework for interpreting Ireland's relatively poor economic performance since 1950. Olson predicts, in the absence of disturbing causes, powerful tendencies for sectional interest groups to become entrenched in an economy. These groups will tend to cause institutional sclerosis and economic stagnation. According to Olson, societies fortunate enough to have been spared military invasion or serious political unrest for a long time, such as the UK, pay a price in that their very stability gives such interest groups ample scope to plan collective actions which restrict competition and retard growth. Only an external shock such as defeat in war or economic and political integration can destroy the influence of such groups.

There is plenty of evidence for rent-seeking in Ireland (see Chapter 10). Many non-traded services in Ireland – telecommunications, electricity, transportation – have traditionally been provided by semi-state companies who have used their monopoly position to force up prices, reducing the competitiveness of the rest of the economy. Private non-traded services – public houses, taxis, and lawyers, for example – similarly enjoy monopoly profits by restricting entry (see Chapter 10). Government expenditure as a percentage of GDP has been higher in Ireland, although not spectacularly so, than in other countries at the same level of development, implying relatively high tax rates. In all of these cases, 'muscle'· has clearly been used by powerful lobbies to extract benefits from the rest of the community. These lobbies' clout has also been used to block technological or organisational change in the sectors concerned, with negative implications for innovation and growth.

One institutional feature of Irish life that has often been blamed for some of the rent-seeking that occurs in the country is the multi-seat constituency, which pits party member against party member, and places a premium on 'constituency service'. It also makes for more marginal seats, giving greater weight to regional issues than would be the case under either a 'national list' or a single-seat constituency system. Perhaps more important is the fact that Irish political constituencies are too small. Ireland's Dáil has 166 members serving a population of 3.5 million; the UK's House of Commons has 630 members serving a population of over 50 million.

Institutions and politics can matter in other ways. Did Ireland's pay-bargaining structure retard output and productivity growth? The Olson model would seem to have a definite bearing here. Olson argues that interest groups such as trade unions and producers' groups inflict most damage when they are big enough to cause widespread·disruption but small enough for the social cost of their actions to remain an externality to themselves. In this view, either very weak (as in the US) or all-powerful (as in Sweden) lobbies may be preferable to something in between. Thus it is often argued that corporatism works, both in pay bargaining and strategic policy decision-making, because it takes account of macroeconomic constraints and minimises the risk of inter-union disputes (see Chapter 4). Many analysts consider the cost of reduced wage dispersion worth paying. In Ireland, the experience of the Committee on Industrial Organisation, which united management, unions, and the public service in analysing the shortcomings of protected industries in the early 1960s and in proposing rationalisation schemes seems a good case in point.

The experience with centralised bargaining since 1987, after decades of decentralised or poorly planned centralised bargaining, would also appear to bear out the above. The result has been wage restraint, with the government pre-announcing the wage increases it would accept. Macroeconomic constraints were explicitly recognised by the main players, in classic corporatist fashion; the result was that when demand eventually expanded, the outcome was an increase in employment, rather than wage inflation. This political economy turnaround is a plausible cause of the Irish growth upturn of the late 1980s.

5 CONCLUSION

Observers of the Irish economy, worried about its lowly and laggard status in the growth stakes, have long looked to history and to the achievements of neighbouring economies for inspiration. In the 1840s Young Irelander Thomas Davis pointed to the Prussian system of technical education and the Norwegian system of succession; in the 1900s agrarian reformer Horace Plunkett urged his countrymen to make Ireland 'another Denmark' and economic nationalist Arthur Griffith saw a lesson in the 'resurrection of Hungary'. Though their diagnoses differed radically, Davis, Plunkett, and Griffith believed that the performance of the Irish economy was far from optimal. Most subsequent assessments concur. Our own comparative perspective on the growth record over the last half-century or so confirms the gloomy assessments of earlier studies.

The outcome will hardly come as a surprise for the 1950s, conventionally deemed a 'lost decade' in Irish economic history. Yet even the 1960s, usually considered a 'golden age' for Irish economic growth, emerge in a less favourable light, when assessed in the context of a European pattern of 'convergence'. Economic growth throughout Europe declined in the wake of the oil crisis of 1973, and the achievements of the previous two decades have not been matched since. Ireland's problems in the 1970s and 1980s were thus partly a reflection of a general slowdown in economic growth, but they were aggravated by a growing and ultimately crippling public debt. However, this rather gloomy assessment of the record since the 1940s must be tempered with the key caveat that the performance of the Irish economy over the last half-decade or so seems to have been excellent. Real GNP rose by more than six per cent in 1994 and a further rise of over five per cent is predicted for 1995, with associated rises in employment and living standards. But whether this relatively rapid growth is more than a transient phenomenon is something which remains to be seen.

Why, then, has Ireland's record been poor until very recently? We have seen that low investment rates, low-quality investment decisions, restrictive tariff policies, and rent-seeking all played a role at some time or other over the past half-century or so. For some of the period, too, government spending was on the high side for an economy at Ireland's stage of development. On the other hand, low rates of investment in human capital do not seem to have been a factor, at least from the 1960s on. Finally, one dimension not addressed in this chapter – and this is a shortcoming that it shares with most of the convergence literature – is the role of geography. Could Ireland's proximity to Britain, a slow grower in absolute terms (although not an underperformer in the convergence sense) have led to slow Irish growth rates? Adding a spatial dimension to the empirical growth literature may prove a fruitful research programme for the future.

Endnotes

1 A. Maddison, *Dynamic Forces in Capitalist Development*, Oxford University Press, Oxford 1991, Table 1.3, p.10.
2 In fact, output is also produced with land, and thus land per capita should also belong in the aggregate production function. In previous centuries, Europeans have indeed increased their living standards by increasing the acreage under cultivation; but this sort of growth is hardly of great importance today, which is why we ignore it.
3 Of course, technological progress will typically only come about as a result of investment, of which more later. Moreover, technological progress, by shifting OA (and therefore OC) upwards, will lead the economy to converge to a new equilibrium involving a higher level of the capital stock.
4 N. Mankiw, D. Romer and D. Weil, 'A Contribution to the Empirics of Economic Growth', *Quarterly Journal of Economics*, CVII(2) 1992.
5 R. Easterlin, 'Why Isn't the Whole World Developed?', *Journal of Economic History*, 41(1) 1981.
6 For an accessible overview of the literature, see the articles on the subject in the Winter 1994 issue of the *Journal of Economic Perspectives*.
7 The terminology is taken from Baldwin, 'The Growth Effects of 1992', *Economic Policy*, no. 9 1989.
8 For an accessible survey, with a focus on Ireland, see F. Barry, 'Peripherality in Economic Geography and Modern Growth Theory, Evidence from Ireland's adjustment to free trade' (UCD Centre for Economic Research), Dublin 1994.

9 See for example P. Krugman and A. Venables, 'Integration and The Competitiveness of Peripheral Industry', in J. de Macedo and C. Bliss (editors), *Unity with Diversity within the European Periphery: The Community's Southern Frontier,* Cambridge University Press, Cambridge 1990.

10 J. Lee, *Ireland 1912-1985: Politics and Society,* Cambridge University Press, Cambridge 1989; K. Kennedy, T. Giblin and D. McHugh, *The Economic Development of Ireland in the Twentieth Century,* Routledge, London 1988.

11 Kennedy *et al.,* Table 6.1.

12 Lee, *op. cit.*

13 Here defined as: Austria, Belgium, Denmark, Finland, France, Germany, Greece, Italy, the Netherlands, Norway, Portugal, Sweden, Spain, and Switzerland.

14 Ireland's profit taxes are lower than elsewhere, so multinationals want their profits to show up as having being generated in Ireland. For an analysis of the effects of transfer pricing on GDP estimates see O. Mangan, 'The Irish National Accounts: How Do They Measure Up?', *Irish Banking Review,* Winter 1994.

15 See Mankiw, Romer and Weil, *op. cit.*

16 See J. Sheehan, 'Education, Training, and the Culliton Report' (UCD Centre for Economic Research), Dublin 1992.

17 K. Kennedy, 'The Context of Economic Development', in J. Goldthorpe and C. Whelan (editors), *The Development of Industrial Society in Ireland,* Oxford University Press, Oxford 1992, p.28.

18 M. Daly *Industrial Development and Irish National Identity,* Gill and Macmillan, Dublin 1992, p.108.

CHAPTER 8

Employment and Unemployment

John O'Hagan *

1 INTRODUCTION

This chapter follows logically from Chapter 2, where economic growth and full employment as objectives of economic policy were discussed in some detail. In that chapter the meaning of these objectives was explained, as were the problems of measurement, and the desirability of each objective and possible policy conflicts were examined. This chapter also draws on the last chapter, as policies to promote economic growth are also those needed to stimulate increased employment: one of the apparent paradoxes in Ireland, though, is that in the last fifteen years or so an above-average (compared to other OECD countries) growth in GDP has been accompanied by a well below-average increase in employment. This is a topic that will be discussed later in the chapter.

This chapter also links into the later chapters. Any policies to deal with unemployment must be compatible with the country's foreign payments position and policy with regard to exchange rate and inflation (Chapter 9). Besides, any policy at a macroeconomic level must translate into sectoral policy, with the emphasis always for a small open economy such as Ireland's on competitiveness (Chapters 10, 11 and 12).

The next section of this chapter examines the issue of labour supply in Ireland and emphasises the critical role that emigration plays in this regard, a factor that marks Ireland apart from other OECD countries. Section 3 looks at the issue of employment, its growth and composition, and compares Ireland's performance to that of a number of other countries. Section 4 does likewise in relation to unemployment, highlighting the extraordinary position

* I would like to thank Cloda Lane for research assistance with this chapter. I would also like to thank David Hegarty for his assistance with many parts of this chapter, including the provision of data for tables, drawing my attention to various reports, and the many helpful comments he made on earlier drafts. The chapter also benefitted greatly from the joint work we did on the topic of unemployment for the National Economic and Social Forum over the last two years.

in Ireland with regard to long-term unemployment. As emphasised throughout the chapter, the labour market in Ireland is very small and forms part of a wider and much greater international market, particularly that of the UK, to a lesser extent that of the US and, in some occupations, that of continental Europe.

The rest of the chapter examines the various factors that may influence the level of employment, and hence the level of unemployment, in the economy. Given that unemployment has increased significantly in most OECD countries in the last twenty years, it is important not to view the problem of low levels of employment creation in Ireland in isolation from what is happening elsewhere in the OECD countries. The OECD in fact has produced some major reports in the last few years dealing with the issue of employment and unemployment and these will very much inform the discussion that follows. Many small countries and many regions of larger countries, of course, with labour forces much larger than Ireland, have experienced much lower rates of unemployment than the OECD average or the national average in their own countries. This would tend to suggest that there are strong 'domestic' factors at play in explaining employment growth and therefore in solving the unemployment problem.

With the above in mind, Section 5 will examine three factors that impinge on job creation, namely globalisation of trade, technological change and skills mismatch. The first two of these are clearly international in origin, yet different countries have been affected by and/or responded to them in very different ways, particularly in relation to the problem of skills mismatch that inevitably results from these factors.

A major reason perhaps for the different responses in different countries to the phenomena of technological change and the globalisation of trade relates to the flexibility of the labour market and this is the subject matter of Section 6. Issues such as the real wage and the wage-setting process, the effects of the tax and social welfare systems on labour supply and demand, the effects of rigidities in the product market on the labour market, and the effects of employment legislation on employment creation are all discussed. Whatever the causes of, and therefore solutions to, unemployment, one thing is clear, especially in Ireland, and that is that the failure to prevent the rise in unemployment in the last fifteen years has led to a huge build-up of those categorised as long-term unemployed (i.e. unemployed for twelve months or more). This is the subject matter of Section 7. The existence of large-scale, long-term unemployment poses very different challenges to those of short-term unemployment, as many of those in this category are, because of the deskilling and demotivation that results from long periods of inactivity, largely outside the labour market. Policies therefore that improve employment creation may make little impact, at least in the short term, on this problem. In this context, the effects of prolonged payment of unemployment and related benefits and the effectiveness or otherwise of active labour market policies will be examined in this section. Section 8 concludes the chapter.

2 LABOUR SUPPLY

Labour supply in any country depends on three factors: the total size of the population, the proportion of that population of working age, and the proportion of the working-age population seeking or in work. This is illustrated by the identity:

(1) $$L = P. P(A)/P. L/P(A)$$

where L is the size of the labour force, P the size of the population, and P(A) the size of the working population. The labour force, in turn, consists of those in employment (E) and those unemployed (UE). Hence:

(2) $$L = E + UE$$

These simple identities are useful reference points for the rest of the discussion in this section.

Population
The total population of a country depends on three factors: the birth rate, the death rate and the rate of emigration. The difference between the birth and death rates is known as the rate of natural increase and in most countries the natural increase translates directly into a population increase. This has not been the case in Ireland, where in the past the change in population has 'tracked' much more closely the trend in emigration than that of natural increase.

In looking at the natural increase the key factor is the birth rate as the death rate has shown only very small change in the last thirty years or so. Up to the late 1970s the birth rate in Ireland increased significantly from its levels in the 1930s and 1940s, leading to a surge in the natural increase of the population, from 27,000 per annum in the 1950s to 40,000 per annum in the late 1970s, but since then the birth rate has declined quite dramatically and may decline even further in the next ten years. As a result, from having one of the highest birth rates in Europe only ten years ago, Ireland now has a birth rate little above the levels pertaining in Northern Europe. This means that the natural increase in the population now is averaging only 20,000 per annum.

While this is a significant change in the natural increase, it is slight compared to the huge swings in net migration that can occur in Ireland: net immigration of 15-20,000 per annum in some years in the 1970s, to net emigration of 40,000 per annum in some years in the 1980s, to a level of

2,000 or so in the early 1990s, with a prediction that this will rise to 18,000 or so in the second half of the 1990s. The picture that is emerging in the 1990s then is that on average the natural increase will be much lower than in the past and that it will not translate into any increase in population because of emigration.

Working-Age Population
There will however be significant changes in the composition of the population. As Table 8.1 shows, there will as a result of the fall in the birth rate in the last decade or so be a large fall in the population aged 15 and under and a large increase in the population aged 25 to 64, i.e. the prime working-age population. The decline in the population aged under 15, and by the beginning of the next decade in that aged 15 to 24, clearly will have major implications for the economy in, for example, the area of education, but what is of most interest here is the predicted increase in the prime working-age population in Ireland over the next ten years. Despite the fact then that no increase in population is expected, the large predicted increase in the prime working-age group population will, *ceteris paribus,* lead to a similar increase in the labour force.

Table 8.1
Age Composition of Population (000s) in Ireland, 1991-2005

Age	1991	1995	2000	2005
Less than 15	941	856	749	680
15-24	602	663	629	541
25 to 64	1,581	1,649	1,769	1,865
Over 65	403	411	422	440
Total	3,526	3,579	3,568	3,526

Source: S. Cantillon, J. Curtis and J. FitzGerald, *Medium-Term Review: 1994-2000,* Economic and Social Research Institute, Dublin 1994, Table 3.5.

Participation in Labour Force
The working-age population is traditionally defined as that aged 15 to 64 years, but with an increasing proportion of those aged 15 to 24 staying on in education the working-age group of most interest is that aged 25 to 64, the so-called prime working-age group.

As seen above, the population aged 15 to 24 will decline in the next decade. Besides, the proportion of this age group in education is predicted to rise further, from 50 per cent in 1991 to 65 per cent by the year 2005, implying that the decline in the labour force will be greater than the decline in population in that age group. Changes in the emigration assumptions underlying the ESRI's population projections could seriously affect the projected population figures in this age group, but whether it is likely to be an upward or downward revision is hard to say.[1]

Table 8.2

Labour Force Participation Rates and
Labour Force Growth in Selected OECD Countries

	1993		1983-90
	Participation rates		Annual average growth
	males	females	
Australia	85.0%	62.5%	2.6
Belgium (1992)	72.6%	54.1%	0.1
Denmark (1991)	88.5%	78.9%	0.9
Ireland (1991)	*81.9%*	*39.9%*	*0.0*
Italy	75.1%	43.2%	0.9
Japan	90.1%	61.7%	1.2
Netherlands (1992)	80.8%	55.5%	2.6
Spain	74.4%	42.9%	1.5
Sweden	80.3%	76.5%	0.6
UK	83.3%	64.3%	1.0
US	84.5%	69.1%	1.6

Source: Employment Outlook, OECD, Paris, July 1994, Table J, and July 1993, Table F.

A similar caveat applies to the predicted population in the age group 25 to 64, but the broad trend of a significant increase to the year 2005 is likely to hold. Will the labour force participation rates for this age group also increase, as they have done for the last decade, thereby leading to a faster increase in the labour force than the population in that age group? This largely depends on what happens the labour force rates for females. These have increased significantly in recent years, particularly for the age group 25 to 44: it rose from 28.9 per cent in 1979 to 43.8 per cent in 1990. This trend is likely to continue, and to apply to the age group 45 to 64 as well. As may be seen in Table 8.2, the labour force participation rate for males in Ireland is little below the average in other OECD countries, but that for females considerably less than in most other countries. The figure for Ireland is 39.9 per cent, compared to a figure of 42.9 per cent in Spain (the next lowest country), 64.3 per cent in the UK and 78.9 per cent in Denmark. It is difficult to predict how fast this participation rate will grow in Ireland, but with the decreasing birth rate it could increase very rapidly. If this happened, it would lead to a huge increase in the labour force arising from this factor alone.

The growth in the labour force in Ireland, then, depends primarily on trends in the birth rate, net migration flows and trends in labour force participation rates, particularly for those aged 15 to 24 and for females aged 24 to 64. It is interesting to note from Table 8.2 that throughout the 1980s the labour force showed almost no growth, compared to a growth of 2.6 per cent per annum in Australia, 1.2 per cent in Japan, 1.0 per cent in the UK and 1.6 per cent in the US. The most important reason for this was the high level of emigration in Ireland, at almost 1.0 per cent of the population per annum for the years in question. Assuming that all of those who emigrated would have been in the labour force in Ireland, the growth in the potential labour force between 1983 and 1990 would have been around 2.3 per cent (i.e. between 20,000-25,000) per annum, a figure that is well above that for most countries shown in Table 8.2. This growth in potential labour force will, however, slow down rapidly from the year 2000 on, although again this prediction is very dependent on the assumptions made concerning net migration flows.

Conclusion

A consideration of emigration trends is central to any discussion of labour supply in Ireland. It more than any other factor determines the rate of population increase and the growth of the labour force in the country. The decline in the birth rate, and the labour force participation rates of those aged 15 to 24, and the rise in the labour force participation of females aged 25 to 64 may have been dwarfed by the changes in emigration, but in themselves they are very significant changes which, after the effects of emigration are removed, will have a bearing on the growth of the labour force in years to come, particularly from the turn of the century.

3 EMPLOYMENT: GROWTH AND COMPOSITION

Employment and Employment Growth: International Comparison

The first point worth noting from Table 8.3 is the tiny size of the workforce in Ireland: 1.1 million, as opposed to 26 million in the UK, 64 million in Japan and 117 million in the US. Given that there is an effective common labour market between Ireland and the UK, it is very important for labour policy purposes to bear in mind the relative sizes of the two labour markets.

The most striking fact in relation to employment in Ireland has been its slow rate of growth in the last fifteen years or so, particularly in the 1980s.[2] This is highlighted in Table 8.3. As may be seen, for the countries listed Ireland was the only country that experienced a decrease in employment in the period 1982 to 1990. During this period the annual average percentage change in employment in Ireland was minus 0.2, compared to a figure of around plus 1.5 per cent in Japan, Netherlands, Spain and the UK. Australia and the US experienced even higher growth rates, with figures of 2.6 and 2.1 per cent respectively. The period 1991 to 1995 witnessed employment decreases in many countries and a considerable slowing down in employment growth in others. The exception was Ireland, where employment increased by 0.9 per cent per annum in this period, but this increase was only sufficient to stem the flow in emigration and the rise in unemployment, with the result that by the second half of the 1990s the country still faced a very serious crisis in relation to employment creation and thereby in relation to unemployment.

Table 8.3
Employment and Employment Growth in Selected OECD Countries

	1992	1982-90	1991-95
	millions	annual percentage change	
Australia	7.7	2.6%	0.5%
Belgium	3.8	0.6%	-0.3%
Denmark	2.5	0.8%	0.1%
Ireland	*1.1*	*-0.2%*	*0.9%*
Italy	21.3	0.6%	-1.0%
Japan	64.4	1.3%	0.9%
Netherlands	6.7	1.6%	1.1%
Spain	12.4	1.4%	-1.2%
Sweden	4.3	1.5%	-2.2%
UK	25.3	1.5%	-0.9%
US	117.6	2.1%	1.0%

Source: As for Table 8.2, Table 1.2. Estimates for the period 1991-95.

It is interesting perhaps to look at the sectoral composition of the changes in employment in the 1980s, using the three broadly-defined categories of agriculture, industry and services. In the case of agriculture, the decline in employment in Ireland was large and almost unbroken, a continuation of a very long-term trend, with the rate of decrease above the average for OECD Europe. In relation to industry, there was a significant decline in employment and in the period 1983 to 1990 employment in industry fell by an annual average of minus 0.5 per cent, compared with an OECD Europe average rise of plus 0.3 per cent and a figure of plus 1.3 per cent in the US. It is in relation to services though that there was the most significant contrast. The annual increase in employment in services in Ireland in the period 1983 to 1990 was 0.9 per cent compared to a figure of 2.5 per cent in OECD Europe and 2.8 per cent in the US. It was the failure to increase employment in services and to a lesser extent in industry that marks Ireland out from the rest of the OECD in terms of providing clues as to why the employment performance in Ireland in the 1980s had been so poor relative to other countries. It is of interest to note that the employment level in Ireland in 1979 was 1.145 million, a figure that fell to 1.088 million by 1989 and that was not surpassed until 1994 with a figure of 1.176 million.

Involuntary Part-Time and Temporary Employment
An issue relating to the growth of employment in some countries since 1979 is the extent to which it consisted of part-time employment. What is more important perhaps is the extent to which such part-time employment is involuntary, i.e. chosen by the individual only because they could not get full-time work. This is also an issue that will be looked at later, but the evidence suggests that involuntary part-time employment has not grown

significantly as a proportion of the labour force in the countries for which data exist. For example, in the US involuntary part-time employment consisted of 4.5 per cent of the labour force in 1981 and 3.8 per cent in 1991: the corresponding figures for Ireland are 2.2 and 2.7 per cent and for the UK 1.8 and 2.2 per cent respectively. There is little evidence therefore that the increase in employment in other countries was not 'real', in the sense that it took place in involuntary part-time employment.

A different issue is the extent to which the increase in employment was in temporary work. This is becoming an increasingly debated topic in labour market economics as many economists believe that an increasing proportion of jobs will have to be temporary if labour markets, especially in Europe, are to be sufficiently flexible to cope with the employment/unemployment crisis, a topic that will be returned to later.

Temporary work is where a worker is employed by a firm under a fixed-term contract. The conditions under which someone can be employed as a temporary worker vary enormously across Europe, with Ireland having one of the least restrictive regimes in this regard. Data on numbers of temporary workers are not available for many countries, one of these being the US which is unfortunate given its status as the nation with the most flexible labour markets. Besides, the data may not be directly comparable over time or across countries. None the less, some broad trends can be observed from the data. First, temporary workers account for 5.3 per cent of all employees in the UK, 8.3 per cent in Ireland, 19.7 per cent in Australia, and 32.2 per cent in Spain. This is an enormous variation, but for most European countries for which there are data the figure is 15 per cent or lower. Second, in many countries there has been a growth in this percentage, with the most dramatic increases coming in France and Spain: up from 3.3 per cent in France in 1983 to to 10.2 per cent in 1991 and up from 15.6 per cent in Spain in 1987 to 32.2 per cent in 1991. The increase in Ireland was much less marked, up from 6.2 per cent in 1983 to 9.1 per cent in 1988 and back to 8.3 per cent in 1991.

The story here is confusing though. First, there does not appear to be any relationship between the degree of government regulation on the use of fixed-term contracts and the number of people employed under them. For example, the UK places minimal restrictions on their use but only 5 per cent of all employees are employed under them, whereas Spain where government regulations are highly restrictive has the highest percentage of employees employed under fixed-term contracts. The likely explanation could be to look at the restrictions on temporary work *compared* to the protection provided to the permanent workforce, i.e. compared to the extent of employment-protection legislation. For example, the protection provided to temporary workers in Spain may be strong compared to that in other countries but it may be relatively modest compared to that provided to the permanent workforce in Spain. Second, there does not appear to be any clear relationship between the extent of temporary work in and the employment performance of a country.

Again, it could be argued that what matters is the level of protection offered to the permanent workforce, an issue that will also be returned to later.

Sectoral Composition of Employment in Ireland
Table 8.4 provides a sectoral breakdown of employment in Ireland in 1994 and projected employment in each sector to the turn of the century. (See Chapters 10, 11 and 12 for international comparisons.) The first point to note is that an increase in employment is forecast, arising from quite buoyant forecasts for growth in the economy in the next five years or so. Despite this forecasted growth of output, the increase in employment is rather modest and nothing like what would be needed to absorb the increase in the labour force in the absence of emigration. Thus the situation of the last fifteen years or so where the growth in the labour force (before emigration) outstripped the growth in employment will continue until the turn of the century, although the gap will close considerably. Second, employment in agriculture will continue to decline: by 1993 employment in health and education exceeded that in agriculture, and the former is set to rise substantially to the turn of the century. Third, employment in industry will be three times that in agriculture by the year 2000, with employment in the high-technology subsector of manufacturing alone almost as great as that in agriculture. Last, while it is ·clear that agriculture is no longer a major sector in terms of employment and will account for as little as nine per cent of the workforce at the turn of the century, the rise in the importance of services will, in line with other countries, continue and account for over 60 per cent of total employment within five years.

Table 8.4

Sectoral Composition of Employment (000s)

	1993	1995	2000
Agriculture	144	137	117
Industry			
Food processing	38	34	31
Other traditional manufacturing	103	110	121
High-technology manufacturing	88	94	104
Building and utilities	83	90	103
Services			
Distribution	185	189	211
Transport and communications	70	70	64
Other market services	218	232	284
Health and education	149	156	173
Public administration	66	69	76
Total	1,144	1,180	1,285

Source: As for Table 8.1, Table 4.8.

4 UNEMPLOYMENT: EXTENT AND FEATURES

Extent and Growth: International Comparisons
It follows that since Ireland's labour force before emigration grew rapidly since 1979 and employment declined, then either unemployment increased substantially and/or significant emigration took place. Both outcomes occurred. In the 1980s almost 200,000 people emigrated and in the early 1990s the annual outflow slowed down but is predicted to rise in the second half of the decade, albeit not at the levels of the mid-1980s, once conditions in the UK labour market pick up. Correspondingly, unemployment increased steadily in the first half of the 1980s and remained high thereafter (see below). It should not be forgotten, though, that one of the major impacts on the labour force in Ireland of a poor employment performance is not included in the data below, namely the huge loss through involuntary emigration already alluded to. This point cannot be stressed enough, as the rise in unemployment, huge though it has been in the last fifteen years, would have been considerably greater if this outflow of labour did not take place.

Table 8.5
Unemployment and Unemployment Rates in Selected OECD Countries

	1995 millions	1982-90	1992	1995
		as a percentage of the labour force		
Australia	0.8	7.8%	10.7%	9.2%
Belgium	0.5	11.3%	10.3%	12.7%
Denmark	0.3	9.1%	11.2%	10.5%
Ireland	*0.2*	*15.5%*	*16.3%*	*15.4%*
Italy	2.7	10.9%	11.6%	11.9%
Japan	1.9	2.5%	2.2%	2.8%
Netherlands	0.7	9.8%	6.7%	9.5%
Spain	3.8	19.0%	18.4%	24.4%
Sweden	0.3	2.3%	4.9%	7.4%
UK	2.5	9.7%	10.0%	8.9%
US	7.8	7.1%	7.4%	5.8%

Source: As for Table 8.2, Table 1.3. Estimate for 1995.

Table 8.5 provides the main information on recorded unemployment rates in Ireland and selected OECD countries since 1983. The picture is fairly clear. First, Ireland had the second highest unemployment rate throughout the 1980s, 15.5 per cent, compared to 19.0 per cent in Spain. Other countries had much lower rates, although the rates of unemployment in Belgium, Denmark, Italy, Netherlands and the UK, at around 9 to 11 per cent, were much higher than what these countries had experienced in the two decades prior to the 1980s. Of the countries listed in the table, Japan, Sweden and the US stand out: the US because it had the third lowest rate of unemployment and this rate was little higher than it had been in the previous two decades, and Japan and Sweden because of their extraordinarily low rates of unemployment. Even accounting for the fact that the Japanese and Swedish rates may be underestimated because of the exclusion of discouraged workers and the effect of involuntary part-time employment (see later), and the fact that many of the long-term unemployed in Sweden do not appear on the register because of compulsory training and work programmes or are reclassified into another social welfare category, the experience of these countries in the 1980s in relation to unemployment was remarkable.

The high unemployment rate in Ireland, despite the huge outflow through emigration, was as mentioned a reflection of the country's failure to create sufficient employment growth. This problem continued into the 1990s, as seen earlier, and, with reduced emigration, was reflected in a further jump in the unemployment rate, to over 16 per cent in 1992, with a small decline between then and 1995. In the case of some countries in the table, there was a similar large jump in the first half of the 1990s, the case of Sweden and indeed the other Nordic countries, bar Denmark, being a striking example. Japan and the US stand out again though, the former because the low rate of unemployment in the 1980s was maintained and the latter because the rate of unemployment actually declined in the first half of the 1990s. It is for this reason that increasing attention is being paid to the US experience, but one thing that has become evident is that such success has been gained at a large cost, namely a very significant widening in the dispersion of incomes there.

One final thing to note in Table 8.5 is that despite the high rate of unemployment in Ireland, the number of people unemployed in absolute terms is very small in relation to that in other countries: 0.2 million in Ireland compared to 2.5 million in the UK, 2.7 million in Italy and 7.8 million in the US. This simply reflects again the tiny size of the Irish economy in the context of the OECD as a whole.

Comparison Problems
The discussion above is based on the assumption that the data can be used for valid comparison both across countries and over time. Is this the case? There are three main issues of concern here. The first is whether or not all countries are using the same methods of defining and compiling data on unemployment; the second is whether or not over time there is a consistent series for Ireland; the last is whether or not there are certain categories of persons that are not, perhaps cannot be, included by any country but which should be included in any discussion of labour market slack (i.e. where labour demand is less than labour supply) in an economy. The last of these issues is discussed at some length in the next section and the first two will be discussed briefly in this section.

International comparison of unemployment rates is fraught with difficulty despite the best efforts of the OECD and the EU. The very low unemployment figures for Japan and Portugal, for example, are treated with suspicion by many economists, as are the very high figures for Spain. None the less, there are reasonably reliable comparative data for the EU member states, if not for most of the OECD countries, and these are the data that inform comparative studies and international policy debate.

In relation to Ireland there are two main sources of data on unemployment, the Labour Force Survey and the Live Register. The trends given by these two sources have diverged significantly since 1985 and the Live Register by 1993 for example gave an unemployment total that exceeded by 65,000 that given by the Labour Force Survey. The Live Register is simply a measure of the number of persons registering as unemployed in order to claim social welfare payments or qualify for Social Insurance Credits.[3] A person is classified as unemployed in the Labour Force Survey if the person's own subjective assessment is that his/her principal economic status is that of being unemployed. There are two main reasons for the divergence between the series since 1985. First, greater numbers of females aged over 25 years are signing on the Register following the 1985 Social Welfare Act, which removed restrictions on married women doing so: many of these women are believed to identify themselves as engaged in 'home duties' in the Labour Force Survey. Second, many of those who have effectively withdrawn from the labour force, or are only marginally attached to it, such as for example the very long-term unemployed, but yet are registered for receipt of social welfare benefits, are unlikely to describe themselves as unemployed in the Labour Force Survey: the numbers in this category are likely to have grown considerably with the rise of long-term unemployment in the last ten years.

It is the data from the Labour Force Survey that are used for international comparison, as the methods used in arriving at these data are considered to give the more accurate indicator of the underlying level of unemployment in a country. These data are also used in this chapter, unless indicated otherwise. Data from the Live Register, on the other hand, are published on a monthly basis, with detailed breakdowns, and it is these data that tend therefore to gain the headlines in the media. If the two series were showing the same trends, then this would not be a problem, but as mentioned this has not been the case. The gap between the two also causes confusion, with the Labour Force Survey as mentioned indicating, for example, a figure of 229,000 unemployed in 1993 as opposed to a figure of 294,000 according to the Live Register.

Discouraged Workers and Involuntary Part-Time Workers
Labour market slack manifests itself in many ways, the most common being through open unemployment as measured by the conventional unemployment rate and as discussed above.[4] This rate, though, does not capture all of the slack. Some people leave the labour force because of poor job prospects while

others may decide not to enter the labour force in the first place, for the same reasons. These are commonly referred to as discouraged workers and are considered as forming part of 'hidden' or 'disguised' unemployment. They are not counted as part of the labour force because they fail the 'job-search' criterion, i.e. they are not seeking a job because they believe there is no suitable job available.

Similar to discouraged workers, *involuntary* part-time work also indicates a measure of underutilisation of an economy's labour resources. There are two main ways this type of underutilisation arises: first there are persons who normally work full-time but are working part-time because of recession or some other economic reason; and second there are those who are working part-time simply because they cannot find a full-time job.

Looking at the statistics on these two sources of labour underutilisation, some striking findings emerge from data compiled by the OECD (see Table 8.6). First, in relation to aggregate labour force numbers, discouraged workers account for around one per cent of the total in the OECD member states, but this varies widely from country to country. In general, the inclusion of discouraged workers in the total would tend to reduce the differential in unemployment rates between countries, Belgium and Italy being notable exceptions to this. It is interesting to note that in Ireland discouraged workers account for 0.5 per cent of the labour force, a small figure both in absolute terms, relative to the recorded unemployment rate and relative to other countries. The figure for Japan, at 1.9 per cent, is also interesting as it is almost the same as the recorded unemployment rate: indeed it is believed that one reason for the small change in the latter over time is that women tend to leave the labour force altogether rather than remain unemployed in times of recession, thereby disguising the true rise in the unemployment rate. In general, females tend to account for the vast bulk of discouraged workers, the figure for Ireland being over 70 per cent, i.e. about the norm for the OECD countries.

Table 8.6 also shows the number of involuntary part-time workers expressed as a percentage of the labour force in 1991. This is a measure of *underemployment* and given the figures in the table it is clear that including some fraction of these workers as unemployed would very significantly increase the unemployment rate in some countries. As seen in Table 8.6, the underemployment rate in the US was 4.0 per cent, with only the Netherlands (7.1 per cent) and Australia (5.7 per cent) having higher totals. The figure for Ireland is 2.7 per cent, somewhat above the average but low relative to the recorded unemployment rate. The evidence suggests that there has been some increase in the underemployment rate in Ireland, especially that arising from an inability to find a full-time job. It is important to emphasise though that in most countries the majority of those employed part-time want to be so: over 60 per cent of total part-time employment in Ireland in 1991 was voluntary.

Table 8.6

Discouraged Workers and Involuntary Part-time Workers as a Per Cent of the Labour Force in Selected OECD Countries, 1991

	Discouraged workers	Involuntary part-time workers
Australia	1.5%	5.7%
Belgium	1.7%	2.9%
Denmark	0.2%	3.4%
Ireland	*0.5%*	2.7%
Italy	2.6%	2.1%
Japan	1.9%	1.2%
Netherlands	0.8%	7.0%
Spain	0.1%	1.1%
Sweden	1.5%	0.5%
UK	0.4%	2.2%
US	0.8%	4.0%

Source: OECD Employment Outlook, July 1993, Table 1.5.

Labour market slack then in the form of discouragement and involuntary part-time work is an important phenomenon, accounting in the OECD for almost half of the total unemployed in 1991. It is perhaps less significant in Ireland but this arises more from the fact that the recorded unemployment rate is so high. Besides, the impact of involuntary emigration, which also indicates labour slack, and which would be much more significant in Ireland than in the other countries looked at, is not included in the discussion above.

Long-Term Unemployment

Apart from the level of unemployment, its composition is also of considerable interest to economists, for reasons alluded to already. The most important consideration in this regard relates to its composition between short-term (less than 12 months) and long-term (12 months or more) unemployment. Table 8.7 provides some information on this in relation to Ireland and some other countries for which data exist. As may be seen, the long-term unemployment rate in Ireland amounted to 8.9 per cent in 1991, which, in itself, was greater than the total unemployment rate in many OECD countries. It is also evident that the long-term unemployment rate in Ireland is around three times that of Australia Denmark and Netherlands, more than twice that of the UK, and more than ten times that of Japan, Sweden and the US. In marked contrast, the short-term unemployment rate in Ireland is not greatly out of line with that of other countries. Hence, it is only in relation to its rate of long-term unemployment that Ireland is almost unique among OECD countries.

Table 8.7

Standardised Unemployment Rates,
by Duration, in Selected OECD Countries, 1993

	< 12 months duration	12 months +
Australia	4.6%	2.6%
Belgium (1992)	4.7%	4.7%
Denmark (1992)	8.2%	3.0%
Ireland (1991)	*5.8%*	*8.9%*
Italy (1992)	4.4%	6.1%
Japan	2.1%	0.4%
Netherlands (1992)	3.7%	3.0%
Spain	11.2%	11.2%
Sweden	7.3%	0.9%
UK (1992)	6.5%	3.5%
US	5.9%	0.8%

Source: Employment Outlook, OECD, Paris July 1994, Tables K and P.

The rise in long-term unemployment in Ireland took place largely between 1980 and 1993. Using Live Register data, the long-term unemployment rate was only 2.8 per cent of the labour force in 1980, this figure rising to 8.3 per cent of the labour force in 1988 and rising again in the early 1990s to almost 10 per cent of the labour force.

According to the 1992 Labour Force Survey, over half of the long-term unemployed have been unemployed for over three years and two-fifths for more than five years. These are striking figures and paint a rather stark picture in relation to the duration of long-term unemployment. These figures are complemented and reinforced by data on survival rates which show the probability of persons unemployed for a certain duration at a point in time remaining on to be unemployed into the next period.[5] These data show that the longer a person is unemployed the greater is the probability of the person remaining unemployed. For example, persons unemployed for under a year have a 30 per cent chance of being unemployed a year later, whereas those who have been unemployed for over two years have a 74 per cent chance of being unemployed one year later, this figure rising to over 80 per cent for males aged 25-44 years and to 90 per cent for males aged 45-54 years.

Turning now to other characteristics of the long-term unemployed, Table 8.8 compares the educational qualifications of those at work with those who were short-term unemployed and long-term unemployed in 1993. As may be seen, the educational qualifications of those in work are considerably better than of those unemployed, but especially of those long-term unemployed. Almost half of the long-term unemployed have no formal educational qualification (except in some cases the Primary Certificate), compared with one-quarter of those unemployed for less than one year and 14 per cent of those at work. Only 19 per cent have Leaving Certificate level or higher, compared with 42 per cent for the short-term unemployed and 62 per cent for those at work. Those with the greatest educational disadvantage are the older long-term unemployed: almost two-thirds of the long-term unemployed aged 35 years or more in 1991 were without any qualifications and only 12 per cent of this group had attained Leaving Certificate level or higher.

Table 8.8
Educational Qualifications of Those at Work and Unemployed, 1993

	At work	Unemployed	
		<12 months	12 months+
No qualification	14%	21%	47%
Intermediate/Group Cert	24%	37%	33%
Leaving Cert	35%	28%	14%
Third-level	27%	14%	5%

Source: CSO, *Labour Force Survey, 1993* (special tabulation).

Table 8.9 provides information on the occupational background of those in employment, compared to those unemployed for less than 12 months and to those unemployed for more than 12 months. Around half of the unemployed have a 'manual' background compared to 27 per cent for employees. More striking perhaps is that 30 per cent of those long-term unemployed are in the 'other' category, compared with only 2 per cent of the short-term unemployed, reflecting the fact that they may not consider themselves as having any occupational background, given the length of their absence from employment. It is also noteworthy, given that most new jobs in the future are likely to arise in the services sector, that less than one-quarter of the long-term unemployed have a services/clerical background, compared with 58 per cent of those employed and 43 per cent of the short-term unemployed.

Table 8.9
Occupational Background of Those at Work and Unemployed, 1993

	At work	Unemployed	
		<12 months	12 months+
Manual	27%	48%	42%
Transport/communication	8%	17%	6%
Services/clerical	58%	43%	22%
Others (incl not stated)	7%	2%	30%

Source: As for Table 8.8.

Another noteworthy feature of the 'profile' of the long-term unemployed is that almost two-thirds were classified as 'household head', compared with 42 per cent of the short-term unemployed and 45 per cent for those at work. As heads of households are more likely to have dependants, long-term unemployment carries significant effects on households, with many families affected by long-term unemployment facing almost total exclusion from the labour market and, because of being concentrated together in certain geographical areas, almost total exclusion from society.

An understanding of the extent and nature of the unemployment problem, as outlined above, is critical to an understanding of the scale of the task of solving the unemployment problem in Ireland. The fact that so much of this unemployment problem now arises from the phenomenon of long-term unemployment renders, as shall be seen, the possibility of any immediate solution to the problem all the more unlikely.

5 CAUSES OF UNEMPLOYMENT: GLOBAL FACTORS

Introduction

It was seen in in Section 4 that the increase in unemployment in the last fifteen years was not unique to Ireland, but affected almost every country in Europe, including the Nordic countries since 1990. There is a very high rate of unemployment in Ireland, though, with only Spain having a higher rate. If emigration is added to the Irish unemployment figures, then Ireland would have a level of labour market slack, in relation to its potential labour force (even excluding the possibility of immigration), that is truly exceptional.

What caused the rise in unemployment in Europe since the early 1980s, and particularly since the early 1990s? A number of causes have been suggested. First, there are arguments relating to global factors such as increased competition in international trade and technological change, factors that would have affected every country in Europe, but some to a greater extent than others. These issues will be discussed in this section. Second, there are structural arguments relating to such issues as the role of unions and wage bargaining/setting, employment-protection legislation and the taxation system. All of these issues will be discussed in the next section. Third, there are arguments relating to the persistence of unemployment, the so-called hysteresis effect of being unemployed, i.e. if unemployment is allowed to persist its level will not drop for several years even when the original cause of the unemployment has disappeared. The result of this is the long-term unemployment mentioned earlier, a problem that not only reduces the effective labour supply but poses a very serious 'stock' problem for most governments in Europe, not least that in Ireland where as seen there is an exceptionally high level of long-term unemployment. This will be discussed in the context of the effects of the prolonged payment of unemployment and related benefits and the effectiveness or otherwise of active labour market policies in the penultimate section of the chapter.

What happens with regard to unemployment in Ireland will clearly be determined by international factors. Some of the causes listed above, such as the rate of technological change, are largely outside the control of policymakers in Ireland. Others are partly outside their control: for example it would be difficult for Ireland to alter its social welfare system radically as it relates to unemployment without a similar change in the UK, as otherwise major shifts in emigration levels could result. None the less, as mentioned before, several small European countries, such as Austria and Switzerland, and until recently Norway and Sweden, and many regions of the larger European countries have experienced unemployment levels well below the European average. In contrast, Ireland has experienced unemployment rates well above the European average, and way above the European average if emigration is taken into account. Why is this the case?

There are no easy answers to this question, and hence no easy solutions to the problem of unemployment in Ireland. The approach adopted in this chapter will be to examine each of the issues mentioned above first in an international context and then specifically examine them in an Irish context to ascertain which if any of these factors could explain the unusually low level of employment growth in Ireland and hence the exceptionally high levels of unemployment and emigration. It is difficult, as shall be seen, to demonstrate conclusively the impact of any of these factors on the level of unemployment and emigration in Ireland, but there is little doubt that these are the factors that do exert the decisive influence on employment, unemployment and emigration levels in Ireland even if the precise contribution of each cannot be pinpointed.

Globalisation of Trade

Given the extent of Ireland's trade, factor and corporate links with the world economy, it is inevitable that the increasing globalisation of economic activity, as discussed in Chapter 9, has, and will have, a major effect on economic activity and employment in Ireland.

It is alleged by some that rising imports of goods and services produced by low-skilled labour in the Far East, and more recently in Eastern Europe, are depressing demand for such labour in Western Europe because average wages for this type of labour are much higher in Western Europe, including Ireland, than in these newly-emerging international competitor countries. It is also asserted by some that such a development has been exacerbated by European and US companies 'relocating' their manufacturing operations to the Far East and Eastern Europe in order to take advantage of the low wages there. Is there substance to these arguments? No, according to the OECD and many other commentators.[6] As pointed out in Chapter 9, the evidence for Ireland also supports this conclusion.

It is generally believed by economists that an increasing intensity of trade will lead to higher incomes, but that it will also lead to the displacement of labour in some activities and the expansion of labour in other activities. The net impact on employment should be negligible as long as labour and product markets function well and wages are reasonably flexible. Thus, if decreased overall employment should result from increased trade intensity it is not trade *per se* that is causing the problem but the functioning of the labour and product markets, a topic that will be returned to in a later section. The evidence, according to the OECD, supports such an argument. The evidence also suggests that the opening up of the Far East and Eastern Europe to foreign investment has had minimal impact on the flows of such investment. Net flows to non-OECD countries are still very small relative to fixed investment in both OECD and non-OECD countries, and they appear to have very little impact on total employment in either region. There is certainly no evidence that this factor has had any significant effect to date on investment flows into Ireland, although as pointed out in Chapter 12 Ireland is likely to face much stiffer competition in years to come for such investment, largely though within the OECD region itself but also perhaps from the non-OECD region as well.

Increasing international trade may also have an impact on innovation and the absorption of technological change, the subject matter of the next subsection. It is argued by some that labour-saving technologies are, at least in part, introduced in anticipation of and/or in response to the increased competition both on domestic and foreign markets that arises from the increased globalisation of trade (see Chapter 7). As such the effect of increased international trade and technological change are difficult to separate in practice.

Technological Change
Technology is central to the process of growth (see Chapters 7 and 12): it allows increases in productivity and thereby real incomes. But does it destroy jobs and in the process create unemployment? Is it the cause of the so-called 'jobless growth' being experienced in Europe? There is little doubt that many 'ordinary' people see technological change as a major cause of the present high levels of unemployment in Europe, but as the OECD convincingly argues this is probably not the case.[7]

Fears about widespread job losses associated with the emergence of new technology are not, of course, new and are in the aggregate largely unfounded. It is true that technological change involves a process of job destruction in some older occupations, firms and industries, but it also involves a parallel process of job creation in new and emerging sectors and occupations. There are many historical examples of predictions of large-scale technological unemployment being followed in fact by large net expansions of jobs. For example, just after World War II it was predicted in the US that the invention of the computer would create technological unemployment that would make 'the Great Depression look like a picnic', yet in the following forty years there was a massive increase in employment in the US and almost no increase in the unemployment rate (see earlier).

The argument is made, though, that the *nature* of the new technologies being introduced in the last twenty years is very different to anything experienced previously. The wave of new technologies in electronics, computers, telecommunications, industrial materials and biotechnology, it is argued, are applicable not just to manufacturing and agriculture, like past developments, but across the whole economy, even into areas such as banking, accountancy, retail trading and health care. It is also argued that not only the nature, but also the *pace* of the technological change is new. The central point here relates to the earlier discussion on the increasing globalisation of world trade. This increase in world trade pressures, it is argued, has put pressure on industries everywhere to innovate and absorb new technology in order to survive. Thus the globalisation of trade and changing technology are interlinked and, as mentioned already, their effects hard to differentiate one from the other.

It is clear that technological change makes it possible to produce more output from a given stock of resources or, by creating new products, to expand demand. This in principle provides the basis for sustained expansion over time in both earnings and employment. The issue then really is how long it takes for this process to take effect and what policies need to be put in place to ensure that an economy adjusts to the new technology in such a way that not only will real incomes, but also employment, increase. It is the organisational and institutional change that must accompany technological change that is the key to the job-creating potential of the latter.

As mentioned above, by destroying jobs in some firms, industries and regions, and creating jobs in others, technology can significantly change the structure of employment in an economy. This is a particularly serious problem with the present wave of technological change, which is rooted in information technologies. As the OECD states, 'such technologies have already affected – or have the potential to affect – the production structure and organisation of virtually all manufacturing and services industries while at the same time blurring the distinction between these two categories'[8] (see also Chapter 10). These developments have also contributed greatly to the globalisation of economic activities and the loosening of location constraints that were discussed in the previous section. Information technologies are not only all-pervasive, and therefore widespread in their effect on the structure of employment, but their efficient implementation often requires substantial changes in work organisation and skills requirements. The evidence suggests that it is the countries that have adjusted to these changes that have most exploited the employment potential of new technologies.

Ireland clearly cannot escape the effects of the technological changes occuring worldwide. The government actively encourages the establishment of high-technology industry in the country: in 1992, exports from these industries accounted for a higher share (39.4 per cent) of total manufacturing exports than was the case in any other OECD country. The importance attached to such industries in Ireland can be explained not only in terms of their employment contribution but more by the fact that it is believed that they generate the technologies that are subsequently used throughout the economy. (The discussion in Chapter 12, however, cast serious doubts on how successful has been this policy.) Data in Chapter 12 indicate that there has been major change in the composition of employment in manufacturing in Ireland in the last thirty years, with huge job gains being matched by almost equally large job losses. This would give some measure of the impact of both the increased globalisation of trade and the technological changes that are taking place worldwide. As argued in Chapter 12, it is the country's ability to absorb and adapt to this new technology that will be the key to employment, not only in manufacturing but more important perhaps, given its scale, the services sector as well.

The available evidence does not suggest, though, that increased technology in Ireland has reduced the employment intensity of growth. Taking the period 1960-90 as a whole, employment grew at 0.26 per cent per annum compared to a figure for output growth of 3.2 per cent per annum, the ratio of these two figures giving an 'employment intensity' of growth measure of 0.08. The corresponding employment intensity measure for the 1985-90 period was 0.28.[9] Comparing the Irish figures to those for other countries, it can be seen that Ireland is not much out of line with the rest of Europe in this regard, with an EU average of 0.12 for the 1960-90 period. The real exceptions were Australia, Canada and the US, with figures of over 0.5 in each case. Like with Ireland, the employment intensity of growth in the period 1985-90 was higher in most countries than for the total period 1960-90, again casting doubt on the fact that technology has widened the gap between output and employment growth.[10]

The real issue here is why the employment intensity of growth in the US has been so much higher than that in Europe. The answer to this question is not to be found in technological change, as the US has probably undergone a more dramatic change in this regard than Europe, but, according to many economists, in the differing operation of the labour markets in Europe and the US (see later). It must be noted though that the employment increase in the US was associated with an increasing dispersion in the distribution of earned income there, with many of the lower-income groups experiencing declines in real incomes of 30 per cent or more in the 1980s, as against substantial increases for those in the higher-income groups.[11]

Mismatch
Over the 1980s the structure of work in the industrialised world has, for the reasons mentioned above, been changing. There has been a shift in demand away from low-skilled, low-wage jobs towards high-skilled, high-wage jobs. The change in the nature of work arises not only from the transformation of jobs by technology and international trade but also from

the 'natural' sectoral changes that have occurred with regard to employment. The skills required in services are different to those needed for industry and hence the declining industrial workforce cannot be automatically transplanted into services jobs. The new wave of employment creation leads, as mentioned earlier, to a transformation of the competences required from the workforce. Not only do they need different qualifications and skills but the dynamic, continuously changing nature of work also requires them to have a high degree of flexibility which was not necessary in the past when permanent, stable positions were the norm.

The skills of the labour force then have to be altered to take account of the changing environment and nature of work that goes with this. In the absence of this adjustment, mismatch can, and may have, become a serious problem in the labour market in Ireland. Mismatch is reflected in the fact that different skill groups experience different unemployment rates. In particular, the semi-skilled and unskilled have very high unemployment rates because there is a very large imbalance, within these groups, between the skills demanded and those that the labour force can supply. The variance of different unemployment rates relative to total unemployment then may be used as a measure of the extent of mismatch in the labour market. Layard *et al* use this measure for mismatch and they claim that the more variation there is between the unemployment rates of different groups the higher will be the overall unemployment rate.[12]

The data for 1987 show that the variance for Ireland was exceptionally high, 45.1 per cent as against 18.5 per cent in the US, 11.4 per cent in Germany and 25.3 per cent in Norway. This may mean that mismatch helps explain why Ireland's unemployment rate is higher than that of other European countries. Layard *et al* argue, however, that mismatch has not been rising in Europe. Assuming that this holds true for Ireland, mismatch may not be a major explanation for rising unemployment here. It is highly likely, however, that it may have contributed to its persistence by making a large proportion of the labour supply ineffective in the labour market (see later).

It is for these reasons that the OECD has placed special emphasis on upgrading the skills and competences of the labour force as part of the search for a solution to the unemployment problem.[13] As seen earlier, not all persons have acquired adequate initial education and training before they enter the labour market and these are the people most likely to experience long-term unemployment in Ireland. The first priority then must be to reduce through preventive and remedial measures the number of young people who leave school without some qualification. The next concern is to ensure that those who have acquired satisfactory initial qualifications make the transition to employment and this many people believe may be assisted by a more employer-led approach to education, particularly vocational education. Last, and of most relevance perhaps in relation to the issues discussed in this section, is the need to emphasise continuing education and training, as individuals need the opportunity to upgrade their knowledge and competences to prepare themselves for the changes brought about by increasing international trade and technological change.

6 STRUCTURAL RIGIDITIES IN LABOUR MARKET

It has been mentioned already that structural rigidities in labour markets, especially in those of many countries in Europe, may largely explain why unemployment is at such high levels in these countries. These rigidities, in particular, it is argued may explain why increased international trade and technological change have led to so-called 'jobless growth' in Europe at a time when there was a huge increase in employment in the US. Moreover, the persistence of these rigidities may have led to the build-up of long-term unemployment, which is now such a major problem in many European countries, including Ireland. This section and the following sections will deal with such issues.

The discussion draws extensively on the excellent analysis by the OECD of this topic in 1994 and uses the framework adopted in its final report.[14] First, wage and price adjustment are examined, with the main attention devoted to industrial relations, in particular collective bargaining structures. Unemployment and related benefits are also very important in this regard, but as their main impact appears to be on long-term unemployment, discussion of this topic is left to the section specifically devoted to this issue. Second, quantity adjustments (which refer to barriers facing the movement of people in and out of jobs) are analysed. Policies to enhance quantity adjustment include increased labour mobility, reforms of employment-protection legislation, policies to reduce labour supply (for example, work-sharing schemes), and active labour market policies. The last mentioned has particular relevance to the long-term unemployed and will be discussed in that section. Of the other three, the main one of interest relates to employment-protection legislation. Labour mobility is not a particularly serious problem in a country with such a record of emigration, and reducing the supply of labour is not really a solution to the unemployment problem but simply a device, albeit an important one, for sharing the burden of unemployment and underemployment. Last, the effect of the tax system on the working of the labour market will be looked at briefly, this issue having been discussed already in Chapter 5.

Wage Adjustments
Price formation in the labour market is, as the OECD states, of necessity different from that in other markets. This is because wages are not simply a

price of one type of product among others, but 'determine to a large extent the well-being of the majority of citizens in modern society. Societies' concern about social justice and the distribution of income therefore becomes integrally linked to wage-setting'(p.1). Because of this, distinct social arrangements and institutions intervene in every country in the market-clearing role of wage adjustments. However, even if the operation of the price system for labour is different for that of products, the effects of prices being too high are the same: i.e. wages above market-clearing levels will result in excess supply and therefore lower levels of employment than would otherwise be the case.

It is being increasingly realised in OECD member states that the persistently high levels of unemployment in most of these countries may require changing the balance between the social and market-clearing role of wages. It is against this background that the OECD assessed the extent to which institutional structures may be hampering competitive wage adjustments and identified some areas where changes in government policies could assist employment-creating wage-setting.

(i) Industrial Relations and Competition in the Labour Market

As mentioned previously, the response of wages to market conditions has to be seen against the background of the institutional arrangements, particularly those relating to industrial relations and the role of trade unions, in the labour market in each particular country. These arrangements have been partly designed to encourage stable employment relationships and to avert the income insecurity that can accompany rapid price adjustments in the market for labour, as happened in the US in the 1980s. However, in so doing these arrangements may encourage anti-competitive behaviour in the labour market and, as in all markets, this will result in lower demand because prices are not set at their clearing rate. This of course must be set against the advantages for employees of the protective industrial relations arrangements and the potential advantages for employers in that these arrangements may strengthen cooperation by workers and prevent the harmful behaviour that may be inherent in a more atomistic wage-setting environment.

The degree of unionisation is a possible measure of how powerful trade unions are and, hence, how much influence they have on unemployment. Table 8.9 provides information on the degree of unionisation, as measured by union density (i.e. trade union members as a percentage of all wage and salary earners), in OECD countries. The supposed positive link between union density and unemployment is not at all clear from an examination of these economies over the period shown.

During the 1970s there was an increase in union density in most countries. Spain and the US stand out for having very low union density rates, but yet contrasting rates of unemployment, while the Nordic countries had very high union density rates accompanied by very low unemployment rates. In the 1980s there was a fall in union density in nearly all countries, but this fall in unionisation coincided with a rise in unemployment. The evidence then points to the fact that there is no simple direct relationship between union density and unemployment. The manner in which wages are bargained over and the scope of these wage bargains (i.e. union coverage) may, however, be more significant as these are what directly affect the flexibility of wages in the labour market.

The share of workers covered by collective agreements is substantially higher than the share of employees belonging to trade unions. More workers are covered by agreements than are members of the trade unions because either these agreements have to be extended to all of the workforce by statute or the employers voluntarily agree to include non-union employees in the settlement, probably to avoid damaging wage differentials that would arise within the firm. The extensive coverage of trade union agreements means that a much more significant proportion of the labour market could be characterised by relatively high wages and, if these are set in long-term contracts, they will also be rigid, with consequential effects on unemployment. The interesting thing is that while union density rates fell in the 1980s, the coverage rates showed no marked tendency to fall.

Table 8.9

Trade Union Density (%) in Selected OECD Countries

	1970	1980	1990
Australia	50.2	48.0	40.4
Belgium	45.5	55.9	51.2
Denmark	60.0	76.0	71.4
Ireland	*53.1*	*57.0*	*49.7*
Italy	36.3	49.3	38.8
Japan	35.1	31.1	25.4
Netherlands	38.0	35.3	25.5
Spain	n.a.	25.0	11.0
Sweden	67.7	79.7	82.5
UK	44.8	50.4	39.1
US	n.a.	22.3	15.6

Source: OECD Jobs Study: Part II , OECD, Paris 1994, Table 5.8.

Whether bargaining occurs at a centralised or decentralised level also appears to affect the impact of trade unions on wage levels significantly and therefore on employment and unemployment levels. If wage bargaining is decentralised an increase in the degree of union power may imply an increase in unemployment. This is because the trade union takes the level of national employment as given and probably ignores the effect of their demands on the job opportunities that may be open for others in the labour force. In contrast, with centralised bargaining one trade union represents the whole workforce and thereby takes account of all job opportunities. This may cause them to moderate their wage demands as they incorporate the unemployment rate into their optimisation decision.

The bargaining outcome of course depends on how severe or credible the threats of alternative action are. That is, how much ability has the union to reduce or halt production (e.g. through a strike) and how far can the employers go with regard to the freezing of wages, the laying-off of union members or (in the extreme) the locking-out of the employees. This power is largely determined by legislation on industrial action. The existence of outside options also influences the bargaining solution. For the employer, this involves the probability of getting equally skilled labour at a lower wage (which is quite unlikely if the trade union is centralised). With regard to the union, the existence of unemployment benefits and the level of unemployment influences their bargaining position. If unemployment benefits are high the trade union will be willing to bargain for higher wages as members have a reasonable alternative source of income. The probability of getting another job is also crucial. This has become very evident recently because the current high levels of unemployment across the OECD are imposing certain constraints on the actions of trade unions. Union pressure on wages has subsided (evidenced by declining real wage growth) as the organisations have become more employment conscious.

Imperfect competition in the product market can also affect the wage level and thereby the level of employment and unemployment. If there is an absence of competition in the product market then firms have an option of choosing 'supranormal' profits ahead of increased employment. They also have the option of retaining all the surplus for themselves or sharing it with existing employees. The latter will happen if the workers have bargaining strength (see above) or the rents may be willingly shared with workers to encourage efficiency and to boost work motivation, i.e. the employers may be prepared to pay what are called 'efficiency wages'. Whatever the rationale for rent-sharing with workers, such arrangements favour the 'insiders' at the expense of the 'outsiders' and create a united lobby between unions and employers to oppose the removal of the imperfect competition in the product market that is giving rise to the rent. The solution to reducing the distortionary effects of imperfect product market competition on labour market outcomes is clearly to remove the opportunity for producers to earn rent and this calls for a strict and tough competition regime, a topic that is covered at some length in Chapter 10. There appears to be little doubt that there is imperfect competition in several product markets in Ireland, but the effects of these on the wage level and thereby on employment and unemployment levels has not been precisely ascertained.

(ii) The Irish Experience
It may be of interest in view of the discussion above to look at the trend in the real wage in Ireland over time. Data indicate that Irish manufacturing unit wage costs increased up to 1986 and post-1986 unit wage costs fell and continued to do so up to 1994. The decline of real wages in manufacturing in Ireland in the late 1980s and in the early 1990s is particularly significant when it is considered that unit wage costs in *manufacturing* in her major trading partners were increasing at a rapid pace up to 1994. Ireland therefore cannot be considered as having exceptionally high unit wages in manufacturing.

There is considerable doubt though as to what conclusions can be drawn from the above. Unit wage costs in manufacturing may be artificially low because of the inflation of output figures arising from the phenomenon of transfer pricing discussed in Chapter 9. Second, they relate only to a small section of the economy and generalisations in relation to the overall wage level cannot really be inferred from these data.

While the unionisation rate in Ireland fell in the 1980s, in line with many other countries, the rate in Ireland was still above that in the UK and way above that in the US, although well below that in the Scandinavian countries. In relation to the wage-bargaining process, there is a degree of corporatism in the Irish labour market with a large proportion of wages being determined by national wage agreements (see Chapter 4). In October 1987, the Programme for National Recovery was launched, this was followed in 1991 by the Programme for Economic and Social Progress, and in 1994 by the Programme for Competitiveness and Work, which provided what many see as modest wage increases for the years covered by these programmes. Ireland therefore appears to have adopted in recent years the preferable system of wage bargaining (i.e. centralised) where participants are more likely to take wider economic interests into account. The wage demands of Irish trade unions then may have been moderated because of the centralised bargaining process: they may also have been restrained by the high unemployment rate, but this effect may be condsiderably lessened by the high replacement rate in Ireland (see later) and the phenomenon of large-scale emigration.

It is generally recognised that income restraint is essential to employment creation in Ireland and that there is a trade-off between pay and employment. As argued by the National Economic and Social Forum, this trade-off can be looked at in four ways.[15] In the multinational high-tech sector of the economy pay moderation can lead to more employment in the medium to longer term through increased profitability and its effect on investment location decisions. In the more traditional labour-intensive parts of the traded sector there is likely to be a substantial trade-off between pay and employment, as in many cases pay moderation is essential in this sector simply to retain existing jobs. In the sheltered private sector pay moderation is necessary to underpin the competitiveness of the traded sector and also to generate increased employment in this sector. Last, in the public sector pay restraint could translate in a direct way into increased employment almost immediately.

Employment-Protection Legislation

Employment protection relates to the 'firing' and 'hiring' rules governing unfair dismissal, lay-offs for economic reasons, severance payments, minimum notice periods, administrative authorisation for dismissals and prior discussion with labour representatives. A number of benefits are alleged to justify employment-protection legislation: encouraging increased investment in firm-specific capital, reduced contracting costs by setting general rules and standards, and early notification of job loss to allow job search prior to being laid off. As against this, employment-protection legislation imposes constraints on firms' behaviour that can raise labour costs and adversely affect hiring decisions. It may also provide strong incentives for employers to use forms of employment (e.g. short-term contracts) that do not involve high firing costs. Labour-security legislation doesn't only affect the actions of employers. It also influences the bargaining power and, hence, strategy of the insiders (see earlier). With the legislation in place workers' fear of job loss will be greatly diminished and they will push for higher real wages. This will then have an impact on labour demand. Labour-security legislation therefore could cause labour demand to be inflexible both directly (i.e. through employers' immediate decisions) and indirectly (i.e. through its promotion of higher real wages).

It appears though that a certain level of employment protection is justified to protect workers from arbitrary or discriminatory dismissals. However, the OECD believes that dismissals which are required on economic grounds must be allowed and that the provision of more explicit long-term commitments to job security should not be imposed on all firms but decided on a firm-by-firm basis. Whether and to what extent reform is required clearly depends on the country-specific circumstances.

Attempts have been made to construct various summary indicators to describe the 'strictness' of employment protection in each country, including Ireland. Given the complexity of constructing such indicators, they are inevitably somewhat arbitrary, but none the less are indicative. An OECD study ranking EU countries according to 'strictness' of protection in the areas of individual dismissals of regular workers, fixed-term contracts and employment through temporary employment agencies, using objective methods and surveys of employers, showed that employment protection was ranked relatively low in Ireland (3.0 in relation to regular workers), as well as in Denmark (4.0), Switzerland (1.0), and the UK (2.0). Greece (12.0), Italy (14.0), Portugal (16.0), Spain (15.0), and Sweden (11.0) were ranked as high in terms of employment protection, with the other countries ranked as having intermediate levels of protection.[16] Compared to other European countries, therefore, there does not appear to be excessive employment-protection legislation in Ireland. It is noteworthy, though, that in relation to the most relevant other European labour market from Ireland's point of view, namely that of the UK, Ireland is ranked higher in terms of strictness of employment-protection legislation. It is also the case that employment-protection legislation in Europe in general is much stricter than in Canada and the US, although the opposite appears to be the case in comparison to Japan.

Reform of employment-protection legislation could increase vacancy flows and hirings. In the absence of such reform, the policy adopted may be, as mentioned, to rely more on short-term contracts to loosen up the labour market and this has certainly been a tendency in Ireland, as elsewhere, in recent years. Such contracts may have beneficial effects on employment creation but they also tend to create a dual labour market and have generated a new and relatively artificial source of labour turnover. It appears more equitable in this case to reform the legislation in relation to permanent contracts. As the OECD states, 'a loosening of existing employment-protection legislation may give rise to concern about equity, but this has to be seen in relation to the perhaps even greater inequality represented by persistent denial of access to jobs for some workers. Long-term unemployment affecting a significant and growing number of the labour force, on the one hand, and highly-protected and well-paid jobs, on the other hand, are clear signs of both inefficiently-working labour markets and inequality'.[17]

Taxation

Payroll taxes, such as employers' social security contributions raise the costs of employing labour over and above the wage paid. Income taxes and employees' social security contributions reduce the return to working. These taxes therefore are important because they directly affect the rate of return from decisions to enter the labour market and thereby affect the supply of labour (see Chapter 5). They may also influence the choice between working in the black economy and declared paid employment. These taxes may have an even greater impact on employment and unemployment through their influence on wage determination and therefore on the demand for labour. In a perfectly competitive labour market these effects would be minimal, but as seen earlier most labour markets are far from perfectly competitive. Hence, cuts in real wages through the imposition of increased personal income taxes or social security contributions may be resisted by workers and compensated for by higher nominal wages – but at the cost of higher unemployment. Likewise, an increase in employers' social security contributions can also result in unemployment when workers resist offsetting wage cuts.

Marginal tax rates (and in some cases average tax rates) on high-income earners have fallen in recent years, including in Ireland (see Chapter 5). But with a few exceptions, these tax reforms have barely affected the position of low-income earners, a problem that Ireland has attempted to address in recent years. Reductions in average tax rates at low levels of earnings are clearly one way of increasing the income differential between being in and out of work, for the groups for which this is the most serious problem. It appears that particular attention needs to be devoted to social security contributions in this regard, not just to the level of these contributions but also their structure. Employers' taxation does not only influence the amount of people that are employed but may also influence the type of worker that is hired. Employers' social security contributions are often differentiated in such a way as to promote the employment of particular groups (e.g. high-skilled labour) and to encourage employment in particular activities. In particular, in Europe, there is an in-built bias in the system towards the employment of high-skilled workers. This contributes to a high proportion of low-skilled workers in the ranks of the unemployed and it also induces a general increase in the level of unemployment.

The rate at which social benefits are withdrawn, as seen in Chapter 5, is also another important aspect of the problem. A feature of many tax and benefit systems, including that in Ireland, is that they embody very high marginal tax rates for those on low incomes, especially those with large families, as benefits are reduced and earnings are taxed, and as indicated in Chapter 5 there have been some moderately successful attempts to address this problem in Ireland in recent years.

7 LONG-TERM UNEMPLOYMENT

Introduction

It was seen earlier that over half of the unemployed in Ireland can now be classified as long-term unemployed. We will look in a moment at the possible reasons for this, but first it is worth noting the implications of long-term unemployment. As seen in Section 4, the probability of escaping from long-term unemployment decreases rapidly the longer the duration. At an individual level long-term unemployment may lead to significant deskilling and demotivation. At a macroeconomic level, and partly as a result of this, the long-term unemployed may not be regarded as 'employable' and in a sense the long-term unemployed cease to be part of the labour market. As such the level of long-term unemployment does not lead to greater competition for jobs in the labour market and thereby to any moderating pressure on wages. 'In essence, therefore, long-term unemployment does not trigger any adjustment in the labour market which might lead to its reduction'.[18]

Apart from the above, there are also a number of significant barriers facing the long-term unemployed. An important aspect of this is that employers may use duration of employment as a screening device in assessing job applications. There is evidence to support this in Ireland and other countries.[19] A study in the UK for example found that the long-term unemployed came second last in a list of six sources of potential recruits by companies, while those with disabilities came last. An ESRI survey of private companies in 1991 found that the long-term unemployed accounted for just 6 per cent of recent recruits compared with 16 per cent from the short-term unemployed, 29 per cent from persons employed and 26 per cent from new entrants. One reason for this may be that the long-term unemployed may not have access to information about job vacancies. Whatever the cause, this reinforces the view that many of the long-term unemployed are considered unemployable, not only by themselves but by the majority of employers. If this is true, it poses a very significant challenge for policymakers.

Why has this situation come about? Clearly before someone becomes long-term unemployed they must first have been short-term unemployed, and hence the original cause of the problem lies with the factors discussed in earlier sections. However, why do so many of the short-term unemployed in Ireland and some other countries drift into long-term unemployment? One suggested cause is the operation of unemployment and related benefits for those long-term unemployed and this is a factor that the OECD looked at in some detail and will be examined first below. The second major suggested cause relates to the lack of an active labour market programme to overcome the problems listed above, as it is argued that the best way to prevent people drifting into long-term unemployment and to facilitate a return to the labour force for those already long-term unemployed is by means of an active labour market policy. This issue will be the subject matter of the second subsection below.

Unemployment Payments
The rationale for unemployment insurance payments is 'to relieve people who have lost a job through no fault of their own from immediate financial concerns, and thus allow efficient job search. Insurance benefits, therefore, have an economic efficiency as well as a social equity objective'.[20] In relation to unemployment assistance payments, which apply in Ireland after twelve months and effectively for an indefinite period, the social or equity role, in reducing poverty among unemployed people and cushioning the adverse effects of high and rising unemployment, becomes paramount. As a result of the above, there would be strong political objections to resist any cuts in unemployment benefits or assistance and this clearly 'flavours' any debate on the causal connection between unemployment benefit/assistance and unemployment. However, the possibility of such a causal connection, and its extent, must be addressed, especially in countries where unemployment has persisted, at high levels, and has led to a build-up of large-scale, long-term

unemployment and 'handout' dependency. This is clearly the case in Ireland, where as seen earlier despite almost boom conditions in terms of economic growth long-term unemployment is set to stay stuck at present levels for the foreseeable future.

Few economists question the fact that there *is* a link between the benefit system and unemployment. At the simplest level, unemployment payments may create an option of leisure and low income, which some people might choose in preference to full-time work and a higher income. However, such payments could affect employment in many other ways. First, receipt of such payments may prolong intervals of job search, even for those who want to work. Second, because unemployment payments reduce the cost of becoming unemployed, employed people may take a tougher stance in industrial relations disputes or in collective bargaining over wages (see earlier), thereby exacerbating the high real wage problem. Last, payments may increase employment in high-turnover and seasonal industries, by subsidising these industries relative to those which provide long-term contract jobs.

The adverse effects of unemployment payments may, however, result not so much from the existence and level of these payments, but more from the entitlement conditions, the administration of the system and other institutional background factors. For example, payment of unemployment benefits is conditional upon the claimant being available for, and willing to take, full-time work, but if this condition is not effectively implemented then people *not* in the labour force (i.e. not available for or not seeking work) may register as unemployed simply to collect unemployment payments. If this condition is strictly enforced and payments stopped if it is not met, then many of the effects of unemployment payments could be substantially reduced. A related issue is that the employment agency must not only enforce this condition but must also facilitate effective job search (see later).

Examining the relationship between unemployment payments and the level of unemployment is fraught with difficulty. Depending on which 'side' one is taking in the debate, both positive and negative correlations can be found. For example, it could be pointed out that during the 1960s, the countries with the highest unemployment entitlements (e.g. Denmark and Germany) had the lowest unemployment rates (1 to 3 per cent), whereas those with low entitlements (e.g. Italy and the US) had the highest unemployment rates (around 5 per cent). In a similar vein, it could be pointed out that in several countries where entitlement levels have not increased markedly since the 1960s (e.g. Belgium and the Netherlands) unemployment rates increased greatly in the 1970s and 1980s. Last, during the 1980s benefit entitlement rose markedly in only one or two countries, including Portugal where unemployment fell, and declined or remained steady in many countries (e.g. New Zealand and Ireland) but unemployment increased.

The contrary evidence is that Japan and the US, among the few OECD countries where benefit entitlements have remained unchanged and at relatively low levels, especially after the first twelve months of unemployment, for the last thirty years, have largely avoided any long-term rises in their unemployment rates. It is also noteworthy that the countries with high entitlement levels in the 1960s and 1970s were the countries which experienced the most serious jumps in the levels of unemployment in later decades. In particular it could be pointed out that Ireland substantially increased benefit entitlement levels between the mid-1970s and mid-1980s and that this was followed in years to come by very large increases in unemployment.

The OECD suggests that the relationship between unemployment rates and entitlement levels may be a lagged one, in the case of some countries the lag being 10 to 20 years. In particular they note that the tendency for unemployment to persist in recovery periods was most evident in countries with high entitlement levels, i.e. increases in unemployment which initially were due to some macroeconomic shock such as technological change or free trade persist in countries where benefits are high and the duration of such payments is almost indefinite.

In terms of replacement rates (i.e. benefit entitlement before tax as a percentage of previous earnings before tax), Ireland belongs to the upper range countries of Europe, with an overall average of 29 per cent (as measured by the OECD), compared to figures of 52 per cent in Denmark, 43 per cent in Belgium, 37 per cent in France, 33 per cent in Spain and 28 per cent in Germany. The figure for the UK, the country with which Ireland has the closest labour market links is only 18 per cent, and those for Japan and the US only 8 per cent and 11 per cent respectively. The low figures in the last two countries arise from relatively low replacement rates in the first year of unemployment and, more importantly, the effective withdrawal of benefit in subsequent years.

While acknowledging that the precise effect on unemployment levels of the high replacement rates in some European countries may be unclear, the OECD is unequivocal concerning the changes that need to be effected in benefit administration in these countries. They suggest, for example, much more in-depth verification of eligibility, much better matching of workers to job vacancies, and field-work investigation of concealed earnings and related fraud. A more fundamental problem they claim is making unemployment payment, especially to the long-term unemployed, effectively conditional on availability for existing vacancies. In particular, they stress that the long-term unemployed should be expected to take, and unemployment payments made conditional on them taking, low-status jobs. Since already-employed people will not move into these jobs, the danger then is that there may be a steady tendency for these jobs to disappear altogether, resulting in the progressive erosion of total employment. As the OECD notes, 'much may depend upon achieving a social, political and analytical consensus on this, rejecting the opposite idea that modern economies should be able to afford to make work optional'.[21]

Active Labour Market Policies
What is being suggested above is effectively a much more active approach to labour market policy on behalf of the employment service in each country. The purpose of active labour market policies is threefold: first to mobilise labour supply, second to improve the quality of the labour force, and third to strengthen the search process in the labour market. They are particularly appropriate for those experiencing long-term unemployment, because as mentioned many of them are effectively not participating in the labour force, because of the deskilling and demotivation that has taken place they need assistance with education and training, and last because of demotivation and the indefinite nature of unemployment and related payments the search for jobs may not be as active as might be desired.

Active labour market policies can be classified into four categories: first, there are state employment services (e.g. placement and counselling); second, there is labour market training (i.e. for unemployed and employed adults); third, there are youth measures (e.g. remedial education, training or work experience for disadvantaged young people); and last, subsidised employment (i.e. subsidies to increase employment in the private sector, support the unemployed persons starting their own enterprises and direct job creation in either the public or non-profit sector). All OECD countries have had a mixture of such policies for many years, but there is very considerable variation in the proportion of GDP devoted by each country to such active labour market policies. Germany and Sweden devote the most expenditure to such programmes and both countries have managed to sustain relatively low unemployment rates, certainly compared to those in Ireland.

The most significant of the active labour market policies relates to the public employment service (PES), mainly because they tend to play a central role in promoting coherence between all elements of labour market policy. These elements include job information and counselling, administration of income maintenance (in some countries) and the admission of participants to active programmes. The evidence from various countries suggests significant positive effects from individual counselling for the long-term unemployed and such a policy was initiated on a phased basis in Ireland in 1995.

8 CONCLUSION

This chapter has attempted to look at the nature and extent of the employment and unemployment challenge facing Ireland and, indeed, most of Europe in the 1990s. It was emphasised throughout that in the Irish case the existence of large-scale emigration is just as much a reflection of failure on the employment front as is the rise in unemployment.

The outstanding failure appears to have been the inability to increase employment in Ireland in the 1980s, despite the huge increase in the potential labour force in this period. The result of this failure was a large increase in the unemployment rate and emigration of almost 200,000 people in this period. More seriously, perhaps, the sustained failure to increase employment meant not only that the high level of unemployment persisted but also that an increasing proportion of that total were drifting into long-term unemployment and, in many cases therefore, effectively out of the labour market. Employment levels have increased in the 1990s, but only at a rate high enough to stem the increase in unemployment and the flow of emigration. The high level of unemployment, and the attendant and almost intractable long-term unemployment problem, remain and may last to the end of the decade at least.

There have been similar failures in relation to employment and unemployment in several European countries, most notably in Spain. This, of course, does not lessen or mitigate the seriousness of the problem, but it does suggest that when looking for causes and/or explanations adopting a purely Irish perspective may be quite wide of the mark. The later sections of this chapter, therefore, attempted to outline the factors which it is believed – most notably by the OECD, the body which perhaps has done the most extensive research into the causes of unemployment in Europe – have brought about the huge increase in unemployment in Europe in the last twenty years and to see in what way, if any, the situation in Ireland differed from that in these other countries.

The impact of global factors such as technological change and increased international trade were looked at and it was suggested that it was the failure to adapt to these factors rather than these factors *per se* that may have been responsible for some of the increase in unemployment in Europe and therefore Ireland. The lack of an appropriate retraining programme may have been one of the key factors in the failure to adapt to these global factors, but rigidities in the labour market many economists appear to believe were the root cause. The role of trade unions, distortions in product markets, employment-protection legislation, taxation and the unemployment payments system are all mentioned as possible factors distorting the labour market and therefore its capacity to adjust, especially to technological change and increasing trade levels. One thing is clear, though, the causes of, and solutions to, the employment and unemployment problem in Ireland are varied and are not easy to verify precisely from empirical analysis.[22]

Whatever the causes in the past, though, the problem for Ireland in the 1990s is that a large proportion of the unemployed are now long-term unemployed, an issue which poses problems of a quite different dimension to those whose solution may be sought in such policy measures as 'freeing up' the labour market or increasing output growth. The long-term unemployment problem is as much a social and political problem as an economic one and its solution will require a sea-change in thinking if it is to be resolved. In the meantime the emphasis must be on ensuring that the numbers drifting into long-term unemployment are brought to a halt.

It must not be forgotten, though, that the labour market will never be quite the same as that for products or services: the price in this case is the income for some person/family. In this regard, the advantages of large increases in employment through a US-style labour market policy must be set against the huge increase in the dispersion of incomes, and insecurity for many, that accompanied such a policy. The dilemma for policymakers is how to bring about a large increase in employment while at the same time avoiding a widening of the gap between high- and low-income earners, a serious diminution of state support for those genuinely in need, and an unacceptable increase in insecurity for most of those in employment.

Endnotes

1 The Central Statistics Office predictions for population and labour force assuming a lower level of emigration, and a smaller decrease in the fertility rate, than that assumed by the ESRI indicate that the total population in 2006 could be almost 200,000 higher than that predicted by the ESRI. See CSO, *Population and Labour Force Projections, 1996-2026,* Stationery Office, Dublin 1995.

2 Between 1968 and 1982, employment increased at an annual average rate of 0.6 per cent in Ireland. During this period, there were employment declines in Spain and the UK, and lower employment increases than in Ireland in Belgium, Denmark and Italy. Employment grew at a much higher rate than in Ireland, though, in the US.

3 See P. O'Connell and J. Sexton, 'Labour Market Developments in Ireland, 1971-1993', in S. Cantillon *et al , Economic Perspectives for the Medium Term,* Economic and Social Research Institute, Dublin 1994.

4 This section of the chapter draws on, *Employment Outlook*, OECD, Paris, July 1993, Chapter 1, 'Labour Market Prospects and Recent Developments'.

5 See, *Ending Long-term Unemployment*, National Economic and Social Forum, Dublin 1994, for further details.

6 See, *OECD Jobs Study: Part I*, OECD, Paris 1994, Chapter 3, 'Trade and Foreign Direct Investment'.

7 *Ibid.,* Chapter 4, 'Technological Change and Innovation'.

8 *Ibid.,* p.165.

9 See, *The Association Between Economic Growth and Employment Growth in Ireland* (NESC Report no. 94), Stationery Office, Dublin 1992.

10 A difficulty also in the Irish case is the calculation of the employment intensity measure. There are many factors that may prevent increases in GDP translating into increases in real resources in the economy, the net effect of these factors being that in the last fifteen years the growth of real resources available to Irish residents may have been considerably less than the growth of GDP (see Chapters 1 and 7). The main issue here surrounds the activities of multinational corporations which, because of transfer-pricing practices (see Chapter 9), may lead to a considerable overstatement of their output and hence the output of the economy and, in the process lead to profit outflows that are large but probably also overstated. For this reason alone, the use of GNP rather than GDP would be preferred as a measure of the true output growth of the economy, a measure that would lead to a greater employment intensity measure for Ireland than the previous figures would suggest.

11 See, *Employment Outlook,* op. cit., Chapter 5, 'Earnings Inequality: Changes in the 1980s'.
12 See R. Layard, S. Nickell and R. Jackman, *Unemployment: Macroeconomic Performance and the Labour Market*, Oxford University Press, Oxford 1991.
13 See, *OECD Jobs Study, Part II*, OECD, Paris 1994, Chapter 7, 'Skills and Competences'. See also P. O'Connell and M. Lyons, *Entreprise-Related Training and State Policy in Ireland*, Economic and Social Research Institute, Dublin 1995.
14 See, *OECD Jobs Study: Part II*, op cit.
15 See, *Negotiations on a Successor Agreement to the PESP*, National and Economic Social Forum, Dublin 1993.
16 See, *OECD Jobs Study: Part II*, op. cit.
17 *Ibid*, p.108.
18 See, *Ending Long-term Unemployment*, op. cit., p.23.
19 *Ibid.*, p.22.
20 *OECD Jobs Study: Part II*, op. cit., p.171.
21 *Ibid.*, p.213.
22 See D. McGettigan, 'The Causes of Unemployment: A Review', in Cantillon *et al, op. cit.*, for detailed references.

CHAPTER 9

European Integration, the Balance of Payments and Inflation

Dermot McAleese and Fiona Hayes *

In Chapter 3, inflation and the balance of payments were considered in a general context and the reasons for assigning them the status of secondary policy objectives were explained. This chapter looks at these matters in a specifically Irish context. In particular, the policy measures available to secure these objectives are discussed.

The analysis emphasises the empirical dimensions of Ireland's involvement in the global, and particularly the European, economy. This involvement has implications not only for the balance of payments and inflation but also for the attainment of the primary objectives of economic growth and employment (Chapter 2) and for determining the pattern of economic development (Chapter 7).

The opening section deals with foreign trade. The pattern of Irish trade is analysed under four headings: the level of trade (trade dependence); the commodity composition of trade; the geographical distribution of Irish exports and imports; and the terms of trade. The Irish balance of payments is then discussed. The components of the balance of payments statements are described and the automatic adjustment mechanisms are sketched. Because of the high import content of aggregate spending, these automatic mechanisms are more powerful in the case of Ireland than for larger countries. In some circumstances, they will need to be supplemented by non-automatic policy measures such as expenditure reduction (deflation), commercial policy, exchange rate change and domestic competitiveness. It is argued that only the last option possesses real contemporary relevance for the Irish economy.

---

* The authors wish to thank the editor for helpful comments on an earlier draft.

Next, the implications of EU membership for Irish trade and payments are assessed. This involves discussion of the EU's Common Commercial Policy, the Structural Funds, the 1992 Programme and the Maastricht Treaty. In addition, the effects of EU enlargement and the completion of the GATT Uruguay Round will be analysed.

Ireland's policy towards inflation and the exchange rate is then examined. Irish policy on these fronts has been determined in the context of membership of the European Monetary System (EMS), with a view to the attainment of Economic and Monetary Union (EMU). However, since the currency crisis of 1992/93 the exchange rate mechanism (ERM) of the EMS has been radically changed, and the Maastricht process of convergence to EMU has been interrupted. It is against this background that Ireland's future within the EMS and EMU must be examined.

1 INTERNATIONAL TRADE

Like most small economies, the Irish economy is heavily dependent on foreign trade. In 1994, imports of goods and services amounted to 54 per cent of GDP, compared with an EU average of 25 percent; the corresponding figures for exports of goods and services were 65 per cent and 27 per cent (Table 9.1).

Table 9.1

Comparative Figures of Trade Dependence

	Percentage ratio exports (goods and services) to GDP		Percentage ratio imports (goods and services) to GDP	
	1964	1994[1]	1964	1994[1]
Belgium	43	68	44	64
Denmark	30	35	32	29
France	13	23	13	21
Germany[2]	18	22	17	21
Greece	9	25	19	34
Ireland	*32*	*65*	*40*	*54*
Italy	13	25	13	21
Luxembourg	79	87	79	88
Netherlands	42	52	44	46
Portugal	26	29	30	38
Spain	11	22	12	21
UK	19	25	21	27
EU 12	18	27	19	25

Sources: Commission of the European Communities, *European Economy,* No. 58, Brussels 1994.

[1] Estimates.

[2] 1964 figures refer to West Germany only; 1994 figures to Germany after unification.

The trade ratios for Belgium and Luxembourg are higher, while those of the larger countries of the EU are considerably smaller. Trade ratios in most EU countries have been increasing rapidly during the last two decades. The Irish economy also has become more open, reflecting an accentuated level of specialisation in the industrial and agricultural sectors.

This openness makes it possible to reap the gains from international exchange; it also means greater sensitivity to world economic fluctuations, less autonomy in the formulation of domestic economic policy and a growing interdependence with the outside world. Comparison with Scandinavian countries on the northern periphery of Europe shows, however, that while trade dependence is a feature of all small countries, Ireland's degree of trade dependence is exceptionally high, reflecting its pattern of development with comparatively heavy emphasis on export-oriented overseas subsidiaries (see Chapters 7 and 12).

The commodity composition of Irish trade has changed dramatically in recent decades. Three decades ago, live animals and food accounted for 61 per cent of all exports whereas now the share has fallen to 20 per cent (Table 9.2). The import content of these food exports is much lower than that of other goods, so their net balance of trade contribution is much higher than the gross figures suggest. The shift away from Ireland's historical dependence on primary products is nevertheless the most significant change in our pattern of specialisation.

Table 9.2

Composition of Merchandise Trade by
Commodity Group, 1961 and 1995

	Exports			Imports		
	1961	1995[1]	1995[1]	1961	1995[1]	1995[1]
	%	%	IR£m	%	%	IR£m
Live animals and food	61	20	4,896	16	8	1,447
Beverages and tobacco	4	2	490	3	1	181
Raw materials, fuels & oil	9	3	734	19	8	1,447
Manufactured goods	18	68	16,648	54	74	13,380
Other	8	7	1,714	8	9	1,627
Total	100	100	24,482	100	100	18,082

Sources: CSO, *Trade Statistics of Ireland,* Stationery Office, Dublin, various issues.
[1] Authors' own estimates, based on 1993 data.
Note: Following the completion of the internal market at the end of 1992, customs declarations for intra-EU movement of goods are no longer required. Since trade statistics can no longer be based on customs data, a new EU-wide system for collecting intra-EU trade statistics, Intrastat, has been introduced. The system has two components: (i) the Intrastat survey itself, in which large traders make a monthly return detailing the quantity and value of all exports to and imports from other EU countries; (ii) VAT returns, on which all traders record the value of their exports to and imports from other EU countries. For this reason, care must be exercised in comparison of pre- and post-1992 figures.

Manufactured goods have increased their share in both exports and imports. There are several reasons for this. First, firms exporting industrial goods rely on imports for their supplies of raw materials, components and capital goods. The direct import content of Irish non-food manufactured production is about 36 per cent of gross output. Second, as nations become more industrialised, the share of *intra-industry trade* tends to increase. That is, countries tend to exchange goods which are broadly similar but none the less differentiated. Within consumer goods categories this phenomenon is familiar. Ireland exports Ballygowan and imports Perrier; exports Irish cheddar and imports French brie; exports Cross pens and imports Parker pens – examples can be multiplied. The same process also operates in intermediate and capital goods: Ireland is a major exporter and importer of electrical and data-processing machinery. According to Brülhart and McAleese, 44 per cent of Irish trade in manufactured goods in 1990 consisted of intra-industry trade.[1]

About three-quarters of Irish manufacturing exports originate in subsidiaries of foreign firms. These overseas subsidiaries export on average 86 per cent of their production compared with 33 per cent in the case of indigenous firms. Their exports are heavily weighted towards high-technology, 'sunrise' industrial products which explains the favourable technology profile of Irish exports. Overseas firms are almost wholly responsible for the increase in the share of office machinery and data-processing equipment from 5 per cent of Irish exports in 1980 to 18 per cent in 1993. Similarly, multinational enterprises such as Microsoft and Lotus account for the build-up of Irish PC software exports. Indeed, according to IDA estimates, about 40 per cent of all European PC software is produced in Ireland. However, in interpreting Irish trade data, account should be taken of certain practices (the best-known being transfer pricing) which result in an exaggeration of export values.

Transfer pricing is a device used by multinational enterprises to limit their overall tax burden. It arises from the existence of different tax regimes in the global economy. Multinationals have an incentive to locate in a country with a comparatively low rate of taxation on profits, such as Ireland. Not only do they pay lower taxes on profits from operations located in the low-tax country, they may also engage in transfer pricing – reporting profits earned in a high-tax country in the low-tax country. In this manner, the subsidiary in the low-tax country shows high profits, while low profits are reported for the operation in the high-tax country. Profits are 'transferred' from the high-tax country to the low-tax country, and the company's overall tax burden is greatly reduced.

For example, suppose that a multinational company has a plant in Ireland, which produces an intermediate product for export to another plant located in a high-tax country, say Germany. The Irish subsidiary pays corporation profits tax at 10 per cent; the German subsidiary pays 30 per cent. If the two tax rates were identical, the Irish plant would sell the components to the German plant at a 'transfer price' of IR£10 million. However, with different tax rates, the multinational has an incentive to inflate this price. Suppose it charged IR£20 million instead of IR£10 million. The amount of profit reported in Ireland is increased by IR£10 million, profits attributed to Germany fall by the same amount and the company's tax bill is reduced by IR£2 million. The Irish exchequer also benefits – it gains IR£1 million in tax revenue while Germany loses IR£3 million. There is no loss to the Irish economy; however, as a result of the transfer-pricing policy, Irish export figures are artificially inflated by IR£10 million. Given that a very large part of Irish manufacturing output and exports is concentrated in the hands of a few multinationals, and with output per employee as high as IR£824,000 for the top ten multinationals in 1992/93, it is clear that the extent of transfer pricing is significant. This explains the large gap between Irish GDP and GNP figures. It also means that Irish export figures are exaggerated.[2] Note, however, that this does not affect the balance of payments current account, since profit outflows are deductible under trading and investment income.

At the time of Independence, most Irish merchandise trade was with the UK, making the economy heavily dependent on the fortunes of the British economy. The degree of dependence has fallen markedly since then (Table 9.3). The UK is still the largest customer, but its share of Irish merchandise exports has fallen from 75 per cent in 1960 to 28 per cent in 1993. About 40 per cent of Irish exports are now sold on continental EU markets and one-fifth of imports originate there. (The member states of the EU, excluding the UK, are the only group of countries with which Ireland runs a trade surplus.) The Scandinavian countries are also major trading partners for Ireland. Outside of Europe, Ireland's two most important trading partners are the US and Japan.

Table 9.3

Percentage Composition of Merchandise Trade by Geographical Area, 1960 and 1995

Area	Exports		Imports	
	1960	1995[1]	1960	1995[1]
UK	75	28	49	36
Rest of EU	7	40	15	20
Others	18	32	36	44
Total	100	100	100	100

Sources: As for Table 9.2
[1] Authors' own estimates, based on 1993 data.

As can be seen from Table 9.2, Ireland enjoys a large overall balance of trade surplus, and has done so since 1985. There is a changing pattern of surplus and deficit as between different types of goods and different areas of the world. Ireland is a large net exporter of food (as one would expect) and also, less expectedly, of chemicals and electronic data-processing machines. Large surpluses are earned in trade with France (IR£1.2 billion) and Germany (IR£1.5 billion), whereas large trade deficits are the rule with Japan and the US. In 1993, a trade deficit of IR£750 million was recorded in trade with the US and IR£240 million in the case of Japan. It is tempting, but incorrect, to identify such deficits as a loss. Imports are the source of gains from trade; exports the price which must be paid to secure them.

The geographical diversification of export markets can be attributed to four factors: the influx of overseas manufacturing enterprises with worldwide and European-oriented market strategies (Irish-owned manufacturing firms still sell 43 per cent of their exports to the British market compared with 23 per cent in the case of foreign subsidiaries[3]); the increased penetration of the continental market for Irish agricultural produce; and the development of new export markets in the Middle East and in LDCs, particularly for food products. Of the four, there is little doubt that the first is the most significant. The more diversified market structure for Irish trade is welcome from an economic viewpoint in that it protects the country from the effects of a recession in one particular market. However, since the economy has become more than ever dependent on foreign markets, the diversification of trade has altered the form rather than the degree of economic dependence.

The commodity terms of trade is an important concept for a small trading economy. It represents the ratio of export prices to import prices. If import prices rise and export prices stay constant, the terms of trade deteriorates. If export prices rise faster than import prices, the terms of trade improves. As Table 9.4 shows, Ireland's terms of trade has fluctuated widely over time. In the period 1968-73 the terms of trade improved because of the boom in agriculture prices. A drastic 18 per cent deterioration was recorded in 1974 because of the oil price rise. The decline in Ireland's terms of trade from its high point in 1973 offset much of the value of increased GNP during the 1970s. That is, more was being exported, but the purchasing power of these exports in terms of imports had diminished. Between 1981 and 1986 the terms of trade improved from 98.1 to 108.7 as a result of the fall in oil prices, weak world commodity prices and the decline in the value of the US dollar relative to the Irish pound. The deterioration since then is primarily due to depressed food prices.

Table 9.4

Terms of Trade (Goods and Services): 1968-95 (1980=100)

	1968	1973	1974	1981	1986	1990	1995[1]
Ireland	110.8	127.2	108.4	98.1	108.7	109.4	99.6

Sources: As for Table 9.1.
[1] Estimate.

Trade in services was, until recently, a neglected aspect of international trade. Yet services are an important component of world trade, amounting to an estimated 20-25 per cent of total trade. Ireland's trade in services is difficult to measure and no comprehensive record of its components exists. Tourism and travel is a traditional item of services expenditure. Although nowadays associated with extensive two-way flows, tourism and travel is still a net earner of foreign currency for the Irish economy. In 1993, a net surplus of IR£250 million was recorded. A feature of the services industry is the rise of new types of activity, hitherto untraded, where the potential for trade has been unleashed by the information technology revolution, the relaxation of exchange controls and the completion of the Single European Market.[4]

One example is the financial services industry. The Irish Financial Services Centre in Dublin is largely export-oriented. Also data-processing activities (notably insurance claims processing and hotel bookings), which feed their statistics back to the US, have been set up in many parts of Ireland. Over the years, a growing contribution to Irish export activity has been made by firms engaged in construction-related activities and by consultancy organisations in the public and private sectors. Irish building contractors have been working in Africa and Middle Eastern countries. Some Irish contractors have by now achieved a significant international reputation. Computer software, medical and other consultancy services have also contributed to trade in services. Public sector enterprises such as Air Lingus, the ESB, CTT and the IDA have also been active in this field. The net foreign exchange flows arising from these types of export activity are as yet small in aggregate, but they are becoming increasingly important.

The opening of the Eastern European economies has stimulated interest in establishing East-West trade links, both in the goods and services sectors. Goods trade with these countries is negligible: about 1 per cent of total exports. Since liberalisation of these economies took place against a background of declining economic growth, rapid expansion of trade was not to be expected. Yet, relative to the size of economy, proximity and economic status, these economies trade less than would be expected and, as their economies recover from the transitional shock of moving to a market system, they offer good long-term prospects for further trade.

2 BALANCE OF PAYMENTS

Balance of Payments Position
Trade data relate to only part of a country's total transactions with the outside world. The nearest to a complete statistical picture is given in the balance of payments (Table 9.5).

Table 9.5

Balance of International Payments (IR£m), 1985-95

	1985	1989	1993	1994[1]	1995[2]
Merchandise	137	2,244	4,829	5,760	6,400
Services	205	-467	-453	-662	-763
Trading and investment income	-1,966	-3,233	-3,804	-4,090	-4,637
International transfers	974	1,108	1,890	1,392	1,800
Balance on current account	-650	-348	2,462	2,400	2,800
(as % of GNP)	(-3.9)	(-1.6)	(8.6)	(7.8)	(8.3)
Private capital	-108	-1,870	-922	n.a.	n.a.
Official capital	1,029	964	537	n.a.	n.a.
Banking transactions	286	-186	-844	n.a.	n.a.
Official external reserves[3]	-196	640	-1,756	n.a.	n.a.
Net balance on capital account	1,011	-453	-2,984	n.a.	n.a.
Net residual[4]	-361	801	522	n.a.	n.a.

Source: CSO, *Balance of Payments Statistics,* Stationery Office, Dublin, various issues.

[1] Estimates.

[2] Forecasts.

[3] For accounting reasons an increase in reserves is shown as a negative number and a decrease as a positive number.

[4] This is the balancing amount, credit or debit as appropriate, which must be included to ensure an accounting equivalence between the total of all credit entries and the total of all debit entries, i.e. this balance plus the balance on the current account plus the balance on the capital account must by definition sum to zero.

Ireland's balance of payments has been subject to much change in recent years. The major change has been the transformation of an enormous current account deficit of 14.6 per cent of GNP in 1981 into a surplus of 8.6 per cent of GNP in 1993. This changeover from deficit to surplus occurred notwithstanding the high and growing deficit on trading and investment income. Investment income outflows include interest payments due on foreign debt (see Chapter 6) and the outflow of profits and interest payments from foreign manufacturing firms in Ireland which, together with other items, involved foreign exchange outflows of almost IR£4 billion in 1993 alone. To a certain extent, profit outflows are the corollary of the export growth driving the trade surplus – it is to be expected that overseas subsidiaries should earn profits and wish to repatriate them. One would expect the extent of multinationals' profit repatriation to be greatly influenced by their transfer-pricing activity. Surprisingly, the scale of profit repatriation has remained constant at about 17 per cent of the value of exports since the late 1980s, despite the huge increase in multinational activity in Ireland as reflected by output and export figures. (This is partly explained by the increase in outflows classed as service charges, such as management fees and charges for research and development – see below.) Finally, the large surplus on international transfers merits attention. It arises because of CAP transfers (see Chapter 11 and later in this chapter) and Structural Funds from the EU. By the early 1990s, Ireland had graduated to the unaccustomed position of being in surplus both in trade account and current account.

That the balance of payments must always balance is a truism. The difficulty lies in identifying its separate components. The distinction between autonomous transactions, which occur independently of the overall condition of the balance of payments, and accommodating transactions, which react passively to it, has been made in Chapter 3. The strength of this approach lies in its recognition of the organic link between capital and current transactions. For example, suppose Air Lingus were to decide to purchase an aircraft for IR£100 million, credit being supplied by the vendor. Imports would rise by IR£100 million, and the contra-entry would be a IR£100 million capital inflow. It would be wrong to infer that a current account deficit 'forced' the country to borrow IR£100 million abroad; causality could have gone the other way. The two variables are clearly interdependent. The main problem lies in classifying transactions into accommodating and autonomous categories. There is the difficulty of distinguishing a long-term loan from a short-term capital flow (the rule of thumb definition of long-term as investment in bonds of more than one year's maturity is clearly unsatisfactory). Suppose the government borrows long; how can one say whether this is to bolster reserves and stave off balance of payments adjustment (accommodating) or to finance its capital programme (autonomous)? Hard and fast rules are impossible to apply.

The scale of private capital outflows in the early 1990s has been a source of some concern. These exceptionally large outflows are in part accounted for by the relaxation of exchange controls. They have been partly matched by capital inflows in the form of non-resident purchases of government securities. Capital flows are sensitive to UK capital market developments, expectations about currency realignments, Irish interest rate policy, the taxation of savings and deposits, and the monetary authorities' approach to external reserves. But, at present, we know little about the precise degree of sensitivity of capital flows to these variables.

Ireland's perception of the balance of payments has altered in recent years. For one thing, the current balance of payments deficit has disappeared This was mainly due to exceptionally strong export growth, with multinationals playing a lead role.[5] Another structural factor was the commercial exploitation of natural gas, providing a domestic source for 14 per cent of Ireland's primary energy requirements by 1986. The terms of trade was also favourable from the mid-1980s with low oil and other commodity prices. While the slow growth of domestic demand up to the late 1980s also restrained import demand, the post-1987 upsurge in demand was not accompanied by a destabilising increase in imports. The improvement in Ireland's competitive position during this period undoubtedly helped matters.

A second major change in perception applies to the private capital account. In the past, with inefficient and expensive telecommunications, capital controls and foreign exchange restrictions, there was comparatively little concern about this aspect of Ireland's balance of payments. After 1992 (see below), the position changed in a fundamental way. Irish institutions must now compete for Irish private capital and, if the return is not sufficient, Irish capital can and will leave the country. A feature of the capital account which merits attention is the large volume of two-way trade in slightly differentiated 'products'. This is analogous to intra-industry trade as described in connection with current account flows.

Current account deficits and surpluses can each cause serious problems. Hence the government may want to restore the balance of payments to equilibrium. There are two means by which equilibrium might be restored: *automatic adjustment mechanisms and balance of payments policies.*

Although traditionally a deficit country, Ireland now has a current account surplus which is forecast to last for some time. In a sense, the balance of payments 'problem' has changed from one of chronic deficit to chronic surplus. Yet it is premature to see the surplus as a problem, for three reasons. First, the extent of the surplus is a matter of continuing controversy. In 1993, a major revision of the Irish current account balance of payments statistics resulted in a cumulative downward revision of nearly IR£2 billion for the period from 1986 to 1990. The revision reflected the fact that insufficient attention had been devoted to the amount of money leaving the country through multinationals in the form of service charges. The revised statistics showed that in some years where the balance of payments was believed to be in surplus, it was actually in deficit. The revised 1989 figures, for example, changed a recorded surplus of IR£261 million into a deficit of IR£348 million. Second, Ireland's balance of payment position under full employment might not be as favourable as the present balance of payments position. Third, the balance of payments surplus has been bolstered by transfers which will be unlikely to be maintained at their current level indefinitely. For these reasons, and also for ease of exposition, the analysis of balance of payments adjustment in the next section focuses on the deficit side. A reader interested in ways of reducing a chronic balance of payments surplus need only note that the processes that reduce a deficit will also – if operated in the opposite direction – reduce a surplus.

Automatic Adjustment Mechanisms
Automatic adjustment mechanisms refer to the processes whereby *ex ante* imbalances between the supply and demand for external funds are brought into *ex post* equilibrium. Starting from initial current account balance, suppose foreign demand falls, causing a reduction in manufactured exports. Two processes are immediately set into operation which tend to reduce the deficit thereby created. First, a fall in demand for exports automatically

reduces demand for imports required as inputs for their production. Second, the fall in aggregate demand generated by the decline in export demand (i.e. exports minus imported inputs) percolates through the economy. The amount of income affected in this way hinges crucially on the value of the foreign trade multiplier, i.e. on the marginal propensity to import, the marginal propensity to save and the marginal tax rate. The higher the marginal propensity to import, the greater is the extent to which a fall in demand will be translated into a decrease in imports. Note, however, that the adjustment mechanism is still only a partial one. The initial deficit is greatly reduced but not eliminated.

At this stage, capital account transactions can be introduced into the analysis. The net deficit will appear in the form of a decline in deposits in domestic banks. The balance of payments deficit in other words reduces the domestic money supply and, at constant prices, the value of real balances. If it is accepted that households maintain a given relation between their cash balances and levels of expenditure, further changes in income and imports must occur in order to preserve monetary equilibrium.

There are a number of ways in which this adjustment could occur. Reduced cash balances could cause a fall in consumption, directly reducing import demand. Alternatively, these balances may be replenished by sales of bonds, in which case bond prices tend to fall, and interest rates to rise, causing a fall in aggregate demand. This again could lead to lower imports. Financial intermediaries can also be introduced into the analysis. The adjustment process might be viewed as leading from reduced reserves in the banking system, to increases in the interest rate on overdrafts, to reduced borrowing and spending. The decrease in aggregate demand, by whatever process it comes about, must continue until full equilibrium can be restored.

This automatic adjustment mechanism stresses the link between the net deficit on current account, the deterioration in liquidity position of individuals and/or domestic banks, and the translation of the latter into a reduced level of advances and, eventually, into lower aggregate demand. While simple in theory, in practice the process may take a long time to work through the system. When private capital is internationally mobile, a very small increase in domestic interest rates may attract net private capital inflows which offset the current account deficit and temporarily ease the liquidity constraint. However, private capital will continue to flow into a country only if it is convinced that the underlying balance of payments position is secure. Official policy could also encroach upon the automatic adjustment mechanism by 'sterilising' the monetary effects of balance of payments disequilibrium. For example, the Central Bank might offset the liquidity-reducing effects of the deficit by short-term measures designed to increase domestic liquidity. Alternatively, the government might borrow abroad in order to restore the liquidity loss without detriment to the level of gross official reserves. But since reserves are not finite and a sustained deterioration in the *net* reserves position (gross official reserves less public foreign debt) would not be acceptable, eventually some action would have to be taken to restore balance of payments equilibrium.

The argument so far can be summarised as follows. A strong automatic adjustment mechanism is at work in a small open economy. Changes in the demand for exports quickly translate into changes in the demand for imports. In the short run the adjustment mechanism tends to be incomplete and the process of adjustment may be delayed by *ad hoc* government interventions. In a *laissez-faire* world, the automatic adjustment process would eventually be complete. The way in which adjustment is effected may, however, be costly in terms of employment and growth. The aim of the balance of payments policy is to ensure that the process of adjustment is carried through with minimum loss of output and efficiency. Rather than waiting for reserves to run out and for foreign borrowing capacity to be exhausted, the objective is to head off such difficulties by appropriately designed policies. This gives economic 'actors' an opportunity to make structural changes in good time before a crisis point is reached.

Balance of Payments Policies

Suppose a country with a current account deficit reaches a stage where reserves and borrowing capacity are depleted. In such circumstances, the country does not go bankrupt – there is no mechanism by which a sovereign state can be wound up and its assets disposed of as would happen in the case of an individual firm. However, the country will find it progressively more difficult to secure essential imports. Firms supplying imports will demand payment in advance, and where is the foreign exchange to come from? The result will be a shortage of spare parts, factories which cannot operate due to delays in obtaining raw materials and components, a breakdown in transport due to petrol shortage, etc. Cumulatively, these effects are seriously damaging to growth. Corrective action taken earlier could have avoided many of these losses. Accepting this, what policy instruments are available to the government to remedy the situation?

One method is through *expenditure-reducing policy*. A reduction in the real level of spending brings about a decrease in the level of import demand. This policy can be highly effective in restoring balance of payments equilibrium. It may not, however, be the most efficient method. Balance of payments equilibrium is a secondary, not a primary, policy objective.

Expenditure-switching policies are designed to achieve a change in the balance of payments by redeploying resources between the traded and non-traded sectors. There are three standard models of expenditure-switching: (i) commercial policy, (ii) exchange rate changes, and (iii) competitiveness.

Commercial policy comprises price and non-price measures designed to reduce imports and stimulate exports, e.g. tariffs, quotas, export subsidies. Since discrimination against trade with member countries is explicitly ruled out by the Treaty of Rome and extra-EU trade is covered by the Common Commercial Policy, the Irish government has little independent discretion in this matter. Even if it had, commercial restrictions might not be an appropriate policy for rectifying the balance of payments (see Chapter 1).

Devaluation, or *a depreciation of the exchange rate,* makes exports more attractive to purchase. Devaluation is not discriminatory between different types of imports, nor does it create a bias against exports. For these reasons, economists consider it a superior policy to protection as a method of improving the balance of payments. The effectiveness of a devaluation in the Irish context is limited by practical and institutional constraints. For one thing, a devaluation raises exporters' costs by raising the price of imported inputs, an effect which tends to be more pronounced in a small trade-dependent country. Ireland's low price elasticities for imports and the uncertain price responsiveness of the export sector means that a large percentage devaluation would be required in order to achieve a modest proportionate improvement in the balance of payments. Only in the medium to longer term do the favourable competitive effects (assuming no compensatory income claims) come into play. At the same time, experience shows that compensatory income claims often are exacted.[6]

There have been many instances of small country devaluations. Sometimes such devaluations are forced upon the country by a change in external circumstances. The collapse of Finland's markets in the former Soviet Union, for example, necessitated a radical realignment of the markka in the early 1990s. Devaluations can also occur in order to protect a country against competitive disadvantages arising as a result of devaluation in the currency of the country's trading partners. But in Ireland's case the scope for independent action is constrained by institutional obligations and, as we shall see, membership of the European Monetary System (EMS) and the prospect of a single currency further constrain Ireland's discretion in this regard.

This leaves improved *domestic competitiveness* as a third major policy option (see also Chapters 7, 8, 10, 11 and 12). Competitiveness must be defined in a broad sense to include price and non-price factors such as product quality, reliability of supply and back-up marketing services. Raising a nation's competitiveness must involve incomes restraint but it can take many other forms as well: improvements in productivity, in infrastructure, in the supply of skilled labour, and in the industrial relations system. All of these have the effect of cutting down production costs and raising the competitiveness of export- and import-competing industries. A country's long-run competitive position can also be profoundly influenced by its policy towards research and development, and by its success in product innovation and technology, as Japanese success testifies. In the short run, however, incomes restraint is essential, for it brings with it all the advantages of devaluation without any of its inflationary disadvantages. Improving competitiveness in the broad sense of the term will be the key objective for the Irish government as integration with Europe becomes closer.[7]

3 INTEGRATION WITH THE EUROPEAN ECONOMY

Paralleling Ireland's move from home-market-oriented to export-oriented policies during the 1960s were a series of commitments to international institutions. Ireland joined the IMF and World Bank in 1957, applied for membership of the European Economic Community (EEC) in 1961, became a member of GATT in 1967, and entered the EEC in 1973. Of these steps, the last one was the most significant. The EEC (now the European Union) brought with it more far-reaching obligations and opportunities than any previous economic arrangement since Independence.

The European Union has evolved considerably since 1973. Economic integration among member states has been 'deepened' by the Single European Market (or 1992) Programme, the Maastricht Treaty and the proposal for EMU. Participation in these programmes has extensive implications for the Irish economy. To ensure that Ireland, as a peripheral region of the EU, is in a position to reap the benefits from trade and integration, substantial contributions from the EU's Structural Funds have been made available. Also on the EU agenda has been the enlargement of the Union. Austria, Finland and Sweden, joined on 1 January, 1995. Many more potential candidates wait in line. Ireland's role in the international economy will also be affected by the completion of the Uruguay Round of GATT negotiations. We will consider each of these developments in turn.

Trade Policy
Theoretical analyses of customs unions frequently proceed in terms of trade creation and trade diversion, the former referring to the creation of trade arising from the shift in production from domestic sources to cheaper sources in other member states, and the latter representing the diversion of supplies from cheaper non-member sources to dearer member sources. Such analyses have little relevance to Irish membership of the EU. The pattern of trade precluded the possibility of any significant trade diversion and only a limited amount of trade creation was to be expected following free access to continental European markets (the main impact of free trade had already been felt as a result of the Anglo-Irish Free Trade Area). Far more important were the dynamic gains from integration for industry (enhanced attractiveness of Ireland as a location for overseas manufacturing investors, further possibilities of specialisation for existing firms) and the long-term price gains expected in agriculture (see Chapter 11).

At its simplest level, the EU is a customs union. Hence trade among member states cannot be impeded without reference to the Commission in

Brussels. The conduct of this trade is governed by the Union's policies, such as competition policy and the CAP, and it is in this context that allegations of predatory pricing, implicit subsidies or other unfair trading practices have to be investigated. The government's control over trade with countries outside the EU is similarly circumscribed. Extra-EU trade falls within the ambit of the EU's Common Commercial Policy. Under this, a common external tariff applies to imports from all countries outside the Union. However, there are numerous exceptions: the members of the European Economic Area, those developing countries which are party to the Generalised System of Preferences, the Mediterranean Agreement or the Lomé Convention, and Eastern European countries which have signed special agreements with the Union.[8]

The 1992 Programme

The 1992 Programme originated with the White Paper on Completing the Internal Market in 1985. This paper recognised that the existence and growing incidence of internal barriers to trade was not only contrary to the spirit of the Treaty of Rome, but also posed a danger to the degree of integration that had already been achieved. The White Paper became effective with the passing of the Single European Act 1987, which set a target date of December 1992 for the creation of a unified internal market. This was to be accomplished by removing all remaining impediments to the free movement of goods, persons, services and capital. Of particular concern were three types of non-tariff barriers: (i) *fiscal* barriers, understood as emanating from different indirect tax regimes among member states; (ii) *physical* barriers, such as delays at customs posts, administrative hassle; and (iii) *technical* barriers, defined as technical stipulations with the objective of protecting the home market from competition such as public rules, technical standards and regulations, barriers to entry and public monopolies.

A considerable amount of study was undertaken both at aggregate and sectoral levels in order to identify the expected effects of 1992 on the Irish economy.[9] Among the positive aspects, the most significant was the expansion of exports to be expected from improved access to continental EU markets, especially for machinery, high-technology goods and foodstuffs previously subject to non-tariff barriers. Given its high export propensity, and high import content of exports, Ireland stood to gain from the reduction in physical access costs following the abolition of customs frontiers. These reductions were expected to be particularly relevant to firms contemplating further investment in Ireland. Much of the 1992 debate focussed on how industry could be expected to respond.

On the negative side, the most pressing concern related to the cost of fiscal approximation. This could have involved a large loss of tax revenue to the exchequer, with the reduction of Ireland's VAT rate and the high excise taxes on alcohol, tobacco and petrol to an EU average (see Chapter 5).

However, the Commission adopted a much more flexible approach to fiscal approximation than was originally expected.

The completion of the Single European Market also raised concerns about the future of Irish service industries such as insurance, banking and construction, in the context of strong EU competition on both domestic and European markets (see Chapter 10). While Irish consumers might gain from lower prices, in manufacturing industry there was some fear that overseas' subsidiaries might be rationalised, with facilities being withdrawn from Ireland to the Continent. The 1992 Programme also has consequences for agriculture in terms of both technical barriers and the reduction of CAP expenditure but consideration of this aspect is deferred until Chapter 11.

The 1992 Programme was concerned with the free movement of capital and labour as well as goods and services. The Programme provided for the elimination of the last elements of exchange controls. This, combined with the increasing ease of communication, has made capital extremely mobile, both inwards and outwards of the Irish economy. The Programme also aimed to consolidate the rights of citizens of any member state in the EU to work and study in another member state. However, labour mobility within the Union is still very low, and anglophone countries continue to be the most popular destinations for Irish emigrants.

Regional Convergence: the Role of the Structural Funds
The EU has been associated with considerable net trade creation, yet there is concern that the benefits from trade and integration have not been evenly distributed. Significant regional disparities in economic performance persist and some theories suggest that, far from converging, these disparities will widen over time in the absence of an appropriate regional policy. Furthermore, the burden of EU unemployment has fallen disproportionately on the poorer regions, exacerbating their problems of underdevelopment. The EU Structural Funds were created specifically in order to alleviate the economic problems of the poorer regions.

Ireland is a large net recipient of funds from the EU. Most consist of non-repayable transfers, but more resources are obtained at more or less commercial rates from the European Investment Bank. The largest single item is the transfer under the Guarantee Section of the European Agricultural Guidance and Guarantee Fund (EAGGF), designed to achieve the objectives of the Common Agricultural Policy (see Chapter 11). This takes the form of subsidies on agricultural exports sold on the world market and other supports. In addition, there are three Structural Funds: the European Regional Development Fund (ERDF), which is designed to assist the development and structural adjustment of the poorer regions of the EU, the European Social Fund (ESF), which aims to increase the geographical and occupational mobility of EU workers through vocational training, and the Guidance Section of the EAGGF, devoted to structural change in the agricultural sector. The Treaty on European Union (Maastricht, 1993) established a fourth fund, the Cohesion Fund, which aims to improve transport infrastructure, and is available only to the four poorest member states – Ireland, Greece, Portugal and Spain. An estimated IR£2,255 million was transferred to the Irish economy under the various headings in 1994 (Table 9.6). Over the decade to 1994, the average annual subvention from Brussels amounted to 5.7 per cent of Irish GNP. This is by any standards an enormously generous scale of assistance.

Table 9.6
Ireland's Net Receipts (IR£m) from the European Union

	1985	1990	1994
ERDF	76	225	306
ESF	141	128	321
EAGGF guidance	56	94	170
EAGGF guarantee	837	1,287	1,300
Cohesion fund	n.a.	n.a.	145
Other	18	7	13
Gross receipts	1,128	1,741	2,255
Less Irish govt. contributions	214	284	493
Net receipts	914	1,457	1,762
Net receipts (% GNP)	(5.8)	(6.4)	(5.7)

Source: Department of Finance, Dublin 1994.

Concern that deeper integration would intensify regional tensions resulted in new measures to deal with 'economic and social cohesion'. The 1992 programme agreed that the Structural Funds were to be doubled in size, and their role in the EU's overall regional policy has been more clearly defined:

> Regional policy must be directed at enabling the peripheral regions to compete, not at subsidising them in continued deprivation: it must be far more than financial transfers, and those transfers should be directed towards reducing costs and raising productivity; it should mean a regional dimension to every policy, and not simply a fund, however well spent.[10]

A number of measures to improve the effectiveness of the funds have been implemented. Under the programme to 1999, they are to be targeted specifically at the development of physical and social infrastructure to enable Ireland and other peripheral regions to compete successfully with other EU countries; EU money is complemented by government and private sector funding; and the effectiveness of the funds is to be subject to regular review.[11]

A Community Support Framework (CSF) for Ireland set out the development strategy by which the Structural Funds are to be administered.

The CSF was then given effect by operational programmes which detailed the measures to be taken. The current CSF covers the five years from 1994-99. Total funding for the period (including allocations under the Cohesion Fund) will amount to IR£5.75 billion. The allocation of funds is determined according to priority sectors for the period: industry and human resources, with emphasis on transport and tourism.

The purpose of the Structural Funds is to enable Ireland to compete unaided in the Single Market. With the likely enlargement of the EU (see below), Ireland must recognise that the generous level of funding which it receives at present will be a thing of the past. Experience shows that it is not sufficient to rely on EU regional policy to improve domestic competitiveness. Domestic policy must also be appropriately managed. Sean Cromien, former Secretary of the Department of Finance, observed that 'it is the quality of the small decisions that differentiates the successful economies from unsuccessful', and these small decisions, more often than not, are taken by national governments.[12]

EU Enlargement
European integration concerns more than the deepening of EU integration among existing member states. It also involves widening the number of participants. Indeed, it can be viewed as a sign of great achievement that almost all of the EU's immediate neighbours have expressed a wish to join.

The candidates fall into three groups: first in line were the prosperous former-EFTA countries. Not only did they meet the strict criteria for membership, the level of cooperation between the EU and EFTA was already substantial, with the European Economic Area in existence since 1994. Sweden, Finland and Austria joined the EU on 1 January, 1995 but Norway, Iceland and Switzerland decided not to follow their example. Turkey, Cyprus and Malta have also made formal applications. Also waiting in the wings are the transition states of Eastern Europe. It is understood on both sides that the Eastern European states will eventually join, but given the level of economic restructuring needed for transition to the market system, and the huge performance differentials between East and West, full membership is still a long way off.

Some people believe that a wider Union will of necessity be shallower, as it becomes increasingly difficult to secure agreement on the various dimensions of integration. For example, a larger number of net recipients of EU funding would place severe limits on the ambitions of a revised programme of regional development for the Union. Current net recipients of EU funding, such as Ireland, would lose out as newer, poorer countries join. However, provided the EU adheres to its strict eligibility criteria when appraising new applicants, and admits only those countries which can participate fully in the integration process, there is no compelling reason why a wider Union need be a weaker Union.

Maastricht: the Treaty on European Union

The Treaty on European Union was signed in the Dutch city of Maastricht in February 1992 and became effective in November 1993. It was the result of a general consensus that the EU needed to evolve in response to a changing external and internal environment. The major item on the external agenda was the collapse of communism in Eastern Europe and the subsequent reunification of Germany. Germany wanted to ease worries among other member states that its unification would interrupt progress towards deeper European integration. Further, institutional changes were needed to facilitate the enlargement of the Union. Internal motivations were based on 'spillover logic'. It was felt (i) that the economic union could advance no further without strengthening the political and social dimensions of integration and (ii) that the internal market would never be truly completed, and its continued existence might even be endangered, in the absence of a single currency.

The resultant Treaty has a structure resembling *three 'pillars'*. The *first* and most important pillar outlines the conditions and timetable for the achievement of Economic and Monetary Union (EMU) by the end of the century. The agreement of Ireland and other peripheral regions was secured through a further expansion of the Structural Funds and the introduction of the new Cohesion Fund. The UK and Denmark secured a special 'opt-out' clause granting them permission to decline participation in the single currency programme. Following objections by the UK (tacitly backed by other member states), the 'Social Charter' was not included in the Treaty proper. Its status was reduced to that of a protocol. The first pillar also provides for the extension of the EU's powers to cover a broad range of policy areas: health, education, consumer protection, transport, tourism, energy, the environment and culture.

The *second pillar* brings justice and home affairs under the ambit of EU policy, addressing fears that the removal of internal borders would reduce member states' ability to control crime, international terrorism, drug-trafficking and illegal immigration. The *third pillar* provides for a Common Foreign and Security Policy. This is an important element in a more integrated Europe. It involves the revival of the dormant Western European Area to the status of a common EU defence force, linked to NATO. Ireland objected on grounds of its neutrality, and an opt-out clause was granted.

The various 'opt-out' protocols, combined with the failure of the Danes to ratify the Treaty first time round, reflect internal disagreements as to how the EU should evolve. While a core group led by Germany push towards deeper integration, objections by other member states threaten to undermine this progress. The likely outcome could be a 'variable-geometry' Europe, with members 'opting in' and 'opting out' of different policy dimensions.

Ireland and the GATT

Given that Ireland no longer has an autonomous trade policy, it participates in GATT negotiations as a member of the EU. GATT (the General Agreement on Tariffs and Trade) was established in the post-war period with the objective of liberalising world trade, by reducing barriers to trade and eliminating discriminatory behaviour. This support accords with the objective of the EU's Common Commercial Policy, which is, in the words of the Treaty of Rome, 'to contribute to the harmonious development of world trade'. The EU has played an active role in GATT negotiations for multilateral trade liberalisation. Indeed, EU participation in previous rounds has been crucial to their success.

The Uruguay Round of GATT trade negotiations commenced in September 1986, and finally concluded in December 1993. It was the eighth GATT Round, and by far the most ambitious to date, covering new areas such as trade in services and agriculture, as well as addressing problems posed by non-tariff barriers. The draft agreement provided for further tariff reductions, increased control of non-tariff barriers (including the phasing-out of the Multifibre Arrangement[13]) and more disciplined agricultural support. The agreement also provided for the evolution of the GATT into a new World Trade Organisation, thus providing a more solid institutional basis to international rules and disciplines governing trade.

The implications of the Uruguay Round Agreement for the Irish economy have been examined in detail by Matthews.[14] As a small, trade-dependent country, Ireland is expected to gain from more liberal trade. Irish exporters will enjoy improved access to important extra-EU markets, notably North America and South-East Asia. Moreover, the agreement is expected to restore confidence in the multilateral trading system. This will have a positive impact on world growth and trade. Ireland will benefit indirectly, assuming an increase in world trade translates into increased demand for Irish exports. Against this, the agreement will erode some of the gains associated with our preferential access to other member states' markets. Third-country exports are expected to increase their penetration of Irish and other EU markets. Another adverse effect of the Round is the reduction in receipts for Irish agriculture. Matthews' findings suggest that the overall effect on the Irish economy will be positive, but small, and the benefits will be unevenly distributed, gains for the advanced manufacturing sectors being counterbalanced by losses for the clothing and textile industry and for agriculture.

Matthews attempts to quantify the effects of the agreement for the main sectors of the Irish economy. Comparing the effects of the agreement with the status quo scenario, he forecasts job losses/gains as follows: agriculture (-10,500), industry (+4,550) and services (+6,302). Thus the overall effect of the agreement is an estimated 352 additional jobs.

4 INFLATION, THE EXCHANGE RATE AND EMU

The above analysis shows how Ireland's involvement in European and world trade and payments has steadily been extended. As integration proceeds, the task of recording trade and capital movements becomes increasingly difficult. A logical next step is to ask whether separate currencies (and exchange rates) fulfil any useful function in such circumstances. Many believe that they do not. Hence the argument for a European monetary union with a single currency. Such a regime, however, would require certain agreed restraints on the economic policies of the member states in order to be effective. Hence the debate about Economic and Monetary Union (EMU) involves a wider range of issues than the technical aspects of monetary union (see Chapter 6).

Before proceeding to discuss EMU, it is necessary to examine how an essential precondition to EMU – the convergence of Ireland's inflation rate to the EU level – has been achieved.

Ireland's inflation experience in the last decade can be broken down into three phases. First, high inflation prevailed in the early 1980s, peaking at 20 per cent in 1981. Second, steady disinflation took place between 1981 and 1986. Third, since 1987 Ireland's inflation appears to have stabilised at a low level; in the early 1990s it was consistently below Germany's. A decade ago, few would have believed this possible.

Explaining Irish Inflation
Irish inflation has, at one time or another, been attributed to three types of influences: 'imported' price increases, government policy (fiscal and monetary), and 'wage-push' pressures caused by trade unions. These will be analysed in turn.

Given the small size of the Irish economy and its high ratio of exports and imports to GNP, a rise in the price of traded goods must, in the absence of powerful countervailing forces, have a strong impact on the domestic price level. Exactly how strong an impact depends on the 'pass-through effect' from import prices to domestic prices, wages and salaries and profit margins. In Ireland, this effect has been found to operate quickly and effectively. Hence two possible approaches to an anti-inflationary policy are suggested: (i) operate a 'go-it-alone' exchange rate policy with regular exchange rate revaluations to neutralise higher imported prices; or (ii) participate in an exchange rate arrangement which links the Irish pound to low-inflation currencies. Ireland chose the latter course in 1979 through membership of the European Monetary System (EMS) and participation in its exchange rate mechanism (ERM) (see Chapter 6). The UK joined the EMS, but did not participate in the ERM until 1990.

Under the EMS, each member of the system has a fixed 'central exchange rate' against the European Currency Unit (ECU). For each country there is a percentage band which determines upper and lower intervention limits at which central banks must support the currency. Prior to 1993 the band was ±2.25 per cent; it now stands at ±15 per cent.[15] Thus member currencies are pegged to the ECU, which is in turn a weighted average of the member currencies. The logic of the system is that the balance of payments adjustment should rely on internal measures such as 'competitiveness' and expenditure-reducing/expanding policies (as described above) rather than exchange rate changes.

In March 1979, as a result of Ireland's participation in the ERM, the one-to-one parity between the Irish pound and sterling was broken and the currency union between Britain and Ireland which dated back to 1826 came to an end (see Chapter 6). Since Britain did not participate in the EMS exchange rate arrangements, the Irish pound/sterling rate fluctuated throughout the 1980s, often in the process causing difficulties for the Irish authorities. It was hoped that the accession of the UK to the ERM in 1990 would ensure a more stable relationship for the 1990s. But later events proved otherwise.

However, leaving the currency crisis aside for the present, the benefits of the ERM for Ireland are worthy of exploration. The tying of the Irish pound to a low-inflation 'anchor' currency, the Deutsche mark, helped Ireland to attain a low level of inflation. Following from this, the gap between Irish and continental interest rates narrowed, to the benefit of the exchequer and the economy.

But these benefits were not earned without cost. In the initial period there were serious competitive misalignments caused by the failure to take account of the price/wage implications of the new exchange rate regime. A competitive loss of about 40 per cent *vis-à-vis* the continental ERM countries was incurred between 1979 and 1986 which has never been recovered.[16] Another cost, inherent in exchange rate systems of this type, is that the Irish economy was locked into an interest rate regime which responded more to the needs of the centre than to those of the periphery. In this manner, high German interest rates after reunification were forced on the other member states, thus exacerbating their problems of recession and unemployment. There is little a small country can do about this, save to ensure that the size of the absolute gap between centre and periphery interest rates is not widened by domestic policy mistakes, such as excessive borrowing, shortening maturity of debt profile or inadequate external reserves.

At the time of the EMS negotiations, it was expected in Ireland that membership would involve transference to a less inflationary exchange rate regime. This expectation was based on the small open economy model of inflation, outlined in Chapters 3 and 6. Given that most of Ireland's trade is with the UK, the inflation rate (P) is determined in the following manner: $P_{IRL} = W_{UK}(P_{UK} + E_{UK}) + W_{EMS}(P_{EMS} + E_{EMS})$ where the Ws refer to trade weights and the Es to the rate of change in the Irish price of foreign currencies.

If Ireland chooses E_{UK} to be zero, as it did prior to 1979 (i.e. to have a fixed exchange rate with sterling), E_{EMS} is the rate of change in the sterling price of foreign currencies. An essential element of this argument is that if, for example, P_{UK} = 20 per cent and P_{EMS} = 5 per cent, sterling will devalue by 15 per cent annually *vis-à-vis* the EMS, i.e. the exchange rate will respond to differentials in inflation rates between the UK and EMS countries. (This is the so-called purchasing power parity view of exchange rates.) Therefore, P_{UK} = (P_{EMS} + E_{EMS}) and, from the equation above, P_{IRL} = P_{UK}. The key feature is the assumption that causation runs from the exchange rate to the rate of inflation and not *vice versa*.

With EMS membership in 1979, the expectation was that Irish inflation would fall substantially, since EMS inflation rates had been systematically lower than UK rates in the previous decade. This did not happen until well into the 1980s. What went wrong? First, purchasing power parity broke down, i.e. (P_{UK} + E_{UK}) greatly exceeded P_{EMS}. The significant real appreciation in sterling fed into Irish prices. Second, instead of this leading to a large shift in Irish purchasing from the UK to the Continent (i.e. to a dramatic change in trade weights), trade patterns remained broadly stable in the short run. In the early years of EMS, therefore, a substantial part of Ireland's post-EMS inflation was still 'imported' from the UK.[17] The Irish authorities could, in principle, have counteracted 'imported' inflation from the UK by a revaluation of the Irish pound within the EMS. Fear of the competitive consequences of such action because of slow downward adjustment of income claims was the main reason why this option was not followed, though strongly recommended in some quarters.

The nature of this dilemma became acute during the Irish devaluation crises of 1986 and 1992 (see Chapter 6). In each case, the problem arose because of the weakness of sterling relative to the core EMS currencies. Both events demonstrated just how vulnerable the Irish pound is to sterling volatility. The policy of the Irish authorities was to anchor the Irish pound as closely as possible to the low-inflation currencies of the ERM. However, currency dealers took the view that Ireland's high unemployment and relatively rigid cost structure would not prove capable of coping with the loss of competitiveness *vis-à-vis* its major trading partner. Thus sterling, rather than the Deutsche mark, proved the decisive factor in determining the value of the Irish pound. When international currency markets forced the pound sterling to leave the ERM in September 1992, pressure on the Irish pound was immediate. A rapid appreciation of the Irish pound against sterling, resulting in a huge loss of competitiveness for Irish exporters, combined with increasing speculative pressure eventually forced the Irish authorities to devalue in January 1993 (see Chapter 6).

Inflation and Domestic Policies

The statement that, for a given exchange rate, inflation is externally determined needs careful interpretation. It does not mean that domestic inflationary pressures are unimportant. Domestic inflationary pressure in excess of 'imported' levels results in firms, hotels and individuals being driven out of business. It means uncompetitive domestic production and more imported goods in Irish shops. The effects of domestically-induced inflation are 'suppressed' through higher unemployment levels, more import penetration and worsening balance of payments deficits.

A link with a stronger currency does not *per se* make inflation fall painlessly. Having decided on an exchange rate policy, the authorities must ensure that fiscal, monetary and incomes policies are consistent with maintaining their currency's position in the EMS (see also Chapter 6). Between 1979 and 1986, there was no such consistency evident in Ireland. Government expenditure continued to grow and borrowing escalated. Since then, a marked improvement in fiscal performance has been achieved. A sound exchange rate policy with a supportive fiscal policy is a necessary condition for an effective low-inflation strategy. Trade unions, and more generally the social partners, must also play a role.

The place of trade unions in the inflationary process is a contentious issue. The unions themselves claim that they respond to inflation but do not create it and that pay moderation can be readily secured if prices remain stable. There is an element of truth in this. Econometric studies reveal a strong relationship between earnings, on the one hand, and prices and productivity on the other hand. (Unemployment plays an insignificant role in the short run in these equations, both in Ireland and elsewhere in Western Europe.) It is equally true that trade unions have a strong temptation to put their own members' interests first. Even if all unions agreed that a cooperative solution based on low-pay norms was optimal, the incentive to individual unions to seek above-the-norm increases would remain strong.

In a small open economy, trade unions do not cause inflation but they can cause unemployment. Producers in the traded goods sector (which includes manufacturing, agriculture and exposed services ranging from software consultancy to tourism) are constrained in their pricing policy by international competition. Hence, wage claims in excess of productivity increases cannot be recouped through higher prices in the way they can be in the sheltered sector. If the trade unions succeed in forcing them through, the effect is to reduce profitability, lessen the inflow of foreign investment and deter domestic investors. Sooner or later, employment and output suffer. Trade unions and professional organisations can also impede the efficient operation of the labour market through restrictive practices and limitations on recruitment which have the effect of raising labour costs and undermining competitiveness. Strikes in vital sectors of the economy can also damage employment prospects by casting doubt on Ireland's reliability as a supplier to foreign markets. These points illustrate how 'insiders' (those in jobs) can, intentionally or otherwise, make it more difficult for 'outsiders' (the unemployed and immigrants) to find work.

The Irish government has sought to restrain these potentially destructive forces by means of centralised pay negotiations. Since 1987 there have been three formal pay agreements between the government and the social partners (see also Chapters 4, 6 and 8): the Programme for National Recovery (1987), the Programme for Economic and Social Progress (1991) and the Programme for Competitiveness and Work (1994). These agreements have been criticised for failing to give sufficient priority to the unemployment problem, and for burdening the public finances with an enlarged public sector pay bill. However, the first two agreements have had significant success in so far as they have kept pay increases in line with continental Europe. The third agreement allowed for a pay increase of 10 per cent over three years, a figure that helped to consolidate Ireland's low-inflation reputation. In addition, the maintenance of a stable pay system has undoubtedly helped the development of the traded sector and the employment-creating potential of the services sector.

Ready for EMU?
The currency crisis of 1992-93 seriously damaged the credibility of the ERM and the process of EMU, at least in the short run. It has now become fashionable in some quarters to rubbish the ERM and the process of EMU. However, others argue that, despite the crises and the scepticism, the EMU proposal remains on course, even if only a subset of member states agree to go ahead initially. At that stage, the Irish government will have to decide if it is in Ireland's best interest to join the 'fast-track' countries or if it would be preferable to defer monetary union until the majority of EU countries have joined.

The EMU debate began in earnest in 1990. It was proposed as a logical next step for countries which were becoming increasingly interdependent. Monetary union would involve the irrevocable tying of exchange rate parities, a unified monetary policy and ultimately a single currency. A central monetary authority, the European Central Bank, would exercise control over monetary policy and member-country budgetary policies would be closely monitored. Politically, EMU is one more step towards an ever-closer European Union. In addition, there are some very good economic reasons for EMU. The principal gains from an EMU with a single currency are (i) a reduction in foreign exchange transactions costs, (ii) greater transparency of prices in different member states, (iii) consolidation of the Single Market and (iv) increased certainty for business. Furthermore, an autonomous European Central Bank is likely to have greater success in achieving lower inflation for all participating countries. At the same time, there are some important arguments against EMU. The main objection is that EMU will erode individual countries' sovereignty in relation to monetary policy. This is a serious qualification for larger countries. For Ireland, however, this loss of sovereignty has caused fewer misgivings. This is because monetary independence for a small country is something of an illusion in the context of mobile international capital and a strong low-inflation core in continental Europe (see Chapter 6). Indeed, in so far as each member state will have a voice in determining a unified European monetary policy, the proposed system represents an increase in sovereignty for Ireland.

The Maastricht Treaty mapped out the route to EMU in three distinct stages (see Chapter 6):

Stage 1, which began on 1 July 1990, concerned the completion of the SEM, including the abolition of all remaining capital controls. It also aimed at greater convergence in economic performance in the EU through the strengthening of economic and monetary policy coordination.

Stage 2 started on 1 January 1994, with the creation of the European Monetary Institute (EMI), located in Frankfurt. The EMI was intended to be the precursor of the European Central Bank (ECB). Its functions include strengthening monetary policy cooperation between the central banks of the member states and reporting on the convergence of economic policies in preparation for Stage 3.

Stage 3 was scheduled to commence some time following the Inter-Governmental Conference in 1996. At the start of this final stage, exchange rates between the national currencies will be irrevocably fixed, and the ECB will commence operations. Eligibility for EMU will be judged on the basis of a number of convergence criteria: level of inflation, interest rates, budget deficit/GDP, debt/GDP ratios and exchange rate stability within the ERM. The third stage has to begin at the latest on 1 January 1999, with the participation of only those countries which meet the eligibility criteria.

Ireland's policy in the medium term is to ensure that it satisfies the Maastricht criteria. As other chapters have shown, it is in the national interest to pursue these objectives, regardless of EMU participation. Ireland is on target with all but its debt/GDP ratio,[18] and it is likely that a commitment to reduce debt on an ongoing basis will suffice. This is not to say that Ireland does not have serious problems with the prospect of EMU. A key issue from an Irish perspective is whether or when the UK will agree to participate. If the UK decided to join, then full participation as soon as possible would clearly be in Ireland's economic interest. If the UK declined to participate, this would pose a dilemma, both in economic and political terms. The UK remains an extremely important trading partner with which most of our price-sensitive trade is still conducted. One can expect a lively debate on this problem as 1999 approaches.

Many take it for granted that the UK will not participate in EMU. What does this mean for Ireland? Some argue that we should participate in EMU regardless of the UK's decision. The advantages are many: monetary union ensures inflation is kept low, encourages investment by multinational enterprises with a view to export to the Continent and strengthens the financial services industry. Against this, the currency turmoil of recent years has demonstrated the vulnerability of the Irish pound to sterling volatility. There are undisputed arguments for policies to reduce volatility against sterling. Indigenous industry is most trade dependent on the UK; hence new and small Irish firms are most vulnerable to exchange rate fluctuations *vis-à-vis* sterling. Volatility can inflict serious damage on the development of indigenous industry, and also on employment. While trade dependence with the UK is significant at 31 per cent, dependent employment is probably closer to 50 per cent.[19] With the priority being given to the reduction of unemployment, the exposure of indigenous industry to this kind of exchange rate risk is highly undesirable. Furthermore, if the government is to make any sizeable inroad into the level of long-term unemployment, it must strive to make it attractive for business to hire more low- and moderately-skilled workers. These are the very kind of jobs which are most vulnerable to UK competition. On a more political note, integration with Northern Ireland would be facilitated by a stable exchange rate with sterling.

Suppose, as many would expect, that Ireland goes ahead with EMU while sterling floats. How will the Irish authorities cope with the problem of a decline in the value of sterling? One could expect imports to rise, exports to fall, and the balance of trade to worsen. With devaluation no longer available as a policy option, some other adjustment mechanism will be needed. This brings us back to the discussion of policy options to deal with a balance of payments deficit. Irish participation in EMU in such circumstances depends on the development of policy to increase the flexibility and competitiveness of the Irish economy.

Note, however, that UK participation in EMU is not the only cause for concern. The success of EMU and in particular of the objective of price stability hinge critically on the institutions and operations of the ECB, and of its precursor, the EMI. To assume that the ECB will automatically deliver low inflation takes insufficient account of the difficulties a new and untried institution may encounter in achieving credibility. The establishment of an autonomous ECB and the implementation of a unified monetary and exchange rate policy require significant preparatory work in technical and institutional areas during Stage 2. This preparatory work involves detailing the operational rules and procedures for the ECB, including those concerning the execution of monetary and exchange rate policy. The success of EMU hinges critically on whether these institutional arrangements will actually work.

5 CONCLUSION

A major theme of this chapter has been the growing importance of European integration. Closer European integration will impinge on all aspects of the Irish economy. As integration proceeds, Ireland will increasingly assume the features of a regional economy of the EU. This is the context in which analysis of Ireland's balance of payments and inflation must henceforth be undertaken.

The two global trends which have emerged in recent years have been: (i) the trend to liberalise economies to give greater scope to market forces; and (ii) the internationalisation of services and factor markets. Continued growth for the Irish economy will depend on the ability of firms in Ireland to compete successfully in this global market.

The EU has led the way in opening its markets to competition among member states. Deeper integration offers the prospects of a more prosperous Europe. With careful management, there is no reason why Ireland should not participate in, and benefit from, this process. Foley and Mulreany's conclusion that by the early 1990s the Irish economy was 'in a better position to compete in the single market than at any time in the 1980s' remains valid.[20] As a small trade-dependent country, Ireland also stands to benefit from the successful completion of the GATT Uruguay Round. Furthermore, Ireland is well on target to meet the convergence criteria for EMU as specified by the Maastricht Treaty.

Ireland's balance of payments position offers reassurance that sustained fast growth will not be cut short by a balance of payments crisis – as has happened in many countries in the past. As this chapter has shown, the 1980s saw the transition from deficit to surplus on the balance of payments current account, and this surplus has persisted to date. Provided the export sector remains in a healthy state, the balance of payments should be able to withstand the effects of greater competition and there is a reasonable prospect that the more unpalatable adjustment mechanisms evaluated in this chapter will not have to be used.

In an economy such as Ireland's, inflation can best be understood by looking first at the exchange rate policy and analysing its inflationary implications in terms of an 'imported inflation' model. The second step is to recognise the role of government, trade unions and other internal factors which play a decisive role in determining whether the exchange rate regime is sustainable. By the 1990s, Irish inflation has converged to the EU level. This does not mean that inflation is no longer important. The focus of policy has simply shifted to the maintenance of the current low inflation level.

It is clear that the balance of payments, inflation and the exchange rate are interlinked phenomena in an economy such as Ireland's. Inflation through its effects on competitiveness can have implications for the balance of payments. The balance of payments profile, by determining the sustainability of a given exchange rate, can have an important bearing on the rate of inflation. What the Irish economy has needed is an exchange rate regime which exerts downward pressure on the level of inflation and, within that regime, an exchange rate which ensures a strong level of competitiveness relative to our major trading partners. Since the EMS failed so dramatically to maintain Ireland's competitive position, it would be foolhardy to rely on any institutional arrangement, even EMU, to achieve this aim. Hence domestic policy must be targeted at improving competitiveness levels to enable Ireland to reap the full benefits from participation in the global market.

Endnotes

1 M. Brülhart and D. McAleese, 'Intra-industry Trade and Industrial Adjustment: The Irish Experience', *Economic and Social Review,* January 1995.
2 A. Murphy, 'The Irish Economy: Celtic Tiger or Tortoise?', Money Markets International, Dublin, November 1994.
3 M. Gallagher and D. McAleese, 'Ireland's Trade Dependence on the UK', *Irish Banking Review,* Spring 1994.
4 J. Durkan, 'Indigenous Services', in A. Foley and M. Mulreany (editors), *The Single European Market and the Irish Economy,* Institute of Public Administration, Dublin 1990.
5 OECD, *Ireland: Economic Survey 1980-90,* OECD, Paris 1989; D. Mc Aleese and M. Gallagher, 'The Red and the Black: Developments in Irish Trade in the 1980s', *Irish Banking Review,* Autumn 1991.
6 For a valuable analysis of this issue, see A. Leddin and B. Walsh, *The Macroeconomy of Ireland,* Gill and Macmillan, Dublin 1990.
7 For a stimulating discussion of this issue, see L. Wrigley, 'Corporate Strategy and the Competitive Factor', in D. McAleese (editor), *Competition and Industry: the Irish Experience,* Gill and Macmillan, Dublin 1989.
8 D. McAleese, 'EC External Trade Policy', in A. El-Agraa (editor), The *Economics of the European Community* (fourth edition), Harvester-Wheatsheaf, Hemel Hempstead 1994.
9 A. Foley and M. Mulreany, *op.cit;* P. Keatinge (editor), *Ireland and the Single European Act,* Pinter, London 1991. For a brief overview of the issues, see D. McAleese and A. Matthews, 'The Single European Act and Ireland: Implications for a Small Member State', *Journal of Common Market Studies,* September 1987.
10 M. F. Doyle, 'Regional Policy and European Economic Integration', in Committee for the Study of Economic and Monetary Union, *Report on Economic and Monetary Union in the European Union* (Delors Report), Luxembourg 1989, p.79.
11 A. Matthews, *Managing the EU Structural Funds in Ireland,* Cork University Press, Cork 1994.
12 S. Cromien, 'The Implications of the Single Market for Economic Management', in Foley and Mulreany, *op. cit.,* p.218.
13 The EU has engaged in successive Multifibre Arrangements (MFAs) with textile and clothing-producing developing countries. The MFA is a voluntary export restraint, whereby the developing countries agree to restrict the volume of their exports of clothing and textiles to the EU. It is to be phased out under the Uruguay Round.
14 A. Matthews, 'Implications of the GATT Uruguay Round for the Irish Economy', in S. Cantillon, J. Curtis and J. FitzGerald, *Economic Perspectives for the Medium Term,* ESRI, Dublin 1994.
15 There have been a number of exceptions. Italy, Spain and the UK had 6 per cent bands under the previous system and, under the present system, the Netherlands has committed to a 2.25 per cent band *vis-à-vis* the DM.
16 H. Ungerer *et al, The European Monetary System: Developments and Prospectives* (Occasional Paper no. 73), International Monetary Fund, Washington DC 1990.
17 The *'imported inflation'* model was first applied to Ireland in a series of articles in the mid-1970s. See P.T. Geary, 'World Prices and the Inflationary Process in a Small Open Economy: the Case of Ireland', *Economic and Social Review,* July 1976. A more recent

empirical analysis is provided in T. Callan and J. FitzGerald 'Price Discrimination in Ireland: Effects of Changes in Exchange Rates and Exchange Rate Regimes', *Economic and Social Review,* January 1989.

18 European Monetary Institute, *1st Annual Report,* Frankfurt 1994.

19 Ruairí Quinn, Minister for Finance, addressing the Dáil on 28 February 1995.

20 Foley and Mulreany, *op cit.*

PART IV

POLICY ISSUES
AT A
SECTORAL
LEVEL

CHAPTER 10

Competition and Efficiency in the Services Sector

*John Fingleton**

1 INTRODUCTION

A service is an output that is consumed at the moment of its production. The fact that production and consumption are simultaneous means that a service is usually physically intangible and, as a result of being non-transportable, has traditionally been non-traded. Services are important in the economy, constituting up to 75 per cent of output in many developed economies and still growing.

For all economic purposes, a service is just like a physical good. A service can be used either for direct consumption or as an input to production: a music recital or a telephone call between friends is direct consumption; consultancy or a business telephone call is an input to production and is consumed indirectly. Services have direct demand from consumers and derived demand via producers, and individuals get utility from consuming services and from consuming goods which use services as inputs.

The differences between a service and a physical good are that a service is intangible and largely non-traded. Although these differences are not relevant for economic analysis and welfare analysis, they have been responsible for consistent discrimination in economic policy against the services sector in favour of the traded sectors of agriculture and manufacturing industry. This discrimination is an international phenomenon that continues at present and that is based on flawed thinking. It has resulted in the services sector being the poor relation of the economic sectors, taking a back seat to both agriculture and industry in terms of government policy and state aids, at national and international levels.

The discrimination against the non-traded sectors of the economy can be traced back to the mercantilists of the seventeenth century who viewed trade

* I would like to thank David Hegarty and Michael McGrath for help with acquiring data and John O'Hagan and Paulo Moura for comments on various drafts.

as the source of all wealth.[1] Mercantilists defined national wealth as the stock of gold in the economy and advocated a balance of payments surplus to accumulate gold. That such a policy is based on unsound principles is best illustrated by taking the most extreme view: an economy that exported all its produce and imported nothing would be wealthy in gold, but its citizens would consume nothing and have zero welfare. The flaw in the mercantilist doctrine was the false identification of society's welfare with production rather than consumption.

Although extreme mercantilist views were successfully overthrown by later economists, the policy of accumulating wealth via a trade surplus survived and discrimination against services still continued because of the simultaneity of production and consumption. Adam Smith contrasted the productive labour of a manufacturer with the unproductive labour of a servant.

> There is one sort of labour which adds to the value of the subject upon which it is bestowed: There is another which has no such effect. The former, as it produces a value, may be called productive; the latter, unproductive labour......A man grows rich by employing a multitude of manufacturers: he grows poor, by maintaining a multitude of menial servants.[2]

Smith moved beyond the mercantilists, recognising that services contribute to welfare, but he double-counted the contribution of physical output to welfare in two ways. First, because a service may not easily be stored or transported (production and consumption cannot be separated), a service was seen solely as consumption, whereas a physical good appeared to have a separate value in production. Second, because physical goods yield a flow of consumption services, Smith implicitly suggested that a physical good can be consumed and then resold, although this clearly counts consumption twice. As a result of this double-counting of the value of physical output, Smith emphasised physical output similar to the mercantilist emphasis on gold. Both are flawed because the value of all output is determined solely by its value in consumption as measured by the price paid by (and hence utility of) consumers. Hence a service is, for welfare purpose, no different from physical output. The contribution of output to welfare does not depend on whether it is physically tangible or whether it is traded: arguments to the contrary implicitly involve double-counting.

The doctrine that the traded sector holds the greatest potential for growth still prevails. Non-traded output is obviously constrained by domestic demand whereas traded output appears unconstrained because a small open economy may sell as much as it likes on international markets at the world price. The growth of demand for services is seen as entirely dependent on the growth of the traded sectors: as with Adam Smith, a service is consumed by someone who grows rich from trade.

Technological advancement and membership of the European Union (EU) and the World Trade Organisation (WTO, formerly GATT) mean that services are increasingly traded. The fact that policy now emphasises support for traded services illustrates that the doctrine of growth through trade still thrives, and does not reflect any genuine reassessment of this false doctrine. A major report to the government in 1993 advocated the extension of many of the privileges awarded to industry to the traded services sector on the basis that:

> Non-traded activities are in effect dependent on the internationally traded sector.... Those activities...that are internationally traded determine the rates at which the economy can grow.[3]

The view of the demand for traded sector output as unconstrained is very misleading. With imports equal to exports, the output of the traded sector is constrained by the sum of the domestic demand for traded goods (i.e. that part not exported) and the domestic demand for imported goods. Thus increasing exports is only worthwhile if the revenues earned are required for consumption of foreign goods. Although less obvious, the same logic prevails with a balance of payments deficit due to a high exchange rate.

The other basis for discrimination against services, because they are intangible, is more subtle. Unlike theory, policy eschews complex reasoning: there is in general a psychological tendency to give more weight to simple theories than to correct ones that happen to require hard thinking and rigorous analysis. For instance, it requires effort to explain why the labour of a school teacher adds value in the same way as that of a farmer, or why the labour of a civil servant is productive. The belief that tangible physical output is more productive than intangible service output, although without any intellectual or theoretical foundation, still prevails and is clearly manifest in industrial policy in many countries.[4]

In summary, both economic thought and economic policy reveal that the services sector has been seen as dependent on the traded sector and discriminated against because services are intangible and non-traded, even though such a policy has poor economic rationale.

This chapter will present the view that, for policy purposes, it may be more appropriate to view the traded sector as dependent on the non-traded sector. The traded sector is exposed to international competition and production is expected to be efficient. By contrast the non-traded sector is not similarly exposed and competition may be weaker. This lack of competition, especially in semi-state and government services, but also in the private sector, imposes high costs and competitive disadvantage on the traded sector and lowers the standard of living for all.

In order to elucidate these points fully, this chapter shall begin by outlining the salient feature of services in general (Section 2) in order to provide a methodological framework for subsequent work. Section 3 examines the performance and potential of the services sector of the Irish economy in a European context and outlines the manner in which government policy has favoured the agricultural and industrial sectors. A high proportion of services are produced in monopolistic markets and this makes competition policy (including policy to improve efficiency in government services) a critical policy instrument in the growth of the services sector and the economy more generally. The welfare effects of competition are outlined in Section 4 as a preparation for a general discussion of competition policy in Section 5. Finally, Section 6 examines the performance of the Irish economy in terms of competition and efficiency, arguing that competition and efficiency in the services sector offer enormous potential for economic growth.

2 THE NATURE AND DIVERSITY OF SERVICES

Definition of Services

The use of the services sector in the national accounts as a residual to collect together that which is not agricultural or industry suggests an 'anti-definition' of services as that which is not physical output. In fact, many of the components of the services sector have little in common other than the simultaneity of production and consumption. The definition is so broad that it includes an enormous diversity of economic activities, from public services like education to private services like hairdressing, from high-technology, traded services like telecommunications to relatively low-technology, non-traded services like babysitting. The diversity of services has important implications for the political lobbying power of the sector when contrasted with the strong farming lobby that can be clearly identified with a physical output.

The diversity of services has long been recognised: Adam Smith included (in his description of unproductive labour) public defence, public administration, and noted that:

> In the same class must be ranked, some both of the gravest and most important, and some of the most frivolous professions: churchmen, lawyers, physicians, men of letters of all kinds; players, buffoons, musicians, opera-singers, opera dancers &c.[5]

As the services sector includes activities with very different supply and demand characteristics, sub-sectoral investigation is undertaken. In particular, the distinction between market and non-market services and the distinction between traded and non-traded services will be of interest.

This chapter only considers services that are measured in national accounts: in this sense national output and growth are proxies for consumer welfare. Clearly, services such as voluntary work and work within households for which no explicit payment is received can add to welfare. However, as no payment is made for these services, the quantity of them is not known. In addition, they are not priced so even if the quantity was known, it would not be possible to assess their contribution to welfare. This is not to suggest that this contribution is negligible: on the contrary, the increasing participation of women in the labour force means that households may now make explicit payments to others for work previously internalised without explicit payment. Thus part of the growth of services may be a measurement effect whereby activity that has always contributed to social welfare is suddenly measured in national accounts for the first time.

Government Supply of Services
Many services (e.g. justice, education) are produced by the government. These include market services that are priced in the market and for which the user pays (e.g. electricity) and non-market services (e.g. justice) that are not explicitly or fully priced in the market, although they feature in the national accounts as public expenditure funded from taxation. Whereas the growth of market services (those for which an explicit price is paid at the point of use) is determined solely by demand, this is not so for non-market services. Because non-market services are generally priced below marginal cost (often free to users), they face excess demand. The allocation of non-market services is achieved by a variety of non-price mechanisms: for example, entry to third-level education is rationed by allocating places to those students who perform best at second-level examinations. The total supply cost of non-market services must be met from taxation and the growth of non-market services is determined by the overall level of government revenue rather than by demand for non-market services. Some non-market services are produced by the private sector (e.g. charitable foundations) but these comprise only a small proportion of total output.

The principal economic rationale for government supply of services is the existence of positive externalities whereby an action by one person benefits others in a way that cannot be priced in the market (see Chapters 2 and 4). For example, the social benefit of refuse disposal or vaccination against an infectious disease exceeds the private benefit. It is a standard result that goods with positive externalities are underproduced in the market because the producer pays the entire cost but cannot reap the full benefit. An extreme case of a positive externality is a public good. This is one whose production means that it can be enjoyed equally by everybody (e.g. street lighting). The first person to produce the good privately will benefit society, but cannot appropriate that benefit. Hence the good will be underprovided.

The provision of goods with positive externalities at the optimal level requires some collective action. Legislation or subsidies are sometimes used, but the general solution is public provision by the government or an agency funded from taxation. Even if the charges are nominally linked to a particular service, for example local authority charges for water or a television licence fee, the charge is essentially a form of taxation since consumption is not excluded, i.e. individuals are not allowed to opt out of payment even if they claim that they do not personally use street lighting or watch RTE.

A related rationale for government provision of services is that there is an informational failure in the market. For example, some parents might not value education fully and so education would be underconsumed if provided at marginal cost (and there is no intrinsic reason why education could not be priced in the market). For this reason, education is often provided free at the point of use and funded from taxation, even though the free market could provide it. If the informational problem is potentially severe, consumption of the service can be made compulsory (as with primary education), which weakens further the ability to charge for the service.

Often the positive externality and the informational failure may coexist: hence health education and AIDS-awareness campaigns are non-market government services. In both these cases, optimal government action is to increase the production and consumption of the service and this is done by reducing its marginal cost (usually to zero). As a result, these services are intrinsically non-market.

Another instance of government provision of services, especially important in Ireland, is natural monopoly due to economies of scale. The best example of a natural monopoly is a network (railways, electricity grid, telephone cable, television cable, etc.). Because average cost falls over the entire range of output, one network supplying a given number of people is more cost effective than two parallel networks supplying half that number each. Traditionally, government ownership and provision of such services was chosen because these industries were of national strategic importance, involved large and risky investments when capital markets were poorly developed and exhibited economies of scope across industries (especially in administration).

Improvements in capital markets and technological advancements mean that the original motivation for government intervention has completely receded in many markets. For example, telephony, electricity and cable television are now fully marketed. In Ireland, however, there has been little privatisation (relative to other OECD countries) and the current government programme is explicitly committed not to privatise national industries. As a result, Irish government production of market services continues to be very high. Even in cable television, the government indirectly owns a major dominant supplier, Cablelink, via Telecom (60 per cent) and RTE (40 per cent).

Market government services are similar to privately-produced services in that they are constrained by demand rather than by fiscal considerations. However, the supply characteristics of market services will be very different if they are provided by the government rather than the private sector. The government and its agencies have different access to capital, different labour relations, different management constraints and retain a monopolistic character, and all of these features mean that the supply of market government services is somewhat akin to that of non-market government services.

Traded and Non-Traded Services

The distinction between a traded good and a non-traded good is entirely an economic one, determined by the size of transport costs. The transport cost is usually thought of as the cost of delivering the good or service from its point of production to the point of consumption. However, it is more rigorous to define the transport cost as the minimum of the following:

(a) the cost of delivering the good from its production to its consumption;

(b) the cost of moving its consumption to the production point; and

(c) the cost of moving production to the consumption point.

For example, the Louvre produces a cultural service in Paris. This service cannot be consumed outside of Paris (unless by CD-ROM) (a), nor can its production be moved except for touring exhibitions (c). Hence the relevant transport cost is the cost of the consumer travelling to the Louvre (b). As another example, consider a hotel purchasing plumbing services. Delivery of a service produced abroad is not possible (a), nor can the hotel be moved (b). Here the transport cost is the cost of bringing the plumber to the hotel (c).

Hence, whether a good is likely to be non-traded depends on the size of the transport costs relative to the magnitude of the demand. Transport costs are high if the physical characteristics of the product make it difficult to move, the transport infrastructure is poor, trade barriers such as tariffs and quotas exist and travel (for consumers or producers) is expensive.

One of the major objectives of the European Union is to make goods more tradable. The 1992 Programme removed considerable barriers to trade, Structural Funds have been used to improve transport infrastructure, and aviation policy is tackling the problem of un-competitive and high-priced air transport. EU banking directives have made it easier for banks to locate in other member states. The implementation of the GATT Uruguay Round will have a similar effect on the tradability of many goods and services.

Historically, the distinction between the traded and non-traded sectors of the economy has been closely correlated with the distinction between manufacturing and services. Services had prohibitively high delivery costs, often augmented by legislation which restricted competition or importation (e.g. banking, insurance). As a result most services were non-traded. Some physical goods were also non-traded, either because the transport costs were very high (cement or animal foodstuffs) or because legislation prevented

trade to enable high taxation (alcohol, cigarettes and cars). However
agricultural and industrial produce has been freely traded, especially si
the 1960s.

The correlation was sufficiently strong in the past for the non-traded
sector to be regarded as synonymous with the services sector and the traded
sector with the agricultural and industrial sectors. In recent years, however,
this neat classification of services as non-traded has become increasingly
inaccurate as the tradability of services has increased. This has happened for
several reasons. First, technological advances, especially in
telecommunications, have made it easier to deliver services away from the
point of production. Financial and banking services have been most affected
by technology and are now widely traded internationally, as illustrated by the
establishment of the International Financial Services Centre in Dublin. A
good example is provided by telephone banking where all transactions are
carried out remotely and the bank has no branches. Whereas before the
transport cost was that of travelling to the UK, say, now it is the cost of
telephoning the UK. Although consumption and production are still
simultaneous, consumption does not require physical presence, merely
verbal communication. Second, membership of the EU and the WTO have
both contributed to reduced trade barriers. This is also illustrated in the
banking and financial services sectors. Within the EU, much effort has been
devoted to labour mobility, promoting a single market in professional
services by recognising qualifications. Third, consumer travel has become
much cheaper. Although this is partly due to technological advance,
deregulation of aviation markets has led to greater competition and lower
prices (on some routes). Reduced travel costs mean that tourism, for
example, is now more tradable than was previously the case.

Overall, though, many services remain non-traded in the sense that
transport costs are high relative to demand. Examples include hairdressing
and taxi journeys in the private sector and street lighting in the public sector.

The tradability of a good has important effects on consumer welfare via
lower prices. The domestic price of a good (Pd) cannot exceed its foreign
price (Pw) plus the transport cost (t) because otherwise importers would be
able to undercut the domestic price (an arbitrage opportunity), pushing the
domestic price down. Similarly, the domestic price cannot be lower than the
foreign price plus transport costs because exporters would have an arbitrage
opportunity that would increase the domestic price. Hence,

$$p_w - t \le p_d \le p_w + t$$

The extent to which the domestic price is determined domestically
depends on the size of such transport costs. If transport costs are close to zero
and the good is perfectly tradable, the domestic price is determined on world
markets (law of one price). For example, if producers of shoes in Ireland

:e to the monopoly level, importers would quickly
ort costs are high, the domestic sector is protected
1 and domestic competition determines the price.
·competitive practices can prevail in non-traded
:h they could not in traded markets. Hence the
.. ....-competitive behaviour is in the non-traded sector.
ine stout market illustrates many of the above points. Stout is a
distinctive black Irish beer with a white head and can be said to be in a
separate market in that it has few close substitutes. Stout makes up over 50
per cent of all beer consumed in Ireland and accounts for almost 2 per cent of
GNP.

Although stout is a physical product, it may be bought in two forms.
Draught stout (drawn slowly from a tap) is a non-traded service. Canned and
bottled (packaged) stout are traded products. Although the costs of producing
draught stout are different from those of producing packaged stout, changes
in these costs are highly correlated. In a competitive market, one would
expect the prices of both to be similarly correlated.

The actual pattern of prices over the 8 years to 1994 illustrates a stark
divergence between the price of on-sale (public houses, hotels, etc.) and off-
sale (off-licence stout). The real price of draught stout has increased by 1.6
per cent per annum. In contrast, the real price of packaged stout has declined
by 1.8 per cent per annum. These data suggest that the EU Single Market,
which has lifted restrictions on the trade of packaged stout and thereby
increased its tradability, is having an effect in the packaged stout market. The
price of packaged stout in Ireland is constrained by foreign prices whereas
that of draught stout, because it is non-traded, does not appear similarly
constrained.

3 THE SERVICES SECTOR IN IRELAND

Size and Growth of the Services Sector
The services sector in Ireland has grown enormously over the last 20 years
and (in 1993) accounted for over 60 per cent of total employment and 56 per
cent of output compared with just 49 per cent of output and 44 per cent of
employment in 1971. The services sector has contributed 233,000 new jobs
since 1971, compared with net employment creation in the economy of
97,000 jobs in the same period. The higher share of employment suggests
that productivity (and hence wages) are in general lower in the services
sector than in the other sectors.

The growth in the services sector contrasts with that in other sectors. The
agricultural sector is discussed in detail in Chapter 11: suffice it to note here
that agricultural output has grown in real terms since 1971, but not by as
much as national output has grown. This decline in agriculture's share of

Table 10.1

Percentage Share of the Sectors in National Output and Employment

	Output[1]		Employment	
	1971	1993	1971	1993
Agriculture	15.5	8.5	25.9	12.6
Industry	35.8	35.8	30.5	27.2
Services	48.8	55.7	43.6	60.2

Sources: Department of Finance DataBank and CSO, *National Income and Expenditure,* 1993.

[1] At current prices.

output has been a consistent feature of economic growth in Ireland since the 1930s, as would be expected in a growing economy if agricultural products have less than unitary income elasticity of demand. The industrial sector has also grown in real terms, but its total share of output has not changed over 20 years. The share of industrial output in Ireland may have peaked, indicating a break with the pattern of other developed countries where the peak of the industrial share occurred some time ago and exceeded 40 per cent.

The successful performance of the services sector in Ireland has been part of, but significantly less strong than, a general trend in all developed economies. In the European Union, for example, services constituted over 64 per cent of all output in 1992, with Ireland having the lowest ratio of services to GDP of any EU(12) member state. The services sector in the EU is set to continue to grow and if employment and production in Ireland follow the patterns of our developed trading partners (which has not always been the case), then we should expect the services sector to offer the greatest potential for growth in employment and output. N B.

The share of services in output in Ireland, 54.7 per cent (for 1992), is the lowest in the European Union where the average is 64.4 per cent (see Table 10.2). This is accounted for by higher shares in Ireland for agriculture and industry, with Ireland having the highest industrial share in the EU. While the services sectors in Greece, Portugal and Spain may be bolstered to some degree by strong tourist sectors, Ireland's figure is still well behind that of the other EU countries whose standard of living it wishes to emulate.

N B. A sub-sectoral examination reveals that the low share of services in Ireland is entirely a private sector phenomenon. Ireland's share of non- N B. market services, at 15.9 per cent, is above the EU average of 14.8 per cent and is bettered only by Denmark, France and Greece and is equalled by the UK share. This high share reflects the fact that the major growth in the services sector in Ireland in the last 20 years has been in the area of government services rather than in market services. Ireland's low share of services arises solely because its share of market services, at 38.6 per cent, is the lowest of any EU country and substantially below the EU average of 49.6 per cent. In Belgium and the Netherlands, market services account for over 54 per cent of all output. In general, there is a strong negative correlation across EU countries between market and non-market services: a correlation coefficient of -0.4 may indicate that government intervention substitutes for private entrepreneurship.

Table 10.2

Percentage Shares of Sectors in Gross Value Added
(market prices) in EU Member States, 1992

	Agriculture	Industry	Services total	market	non-market
Belgium	1.7	30.5	67.8	54.4	13.4
Denmark[1]	3.5	26.6	69.9	47.1	22.7
France	2.9	29.7	67.4	50.5	16.9
Germany	1.2	37.6	61.3	48.0	13.3
Greece[1]	17.0	27.3	55.6	39.5	16.1
Ireland	*9.1*	*36.2*	*54.7*	*38.6*	*15.9*
Italy	3.1	31.8	65.2	51.2	14.0
Luxembourg	1.5	31.1	67.5	52.7	14.8
Netherlands	3.8	29.8	66.4	55.6	10.8
Portugal	5.9	36.5	57.6	43.8	13.8
Spain	3.8	34.1	62.2	47.1	15.1
UK	1.5	33.1	65.4	49.5	15.9
EU 12	2.6	33.1	64.4	49.6	14.8

Sources: Eurostat, *National Accounts, 1987-1992,* Vol. 2C.
[1] Gross value added at factor cost, not market prices, used for these countries.

Within the market services sector, a number of points need to be noted. First, the stereotypical view of services being provided by small domestically-owned firms is belied by the fact that some of the biggest quoted companies in Ireland trade mostly in the services sector and include banks, insurance companies, hotel groups, etc. Second, the major areas of growth of services in the last decade have been in financial services and telecommunications (see Table 10.3). A decrease in the share of a sub-sector means that it has grown less than proportionately with overall output. Thus although the more traditional services such as lodging and catering and transport have declined as shares of output, they continue to grow in absolute terms. The growth of tourism in Ireland has been slightly above that of other EU member states and Ireland's share of EU tourist receipts (1.0 per cent) exceeds marginally her share of EU GDP (0.7 per cent).

The lower labour productivity for the services sector as a whole masks vastly divergent sub-sectoral patterns. In banking, insurance, communications and other market services in the EU, labour productivity exceeds average productivity across all sectors, whereas the opposite is the case in recovery and repair, distribution, lodging and catering, transport and in non-market services. This suggests that the distinction between capital-intensive and labour-intensive services is important and that much of the growth has been in capital-intensive areas. This trend is likely to continue as developments in information technology are increasingly applied to the production of services, especially in areas such as wholesale and retailing that were previously more labour-intensive.

Table 10.3

Share of Service Sub-Sectors in National Output

	1980	1992
Agriculture, forestry and fisheries	*11.6*	*9.5*
Industry	*27.1*	*32.5*
Building and construction	*10.1*	*5.3*
Market services	*37.7*	*40.7*
Recovery, repair, trade services	10.1	9.8
Lodging and catering	2.4	2.3
Transport	4.4	3.4
Communication	2.2	2.5
Credit and insurance	5.3	7.8
Other market services	13.0	14.8
Non-market services	*18.0*	*16.4*
Public administration and defence	6.8	5.9
Other non-market	11.2	10.5

Source: CSO.

Treatment of Services in Government Policy
Government policy towards the economic sectors is determined by several different policy tools. First, trade policy in the form of tariffs, quotas, export subsidies, export guarantees, etc. may treat sectors differently. Thus if some sectors have substantial trade barriers, transport costs will be higher and domestic production protected from foreign competition. Second, taxation policy may give competitive advantages in certain markets. Taxation relief can be given to producers (lower taxation on profits) or to consumers (i.e. income tax relief). Such markets are said to be 'fiscally privileged' and have a competitive advantage over other domestic markets or the same markets abroad. Third, explicit sectoral policy can take the form of grants or state aids: this clearly confers a competitive advantage. Finally the different application of competition legislation in different markets will affect the relative performance of the sectors. These policy tools determine the total level of government support, including explicit and implicit economic

NB.

transfers and the ability of each market to retain monopoly rent. Each of these policy tools is widely used in Ireland in a way which implies very different levels of support in different sectors and sub-sectors.

The industrial sector has benefited enormously in terms of state aids and fiscal privilege. Profits in manufacturing are taxed at 10 per cent as compared with 40 per cent in other sectors. In addition, Forfás, Forbairt and IDA Ireland give grant aid to new and existing business (IR£156 million estimated for 1995). Although some of this grant aid may go to service sector firms, the main policy criteria has been the export potential of the sector, so that manufacturing industry has been the main recipient. On the other hand, manufacturing industry has been exposed to foreign competition, especially at the export level and to a lesser extent in terms of imports (where practices such as exclusive dealing in retailing may restrict competition). To some extent, it appears that the enormous assistance given to the industrial sector is necessary to enable it to export at world prices, raising serious questions about costs and efficiency in the economy. The construction sector has been systematically aided by fiscal privilege, both by mortgage interest tax relief and by Section 27 relief for urban renewal schemes.

Agriculture is freely traded within the EU, but major external trade barriers exist, protecting this sector from world competition. Within Europe, agriculture is very heavily subsidised directly and indirectly (see Chapter 11). The fact that agricultural income taxation is based on a self-assessment system and that measurement of agricultural income is difficult may convey fiscal privilege.

The services sector has not in general received fiscal privilege, although service providers located in Shannon and financial services at the ISFC in Dublin have been allowed to benefit from the 10 per cent tax rate. Life assurance has benefited from income tax relief (presumably reflecting the informational asymmetry mentioned above). Some sub-sector services have received direct state subvention. In particular, tourism benefits from grants via Bord Fáilte (IR£18.6 million in 1995) and certain state sectors (e.g. Aer Lingus) continue to receive state aids. In all, the publicly-owned transport sectors will receive over IR£150 million in 1995, consisting of an equity injection for Aer Lingus and a subvention for Córas Iompair Éireann. On the other side, the sector has largely been protected from competition by a combination of trade laws and restrictive practices. This has undoubtedly enabled the retention of considerable monopoly rent in this sector.

A major European report on state aids reveals that Irish state aids are more biased towards manufacturing than in most other EU countries.[6] Within manufacturing, the level of state aids per employee is extremely high and Ireland gives the highest proportion of its state aids to export promotion, compared with other countries that give higher subsidies to more productive activities such as research and development. Total support to science and technology, at IR£3 million in 1994, is dwarfed by the enormous amounts of grant aid in other areas.

This brief survey reveals that sectoral policy results in significantly higher support to agriculture and industry compared with services. The rationale underlying this differential treatment is the belief that economic growth depends on the traded sector (argued to be fallacious in the introduction). Even the higher level of support for tourism and financial services, the most obviously traded services sectors, highlights the continuing preoccupation with trade (and especially export revenue) as a justification for support. There is no indication that this misguided policy is changing: the Report of the Task Force on Jobs in Services (mentioned above) comes out strongly in favour of extending existing industrial policy to include traded services. The argument is, yet again, that these sub-sectors need to be assisted in order to be able to compete at world prices.[7]

This preoccupation with trade raises an interesting question: why does the Irish traded sector need so much support to enable it to compete at international prices? The answer is that the traded sector faces higher costs. The production of traded goods requires both traded and non-traded inputs. Traded inputs can theoretically be purchased at international prices so there is no source of disadvantage for Irish producers. Non-traded inputs, however, are purchased at prices determined within the Irish market and there is no reason why these should be the same across countries unless markets are competitive. Thus, for example, if banks in Ireland are less efficient or less competitive than elsewhere, Irish exporters will have to pay a premium for this inefficiency, putting them at a competitive disadvantage on international markets.

In these terms, the traded sector is dependent on the non-traded sector. Measures which reduce the prices of non-traded goods, such as competition policy, would result in cheaper inputs for the traded sector and hence in a better export performance. (Industrial policy is often based on economic models that implicitly assume perfect competition in the domestic non-traded sectors.) Economic welfare would also increase, as direct consumers of non-traded goods would pay lower prices and have greater spending power. This would result in increased demand for goods and services, especially those services that are characterised by high income elasticity of demand, suggesting a pattern of services sector development comparable with that of our wealthier EU partners. In terms of meeting foreign competition, it offers a more attractive policy option than the alternative of becoming a low-wage economy to be able to supply foreign markets at competitive prices. Sectoral policy should therefore focus on competition and efficiency in all sectors. This would enable industry to compete better in international markets, consequently reducing the dependence of industry on state aids and incentives.

More generally, sectoral policy that favours one sector over another is undesirable. First, there is no basis in consumer welfare for valuing the output of one sector above another if both are produced in the market: the value of output is measured solely in terms of its value in consumption and the sector of origin is irrelevant. Second, the existence of unequal sectoral policies creates enormous incentives for rent-seeking and other lobbying behaviour by well-organised sectors (e.g. banana ripening in Cork was defined as manufacturing to avail of the 10 per cent profit tax rate.) These incentives merely reflect the tendency for the market to eliminate the bias. Third, in political economy terms, uneven policy creates strong property rights and is difficult and expensive to reverse (taxation reform illustrates this point). For these reasons, restoring the economic sectors to a level playing field will be neither easy nor rapid.

4 COMPETITION AND EFFICIENCY

The Welfare Cost of Monopoly

There are several reasons for believing that monopolistic outcomes prevail in the services sector. A high proportion of all services is produced under monopoly by government, in both market and non-market areas. Private sector services are often protected from international competition because they are less tradable. Other factors, like the intangibility of services preventing resale, may permit monopolistic practices such as price discrimination. In a perfectly competitive market, price undercutting and free entry or exit combine to make firms price at marginal cost (allocative efficiency) and to produce at minimum average cost (productive efficiency). This efficient outcome maximises consumer welfare.

A monopoly can set the price above marginal cost without risking competition or entry. As a result, the monopoly price will be higher than the competitive price and the level of demand or output and employment will be lower. Consumer welfare is lower because the overall level of output is reduced and some consumers are (unnecessarily) priced out of the market. Monopoly may also have other social costs such as the quality of the good or service provided, the variety of products available on the market or the level of after-sales service. A monopoly, as it is not threatened with competition, has less incentive to exert effort to provide things that the consumer requires because consumers have no alternative source of supply. Even if a firm only has partial monopoly power, the effect on welfare will be similarly negative, albeit smaller. In addition to reducing welfare, monopoly also results in the transfer of surplus from consumers to producers in the form of supernormal profits. In principle this transfer should have no effect on consumer welfare as the profit goes to shareholders who are consumers, although there may be undesirable consequences for income distribution.

Various economic incentives other than direct competition operate to use up the monopoly profit, a phenomenon known as X-inefficiency.[8]

First, the monopoly may engage in rent-seeking activity, where the rent is (the continuation of) the monopoly profit. Rent-seeking involves exhausting part or all of the monopoly profit to maintain the monopoly position. Examples include political lobbying to maintain or alter legislation or legal battles against new entrants.

Second, managerial slack may survive in a monopoly. It can take various forms, from unjustified shorter working hours and generous expense accounts to making costly strategic errors. In a competitive market, good management is compensated according to productivity because a firm that offered excessive compensation would go out of business. Without the competitive force, the existing management (regardless of their quality) can afford better compensation packages than their productivity justifies. This may simply take the form of working less hard: as Hicks remarked, the best monopoly profit is a quiet life.

Third, the existence of monopoly profits gives considerable bargaining power to employees of the firm. A trade union knows that the firm has supernormal profits and can bargain to obtain part of this rent with the threat of a costly strike (which would interrupt the profit flow). Thus we would expect wages to be higher (than marginal productivity) in monopolised industries.

All types of X-inefficiency are manifest as higher costs, absorbing the monopoly profit. For this reason, observed profits in a monopoly may not be any higher than the normal profit that would occur in a competitive market, and one cannot use profit levels to examine the prevalence of monopoly.

Allocative, productive and X-inefficiency are costs of monopoly seen in a partial equilibrium context, looking at a single market in isolation. A general equilibrium analysis of monopoly would include several other manifestations of the costs of monopoly.[9] First there is the effect in dependent markets. The monopolist's demand for inputs (labour, capital, raw materials) will be lower than would be those of a competitive market. Thus unemployment is undoubtedly caused by lack of competition in the product market (see Chapter 8). Second, if the product is an intermediate one, downstream producers will face higher costs and charge higher prices, with attendant welfare losses for consumers.

As an example of these general equilibrium effects, consider monopolistic pricing in the telephone market. Consumers suffer because the price is higher and output is lower. The demand for factors of production for telephone services (e.g. labour, capital) is lower. Businesses using telephones intensively (e.g. exporting manufacturers) have higher costs and pass these onto consumers in downstream markets in the form of higher prices. It may also adversely affect the allocation of talent in the economy, with higher profits or more lax working conditions attracting the most talented workforce into less productive and less competitive sectors. Thus monopoly in the production of telephone services impinges on direct consumers, on indirect consumers via downstream markets and on factor demands in upstream markets. The total effect may be considerably more than that measured by the type of partial equilibrium analysis discussed above.

The Benefits of Competition

The previous section has shown how the absence of competition in a market has negative welfare effects both directly in that market and indirectly in dependent markets. Increased competition in a particular market would be expected to (a) bring prices closer to costs, (b) reduce costs of production and (c) eliminate X-inefficiency. Competition will also be expected to have positive effects in upstream and downstream markets. Of particular importance in Ireland is the fact that competition policy would reduce unemployment.

To see the myriad effects of increased competition in one market on the entire economy, consider increased competition in the telephone market. Consumers would face lower prices, increasing welfare and increasing demand for telephone services (the substitution effect). In addition, the saving would leave them with more disposable income to spend on extra telephone services or in other markets (the income effect). Firms using telephones would have lower costs and, if in competitive markets, would pass these on in the form of lower prices. As with consumers, demand for telephone services and demand in other markets would increase. Although the reduction in telephone costs may only be a small part of cost, a very large number of firms is affected so that the aggregate effect may be large. Downstream firms that are exporting will have an improved competitive advantage owing to lower costs. The increase in demand (in all markets) would lead to increased production, requiring increased demand for labour directly and indirectly through increased demand for technology and capital. The overall effect would be an increase in consumer welfare and an increase in employment.

In addition to these benefits, competition may have some costs. The reduction of X-inefficiency may make some people worse off, especially the workers and management in the previously monopolised industry who may have benefited from managerial slack and union power. The recipients of rent-seeking expenditure (lobbyists, politicians, lawyers, etc.) might also suffer. Economic theory indicates that the benefits outweigh these costs.[10] One way of thinking of this is that more people would be employed but with greater equity in the sense that wages would be closer to marginal product.

The example also indicates the importance of competition in all other markets. If the downstream market is not competitive, then the full benefits of competition upstream will not be attained because the cost reduction will not be passed on to the consumer. This example of the Theory of Second Best highlights the necessity of increasing competition in all markets: otherwise, competition policy might just transfer monopoly rent from one market to another. The result generalises: other microeconomic reforms such as tax reform are more likely to increase welfare if markets are competitive. Similarly, competition policy abroad may not be imported if the distribution system is not competitive. Competition is cumulative: it contributes to creating the climate in which competition is most successful.

The issue of competition in the (former) semi-state sector also highlights a potential problem. These enterprises have been used to absorb unemployment for political purposes over the years with the result that they are overstaffed. One way of thinking of this is that the monopoly rent was used to increase employment beyond the level where it was productive. As a result, the introduction of competition in these sectors may lead to job losses. Competition in the semi-state sector may initially increase unemployment as the industry adjusts. The same problem may apply in improving efficiency in the production of non-market services.

The example also throws light on the political economy of competition policy. It is clear that as competition increases welfare, it also redistributes income from producers to consumers. The beneficiaries are a highly dispersed group of consumers in many different markets and those seeking work. In contrast, the losers are a more focused group of management, unions and political lobbyists. Although the gainers outweigh the losers in welfare terms, the political power of the losers is greatest. For such reasons, competition policy in practice encounters firm opposition from powerful vested interests.

In markets with special characteristics, competition can damage welfare. In risky financial markets, unfettered competition can result in bankruptcy and regulation to ensure prudential standards is necessary. In television broadcasting, excessive competition may result in a proliferation of homogenous television services aimed at the median market rather than a mix of services that would be preferred. It may be appropriate to regulate the market to ensure variety of programme services: measures to ensure efficiency (such as yardstick competition) can also be used. Arguments about excessive competition will always be manipulated by those defending anti-competitive practices and an overly strong recognition of the possibility of excessive competition would seriously impair competition policy.

The above discussion has important implications for competition policy. First, competition policy can increase consumer welfare in a wide variety of markets offering lower prices and greater choice and quality of service. It also increases employment, output, productivity and international competitiveness, increasing economic growth and the standard of living. Second, the effects of competition policy will be greater if it is applied in all markets systematically. Third, competition policy redistributes away from powerful political and economic groups and for this reason may encounter considerable opposition. Overall, however, competition policy addresses the source of market failure rather than the symptoms and its overall effect on the economy is likely to be positive.

5 COMPETITION POLICY

This section examines the detail of competition policy, that is, what measures can be used to increase the performance of markets without full competition. Monopoly can arise in different settings and the appropriate policy to improve welfare varies according to the source and type of the monopoly. First, we consider how the regulation of natural monopoly can improve welfare. Second, we look at how monopoly outcomes can arise in the private sector where competition is feasible but does not occur. Third, we examine the nature of the government's monopoly and ask what market mechanisms can be used to improve efficiency in the supply of non-market services.

The term competition policy will be used to describe all policies that involve the promotion of competitive outcomes in markets where competition is absent or fails. It thus includes encouraging competition where it is feasible, regulating markets where competition is not feasible, and using quasi-market mechanisms to ensure the efficient delivery of non-market services. Although the discussion is relevant to all product markets, it is clear that natural monopoly and the public sector are concerned almost entirely with the services sector.

Natural Monopoly
With natural monopoly, competition would reduce productive efficiency, increasing average costs. Although actual competition is not present, prices and output may be efficient if the market is contestable. A market is contestable if all fixed costs can be recouped on exit, i.e. costs are not sunk. Potential competition for the position to be the monopolist gives efficiency. However, examples of truly contestable markets are difficult to find so that natural monopoly is likely to result in welfare losses.

It is often argued that a small economy may be more prone to natural monopoly because there is insufficient demand to support more than one firm. This is only the case if the output is non-traded, since otherwise the relevant market is international and the number of domestic producers is not constrained by domestic demand. For this reason, natural monopoly may be more of a problem in the non-traded sector than in the traded sector.

The regulation of natural monopoly can involve controls on both market structure and conduct. With many natural monopolies, only one activity exhibits economies of scale. One regulatory choice concerns the market structure in related (usually downstream) markets. For example, the owner of the telephone network could be allowed a monopoly in the supply of telephone services (vertical integration), or could be obliged to allow other suppliers of telephone services also to have access to the network (access) or could be obliged not to supply any telephone services itself (vertical separation). In addition to this structural aspect, the regulator can control the access prices charged and prices charged to final consumers, both forms of conduct regulation. The regulator might also monitor the quality of service and the range of products supplied and may have an input into technological decisions.

A large literature has developed in recent years dealing with the appropriate forms of regulation in different markets. In addition to the features outlined above, this literature highlights problems with regulation. First, the existence of asymmetric information wherein the regulated firm has superior information to the regulator means that it is usually in the regulated firm's interests to overestimate its costs so that the regulator permits a higher price. Solutions exist to this problem such as greater regulatory powers and resources or the use of regional monopolies so that the regulator can compare costs in different regions (yardstick competition).

Second 'regulatory capture' can occur, where the regulator's decisions reflect partly the interest of the regulated firm rather than those of the consumer. Regulatory capture can arise if the regulator is very dependent on the regulated firm, financially or otherwise or if the regulatory personnel are closely connected with the regulated firm. It is important to have a well-resourced and independent regulator with the clear objective of maximising consumer welfare in order to avoid regulatory capture. In institutional terms, the incorporation of a regulatory division within the competition agency would enable the systematic application of policy across markets and would further minimise the risk of capture.

The question of how to regulate monopoly should be independent of its ownership. Often the network that gives rise to a natural monopoly is considered a national asset and publicly-owned. In principle, a publicly-owned natural monopoly should be identical to a privately-owned one, although it is often difficult to achieve a level playing field in terms of access to capital, labour and other inputs. A particular form of regulatory capture can arise if the government regulatory function is not clearly separated from the government's role as an owner. For example, if the government owns the city bus company and also regulates that company it faces a conflict of interest between maximising revenue (or using the bus company to absorb unemployment) and providing services to consumers at low prices. It is clear from the above that the regulatory role of government must be separate and independent from its role in providing any services.

Monopoly Outcomes in the Potentially Competitive Sector
A firm in a seemingly competitive market may be able to set a price above the competitive level if it has market power, that is, if it can increase its price without losing all of its demand. This is measured by the firm-specific elasticity of demand: the more inelastic the firm's demand, the greater its market power. The firm-specific elasticity of demand and hence its market power depend on the existence of substitutes for the product. If there are no close substitutes, the firm can raise its price and act to some extent as a

monopolist because consumers have few alternatives. With close substitutes, the firm's demand will be more elastic as a price increase would reduce demand substantially.

A firm can increase its market power by increasing consumer switching costs (e.g. frequent flyer programmes or other discounts for repeat purchases) and using vertical restraints with retailers to prevent entry (e.g. exclusive distribution agreements). This enables it to extract more monopoly rent, reducing consumer welfare. Other practices such as price discrimination may be anti-competitive. One of the conditions for price discrimination is that the product may not easily be resold so that price discrimination may be more easily practised in the (non-traded) services sector.

A group of firms may act collectively as a monopoly, known as collusion or creating a cartel. This requires that all the firms in a market agree to restrict output or to set a high price. The welfare loss is identical to that with monopoly. Collusion requires entry barriers, credible punishment of defectors (firms that undercut the others), and is thought to be easier with a small number of firms. Collusion is inherently unstable as the competitive force tempts firms to defect. Typically price wars and output surges occur as punishment phases, followed by reversion to collusion. That anti-competitive practices are widely prevalent and bad for the consumers was noted by Adam Smith:

> People of the same trade seldom meet together, even for merriment and diversion, but the conversation ends in a conspiracy against the public, or in some contrivance to raise prices.[11]

Tacit collusion, where firms maintain high prices or low quantities without an explicit (written) agreement is more common within countries because it is more difficult to detect and prove. Most countries outlaw collusion so they it is usually only observed at the international level for a product whose supply is restricted.

In markets such as those described above, competition may be feasible but may not be present either because the market structure is very concentrated or because the behaviour in the market is anti-competitive. The usual approach is to enact competition legislation and to establish a competition agency to implement the policy (with the courts). Within this general framework, competition policy varies enormously between the EU and US models and even within EU member states. First, it can be prescriptive and prevent problems before they arise (e.g. mergers) or reactive and deal with problems that have arisen. With both policies, severe fines are an important tool of policy. Second, the agency may be bound by strict rules (e.g. a market share above 40 per cent is dominant) or may have considerable discretion in the determination of policy. Third, the resources, powers, political independence, personnel and internal structure of the competition agency are crucial to whether competition policy is effective and immune from regulatory capture.

The competition agency may tackle a particular problem via structural change such as preventing a merger, forcing divesting of subsidiaries or limiting vertical integration in order to create a more competitive market structure. Alternatively, it may prevent certain forms of behaviour either by an individual firm or a group of competing firms. Suspect conduct includes excessive pricing, agreeing prices with competitors, resale price maintenance, exclusive dealing arrangements and consumer loyalty schemes, all of which may dampen price competition and/or restrict entry. Often this conduct takes the form of an agreement between firms. Horizontal agreements between competing firms are usually considered anti-competitive. Vertical agreements between upstream and downstream firms may carry benefits for firms and are judged case by case in most jurisdictions. A crucial factor in determining whether behaviour is anti-competitive is whether a firm or group of firms is in a dominant position (the legal term for being a monopoly and usually meaning a market share of 40-100 per cent). If so, then behaviour which might otherwise be considered competitive may harm competition.

Conflicts can arise between static efficiency (at a point in time) and dynamic efficiency (the level of product innovation undertaken), as reflected by the patent system which grants a temporary monopoly. If the competition agency has consumer welfare, both short-run and long-run, as its objective, it can evaluate the arguments in favour of research joint ventures and other schemes to promote innovation that might adversely affect product market competition in the short run.

The level of competition is only one element in the overall competitiveness of an industry, and should not be confused with other policies designed to improve competitiveness which are macroeconomic in nature and typically have to do with keeping wage levels, interest rates, productivity and exchange rates at appropriate levels.

Monopoly in Government

Finally, the government is, by convention, a monopoly provider of many services such as justice and national defence. The government has a monopoly over legislation, making it the ultimate monopolist in that it can outlaw the private supply of services. Some government monopolies arise by legislation (e.g. public broadcasting). Others arise because non-market services are priced below cost so that the private sector could not compete directly. However, because demand for non-market services is rationed the private sector can compete for the rationed demand. This is illustrated well by private hospitals and educational institutions and other facilities that avoid queuing.

The basis of the problem is that the price mechanism is absent in the non-market sector. Prices convey information between supply and demand and provide incentives more generally. Without prices, several differences arise.

The lack of a profit-maximising environment may mean that production costs are not minimised. The absence of a competitive force means that X-inefficiency such as rent-seeking (e.g. diverting productive work into obtaining a promotion) and inefficiency may go unchecked. The allocation of services among the (rationed) public may be inefficient if the people who value them most are not the recipients. The choice of services supplied may not always be those that the public demand and the democratic process is a very crude and inaccurate communicator of consumer preference compared with the market.

A variety of quasi-market mechanisms can be used to substitute for the function of price and to improve the efficiency of delivery of public services. All of these mechanisms attempt to provide incentives aimed at curbing X-inefficiency in the public service. They are thus directed towards improving the quality of decision-making and management, reducing excessive union power, and mitigating rent-seeking within and by the public sector.

At the heart of the public service are the incentives of individual personnel. In many systems, public servants are paid a fixed salary, salary increases incrementally, promotion is awarded on seniority, monetary (and often non-monetary) reward varies very little with productivity and dismissal only occurs for very grave offences. Thus public servants are highly insured against the consequences of their actions and the vicissitudes of life. This arises partly because of a concern that the government should be 'fair' or equitable, necessarily impeding incentives and efficiency. In many instances, this may constrain the ability of the public sector to continue to attract and retain talented and skilled personnel whose return in the private sector is much higher.

Several measures could be used to improve management efficiency. First, salaries can be tied more to individual productivity, such as promotion on merit rather than on seniority. However, productivity can be difficult to measure because of the absence of competition and because outputs are not measurable. Second, salaries can vary with outcomes, like making the salaries of a department of employment vary (negatively) with the unemployment rate. This is a crude device as the outcome may be under the control of many different factors, only one of which is that department. Also, it gives rise to rent-seeking opportunities such as job schemes which make the unemployment rate appear to fall. Third, one can introduce competition for management posts, making public servants compete with external personnel for senior positions. The reduction of job security would result in significantly higher costs per person to compensate for the lack of insurance. Several such measures were introduced in New Zealand with considerable success.[12]

In terms of curbing wage pressure and restrictive practices, government can contract out many services rather than provide them in-house. Public ownership of the roads does not require that they cannot be built by the private sector. Similarly cleaning, catering, building, software and a host of other services can be bought in rather than produced internally. Recent studies have revealed substantial cost savings (up to 20 per cent) in contracting out various services in the UK and have found that divisions of the public service have been able to compete with private sector firms in these newly-created markets. Contracting-out clearly transfers part of government services from the public to the private sector (reducing the share of non-market services). A partial form of contracting-out can involve the establishment of separate internal divisions with explicit payments for services. The costs of such divisions can be compared across divisions and with similar divisions in the private sector (a form of yardstick competition) and these divisions might be allowed to compete for private sector tenders.

Accounting conventions and the allocation of responsibilities may hinder the efficient provision of services. The New Zealand government changed the recording of government accounts from cash flow to an accruals system which counts the actual cost of work carried out in the particular period and make adjustments for depreciation. This tries to ensure that the accounts measure the true cost of providing a service and improves the allocation of resources.

Overall, the improvement of efficiency in the public service, by whatever means, has the same effect as increased competition in the private sector or improved regulation of natural monopoly. Consumers pay the true economic costs for services, have more money to spend in other markets, and demand for all output increases. In addition, exporters from countries with efficient government and competitive markets are at a distinct advantage in international markets.

6 APPLICATION TO THE IRISH ECONOMY

Regulation of Natural Monopoly
In Ireland, most network monopolies were traditionally owned and managed by the government (electricity, gas, telephones, railways, cable television, etc.). Inefficiencies and enormous losses on commercial activities led to a reorganisation in the 1980s that transferred management (but not ownership) to independent organisations (e.g. Telecom Éireann). Although management is now separate, the relevant minister (usually the Minister for Transport, Energy and Communications) still both owns and regulates the monopoly. The lack of transparent and independent regulation raises serious questions about the efficiency of these sectors and about the prices offered to consumers. The 'rebalancing' of telephone charges in 1994 in response to competition on international routes indicates the high prices previously paid.

But change is in the air. Technology is reducing the areas of natural monopoly. In telephony, it is now possible for several telephone companies to use the same physical network of lines and the physical network will be replaced to some extent by spectrum-based services (mobile telephones). Technology also makes telephone services increasingly internationally traded, putting increased pressure for efficiency within the domestic monopoly. In electricity, the government recently decided to accept bids from the private sector for the provision of an electricity-generating facility. Membership of the EU will enable the entry of other suppliers into the Irish market, increasing competition directly.

Public ownership has meant that these industries were used to fulfil a variety of wider social objectives, in particular to create employment. The combination of new competitive pressures and overstaffing may lead former national monopolies to extend activities into neighbouring markets in order to employ surplus labour (for example, the Electricity Supply Board (ESB) has a separate retailing division). It is important that regulation prohibits cross-subsidisation between the network monopoly and any other activity. Genuine economies of scope may arise if the operation of a network gives a competitive advantage in another market. For example, the ESB or Telecom Éireann have to mail bills to all customers and could also use this billing system to advertise other activities. Where such economies of scope arise solely by virtue of a monopoly in another market, it is important that competitors also have access to the economy of scope. Thus other firms should be allowed access to the mailing system on equal terms.

However, despite competitive pressures, natural monopoly is set to continue, especially where national or local networks exist. The regulatory issues outlined above include whether to enforce vertical separation, the regulation of access prices and the regulation of final consumer (or producer) prices. The most important general issue concerns the system of regulation itself. There is a choice between extending competition law to include monopoly regulation (as in New Zealand) or the establishment of independent regulators (as in the UK). The former, if accompanied by equivalent independent regulators within the competition agency, is strictly superior as it enables a consistency of approach across the entire economy, the use of yardstick competition among regulators and minimises the possibility of regulatory capture. It is vital that regulators are well-resourced, have excellent information-gathering powers and are obliged always to act in the interests of consumers.

Competition in the Potentially Competitive Sector
There is considerable evidence that competition is weak or absent in many markets, and especially in the services sector where the lack of trade protects markets from foreign competition. The lack of official statistics in areas such as market concentration inhibits the systematic and rigorous evaluation of the level of competition, but many other forms of evidence exist. In particular, evidence of the lack of competition is provided by barriers to entry (including restrictive practices and government licensing), concentrated markets, rent-seeking to prevent competition and in the improved performance of markets exposed to competition.

The OECD Economic Survey of Ireland 1993 argued that barriers to competition are widespread in the Irish economy and found that prices and costs are high relative to other countries in the food, transport, communications, and medical and health care markets. The Survey is critical of most sectors in this regard but concentrates its attention on the 'sheltered' sector (mostly services) which is less exposed to external competition and notes that 'impediments to domestic competition have distorted a wide range of relative prices in Ireland, at a heavy cost to Irish consumers'.[13]

Barriers to entry arise both from private sector behaviour and from government regulation. In both cases, the effect on restricting competition is the same. Table 10.4 summarises current entry regulations in some parts of the services sector. Entry to the professions (legal, financial, medical, architectural, therapy, etc.) is frequently regulated by the government and, in any case, it is usual for (full) participation in the market to require some accreditation from a professional association. Such professional associations ostensibly have regard to setting and maintaining quality standards but the incentive is to set an unnecessarily high quality standard that restricts entry to the profession. In fact, the economics profession is somewhat of an exception in this regard, where anybody can call themselves an economist!

Table 10.4

Barriers to Entry in Services Markets

Service Activity	Government Regulations			Other
	Licensing	Vocational certificates	Capital requirements	
Legal services	P	Y		Y
Medical services	P	Y		Y
Other professions	P	Y		Y
Retailing: general				Y
Retailing: alcohol	Y			
Retailing: travel agencies				Y
Transport: road, freight	Y			
Transport: road, passengers	Y	Y	P	
Transport: taxis	Y	Y		
Transport: rail	Y			
Transport: air		Y		
Insurance	Y		Y	
Banking	Y		Y	

Source: OECD, *Economic Survey of Ireland 1993.*
Y indicates existence of the type of barrier; P means barriers are partly of the nature indicated.

In the area of transport, government licensing restricts the number of taxis, resulting in a monopoly rent to the current owners of taxi licences in the Dublin area in the region of IR£75,000 and rising. The allocation of landing slots at Dublin airport also gives rise to entry barriers. As a result, direct flights to continental Europe are frequently more expensive than indirect flights via London, although the latter, involving two flights, cost more to produce.

The fact that concentration data are not published might indicate producer capture in that monopoly is protected by poor information. Examination of individual markets reveals considerable concentration. In the beer market, Guinness supplies approximately 75 per cent of all beer sold in Ireland: in 1991 the Commission described the UK market with 77 per cent of the market coming from 6 suppliers as 'very concentrated'.[14] High concentrations occur in the wholesale supply of a wide range of other consumer products, from ice cream to bottled gas.

In retailing and distribution, vertical restraints are common. The OECD has found an unusually small ratio of wholesale to retail outlets in Ireland, suggesting that the distribution network is more concentrated than in other industries. An example that has been through the courts and has finally been resolved by the European Commission concerns the retailing of ice cream where HB (a subsidiary of Unilever), the market leader, with 70 per cent market share, supplied freezers to retailers free of charge, and recouped the costs in higher ice cream prices to all retailers (regardless of whether they took a freezer or not). They additionally required that the freezers only be used to stock Unilever products (exclusivity). The Commission considered this anti-competitive and decided that retailers should pay different prices depending on whether they accepted a free freezer or not. Another example of a barrier to entry in retailing is that of public houses in Dublin, whose number has been broadly static since the nineteenth century. The very high prices attracted by public houses partly reflects the monopoly rents that exist due to current licensing arrangements. Lack of competition in the retail sector can affect the prices consumers (and producers) pay for traded goods, so that the non-traded sector may impinge on prices in the traded sector.[15]

The existence of rent-seeking behaviour provides an indication that an economy is not competitive and the Culliton Report noted the 'acute' prevalence of rent-seeking in the Irish economy.[16] A good example of how rent-seeking can lead to regulatory barriers to entry is provided by the differential licensing laws for public houses and other premises which protect publicans from direct competition.

Evaluating the effects of competition in individual sectors provides evidence of the benefits of competition. For example, the Dublin-London air route witnessed a dramatic fall in fares between 1986 and 1993 and passenger traffic grew from 900,000 to 2.4 million over the period, without appreciable changes in the quality of service. In 1986, it would have been difficult to anticipate the enormous magnitude of the benefits of competition: lobbyists would have argued that high prices were necessary to cover costs and to provide a high-quality service, and that they were in line with other (selected) routes and the data would not have been available to attempt a rigorous independent analysis of the validity of these claims. Experience in the airline industry suggests that the dire predictions of lobbyists (either producers or trade unions) should be treated with caution.

Until recently, competition policy in Ireland was accidental and arose largely as a by-product of other policy decisions and only affected the traded sectors. Manufacturing industry was exposed to international competition by export-led growth policy since the 1960s and has required substantial subsidisation to compete on foreign markets. Additional markets have been subject to European competition law by virtue of our membership of the EU. However, only agreements involving trade between member states and above a certain size *(de minimis)* are affected; the behaviour must relate to a market constituting a substantial part of the EU. Thus EU law does not apply to most services. For example, except for air and sea transport to other member states, the transport sector in Ireland is completely unaffected by EU competition policy. Even in the traded sectors affected, enforcement has not been adequate.[17]

Within Ireland, the Restrictive Practices Acts of 1972 and 1987 were directed towards specific practices and required a ministerial order and an investigation by the Fair Trade Commission.[18] The process was extremely cumbersome and inefficient. Hogan notes that 'the entire process took about two years, by which stage (a) the victims of this anti-competitive behaviour had probably been put out of business and (b) the wrong-doers had often long since moved onto un-competitive behaviour of a hitherto unknown kind...'.[19]

The 1991 Competition Act is the first and only domestic legislation that explicitly exposes markets to competition policy. This Act applies EU legislation (Articles 85 and 86 of the Treaty of Rome) to Ireland and established a Competition Authority. It has considerable limitations in that the Authority relies on being notified by the offending parties, has no enforcement powers, has no ability to impose fines and is underresourced. Another possible problem is that the application of EU legislation, intended to deal with large trades between member states, may not be appropriate to sub-sectoral markets in a single economy which, in the case of Ireland, are relatively small. The ambiguous treatment of mergers (seemingly according to different criteria and to be decided by the Minister) and the continuing use of the Groceries Order suggests only a semi-committed approach to competition policy.

Nevertheless, the work of the Authority to date reveals a strongly pro-competition line, with many high profile decisions (Irish Distillers and Independent Newspapers). It is somewhat surprising that so many anti-competitive agreements have been notified, given that the Authority has no powers to initiate investigations. The lack of resources devoted to the

Authority combined with the enormous volume of work in its initial period has led to substantial delays. These are regrettable both because of the delay and uncertainty costs imposed on the private sector and because the reputation of competition policy could be damaged in the public mind.

Of the 805 decisions made by the Authority by April 1995, a total of 197 (25 per cent) offended against the Competition Act. This indicates a high level of anti-competitive behaviour, given that the most offensive agreements are unlikely to have been submitted to the Authority for approval.[20]

It is clear that existing competition policy, although a marked improvement on what went before, requires substantial change before it can bring competition to all sectors of the economy.

Efficiency in the Supply of Non-market Services
The main features of the production and delivery of non-market services in Ireland remained untouched for most of this century. Management incentive structures are weak with seniority as a major component of promotion, little reward for productivity, promotion largely from within, etc. This has resulted in the haemorrhaging of many senior civil servants whose productivity is better rewarded in the private sector. Accounting procedures have not caught up with best practice in other areas and the separation of commercial and non-commercial activities is incomplete. Contracting-out is only partly used and government is highly centralised with little delegation, even to local government. Government is highly secretive and policy advice from public servants is not open to public scrutiny. Irish consumers may pay a very high price indeed for non-market services provided by the government.

However changes in this area are emerging, albeit slowly. The introduction of the Public Accounts Committee, chaired by a member of the Opposition to improve incentives, will help to eliminate the worst inefficiencies. The Revenue Commissioners have introduced several incentive schemes to improve the collection of taxation. EU membership sets strict rules for the procurement of such services, requiring the government to advertise the service in the Union's *Official Journal,* to accept the best bid, and not to have regard to national origin. Thus, for example, the printing of examination papers for the Department of Education is carried out by firms in several countries. The National Treasury Management Agency illustrates how the use of incentive mechanisms can reduce debt costs significantly. Much more needs to be done in this area and the example of New Zealand (discussed above) where major reform has been successfully undertaken offers a way forward.

7 CONCLUSION

The services sector of the economy is by far the largest sector and, still growing, offers enormous potential for employment creation and economic growth into the 21st century, especially if consumption patterns follow those of wealthier countries. This growth potential can only be fully realised in a competitive and efficient economy, a situation towards which Ireland has a considerable distance to travel. Optimal economic policy towards the services sector comprises several different policy instruments and dimensions of which the most important are competition policy and ending discrimination in favour of traded goods.

This chapter has argued that the introduction of competition policy, in the form of competition (and regulation if necessary) in the market sector of the economy and a quasi-competitive mechanism in non-market services, offers considerable benefits to consumers. It will reduce prices directly in markets affected and indirectly in downstream markets, releasing consumer expenditure for the growth of all markets. It will increase demands for factors of production, of which labour is the most important in the Irish context. It will reduce the costs of exporting firms, enabling them to compete better on foreign markets and strengthening the international purchasing power of our citizens. It will assist in placing Ireland on a firm footing for a single European currency. It will also enable us to compete with Central European economies, likely future competitors within the EU, some of which have decisive and well-resourced anti-monopoly offices that are adopting a competition policy more rigorous and far-reaching than that currently existing in Ireland.[21] In terms of meeting international competition generally, it represents a significantly better policy than the alternative, namely the development of low-wage sectors.

The requirements of good competition policy are manifold. At the most basic level, competition policy should extend to all markets (not just services). The Authority should have proper resources and powers to enforce, investigate and fine. Independent regulation should be introduced, preferably under the aegis of the Authority and subject to the Competition Act. Incentives for the supply of non-market services need to be systematically evaluated and changed.

Competition policy must be firm and resolute with the interests of consumers as its sole objective and be applied across the entire economy. This will increase its effectiveness, be less divisive and may help forge consensus. If there is a question of priority action, this should be directed towards the sheltered sectors as indicated, for example, in the OECD Survey. The application of policy will need to be most determined in the non-traded sectors of the economy, and especially in the professions and the retail sector in which resistance from monopoly firms and trade union lobbying and other vested interests will be greatest. Procedures and criteria should be transparent and subject to appeal in the courts.

The discrimination against the services sector in economic policy is without rigorous economic justification as there is no economic justification for such discrimination. It arose because most services were non-traded and because services are not perceived to add to productivity and growth (unless purchased by foreigners). Ending discrimination should clearly take the form of reducing support to other sectors. The alternative of increasing support to services would be ridiculous: all sectors cannot have special features that make them more important than the others and therefore justify support. The European Union policy of mutual recognition is also forcing steps in this direction. More generally, all sectoral policy, including state subsidies, assistance and other involvement, should be directed towards areas of genuine market failure, such as research and development, capital markets, education and training, environmental policy and coordination of markets.

Endnotes

1   See J. A. Schumpeter, *A History of Economic Analysis,* London, Oxford University Press, Oxford 1954. For a contrasting view see J. M. Keynes, *The General Theory of Employment Interest and Money,* Macmillan, London 1936, Chapter 23.
2   See A. Smith, *An Inquiry into the Nature and Causes of the Wealth of Nations,* 1775, (Glasgow Edition), Book II, Chapter III, Section 1.
3   *Report of the Task Force on Jobs in Services,* Department of the Taoiseach, Dublin 1993.
4   See Smith, *op. cit.,* 'Like the declamation of the actor, the harangue of the orator, or the tune of the musician, the work of all of them perishes in the very instant of its production.'
5   Smith, *op. cit.*
6   EU, *Third Survey on State Aids in the European Community,* Brussels, July 1992.
7   There is some indication of a change in official policy. See *Job Potential of the Services Sector* (Report no. 7), National Economic and Social Forum, Dublin April 1995. In launching this report, the Minister for Enterprise and Employment noted that the 'theory that services are derived from or are subsidiary to economic activity in the manufacturing and agricultural sectors....is no longer valid and services, like manufactured goods, are recognised as contributing to overall welfare and living standards in the same way as the output of other sectors'.
8   H. Leibenstein, 'Allocative Efficiency Versus X-Efficiency', *American Economic Review,* Vol. 56, 1966.
9   For a discussion of general equilibrium aspects of competition policy, see J. Fingleton, 'Economic Theory, Competition Policy and the Irish Economy', *Journal of the Statistical and Social Inquiry Society of Ireland* (forthcoming), 1994/95.
10 See J. Fingleton, 'Competition Policy and Employment: An Application to the Irish Economy', *Economic and Social Review,* October 1993.
11 See Smith, *op. cit.,* p.145.
12 See P. Massey *New Zealand: Market Liberalisation in a Developed Economy,* St. Martin's Press, London 1995.
13 OECD, *Economic Survey: Ireland,* OECD, Paris, November 1993.
14 See *Official Journal,* 1992 C121/2 [1992] 4 CMLR 546.
15 The Groceries Order permits resale price maintenance in the groceries sector and is much criticised for being un-competitive. See *Report of the Fair Trade Commission,* and J. Fingleton, 'The Groceries Order: Competition Postponed', Irish Centre for European Law (forthcoming), 1995.
16 *A Time for Change: Industrial Policy for the 1990s,* Report of the Industrial Policy Review Group, Stationery Office, Dublin 1992. See also P. Honohan, 'Rent-seeking and Economic Performance' (Dublin Economics Workshop, Kenmare Conference Paper), 1992.
17 The Competition Authority has discovered that several agreements notified to it were already in breach of EU law, but had not been notified to the Commission. See P. Massey and P. O'Hare, 'Measuring the Impact of the Competition Act' (Trinity College Dublin Economic Policy Paper no. 3), May 1995.

18 The 1987 Act brought areas such as banking and transport under the 1972 Act. By the end of 1990 there were 13 Restrictive Practices Orders covering 35 per cent of consumer expenditure and concerning practices such as predatory pricing and collusion. The Mergers, Take-overs and Monopolies (Control) Act 1978 was another element of this legislation which is still in force.
19 G. Hogan, 'The Competition Act 1991', in J. Findlater (editor), *The New Competition Legislation,* Irish Centre for European Law, Dublin 1992.
20 See Massey and O'Hare, *op. cit.*
21 See J. Fingleton, E. Fox, D. Neven, and P. Seabright, *Competition and Competition Policy in Central and Eastern Europe* (forthcoming).

CHAPTER 11

Agricultural Competitiveness and Rural Development

Alan Matthews

1 INTRODUCTION

There are three reasons why the competitiveness of the agricultural sector is of interest to students of the Irish economy. First, despite a gradual decline in its relative importance over time, primary agriculture remains Ireland's largest single industry. In 1993, it accounted for 8 per cent of Gross Domestic Product (GDP) and 12 per cent of employment. Within the European Union the only other countries in which agriculture has a comparable significance are Greece and Portugal. To these figures should be added the contribution of the food industry, much of which depends on the output of Irish agriculture for its raw material. Together, the primary agricultural sector and the food and drink industry represent about 17 per cent of GDP and 19 per cent of total employment. Of particular importance is agriculture's contribution to net foreign exchange earnings (i.e. after account is taken of such factors as import content, profit repatriation and EU transfers associated with exports) which was estimated at around 40 per cent in 1988. Thus the performance of the agricultural sector has a considerable bearing on the economy's success in meeting the primary and secondary objectives of national economic policy outlined in Chapters 2 and 3.

A second reason why agricultural competitiveness is of interest is the very great dependence of the sector on government support. One measure of the scale of this intervention is the amount of combined Irish government and EU expenditure in relation to the sector (Table 11.1). In 1970, prior to Irish membership of the EU, total state expenditure in relation to agriculture (including farm price support and items such as agricultural research and education and disease-eradication programmes) was equal to 33 per cent of gross agricultural product (see below for the definition of this term). By 1993 this figure had risen to almost 80 per cent. It is fair to point out that not all spending in relation to agriculture reaches farmers; included are fees to veterinary surgeons, salaries of agricultural advisors, the cost of intervention storage and other payments to persons outside of farming directly. On the other hand, the comparison ignores the support provided indirectly to farming through the higher prices which consumers must pay for their food. There are few other sectors of the economy where public policy has such a profound impact on the prosperity and livelihoods of those working there.

The third reason why the competitiveness of Irish agriculture is of interest is that this framework of support which has protected the sector from the harshest consequences of market forces is beginning, albeit rather hesitantly, to undergo radical reform. Agricultural policy is being gradually pushed in a more market-orientated direction. This began with the MacSharry reforms of the EU's Common Agricultural Policy agreed in 1992 and is reinforced by the disciplines imposed by the GATT Uruguay Round Final Act which takes effect from 1995. Further changes will probably be necessary if the EU admits the countries of Central and Eastern Europe to membership sometime in the next decade. At the same time, there are further pressures for change from consumers and from environmental interests. Consumers are taking an increasing interest in the way food is produced. There is now a more critical attitude to intensive farming arising from, for example, health worries about the impact of chemical and pesticide residues or animal welfare concerns. Environmentalists also criticise agricultural policy for encouraging farming practices which are detrimental to the environment. They would prefer to pay farmers to manage the landscape in an environmentally-friendly fashion rather than paying them to produce additional food for which no market can be found.

Table 11.1

Total EU and National Spending on Agriculture[1] (in current terms)

Year	EU	National	Total	EU share of total spending	Gross agricultural product (GAP) at market prices	Ratio of total agricultural spending to GAP
	IR£m	IR£m	IR£m	%	IR£m	%
1970	-	66	656	0	200	33
1973	37	68	105	35	426	26
1975	103	91	194	53	586	33
1980	413	183	596	69	951	63
1985	893	224	1,116	80	1,477	76
1989	963	174	1,137	85	2,018	56
1993	1,320	273	1,593	83	2,016	79

Sources: Report of the Agriculture and Food Policy Review Group, Stationery Office, Dublin 1991; Department of Finance, *Estimates of Expenditure on the Public Services;* CSO; Department of Agriculture, Food and Forestry.
[1] National expenditure refers to money spent under the vote of the Department of Agriculture, Food and Forestry.

These changes and pressures are described in more detail later in this chapter, but they invite a series of questions. What should be the strategic attitude of the Irish government to changes in agricultural support policy? Should we try to resist these changes or should we try to adjust to them? In part, the answers to these questions depend on how well we think Irish agriculture might fare in a more market-oriented environment. How competitive would Irish agriculture be if EU support was reduced or removed? What measures should be taken to strengthen its competitiveness? And what would be the impact of a more competitive agriculture on rural areas? Would a more efficient agriculture lead to a further depopulation of rural Ireland? What can be done to improve the competitiveness of rural areas in generating alternative employment opportunities if agricultural support is reduced? What will be the impact of greater public concern for food quality and the environment for the competitive position of Irish farming?

This chapter proceeds to try to answer these questions as follows. Section 2 provides a brief overview of some salient characteristics of the Irish agricultural sector and comments on its recent performance. The main features of recent structural change in Irish agriculture are described in Section 3 which highlights the different responses at farm level to changing economic and technological circumstances. Section 4 discusses the price and market policies put in place to try to minimise the adjustment pressures on farmers as a result of market trends. It describes the pressures for change in these policies arising from EU budgetary concerns, the recent GATT agreement and the possible accession to the EU of the Central European countries. Section 5 assesses the competitiveness of Irish agriculture in the light of these pressures and discusses policies designed to improve its competitiveness. Section 6 examines rural development policies designed to promote agricultural diversification and to provide alternative employment opportunities in rural areas. Section 7 discusses the likely impacts of the new agenda issues raised by consumers and environmentalists. The conclusions of the chapter are summarised in Section 8.

2 CHARACTERISTICS OF THE AGRICULTURAL SECTOR

The composition of Irish agricultural output over the period 1975 to 1993 is indicated in Table 11.2. Climatically, Ireland is better suited to grassland than crop production. Of the total agricultural area (including rough grazing) of 4.4 million hectares in 1993, over 90 per cent was devoted to grass. Livestock and livestock products accounted for 89 per cent of total output in 1993 and their importance has increased steadily over the past twenty years. Within this group, milk output increased its share significantly at the expense of other livestock enterprises until 1985 since when the contribution of milk output has fallen because of the introduction of a quota system limiting the amount of milk production. Sheep production has increased significantly in recent years with sheep numbers increasing by 170 per cent between 1980 and 1991. The contribution of cereals to total output has fallen steadily, although the other tillage sector has maintained its share in recent years, in part thanks to promising developments in the horticultural area such as mushroom growing. It is also noteworthy that the upward trend in the share of current inputs in gross agricultural output has been reversed since the mid-1980s.

Table 11.2
Composition of Agricultural Output and Inputs, Selected Years
(per cent of gross agricultural output by value)

	1975	1980	1985	1990	1993
Livestock and livestock products	*83.6*	*84.5*	*88.2*	*86.9*	*89.0*
Cattle	40.1	36.6	37.8	38.4	39.1
Milk	27.7	31.6	35.4	32.3	33.2
Pigs	7.8	7.6	5.5	5.6	5.9
Sheep and wool	3.2	3.4	3.8	4.4	5.0
Poultry and eggs	3.8	4.1	3.7	3.0	3.0
Horses	0.9	1.3	2.0	1.9	1.9
Total crops and turf	*16.4*	*15.5*	*11.8*	*13.1*	*11.1*
Cereals	6.2	7.8	4.9	5.3	3.8
Other tillage and turf	10.2	7.7	6.9	7.8	7.3
Gross agricultural output	*100.0*	*100.0*	*100.0*	*100.0*	*100.0*
Total inputs	*32.3*	*44.4*	*46.5*	*42.3*	*41.7*
Feed, fertiliser and seed	23.0	29.7	29.7	25.6	25.2
Other current inputs	9.3	14.7	16.8	16.7	16.5
Gross agricultural product	*67.7*	*55.6*	*53.5*	*57.7*	*58.3*

Source: CSO, *Irish Statistical Bulletin,* Stationery Office, Dublin, various issues.

The aggregate performance of the agricultural sector can be measured either in terms of Gross Agricultural Output (GAO) or of Gross Agricultural Product (GAP). GAO measures total off-farm sales plus consumption of farm produce by the farm household plus changes in livestock inventory. From the point of view of the food industry growth in GAO is the relevant indicator because it measures the increase in the total availability of raw material for further processing. GAP measures the contribution of agriculture to value added in the economy and is obtained by subtracting purchased inputs (excluding labour) from gross output. It is the relevant measure of agriculture's contribution to the sum total of national output. Trends in both indicators are shown in Figure 11.1 for the period 1973-1995. GAO grew by an average annual rate of 2.2 per cent and GAP by 1.8

per cent. A pronounced cyclical pattern is evident. Inputs of materials and services grew more rapidly than output in the 1970s but more slowly than output in the 1980s. Ireland's usage of these inputs remains much lower than elsewhere in the EU, but the increased capitalisation and intensification which these figures reflect have given rise to some concern about agriculture's impact on the environment, which is considered further in Section 7.

Figure 11.1

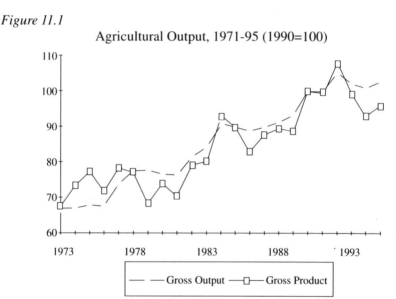

Agricultural Output, 1971-95 (1990=100)

Sources: CSO, *Estimated Output, Input and Income in Agriculture,* various issues; Central Bank, *Quarterly Bulletin,* Spring 1995.

An important characteristic of Irish agriculture is its export orientation. The export market now absorbs more than 80 per cent of dairy and beef output. There has been a marked change in the destination of exports, with a sharp fall in the UK share, a modest increase in the share of other EU countries and a substantial increase in the share of non-EU markets. High export dependence together with relative distance from our main markets has two important consequences. First, it means prices here tend to be lower than those received by producers elsewhere in the EU. If there is downward pressure on the general level of EU market prices, and given a uniform intervention support price across the EU (the nature of intervention is discussed in Section 4), then Irish processors will be the first to find selling into intervention an attractive option to dispose of their produce. This helps to explain why Ireland made such heavy use of the intervention system during the 1980s. Second, the importance of sales to third-country markets outside the EU which are only possible with the aid of export subsidies leaves Ireland vulnerable to any changes in agricultural support arrangements which would target these subsidies. We will see in Section 4 that this is one outcome of the Uruguay Round of GATT negotiations.

Important structural characteristics of agriculture include the number of farms, their size distribution and the resources used. The 1991 Census of Agriculture enumerated 170,000 farms above 1 hectare in size. Their average size in terms of land area is 26 hectares although there is considerable diversity around this average. The average farm area is large in European terms, but because of the relatively low intensity of land use the average size of farm business in Ireland is at the smaller end of the EU spectrum. There is an important regional dimension to differences in farm size, with a predominance of smaller farms in the West and the North-West, and a greater proportion of larger farms in the South and East. Small farm size is frequently associated with a low-margin farming system (mainly drystock) and a predominance of older farmers, many of whom are unmarried.

Finally, farm incomes tend to be lower than average non-farm incomes and to fluctuate very considerably (Table 11.3). The disparity is even more marked when we recall that industrial earnings represent the remuneration for labour supplied, while the family farm income is the return to all the resources invested in the farm business, including management and capital as well as labour. We will see later that examining only the farm income of farm households does not tell the whole story, but the relatively low and variable returns from farming as an activity have been important stimuli for government intervention in the sector.

Table 11.3

Comparison of Farm and Non-farm Incomes

Year	Average family farm income IR£	Average industrial wage IR£
1984	5,370	8,257
1985	4,482	8,915
1986	4,327	9.580
1987	5,779	10,069
1988	7,197	10,547
1989	7,282	10,971
1990	6,682	11,394
1991	6,053	11,878
1992	7,172	12,372
1993	8,075	13,036

Sources: P. Commins and J. Frawley, *The Structure of Irish Farming in 2005,* Teagasc, Dublin 1995; CSO, *Survey of Industrial Earnings,* various issues.

3 STRUCTURAL CHANGE IN IRISH AGRICULTURE

The agricultural structure described in Section 2 is undergoing rapid change as a result of economic imperatives and technological change. The structure of an industry has important economic consequences, and the pattern of agricultural adjustment has important implications for the future competitiveness of the sector. This section examines the nature of the changes underway.

The Pressures for Adjustment

Agriculture in all industrialised countries faces a severe adjustment problem and Irish agriculture is no exception. On the one hand, the supply potential of the farm sector was dramatically increased as the scientific revolution gathered pace, making available to farmers a range of productive new inputs such as improved seed varieties, better fertilisers, more powerful machinery, chemicals and pesticides. As a result of this technological innovation, the supply of agricultural products has increased rapidly. Unfortunately, the market for this increased output has not grown to the same extent. Growth in demand is dependent on growth in population and in per capita incomes. But the rate of population growth in industrialised countries has been slowing down and in some cases has virtually ceased. While per capita incomes have continued to grow, a smaller and smaller proportion of this increase has been spent on food. The consequence has been a downward pressure on the aggregate price level for agricultural products relative to other commodities. This in turn has depressed farm incomes and encouraged the migration of the farm workforce to non-farm job opportunities. In all industrialised countries, the share of the farm workforce in total employment has fallen significantly. In Ireland, the numbers at work in agriculture fell from 330,000 in 1960 to 143,000 in 1993.

The Pattern of Adjustment

This reduction in the agricultural workforce has been accompanied by an increase in the size of the farm business and by increased specialisation. Thus, the number of holdings with several enterprises has declined and there has been a general increase in the average area of crops grown or livestock maintained per farm. Structural change has been most rapid in tillage, dairying and pigs and has proceeded at a slower rate in cattle and sheep farming.

This pattern of increased scale and specialisation has not taken place evenly across farms but has been accompanied by a growing concentration of production and output. Agricultural output is not only produced by fewer farms; it has also become more concentrated on the larger farms. There has been a steady process of polarisation in which the proportion of total output contributed by smaller farms has fallen compared to the share of output produced on larger farms. This polarisation process is illustrated by the divergent trends in family farm income on farms in different size groups in recent decades (Table 11.4). Farm income in each size group is indexed to 100 in the base period 1955-58. By 1983, incomes in nominal terms had increased almost eight times on the smallest size group but by over sixteen times on the largest size group. Figures from the TEAGASC 1990 National Farm Survey indicate that the top 20 per cent of Irish farms based on farm income accounted for 39 per cent of agricultural land but produced 60 per cent of farm output.[2]

Table 11.4

Index Changes in Family Farm Income Per Farm, 1955-83
(full-time farms except for 1955-58 and 1966-67)

| Year | Farm size (acres) | | | | |
	15-30	30-50	50-100	100-200	200+
1955-58	100	100	100	100	100
1966-67	64	97	103	103	112
1975	298	429	381	477	529
1983	744	1,042	1,211	1,288	1,639

Source: R. Breen, D. Hannan, D. Rottman and C. Whelan, *Understanding Contemporary Ireland,* Gill and Macmillan, Dublin 1990.

This pattern of agricultural restructuring reflects a growing tendency towards disengagement from full-time farming in favour of part-time operation of the holding, or even a retreat into retirement or semi-retirement. Recent research documents the growing importance of non-farm income to farm households (in 1987 only 54 per cent of the gross household income of farm families came from farming, compared to 70 per cent in 1973). Non-farm income is made up of state transfers (pensions, children's allowances, social welfare payments, etc.) and other income, including off-farm employment and investment income. The distribution of farm households by their total income is shown in Table 11.5. The average gross farm household income of IR£12,617 compares with the average household income in urban areas in 1987 of about IR£13,700. The contribution of state transfers is much greater in the lower-income groups, while the contribution of other income (mainly from off-farm employment) increases as one moves up the income scale. Clearly farm households where at least one member has off-farm employment have a generally favourable income position. In future, greater emphasis is likely to be put on farm household income, as opposed to income derived solely from farming, in assessing trends in the welfare of the farm population. There may be less emphasis on the gap between farm and non-farm incomes and more emphasis on the sizeable income disparities within the agricultural sector itself.

Table 11.5

Classification of Farm Households by Household Income
(derived from the 1987 Household Budget Survey)

Income group	1	2	3	4	5	Total
No. of households (000s)	27,000	27,000	27,000	27,000	27,000	135,000
Average gross household income (IR£)	3,050	6,000	9,400	15,150	29,450	12,617
Per cent derived from farming (%)	44	52	54	52	57	54
Per cent derived from state transfers (%)	48	38	27	17	8	18
Per cent derived from other income (%)	8	10	19	31	35	28

Source: Report of the Agriculture and Food Policy Review Group, Stationery Office, Dublin 1991.

Table 11.6

Viability Status of Irish Family Farms, 1993

Economic status	Viable	Not viable	Not viable	Not viable
Other activity status		Has job	No job	No job
Demographic status		Viable	Viable	Not viable
Number of farms	47,000	36,000	48,000	34,000

Source: P. Commins and J. Frawley, *The Structure of Irish Farming in 2005,* Teagasc, Dublin 1995.

Farm Viability

The outcome of these structural changes can be summarised in terms of their consequences for the viability of farms and farm households. A family farm business is said to be viable if it is capable of reproducing itself as a business and satisfying the needs and aspirations of family members while perpetuating itself as a domestic group. Viability has three dimensions. In economic terms, a farm is defined as viable if it has the ability to remunerate family labour at a socially acceptable level while making provision for reinvestment in the farm business. A second dimension is whether the farm operator or his/her spouse has an off-farm job. The third dimension is demographic viability, defined as whether an apparent heir to the current landholder exists. An approximate breakdown of the 165,000 Irish farms covered by the TEAGASC National Farm Survey by their viability status is shown in Table 11.6.

Based on the definitions used by TEAGASC, only around 30 per cent of farms could be considered economically viable in 1993. Most of these farms (77 per cent) are dairy farms on good soils and some will have, in addition, off-farm income, mainly because of the occupations of wives and self-employment activity by the farm operators. A further 36,000 farms are made viable by off-farm income even though the farming activity, on its own, is not viable. The largest single group of farms (48,000 in number) are those with relatively young households but without an off-farm job and yet whose farms are economically non-viable. In 1993 these farms had an average value of output of IR£14,500 from which they earned an average IR£4,600. State transfers such as pensions make up an important part of total household income. They constitute the main problem category in Irish farming. The final category is a residual group of some 34,000 households of older people on small farms, operated at low levels of intensity.

In the face of the economic pressures for further agricultural restructuring, it is likely that the survival strategies of farm households will differ depending on the resource base of the family farm and family circumstances. The challenge for currently viable farms will be to maintain their viability by investing to lower costs and, possibly, acquiring additional land in the face of downward pressure on farm prices. For currently non-viable farms with younger families, possible options include intensification to increase the value of the income from farming, attempting to acquire additional land or seeking off-farm employment. Where none of these options are possible, farms will become part of the residual group with a low intensity of farming activity and mainly reliant on state transfers for household income.

4 THE POLICY ENVIRONMENT

Irish membership of the EU in 1973 ensured that Irish agriculture had access to an unlimited market at favourable prices for the first time since Independence (see Chapter 1). Government reports drew up ambitious targets for agricultural growth and considerable investment was undertaken at farm level. Yet although some sectors, such as milk, clearly benefited from the early years of EU membership, the trend in overall agricultural output growth altered little. The structural polarisation in Irish agriculture, described in Section 3, meant that relatively few farms were able to take advantage of the improved conditions. Much of the benefit of higher prices was dissipated through higher land values. By the early 1980s, the warning signs of difficulties ahead were appearing on the horizon. Growing structural surpluses in the EU as a whole led to the imposition of quotas on milk production in 1984 which brought the one dynamic sector in Irish agriculture during the previous decade to a sudden halt. During the remainder of the 1980s, the slack was taken up through expansion in the beef and sheepmeat sectors. In 1992, however, the EU also placed limits on the number of cattle and sheep, and on the acreage of tillage, which could receive subsidies in future as part of the MacSharry reform of the CAP (described below). Within the space of two short decades, the market environment for Irish agriculture has changed from one of unlimited potential to one where there are now ceilings on the expansion of nearly all our major enterprises. The reasons for this change are investigated in this section.

The Common Agricultural Policy

Until the constitutional reforms of the Single European Act (1987) and the Maastricht Treaty (1993) the CAP was often referred to as the EU's only common policy and the cement which held the Union together. Certainly, it dominated the EU's budget for all of its first three decades, often accounting during the 1980s for over 70 per cent of total EU expenditure. However, it is important to understand that the EU did not initiate this policy of agricultural support. A protectionist policy towards agriculture had been pursued by the countries of the original EEC, to varying degrees, since at least the 1870s. The problem for the architects of the Common Market was how to integrate the differing national policies of the six original member states into a common policy. The option of leaving agriculture out of the Common Market (as happened in the European Free Trade Association, for example) was never seriously considered. At the heart of the original Common Market was an economic deal between France and Germany under which France obtained access to the German market for its agricultural exports in return for opening the French market to German industrial goods. Thus a common agricultural policy had to be included in the Treaty of Rome which established the European Economic Community in 1958.

The objectives of this common agricultural policy were spelled out in Article 39 of the Treaty and are worth quoting in full:

The objectives of the common agricultural policy shall be:

(a) to increase agricultural productivity by promoting technical progress and by ensuring the rational development of agricultural production and the optimum utilisation of all factors of production, in particular labour;

(b) thus, to ensure a fair standard of living for the agricultural community, in particular by increasing the individual earnings of persons engaged in agriculture;

(c) to stabilise markets;

(d) to provide certainty of supplies;

(e) to ensure that supplies reach consumers at reasonable prices.

These five objectives of efficient agricultural production, fair incomes for farmers, stable markets, food security and reasonable consumer prices would be broadly acceptable to most people, though the sharp-eyed will note the ambiguity of the wording (what is a fair standard of living for farmers? what is a reasonable price for consumers?) and the potential for conflict between different objectives. The Treaty of Rome did not specify how these objectives should be achieved, but left this for subsequent negotiation. The two key issues were: what support mechanisms should be used to stabilise markets and support farm incomes, and at what level should support prices be set? The mechanisms were finally agreed in 1962 and remained in place until significant changes were required by the GATT Uruguay Round Agreement which came into force in 1995.

For each of the main commodities produced in the EU, each year the Council of Agricultural Ministers establishes a *target price* (or its equivalent). This is the price Ministers would ideally like producers to receive over the coming year. To maintain the market price around this target level the EU has at its disposal a number of policy instruments, including import controls, market intervention, export subsidies and direct aids. The most important form of import barrier in the past was the *variable levy*. This levy was set to equal the difference between the Union target price and the world price, defined as the lowest offer price at which an exporter is prepared to supply the Union. For commodities subject to the variable levy system it ensured that no produce could be imported into the Union below the target price and so undermine the market price received by EU producers. If third-country exporters became more competitive and lowered their offer price, the Commission simply increased the size of the variable levy so that the selling price within the EU remained the same. Thus the variable levy ensured that the EU internal market could not be destabilised by fluctuations in world prices or undercut by falling world prices.

On the internal market, price support to producers of some commodities is further strengthened in the event of excess EU supplies by a guarantee that the Union stands ready to purchase farm produce at a price (called the *intervention price*) usually set some 10-30 per cent below the target price. If there is excess supply on the EU market, farmers have the option to sell to the intervention agency in each state which then takes the produce off the market and puts it in store. This arrangement establishes a floor under the market, although, for various reasons, market prices often fall below intervention levels. In the opposite situation where prices rise significantly above the target price level, then produce may be released from store, tariffs and levies may be suspended and, in exceptional cases, export taxes may be imposed in order to keep internal EU prices down. These measures are designed to fulfil that part of the CAP's objectives which seeks to provide a secure supply of food at reasonable prices to consumers.

For commodities where the EU market was in deficit these arrangements provided almost complete protection against a fall in farm prices. For surplus commodities, however, the problem was that the internal EU price was much higher than world prices in most years. Without some compensatory payment, no country would be interested in purchasing EU exports and surplus production would simply end up in storage. So as a further measure to guarantee prices to producers, provision is made for *export refunds* (subsidies) to enable farm produce to be exported outside the Union. These export refunds bridge the gap between the high internal market prices and the lower world prices in most years. Border levies, intervention purchases and export refunds are the principal means of supporting prices to farmers under the CAP.

The MacSharry CAP Reform

The operation of the CAP price policy ensured a greater degree of internal price stability than in other countries and meant higher per capita incomes for a greater number of farmers than would otherwise have been the case. However, these achievements were bought at a price. Support prices tend to be based on the costs incurred by the average farm producing that output. At these prices the more efficient farmers have an incentive to increase production, while the less efficient farmers do not face sufficiently strong incentives to withdraw from the industry. The resulting increase in output cannot be absorbed by the natural growth in demand, leading to the accumulation of stocks and to dumping on international markets. Thus the EU, which was initially a deficit producer of many agricultural products, is now a major net exporter. An obvious consequence of this was the escalating budget cost of purchasing surplus production for intervention storage or of financing export refunds.

The distribution of support payments was also questioned. Because support is proportional to production, most of the support goes to the largest farmers who need it least. The European Commission has calculated that 80 per cent of the support provided by the CAP goes to the largest 20 per cent of farmers.[3] Furthermore, the costs of the policy are borne disproportionately by low-income consumers who spend relatively larger amounts of their household income on food. Price support also encouraged the intensification of agriculture which has been damaging to the environment. It led to increasing tension with the EU's trading partners who objected to the loss of their markets to EU subsidised exports. The policy was also inefficient as an increasing proportion of the transfers from taxpayers and consumers failed to be reflected in improved farm incomes.

During the 1980s a number of half-hearted attempts had been made to limit the budgetary cost of the CAP. However, the 1992 reforms introduced by Agriculture Commissioner MacSharry, albeit still incomplete, went much further in that they initiated a significant reduction in support prices, especially for cereals and beef. Supply control measures were extended (particularly through the introduction of 'set-aside' for cereals and oilseeds) and the role of intervention support, particularly in the beef sector, was greatly reduced. Compensation for these price reductions and intensified supply controls was provided by means of direct area and livestock payments. Crucially, these payments are limited to the specific numbers of livestock or hectares planted to tillage crops in a base year and if production in any member state were to increase beyond these levels no additional subsidy payments would be made. The livestock payments are also linked to a maximum stocking density limit to promote extensification. These criteria are a strong disincentive to additional production and in this sense the MacSharry payments are partially decoupled from production. Finally, the market regime reforms were accompanied by new agri-environment, forestry and early retirement schemes for farmers.

The transition to the new market regimes was phased in over a three-year period from 1993 to 1995 and had an almost immediate effect. Intervention stocks of beef, dairy products and cereals fell dramatically in the first year. Farm incomes, not least in the reformed sectors of cereals and beef, improved. In future, a much higher proportion of farm income will be accounted for by direct payments. In 1992, for example, the year before the reforms, direct payments accounted for 22 per cent of Irish farm income. These came mainly in the form of compensatory headage payments to farmers in the less-favoured areas and ewe premia paid as part of the support mechanism in the sheepmeat market. By 1996, it is forecast these payments will account for 40 per cent of farm income. In the sheep sector, headage and ewe premia may actually exceed the value of output, while total subsidies in the cattle sector will be equivalent to about 50 per cent of the value of output.[4]

The GATT Uruguay Round Agreement

As noted, the EU's agricultural price-support arrangements were also coming under increasing external pressure from its trading partners, most notably the United States, within the context of the Uruguay Round of GATT trade negotiations. This Round got underway in September 1986 and sought to liberalise trade and tighten the rules covering government intervention in trade over a broad range of areas. When the brief for the agricultural dossier of these negotiations was agreed, world agricultural trade was in considerable disarray. World agricultural prices were very depressed, commodity stockpiles had grown enormously and government expenditures for agricultural support were growing rapidly. Both the United States and the EU agreed, along with the other participating countries, that the objective of the negotiations should be to achieve a substantial, progressive reduction in agricultural support and to bring government interventions in agricultural markets under more effective GATT rules and disciplines.

There are three broad areas where the final Uruguay Round agreement imposes disciplines on agricultural support. The first deals with border protection. All border restrictions, including the EU's variable levies, must be converted into tariffs (i.e. fixed import duties). Furthermore, these tariffs are to be reduced by 36 per cent over a six-year period beginning in 1995. There is also an obligation to ensure that a minimum of 5 per cent of the domestic market is open to foreign competition by the end of this period. The second area deals with restrictions on the use of export subsidies. While, in the past, the EU's use of export subsidies was open-ended (subject only to internal budget constraints), the GATT agreement imposes an obligation to cut subsidised exports by 36 per cent in value and 21 per cent in volume relative to the average for the period 1986-90. The third area deals with the overall value of agricultural support (excluding payments which are decoupled from production in the sense that they do not influence farmers' decision to produce). Non-decoupled payments must be reduced by 20 per cent over the base period 1986-88. In addition, it has been agreed that a further round of negotiations on agricultural trade liberalisation will begin in 1999.

The conclusion of the Uruguay Round agreement set off a heated debate within the EU on whether the restrictions it imposes would have additional adverse effects on farmers to those already introduced (and compensated for) by the MacSharry CAP reforms. It appears that the actual impact of the Uruguay Round disciplines on EU agriculture during the implementation period of the agreement (i.e. to the year 2000) are likely to be minimal, for a number of reasons. The reference period for the tariff cuts was very favourable to the EU, being based on a period of low world prices and thus high EU variable levies. Hence the tariff cuts are being made from very high levels, giving maximum protection in the short run. Credit was given for reductions in EU agricultural support (particularly in the dairy and cereals sectors) which had been implemented since the Uruguay Round talks began in 1986 so that much of the targeted reduction in the aggregate value of agricultural support has already been achieved. Furthermore, the compensation payments payable under the MacSharry reforms are deemed to be decoupled and are therefore excluded from the reductions in this aggregate measure. Even the obligation to reduce the amount of subsidised exports may be relatively easily met by the EU given the expected reduction in production growth (and, for some commodities, increased internal demand) from the implementation of the MacSharry reforms. From this perspective, the GATT deal does not look a bad deal from the perspective of European farmers.

However, this is not the whole story. The full impact of the Uruguay Round disciplines will not be felt until after the transition period. At that point, with continued increases in yields in the EU and limited growth in internal demand, surpluses will again begin to grow and with them the need for exports, so that maintaining the commitments on export subsidies will become increasingly difficult. There is also the prospect that the disciplines will be further tightened in the next GATT negotiating round scheduled to begin in 1999. Now that border protection is entirely transparent in the form of tariffs, it seems inevitable that there will be further pressures for tariff reductions as has happened in the case of industrial goods. Some commentators warn that, in this new round, the 'decoupled' nature of the CAP compensation payments will come under scrutiny and that it will be increasingly difficult to defend their general application to all farms. By then, however, it is probable that the EU will be grappling with the implications of further eastwards enlargement. For the agricultural sector, this could require adjustments far larger than those required by GATT.

Central and East European Enlargement

At the Copenhagen summit in June 1993, the EU held out the prospect of full membership for those Central and Eastern European countries (CEECs) with which it had signed Europe agreements.[5] In all of these countries, agriculture is important in both output and employment terms. This raises the question of the likely impact of the further EU enlargement and its consequences for agricultural policy.

In the immediate aftermath of the transition to market economies these countries experienced a dramatic fall in agricultural output, for a number of reasons. Uncertainty over property rights in land, poorly functioning input markets, unfavourable trends in relative prices, the loss of important export markets in the former Soviet Union, the collapse of domestic demand and adverse weather have all been important causes. Thus, despite limited concessions in the Europe agreements for improved access to the EU market for CEEC agricultural exports, the balance of agricultural trade has actually been improving in the EU's favour.

The extent to and, perhaps more important, the pace at which agricultural output will recover in these countries and whether they will emerge as significant agricultural exporters in the medium term remains very unclear. A number of studies have attempted to estimate the impact of extending the CAP to the CEECs. Where these studies have assumed an unreformed CAP, an early transition to full membership and a rapid growth in the CEECs' agricultural production, the estimated budgetary costs would be crippling (particularly given the likely demand for additional Structural Fund resources as well to promote economic cohesion). In these scenarios further radical CAP reform is inevitable *before* the eastward enlargement can take place. Taking a more realistic view of the likely timescale for the recovery of CEEC agricultural production, taking account of the MacSharry CAP reforms and recognising that the most optimistic interpretation of the institutional timetable makes 2003 the earliest possible date for accession, would all limit the budgetary impact of CEEC membership. Another difficulty for the EU in absorbing the CEECs is likely to be integrating the latter's GATT obligations under the Uruguay Round with those of the EU. These countries have very low limits on their permitted volume of subsidised exports under the GATT. If farm prices were to increase to present CAP levels it is possible the size of their exportable surpluses would exceed the limits allowed. Thus some adjustments to the CAP to prepare for the eastward enlargement would appear to be sensible, although the more apocalyptic pronouncements regarding its agricultural impacts are probably overstated.

Strategic Policy Issues for Ireland

Ireland faces a particular dilemma in assessing appropriate policy options for the future of the CAP. On the one hand, Irish farmers and the Irish economy have benefited from the transfers brought about by the high-price-support policy. This gain to the economy amounts to between 4 and 5 per cent of Irish GDP.[6] If restrictions are required, whether for budgetary reasons or to meet international obligations, the preferred alternative has been supply management under which the high-price policy is maintained but for quantities limited by quota, set-aside or other controls.

But there are dangers in such a 'Fortress Europe' policy. Quota rights eventually become capitalised into costs of production thus eroding the benefits of support for new and expanding producers. Farmers are increasingly irked by the restrictions and rules which they see as limiting their freedom to produce. Consumers lose the benefit of access to cheaper food supplies. Agriculture in the EU would become increasingly detached from market trends. And if the ultimate direction is towards greater market orientation, delaying the necessary adjustments will only make the required changes more painful.

But a pro-active policy of preparing to meet greater market competition creates its own dilemmas for Irish policymakers. One of the voices arguing for such a policy in Ireland has been the National Economic and Social Council. In a 1993 report, it wrote: 'Despite current limitations on production it is clear that the general direction of agricultural policy will be towards greater liberalisation. In this context, structural reform is essential to achieve and maintain long-run competitiveness in agriculture'.[7] This would require greater progress in overcoming the structural weaknesses of the sector, including the large number of non-viable holdings typically controlled by elderly farmers (see Section 3). The Council did not flinch from the logic of its recommendation. Its view was that 'future Irish structural policy should give priority to achieving effective land use rather than to maintaining the maximum number of holdings at inadequate income levels'. However, it qualified this by making this recommendation only within the context of complementary development policies for agriculture as well as effective non-agricultural programmes for rural areas. But are rural development policies likely to be sufficiently powerful to be able to absorb the fall-out from a more commercially-oriented agricultural policy?

Another dilemma concerns the integration of consumer and environmental concerns into agricultural policy. The 1991 report of the Agriculture and Food Policy Review Group argued that, at national level, an increasingly environmentally-friendly agricultural and food industry should be developed based on sustainable production processes, and that the highest internationally-accepted food-quality and safety standards should be attained throughout the production chain from farm level to the consumer. However, it is also clear that meeting the highest environmental and food-quality standards will be costly and, in the short run at least, may conflict with attempts to improve agriculture's market competitiveness. These issues are explored in the remainder of this chapter.

5 POLICIES TO MAINTAIN AND IMPROVE COMPETITIVENESS

The discussion in the previous section suggested that, whatever about the pace of reform of agricultural support policies, the direction of reform is towards a more market-oriented framework for EU agricultural production with income assistance increasingly given in the form of direct payments. A key question is how well will Irish agriculture perform in such a context, and what needs to be done to strengthen the competitive position of Irish farming in such an environment? The competitive position of Irish agriculture and the policies available to improve its competitiveness are the subject matter of this section.

Agriculture's Competitive Position

A useful approach to measuring competitiveness is to examine relative costs of production for different farm enterprises across countries. The argument is that countries with lower costs of production for a particular enterprise have a competitive advantage in the production of that commodity. Table 11.7 presents information on Ireland's costs of producing milk relative to a number of competitor countries. Milk is chosen because of its key importance in the Irish agricultural economy. Two different cost of production series are shown. One index is based on cash costs of production. Cash costs include all actual cash outlays on purchased inputs by producers. The second index is based on total costs of production, i.e. cash costs plus capital depreciation plus imputed resource costs. Imputed resource costs refer to the opportunity cost of using family-owned resources in the farm business. For example, where the labour used on the farm is family labour, it has no cash cost. None the less, it is clear that, in the long term, the farm business must earn enough to remunerate the family labour or otherwise it will go out of business. The difficulty is that the appropriate opportunity cost must be imputed and is not known with certainty. If different assumptions are made in different countries about the size of these imputed costs then this will bias the ranking of countries based on the total cost of production index. For this reason, some analysts prefer to focus on the index based on cash costs as these are known with certainty.

The cash cost index may be quite a reliable guide to countries' relative competitiveness in the short run as the non-priced inputs (such as family-owned labour and land) are relatively fixed factors of production. In the long run, however, the total cost index is the preferred index to use in ranking countries' relative competitiveness. On the cash-cost-index basis Ireland emerges as a very competitive milk producer. However, this ranking is reversed when total costs of production are considered. The reason is that the Irish milk production system requires relatively fewer purchased inputs than our competitors, but conversely has a greater relative dependence on resources whose costs must be imputed. It is generally accepted that dairying is Ireland's most efficient enterprise, so Ireland's lack of long-run competitiveness in milk production is deeply worrying. Incidentally, it is worth noting that in nearly all EU countries total costs of production exceed the value of milk produced. This is another way of saying that the resources employed in milk production do not, in fact, earn a return equivalent to their imputed opportunity cost and thus we can predict a further reduction in the resources employed in dairying including the number of dairy farmers, even with no further reduction in dairy prices. A similar pattern to the story for milk emerges from an examination of the competitiveness of the other main Irish farm enterprises.[8]

Table 11.7
The Competitive Advantage of Irish Dairying in the Late 1980s

Country	Cash costs as a percentage of the value of output	Total costs as a percentage of the value of output
Australia	64	n.a.
Belgium	46	99.3
Canada	52	n.a.
Denmark	74	129.8
France	60	123.5
Germany	60	118.6
Ireland	*52*	*130.0*
Italy	52	127.7
Netherlands	57	113.6
New Zealand	68	n.a.
UK	64	117.2
US	77	n.a.

Source: G. Boyle, B. Kearney, T. McCarthy and M. Keane, *The Competitiveness of Irish Agriculture,* Allied Irish Banks, Dublin 1991.

Structural Policies
Policies to improve the structure of Irish agriculture and its competitiveness are regulated and partly funded by the EU's agricultural structures policy. The Common Agricultural Policy has two arms, price and markets policy and structural policy respectively. Price and markets policy is funded by the Guarantee Section of the agricultural budget (known as FEOGA, after its French initials), and structural policy is funded by the Guidance Section of FEOGA. Originally, it was expected that the Guidance Section would account for up to one-third of total agricultural spending. As surpluses grew, so did the demands on the FEOGA Guarantee budget and,

in practice, structural policy expenditure never accounted for more than 5 per cent of the total. Following the passage of the Single European Act, the EU undertook a reform of its Structural Funds. These include the FEOGA Guidance Section as well as the Regional and Social Funds. The reform doubled the resources available to the Structural Funds, introduced a greater focus on the disadvantaged regions in the EU and required the adoption of a programming approach to the disbursement of these funds.[9] Disadvantaged regions are known as Objective 1 regions and must produce a development plan indicating how the Structural Fund resources will be used to promote economic and social cohesion. This development plan then forms the basis of a contract between the European Commission and the national government known as the Community Support Framework (CSF) which sets out how the Structural Funds, including FEOGA Guidance, will be used.[10] The main measures designed to improve the structure and competitiveness of Irish agriculture are now included in the CSF.

The current CSF covers the period 1994-99 and was drawn up on the basis of the National Development Plan 1994-99 submitted to Brussels in 1993. Under this CSF Structural Fund assistance is disbursed through nine Operational Programmes, one of which is the Operational Programme for Agriculture, Rural Development and Forestry. The CSF is funded through a combination of state, European Union Structural Fund and private expenditure. For the Agriculture Operational Programme EU funding comes primarily from the FEOGA Guidance Section with some additional support from the European Social Fund for agricultural education and training. Total expenditure on agriculture, rural development and forestry over the period will be IR£1,518 million while Ireland's receipts of FEOGA Guidance Section resources will be IR£846 million (in 1994 prices). A significant proportion of this amount is used to fund compensatory headage payments to farmers in disadvantaged farming regions (which now cover 72 per cent of the country). The remainder is used to fund a variety of investment and structural improvement measures.

Investment Measures
The evidence on Ireland's competitiveness in dairying suggests that Irish agriculture might be in a better position than many of its competitors in the short run to withstand a regime of lower support prices, but that to survive in the longer term will require a vigorous programme to assist farmers to adjust by reducing costs. This will require substantial capital investment on farms to increase efficiency and improve quality while at the same time protecting the environment. The investment schemes for agriculture currently in operation are the Farm Improvement Programme (FIP) and the Control of Farm Pollution Scheme (CFP). The FIP provides capital grants to farmers to improve housing facilities for cattle and sheep, to build storage

facilities for fodder, animal waste and effluent and to promote horticulture. It is confined to full-time farmers with training and experience whose income is below a reference income and who carry out the investments under an agreed farm plan. Around 23,000 full-time farmers (out of a total of 112,000) are expected to benefit from this measure over the decade 1989-99.[11] The CFP scheme aims to control farm pollution by providing grant aid to farmers for this purpose and is also focused on the needs of smaller farmers. It is estimated that up to 30,000 farmers will benefit from this programme over the period 1994-99. The government has accepted that the introduction of new dairy hygiene standards and animal welfare requirements from January 1994 will require considerable investment aid in these areas in the coming years and grant aid is also available for these purposes under the CSF.

Investment in Agricultural Research, Education and Training
Fundamental to any strategy to improve agricultural competitiveness must be efforts to improve the quality of the agricultural workforce and to provide through research a stream of innovations designed to cut costs and improve efficiency. TEAGASC, the Agriculture and Food Development Authority, is the statutory body with responsibility for the provision of integrated research, training and advice to agri-industry. International and Irish research shows that the returns to investment in human capital and research are very high – in most countries exceeding 30-50 per cent.[12] Agricultural research and advisory services have traditionally been provided by the state. In the case of research this is justified by its collective and public good nature. The economies of scale associated with research make it impractical for individual farmers to consider undertaking it, while its public good nature means that private firms will underinvest in agricultural research because of the difficulty of ensuring that they can recoup their investment (see Chapter 4). However, private research investment has been increasing in response to recent legislation which permits the patenting of plant varieties and other life forms. These have established a property rights framework under which commercial investors are assured the right to retain the profits of investments in biotechnology and genetic engineering. Agricultural advisory services are also provided by the state as a developmental service and as an extension of the vocational training system. In 1987, charges for TEAGASC advisory services were introduced and TEAGASC advisors are increasingly competing with coops, private consultants and agribusiness in offering technical, market and financial advice. Despite these developments in private sector research and advisory services, there remains a strong case for publicly-funded research and advice and a significant proportion of investment under the Agriculture Operational Programme in the CSF will be used to strengthen these services.

Land Policy

Land tenure in Ireland is now dominated by the owner-occupier system. Various characteristics of this system have proved obstacles to improved land use. The 1991 Census of Agriculture showed that 23 per cent of all farm holders occupying almost 18 per cent of all land are over 65 years of age. Only about 12 per cent of the total area farmed is rented land, and most of this is let on leases of under one year. Virtually all land (estimates suggest between 75 and 85 per cent) is transferred within families so little land becomes available for purchase by others who potentially might make more efficient use of it. In the context of maintaining the competitiveness of Irish agriculture in relation to other countries, the inflexibility of the tenure system and the immobility of land to which it gives rise are major barriers.

For most of the period since Independence land policy was primarily geared to achieving the structural objective of creating the maximum number of viable family farms. Since the 1970s, the goal of bringing about more efficient land use has gained more prominence for a number of reasons. The Land Commission's operations of acquiring, sub-dividing and reallocating land to increase farm size became increasingly slow, expensive and of doubtful effectiveness. Farm size was less and less correlated with farm household viability given the growing importance of non-farm income to farm households. The accumulating evidence showing the widening gap in productivity across farms also focused increasing attention on land use rather than farm size. Land policy based on farm size alone no longer seemed appropriate and the Land Commission's activities were wound up in the 1980s.

Since then land policy has focused on encouraging earlier farm transfer within the family to bring about a higher rate of recruitment of young people into agriculture. The policies implemented include the new EU Early Retirement Scheme in 1994, Young Farmer Installation Aid and concessions for young farmers on the payment of Stamp Duty and Capital Acquisitions Tax.

Incentives to encourage earlier farmer retirement have been tried on previous occasions without significant impact. In the case of the EU-funded Farmer Retirement Scheme which operated in the 1970s the monetary benefits were deemed insufficiently attractive in relation to competing entitlements accruing to farmers who remained in agriculture. Even if it had attracted more interest, however, it would have had limited national impact as it did not apply to the great majority of land transfers which take place within the family. The 1994 scheme is considerably more generous. A farmer (or his or her spouse) who retires between the ages of 55 and 66 and who has been farming full-time for the previous ten years is eligible for a payment of up to IR£9,764 per annum provided he or she transfers the entire farm by gift, sale or lease to a qualified young farmer aged between 18 and 50 years. This younger farmer can be a relative but must already have been farming an acreage equivalent to at least 10 per cent of the land transferred. Around 3,000 farmers are expected to retire under this scheme in 1995.

Long-term leasing is also suggested as a way to promote greater land mobility by separating the question of land ownership from its management control. A number of factors have inhibited the emergence of long-term leasing, including public attitudes which presume a right for persons in occupation of lands for a considerable length of time to retain possession when a letting contract expires, the difficulty for credit agencies in securing advances made to leaseholders, and a tendency in earlier years for the Land Commission to discourage leasing. In order to encourage medium-term leasing a tax break on income from land leasing has been introduced.

Critique of Structural Policies
Greatly enhanced funding for structural policies to improve the competitiveness of Irish agriculture is now available under the 1994-99 Community Support Framework. From an Irish perspective, the requirement to operate structural policies within the broad framework of EU rules has its drawbacks. For example, grant aid to farmers to promote investment and reduce costs is restricted because of EU fears that such aid would lead to increased production and exacerbate its surpluses. The tension between the objectives of improving competitiveness and maintaining the maximum number of farming families is evident in the high proportion of the resources in the Operational Programme for Agriculture, Rural Development and Forestry which are devoted to headage payments to support the incomes of farmers in less-favoured areas. Such payments have little developmental impact and it is odd that they must be funded from the FEOGA Guidance Section rather than the more appropriate Guarantee Section. The additional resources being made available to strengthen research and advisory services are welcome. However, until the basic structural weaknesses in Irish farming are tackled, the number of farmers willing and able to adopt more productive techniques will remain a minority. From a developmental perspective, an important objective should be to try to ensure that the control of land is in the hands of energetic, committed farmers. Such land-use policies have had little success in the past, but it is hoped that the new Early Retirement Scheme and associated moves to encourage medium-term leasing will encourage a greater degree of land mobility in the future.

6 RURAL DEVELOPMENT

Rural development has now a much higher place on the policy agenda. In the past it was often seen as synonymous with agricultural development, on the assumption that greater agricultural output would automatically lead to greater rural prosperity. With cutbacks necessary in farm support there is now greater recognition that sustainable development in rural areas must be based on non-agricultural enterprises, or possibly farm enterprises outside the mainstream of agricultural production. This recognition was reflected in the publication by the European Commission in 1988 of its document The Future of Rural Society which explicitly linked cutbacks in farm support with the need to encourage rural diversification.[13]

In Ireland, the debate on rural development has been given added urgency by the evidence of accelerating rural population decline in the second half of the 1980s. Historically, of course, the Irish rural population has been declining since the 1840s. But this historical pattern was reversed in Leinster from the late 1960s onwards, and the demographic recovery spread to all provinces during the 1970s. Between 1971 and 1981, the population of aggregate rural areas grew by 10 per cent, and by a further 3 per cent between 1981 and 1986. This recovery in rural population numbers came to an end in the mid-1980s. The scale of the turnabout is indicated by the fact that all regions apart from the East region experienced a fall in rural population in the period 1986-91.[14] Apart from the contribution of agricultural restructuring (discussed in Section 3), it appears that rural areas were less attractive to the type of modern industry locating in Ireland in recent years compared to the 1970s. Also, much of the growth in employment has occurred in services, and service employment tends to cluster predominantly in urban areas. There was growing pressure for a government response to what was perceived as a 'rural crisis' and for the adoption of a wider rural development strategy.[15]

In Ireland, while the rhetoric of rural development is relatively new, there is a long history of rural development initiatives which can be traced back to the establishment of the Congested Districts Board by the British administration in 1898 (see Chapter 1). More recently, regional policy measures undertaken since the 1960s encompass many elements of a rural development policy. Given the dominance of the Dublin conurbation, regional development in Ireland might be seen as virtually the same as rural development. However, the term 'rural development' has developed a number of additional connotations. It often implies not just the creation of viable employment opportunities in rural areas but also a particular *style* of development identified by a 'bottom-up' rather than 'top-down' approach. Bottom-up approaches are characterised by an emphasis on local participation in the formulation and implementation of development objectives for an area, by a preference for exploiting indigenous skills and resources rather than relying on 'imported' expertise and capital, by the attempt to integrate social as well as economic development and, for some at least, by a concern that development should benefit the more marginal and disadvantaged groups. Another term which tries to capture the essence of this developmental approach is 'area-based development'.[16]

The Framework for Rural Development Policies

Rural development initiatives are supported by both EU and national programmes. The most important EU initiative is the LEADER programme, introduced as an EU-wide pilot programme designed 'to find innovative solutions which will serve as a model for all rural areas and ensure maximum integration between sectoral measures'. LEADER I operated during the period 1991 through 1994. In Ireland 16 rural development groups covering areas of up to 100,000 people were selected to receive funding of IR£35 million on the basis of 'business plans' submitted to the EU Commission through the Department of Agriculture, Food and Forestry. Each LEADER group then invited local applications for development aid and the funds were disbursed on the basis of criteria agreed with the Department and the group's own business plan. Activities which could be funded included vocational training, rural tourism, small firms, craft enterprises, local services and the marketing of local products. LEADER II will run from 1995 through to 1999 with a budget of IR£77 million with the important difference that it will operate on a national basis.

A number of national initiatives have also been undertaken to promote rural development. A commitment in the Programme for National Recovery (1987) led to the launch of a Pilot Programme for Integrated Rural Development in 1988. Under this programme rural development coordinators were appointed for a two-year period to twelve rural communities to gain experience on appropriate rural development strategies. A number of rural communities are also involved in the pilot programme agreed in the Programme for Economic and Social Progress (1991) for area-based schemes known as PESP Partnerships to tackle long-term unemployment. The distinctive characteristic of this programme is its focus on long-term unemployment and disadvantage (see Chapter 8). The Programme for Government (1993) established County Enterprise Boards with a dual mandate to draw up enterprise action plans at county level covering all sectors and to grant-aid commercially viable small enterprise projects (micro-enterprises) which are not otherwise eligible for support from the main agencies.

The 1994-99 National Development Plan proposed to build on this series of local initiatives and a Local Urban and Rural Development Operational Programme is included as one of the nine operational programmes funded under the 1994-99 Community Support Framework. This Operational Programme is implemented through three sub-programmes, dealing with local enterprise, partnerships with disadvantaged communities and urban and village renewal respectively.

The local enterprise sub-programme will fund the work of the County Enterprise Boards in providing a range of support measures to micro-enterprises including not only financial aid but also advice, mentoring and training. These functions are undertaken in the context of County Enterprise

Plans which are intended to provide a strategic framework for business development in each county through the identification of market opportunities and the coordination of the various support mechanisms for business.

The objectives of the partnerships sub-programme are to use a range of integrated actions in 33 disadvantaged urban and rural areas (thus including additional areas beyond the original PESP Partnerships) to improve the chances of the long-term unemployed finding employment or setting up their own businesses, to enhance community life and the capacity of local organisations and to improve the physical environment of the areas concerned. The funding for the sub-programme is administered by a body known as Area Development Management Ltd. with a membership drawn from representatives of the social partners and a wide range of community and voluntary groups.

The urban and village renewal sub-programme supports investment in the physical renewal and economic regeneration of the major cities, smaller towns and villages.

Rural Development Measures
A characteristic of theses rural development initiatives is that they recognise that rural development is a multi-sectoral phenomenon which will be affected by state policies over a wide range of areas, including the regional emphasis given to industrial policy, the location of public services, settlement planning and the provision of infrastructure. Three measures are particularly linked to farm households and are briefly reviewed here.

Agricultural diversification. Its aim is to encourage agricultural resources to diversify out of the production of mainstream commodities into niche products and activities such as horses for sport, deer, rabbits, greyhounds and on-farm processing such as the production of farmhouse cheese. TEAGASC has launched a Rural Enterprise Service to provide advice, information and training in alternative farm enterprises and generous grant aid (50 per cent in the Disadvantaged Areas and 40 per cent elsewhere) is available under the Operational Programme for Agriculture, Rural Development and Forestry. Organic production is also being encouraged through an Organic Unit in the Department of Agriculture and Food, supporting research and training by TEAGASC, and the development of a labelling system to identify organic products in the marketplace. Early research shows that those adopting alternative enterprises are a select group who already had a favourable attitude towards and the resources to embark on development. Diversification is unlikely to be an option for low-income farmers seeking ways to improve their current standard of living.

Agri-tourism and rural tourism. There is significant potential for tourism to contribute to increased income generation both on farms and in rural areas. Rural tourism is the most significant of all rural development enterprises, accounting for about half of their total value of IR£170 million in 1993. Tourism was also the largest single sector supported under LEADER I programmes, accounting for 51 per cent of all funding disbursed. The provision of farmhouse accommodation was the initial response of farm households to the demand for rural holidays.[18] Subsequently, this has been extended to the provision of more diversified accommodation (e.g. self-catering chalets) and leisure pursuits (e.g. horse-riding). More recent approaches place emphasis on marketing a group agri-tourism product based on the overall accommodation, entertainment and amenity capacity of specific districts. Grant aid for tourism projects is available under the Operational Programme for Agriculture, Rural Development and Forestry as well as from LEADER groups.

Afforestation. More than one-fifth of Ireland's marginal land has been classified as highly productive for forestry so there is considerable scope for afforestation. Afforestation has traditionally been undertaken by the State but supports for private forestry were improved in the Forestry Operational Programme for 1989-93 (part of the first EU-funded Community Support Framework). Further measures to promote forestry are included in the 1994-99 CSF. These include a New Planting Programme of 30,000 hectares a year to the year 2000 (up from 7,000 hectares in 1980 and 23,000 hectares in 1993) promoted by afforestation grants and the payment of annual premia to landowners for 15-20 years, and a Forestry Development Programme consisting of back-up measures such as roads and research and development. Of the area under private afforestation in this period an increasing percentage (from less than 20 per cent rising to over 70 per cent) was taken up by farmers planting trees on their own land. There is a marked regional differentiation in the pattern of applications for forestry grants, however, with commercial farmers showing greater interest in planting trees than low-income farmers on poor agricultural land.[19]

Critique of Rural Development Policy

The current emphasis on rural development arises from the recognition that agricultural policy can no longer be the mainstay of rural economic development and that the emphasis must shift to creating sustainable employment opportunities outside of farming. However, despite the range of schemes and initiatives the amount of funding available for rural development projects is insignificant when compared with the amounts spent on agricultural policy alone. This has consequences beyond the scarcity of funding *per se*. The fact that major support is provided to one particular use of land, namely food production, inevitably creates disincentives for alternative uses (for example, forestry or recreation) and delays the desirable shift from one type of land use to the other. A uniform set of incentives for all rural-based activities would provide the required support for rural development without distorting choices between these activities.

The earlier discussion highlighted the wide range of institutions and initiatives now in place to support rural and area-based development. In the light of the macroeconomic forces at work shaping the spatial distribution of economic activity, and the various sectoral policies (e.g. industrial, tourism, mining, fishing) already in place, it must be asked what these measures can hope to achieve. It is worth investing in rural development initiatives only if they can contribute added value in ways which are not available to mainstream agencies. NESC has argued that added value can arise because local involvement generates voluntary commitment; because the partnership of local groups, statutory agencies and private interests increases the coordination and effectiveness of policy; because information and consultation can improve the design of national policy; and because the coordination of individuals, enterprises and groups encourages the identification of new opportunities for economic activity.[20] Area-based development also has a pronounced focus on combating the disadvantage and social exclusion which may result from conventional market-based approaches to economic development.

It is too early to say whether these claims will be supported in practice. LEADER I claimed to create over 1,400 additional jobs over its three-year life but an independent evaluation suggested this was a considerable overestimate. Problems arise in measuring deadweight (the extent to which the project would have happened anyway) and displacement (the extent to which the new project displaces existing economic activity) effects. An indication of deadweight is that 40 per cent of surveyed recipients acknowledged that the project would have gone ahead without LEADER assistance. Displacement effects must also exist; for example, funding an additional golf course may attract more overseas visitors to play golf in Ireland, but it may also simply attract golfers from already-existing courses. There have also been problems of accountability in the disbursement of funds. To the extent that this leads to a tightening of central financial controls, it tends to crush the element of local initiative the programmes are designed to foster. There are clearly dangers of overlap where different agencies (e.g. LEADER and the County Enterprise Boards) are grant-aiding similar types of projects. Whether the area-based approach to rural development can make a genuinely additional impact in creating sustainable employment in rural areas remains as yet an open question.

7 CONSUMER AND ENVIRONMENTAL CONCERNS

In a more market-oriented environment competitiveness will depend on the ability to assess and meet consumer food preferences accurately. These preferences are rapidly changing, more in response to lifestyle changes than changes in income, and often in contradictory directions. For example, much consumer food purchasing is now driven by health concerns. The message that there is a link between diet and health is now widely accepted and is reflected in increased consumer resistance to the consumption of animal fats and sugar and a growing demand for fresh and natural foods. At the same time, the increased value placed on time (and particularly, women's time as more women enter the labour market) has led to greater consumption of prepared foods and ready-to-eat meals. Government policy can try to ensure that these changing consumer preferences are reflected back to producers through appropriate price signals and other forms of market information.

Increasing environmental awareness must also be factored into agricultural and rural policy. A high-quality environment will be an important source of competitive advantage for agriculture and rural areas in coming years. It can be used to advantage in the marketing of agricultural produce abroad and may help to obtain a premium price in the market place. A high-quality environment may also be an important factor in facilitating alternative income-earning opportunities for the rural population, particularly in disadvantaged farming areas through farm-based tourism. For these reasons the report of the Agriculture and Food Policy Review Group concluded that 'the environment must be brought into the mainstream of agricultural policy'. Because Ireland, in general, has a higher-quality and less-polluted natural environment than most other EU countries, higher environmental standards will require other countries to make more substantial and expensive adjustments and some competitive advantage should shift in Ireland's favour. The Review Group thus argued that Ireland has a clear strategic interest in pressing for high environmental standards to be enshrined in EU legislation.

Food Standards and Quality
From earliest times food has been particularly susceptible to exploitation, and there is a long history of food legislation with the purpose of preventing consumers being either cheated or poisoned! Measures for the protection of the consumer against the adulteration of food and drink are among the earliest examples of social legislation. Since then the scope of food law has been greatly widened. Examples of some of the matters now covered by legislation include the produce of diseased animals posing a threat to human health; the sanitary conditions in food preparation, packaging and handling; pesticide and hormone residues in food; packaging materials which may pose a threat to health; food additives; the labelling requirements for food products; and weights and measures legislation.

Despite the undoubted improvement in food purity and in merchandising practices brought about by this legislation there is a perceptible feeling of unease among consumers about the safety and quality of the modern food supply. Issues of recent concern include the widespread use of chemicals in both food production and manufacturing, the increasingly processed nature of the modern diet, and the existence of nitrates in drinking water. There have been sharp falls in the consumption of particular foods caused by publicity given, for example, to listeria in cheese or salmonella in eggs. The issue of food safety is complicated by the fact that consumers are reluctant to accept the idea of any risk associated with food. Nor is it solely a domestic issue; Latin American countries have refused to accept consignments of Irish dairy products because of alleged high radioactivity while Middle Eastern markets for beef have been lost because of fears of 'mad cow' disease.

The quality and purity of Irish food can be a major positive factor affecting agricultural competitiveness in the years ahead, always provided, of course, that the reality matches the image being promoted. Current legislation and enforcement may be inadequate to ensure the quality and safety of Irish produce, particularly meat. The virtual elimination of antibiotic residues in liquid milk due to comprehensive testing and severe penalties for offending producers shows what is required.

Pricing schemes should reflect consumer preferences and reward producers for producing what consumers want. Milk, for example, has two components of value, fat and protein. Consumer preferences have moved strongly away from the milk fat component in favour of protein. Yet relatively few Irish creameries reflect this situation in the way they pay for milk. Consumers have also turned against fat when purchasing beef and prefer much leaner meat. The meat factories use a payments scheme which penalises producers for over-fat animals and rewards those who produce lean meat. However, purchasers for the live export trade to third countries pay farmers solely on a weight basis, thus giving farmers an incentive to produce the heaviest animal even if much of the additional weight is fat.

The record on animal disease eradication must be improved. While Ireland has a generally excellent animal health status there are a number of economically important diseases, particularly bovine tuberculosis and brucellosis, for which control and eradication programmes are in operation. While considerable progress has been made in reducing the incidence of brucellosis and complete eradication may be possible within a few years (officially the country was declared free of the disease in 1984!), after an early improvement there has been little progress towards eradicating bovine TB despite massive amounts of state aid and on-farm losses.

This last point emphasises the fact that veterinary regulations and food laws can have important trade effects. As tariffs on food and agriculture have been reduced or eliminated, differences in veterinary rules and food laws have emerged as important non-tariff barriers to trade. For example, the EU prohibits the use of growth hormones in beef production while they continue to be allowed (on scientific advice) in the US. As a consequence, the EU bans the import of beef from the US unless it can be shown to come from hormone-free herds. As food-quality regulations are tightened in Europe in response to consumer pressure, the authorities will come under increasing pressure to take similar action against food imports from countries with less stringent standards. New rules to deal with trade disputes arising from issues of this kind were an important subsidiary topic in the agricultural negotiations in the GATT Uruguay Round.

Agriculture and the Environment

Agricultural production has both positive and negative impacts on the environment. On the positive side, many of the landscapes we enjoy today are the product of many years' interaction between man and nature. But this positive contribution is increasingly overshadowed by concern over possible negative impacts. Pollution problems may arise from the increased use of fertiliser and problems of waste disposal from large, intensive livestock units. There are conservation worries that the number and diversity of flora and fauna may be reduced by the practices of hedgerow removal, wetland drainage and monoculture, over the rapid rate of removal of field monuments, and over possible soil erosion in hill areas due to overgrazing. Finally, the amenity value of the countryside may be threatened if agricultural practices reduce the scenic diversity of the countryside or restrict rights of access.[22]

It must be stressed that agriculture is not the only source of pressure on the rural environment. There is also controversy over the coniferous-covered slopes of upland areas, Bord na Móna activities on the peat bogs in the midlands and mining activities in the West, as well as planning battles over the siting of chemical industries and the building of rural bungalows. Because of the combination of lower population density and a predominantly grassland agriculture, environmental pressures are rarely as significant here as in the more intensively-farmed areas of continental Europe. None the less, they are growing and may be significant in localised areas.

How are conflicting interests in the countryside to be reconciled? And at whose cost? Seeking the voluntary cooperation of farmers to avoid environmental damage is an obvious first requirement. TEAGASC is now involved in the provision of advice, information and training in environmental management. Codes of good farming practice have a role to play in avoiding soil erosion, water pollution and damage to amenity. However, voluntary cooperation may break down where there are clear conflicts between commercial gain and the requirements of conservation.

Public acquisition will have a role to play in the case of relatively small areas with high conservation or amenity value. The government, through the National Parks and Monuments Branch of the Office of Public Works, has already established five national parks for conservation purposes with a total area of 41,000 hectares. In addition, nature reserves (places of high scientific or biological interest protected and managed for that interest) can be created under the 1976 Wildlife Act. However, there will still be a need to adjudicate between farming and conservation objectives over the great bulk of privately-owned land.

The government has various food-production objectives which it pays farmers handsomely to meet. If it also has conservation objectives in the countryside why not pay farmers to meet those too, or perhaps to meet those instead where they conflict? Some moves have already been made in this direction. The Disadvantaged Areas Directive introduced in 1975 under which headage payments are made to farmers has as its objective to assist 'the continuation of farming, therefore maintaining a minimum population level or conserving the countryside'. A much bigger step in this direction was the launch of the Rural Environment Protection Scheme in 1994 as one of the accompanying measures of CAP reform. Farmers who enrol for this scheme must implement farming and environmental plans for their farms and in return become eligible for direct payments of IR£122 per hectare, up to a maximum of IR£4,880 per farm per annum, for a five-year period. Some IR£230 million has been set aside for this scheme over the next five years.

An alternative to providing incentives for compliance is greater use of planning controls. Currently most use of land for agriculture or forestry purposes is exempt from planning control, permitting land drainage and reclamation to proceed without restriction. Some environmental objectives (for example, the preservation of wetlands) might be met by removing this exemption. If farm development was restricted as a consequence, it would immediately raise the question whether farmers would be entitled to compensation for the loss of profits that would result. Where restrictions go beyond normal good farming practice it might be argued that farmers ought to be compensated. However, the 1990 Planning Act lists a wide variety of justifications for planning restrictions for which compensation need not be paid, including the protection of amenity and the environment. Whether farming activity is restricted on environmental grounds, or whether farmers are paid for environmental improvements, clearly will have opposite effects on the market competitiveness of the sector in the future.

8 CONCLUSION

This chapter has examined the competitive position of Irish agriculture and rural areas generally in the light of the changes underway and likely to come about in the EU's Common Agricultural Policy. Like agricultural policy in other industrialised countries, the CAP can largely be interpreted as a response to the structural problem of excess farm capacity. There are simply too many resources involved in agricultural production in Europe. Excess capacity exists because the industry's supply potential exceeds effective demand at current prices. The European Commission estimates that over the past fifteen years EU farm production has grown by around 2 per cent annually, while internal demand has increased by less than 0.5 per cent.[24] This imbalance was absorbed, initially, by import substitution as EU production displaced imports from the EU market, and subsequently, by export demand. But the budgetary and foreign policy implications of continuing along that road proved too much. In 1992 the EU took a decisive step to reform the CAP but, in so doing, cut off most opportunities to increase agricultural output. In Ireland, the major enterprises of cattle, milk, sheepmeat, cereals and sugar are subject either to explicit quotas or limits on direct payments which have the same effect. While there are opportunities to increase pig and poultry production and some horticultural products, as well as to diversify farm production into non-conventional enterprises, their collective contribution will make relatively little impact on either the level or trend of agricultural output in the medium future. In the absence of changes in policy, the level of Irish agricultural output will change little between now and the end of the decade.

From one perspective, it is tempting to argue that the maintenance of high prices for a limited volume of production may not be a bad deal as far as Irish agriculture is concerned. But the prospect of a further round of GATT trade negotiations and the possible accession of the Central and East European countries to the EU suggests that this may not be a sustainable option much beyond the end of this decade. Irish agriculture could face difficulties in competing in a more market-oriented environment. The pattern of structural adjustment, shaped by the constraints of a rather rigid land tenure system and weak off-farm demand for labour, has led to increased dualism within farming. Production has become increasingly concentrated on a small minority of commercial farms while significant numbers of farmers struggle to survive or retreat into semi-retirement. A formal analysis of competitiveness in milk production relative to other countries confirms that structural weaknesses exist.

Structural policies to address these weaknesses have been strengthened by the receipt of additional funding under the EU's Community Support Framework 1994-99 which will be used to grant-aid farm investment, expand research capacity and improve human resources through agricultural education and training. The Early Retirement Scheme provides an opportunity to increase the rate at which land is transferred into the hands of the younger generation. Farm viability can also be addressed by rural development measures, particularly to encourage alternative enterprises and farm diversification, agri-tourism and afforestation. The ability to meet consumer food demands arising from changed lifestyles, as well as the value placed on producing food in an environmentally-sustainable way, were also highlighted as key issues in building future competitiveness.

The Agriculture and Food Policy Review Group considered these issues at the beginning of 1991. Its conclusions are worth repeating here.

> Both in farming and in the food industry, the key to successful
> development towards the sort of future envisaged by the Group is

an emphasis on human resources... What is needed above all is a sufficient number of people in the farm and food sectors who are able to adapt effectively to new situations. It is they, not the state or the EU, who in the last analysis will determine whether the sector succeeds or stagnates. Public institutions can only assist the process. They can do this by devoting more finance to developing human resources and less to 'bricks and mortar'. The state also has a fundamental role in providing the right economic conditions and in guarding against high inflation and interest rates. It can facilitate new rural income-generating initiatives, through locally initiated development. It can try to arrange that, right across the agriculture and food spectrum, all of the conditions needed to ensure that Irish products are outstanding in terms of quality and safety apply and that the rural environment is safeguarded. In the Group's opinion the state should do all this, but a vigorous resourcefulness and creativity on the part of those actually engaged in farming and food remains the basic pre-condition of success. (p. 3)

Endnotes

1 E. O'Riordan, *The Net Contribution of the Agri-Food Sector to Earnings of Foreign Exchange* (Situation and Outlook Bulletin no. 20), Teagasc, Dublin 1989.
2 National Economic and Social Council, *New Approaches to Rural Development* (Report no. 97), Stationery Office, Dublin 1995.
3 Commission of the European Communities, *The Development and Future of the CAP*, COM(91)100, Brussels 1991.
4 B. Kearney, 'Scenarios for the Next Decade in Agriculture', in B. Kearney (editor), *What Price CAP?*, Institute of European Affairs, Dublin 1995.
5 At the time, these included Bulgaria, the Czech Republic, Hungary, Poland, Romania and Slovakia.
6 A. Matthews, 'Common Agricultural Policy Reform and National Compensation Strategies', *Journal of the Statistical and Social Inquiry Society of Ireland,* 26, Part 1, 1988/89.
7 National Economic and Social Council, *A Strategy for Competitiveness, Growth and Employment* (Report no. 96), Stationery Office, Dublin 1993.
8 G. Boyle, B. Kearney, T. McCarthy and M. Keane, *The Competitiveness of Irish Agriculture,* Allied Irish Banks, Dublin 1991.
9 A. Matthews, *Managing the Structural Funds in Ireland,* Cork University Press, Cork 1994.
10 Not all structural measures are included in the CSF. The Early Retirement Scheme, for example, is one of the measures which accompanied CAP reform and is funded from the FEOGA Guarantee Fund. Also, national governments still have autonomy to influence agricultural structures through, for example, land policy or taxation policy.
11 Government of Ireland, *Operational Programme for Agriculture, Rural Development and Forestry 1994-1999,* Stationery Office, Dublin 1994.
12 G. Boyle, 'An Exploratory Assessment of the Returns to Agricultural Research in Ireland 1963-1983', *Irish Journal of Agricultural Economics and Rural Sociology* 11, 1986.
13 Commission of the European Communities, *The Future of Rural Society,* COM(88)501, Brussels 1988.

14 P. Commins and M. Keane, *New Approaches to Rural Development* (National Economic and Social Council, Report no. 97), Stationery Office, Dublin 1994.

15 A good example was a study of the West of Ireland undertaken at the request of the Catholic Bishops of Connacht and Donegal acting through the organisation 'Developing the West Together', which opened with the words: 'The West of Ireland is in crisis. If current net out-migration trends continue, the Region stands to lose 110,000 people, one fifth of its total population during the next 20 years'. See Euroadvice Ltd., *A Crusade for Survival,* Developing the West Together, Galway 1994, p.1.

16 Commins and Keane, *op.cit.*

17 L. Downey and L. Connolly, *Rural Development: The Role for Tourism,* Teagasc, Dublin 1994.

18 B. Kearney, G. Boyle and J. Walsh, *EU LEADER I Initiative in Ireland: Evaluation and Recommendations,* Department of Agriculture, Food and Forestry, Dublin 1994.

19 National Economic and Social Council, *New Approaches to Rural Development,* op.cit.

20 *Ibid.*

21 Kearney *et al., op.cit.*

22 Commission of the European Communities, *Environment and Agriculture,* COM(88)338, Brussels 1988.

23 Recent legislation has removed the statutory exemption for large-scale conversion of uncultivated land to intensive agriculture, large-scale afforestation and large-scale peat extraction.

24 Commission of the European Communities, *The Development and Future of the CAP,* op.cit.

CHAPTER 12

Manufacturing and Global Competition

Mary O'Sullivan*

1 INTRODUCTION

This chapter analyses the extent to which the foundations for a sustained process of industrial development, that could serve as the basis for sustained higher living standards of Irish people, have been laid in the Irish industrial sector.[1] It also considers the extent to which Irish industrial policies have fostered this outcome. In Section 2 the broad outlines of Ireland's industrial performance and policy from the late 1950s to the early 1990s are discussed. The main elements of Irish industrial policy in the 1990s – the provision of direct investment incentives and tax concessions to stimulate industrial investment, the attraction of foreign direct investment and the maintenance of a regime of free trade – have remained the same for nearly forty years. There have however been a number of changes in the composition, focus and mix of the three major policy instruments since the late 1950s. Alternative theoretical approaches to the process of industrial development are outlined in Section 3. The shortcomings of mainstream economics in the study of the development process and in particular its neglect of the social foundations of that process – business enterprises and social institutions – are emphasised. Drawing on recent empirical and theoretical work the broad outlines of an emerging alternative perspective on the process of development in the academic literature and its implications for industrial policy are sketched. In Section 4 the organisation of manufacturing activity in Ireland, in the indigenous and foreign-owned sectors of the economy, are analysed in comparative perspective to evaluate the extent to which the social foundations for a cumulative process of industrial development have been embedded in the Irish economy. In light of this discussion Section 5

---

*   I would like to thank Philip Lane and John O'Hagan for their assistance with earlier drafts of this chapter. I also appreciate the helpful comments of the participants in a recent conference on 'Indigenous Innovation' at University of Massachusetts, Lowell, and in particular those of William Lazonick, Qiwen Lu, William Mass and Mohan Rao.

contains an assessment of the contribution of Irish industrial policy to the development of Irish industry.

The most important features of industrial policy and performance in Ireland are deeply rooted in her social, political and economic history. Thus it will be helpful to read this chapter in light of the discussion in Chapter 1. Chapter 7 analyses the aggregate output experience of the Irish economy in comparative-historical perspective. In the past many mainstream economists have regarded this type of aggregate analysis as a substitute for more microeconomic analysis of the process of development of the type that is contained in this chapter. However, this type of aggregative economics has encountered serious problems in accounting for the record of economic growth in the advanced countries and for this reason macroeconomists have invoked the term 'total factor productivity' for the sources of growth that they cannot explain. A relatively recent development in growth theory is the endogenous growth literature which takes a broader perspective than 'old growth theory' on the possible sources of industrial growth. However, the assumptions about technological development and utilisation on which this work is based are not grounded in empirical facts or theoretical arguments. It is increasingly recognised in the mainstream of the economics profession that there is a need to understand the importance of organisations in economic activity. A leading American economist, Joseph Stiglitz, recently remarked that the key element in the explanation of the process of economic growth is 'economic organisation' because the performance of an economy depends on the internal organisation of its firms as well as the overall structure of the industrial sector.

2 INDUSTRIAL POLICY AND TRENDS IN INDUSTRIAL OUTPUT 1950-1995

Framework for Industrial Policy
The main elements in Ireland's current industrial policy were introduced in 1958 in Economic Development, the country's first comprehensive national plan. The fundamental weaknesses in technology and marketing that had been evident in the Irish industrial sector in the late 1920s had persisted until mid-century despite the fact that the Irish industrial sector had expanded considerably in the interim (see Chapter 1). Economic Development proposed a remedy to these problems that entailed a change in focus from the prevailing economic policy of import substitution behind tariff barriers to a policy intended to promote the development of an export-oriented industrial base.

There were three main elements in the strategy outlined in Economic Development: the introduction of substantial capital grants and tax concessions as a 'carrot' to encourage export-oriented manufacturing, the inducement of direct investment by foreign export-oriented manufacturing enterprises in Ireland, and a transition to free trade.

The encouragement of export-oriented manufacturing was undertaken by the Industrial Development Authority (IDA) and other state-sponsored bodies. The IDA was given authority to issue grants to export-oriented companies, domestic and foreign, to help them finance investments in fixed industrial assets. Córas Tráchtála (the Irish Export Board) was established to promote Irish exports abroad and to offer advice to Irish companies in their efforts to develop exports. From 1958 a 100 per cent tax remission – Export Profit Tax Relief (EPTR) – was made available on profits from exports.

The second element of the new strategy was the attraction of export-oriented foreign direct investment by extending to foreign investors the same capital grants and tax concessions that were available to indigenous companies. The rationale offered for this element of the strategy was that foreign companies would supplement the allegedly withered entrepreneurial initiative of the Irish, upgrade Irish industrial skills through the training of Irish managers and workers, and contribute to the development of the indigenous industrial sector through profit reinvestment and the establishment of supply linkages with domestic companies.

The third element of the policy reorientation was a move to free trade. Although quotas were dismantled in the 1950s, the first definite decision to remove tariffs was Ireland's application to join the European Economic Community (EEC) in 1961. The UK also applied, but was denied membership, and Ireland withdrew her application due to her trade dependence on her neighbour. Nevertheless, Irish tariff protection was progressively removed in the 1960s, particularly in trade with the UK. When Ireland joined the Community in January 1973 she agreed to a timetable of tariff removal against other EEC manufactures. The level of industrial protection thus fell from an average nominal tariff of 25 per cent and an average effective tariff of 79 per cent in 1966 to one-fifth of this level within 10 years.

The framework for industrial policy set out in Economic Development was to remain in place until the middle of the 1990s although there were some changes in the composition, focus and mix of the three major policy instruments of which it was comprised. The IDA assumed increasing responsibility for the implementation of industrial policy and in 1969 the government effectively abdicated its role in the promotion of Irish industrial development to that body.

Output and Employment Growth
As Table 12.1 shows, the aggregate performance of the Irish industrial sector began to improve in the 1960s; from 1960 to 1973 the volume of industrial output grew by 6.5 per cent per annum although employment in manufacturing increased at a slower annual rate of 2.3 per cent. From 1973 to 1979 the Irish manufacturing sector sustained an average growth rate of over 5 per cent but industrial employment increased at only 0.8 per cent per annum. The country's comparative performance improved dramatically after the international recession

of 1974 to 1976; in the late 1970s the Irish manufacturing sector sustained an average growth rate of over 7 per cent per annum which was the highest rate of growth in output in the EEC. The volume of manufactured exports grew at an annual average rate of 18 per cent per annum, albeit from a low base.

Table 12.1

Growth Rates of Manufacturing Output, Employment and Output per Head, 1950-92

Period	Output	Employment	Productivity
1950-60	3.1	0.8	2.3
1960-73	6.5	2.3	4.0
1973-79	5.1	0.8	4.3
1979-86	4.1	-2.7	7.0
1986-89	11.5	0.8	10.6
1989-92	6.0	1.0	4.9

Source: CSO, *Census of Industrial Production,* various issues.

An increase in investment in Ireland by foreign-owned manufacturers in Ireland was the primary source of this expansion in industrial activity. Most of the grants and tax concessions made available by the IDA were taken up by the foreign sector and by 1973 foreign companies accounted for 32 per cent of total industrial employment.

Employment in the indigenous sector grew in the early 1960s, while protection still remained, but declined in the latter part of the decade. Employment in the indigenous sector as a whole increased by 5 per cent from 1973 to 1980 but fell by 13 per cent in the firms established prior to 1973. The IDA introduced a Small Industry Programme (SIP) in 1967 to provide financial incentives for the development of small enterprises. This programme prompted an increase in industrial activity by firms with less than 50 persons engaged; from 1973 to 1983 the share of total manufacturing employment in firms receiving SIP grants increased from 5.5 to 11 per cent but few of them developed into medium-sized enterprises.[2] The sector remained weak in international product market competition and even the home market began to slip away as import penetration increased from the late 1960s. The percentage of output exported by indigenous manufacturing companies did rise from 18 per cent in 1960 to around 31 per cent in 1984 but low-value-added food products remained the dominant indigenous export. Few linkages had been established between foreign and domestic companies by 1980. Most high-skill supplies required by foreign companies in Ireland were imported, sometimes at a high transportation cost penalty, and no sub-supplier of Irish origin had developed an export business based on serving multinational companies in Ireland.

The IDA responded to these trends by focusing to an even greater extent on the promotion of foreign direct investment. In 1973 it set out a plan to concentrate, in attracting such investment, on the electronics, chemicals and other 'high-technology' sectors. The rationale for this focus was that these industrial activities required high levels of industrial skills and would give Ireland, with her relatively well-educated workforce, an advantage in competition for foreign investment with newly-industrialising countries (NICs). In the late 1970s and 1980s there was substantial growth in the Irish-based electronics, pharmaceuticals, instruments and machinery sectors.

As the 1970s unfolded foreign companies that had located in Ireland before 1973 showed disturbing signs of weakness. From 1973 to 1980 the older foreign firms that had located in Ireland without the inducement of grants reduced their employment by 15 per cent. But even among the newer grant-aided firms, established before 1973, employment decreased by 2.3 per cent from 1973 to 1980. The number of jobs provided by grant-aided foreign companies typically peaked a few years after the receipt of grants and the initial establishment of a plant in Ireland.

In July 1980 the Telesis Group was commissioned by the National Economic and Social Council (NESC) to assess Irish industrial policy. Following an extensive review of Irish industry Telesis criticised what it regarded as an overemphasis on foreign industry in the policies to promote industrial development in Ireland. The Group argued that this approach was at best a short-term solution to the challenge of industrial development, a challenge that it contended could only be surmounted in a sustained way by the development of an internationally competitive indigenous base. In its current condition the indigenous industrial sector, according to Telesis, fell far short of this ideal.

The group recommended not only a reallocation of resources toward indigenous industry engaged in export and sub-supply activities but also a more active approach by the government to the development of the indigenous sector. In particular, it promoted 'the building of structurally strong Irish companies rather than strong agencies to assist weak companies'. It argued that the pursuit of this objective would require a concerted effort to build strong internal capabilities in a few big companies to allow them to compete on international markets. However, the group did not provide any guidance as to how an industrial policy based on developing 'winners' would be implemented. It did not specify how companies might be selected nor how their internal capabilities might be developed.

The Group published its report in February 1982 and a fractious debate in Irish policy circles ensued. Most of the controversy focussed on two related questions: whether 'picking winners' was possible and if so whether the Irish government and/or the IDA had the capabilities to play such an active role in the development of strong Irish companies. When the White Paper on Industrial Policy was published in July 1984 the main Telesis recommendation was not adopted. Rather than building strong companies the White Paper proposed the identification and support of companies with already displayed growth potential. To this end the Company Development Programme was established in 1985 to coordinate the support package offered to a company by the IDA, CTT and EOLAS (the Irish Science and Technology Board), on the basis of the individual objectives and requirements of the particular company. The National Linkages Programme was also established in 1985 to help develop a competitive sub-supply base in Ireland.

Besides these initiatives the main elements of the industrial policy outlined in 1958 remained in place although there was as mentioned some change in their focus. The tax concession for exporting industry had been replaced in 1981 with a 10 per cent corporate tax rate on the profits of all manufacturing industry and a commitment was made by the Irish government to keep this concession in place until 2010. There was a modest shift away from fixed-asset grants toward employment, training and R&D grants. Monies were also made available to industry under the Technology Acquisition Grant scheme that was introduced in 1986. Indigenous companies' share of the total grant budget was increased from 51 per cent in 1985 to 54 per cent in 1989 although their total allocation fell far short of the 1990 target of 75 per cent that Telesis had proposed.

In the early 1980s the level of employment in industry declined although output continued to grow at an impressive rate (see Table 12.1). After 1987 the divergence between industrial output and employment trends persisted; industrial employment remained static despite record growth in industrial output. Although the overall trend in employment was unhealthy it concealed the true extent of the problems in Irish-based industry and in particular the massive turnover of industrial jobs and the stark disparity between the performance of the indigenous and the foreign sectors.

As Table 12.2 indicates the net loss in total employment in the Irish industrial sector in the period from 1973 to 1994 was 10,491 jobs. However, the gross number of jobs lost was a massive 404,376 which represents 189,173 more than the total number of industrial jobs that existed in the economy in 1973! In the foreign-owned sector there was a net gain of 20,711 for the entire period but a total of 141,175 jobs – more than twice the total number in existence in foreign companies in 1973 – were lost. In the indigenous sector there was a net decline of 31,202 in the total number employed from 1973 to 1994. Once again this concealed a more substantial gross loss of 263,201. The net employment performance of the industrial sector over the entire period was thus only achieved by the creation of jobs on a massive scale; 393,885 jobs were created in total of which 161,886 were in the foreign sector and 231,999 in indigenous industry.

Table 12.2

Changes in Industrial[1] Employment[2], 1973-94

	Irish	Non-Irish	Total
Total employment 1973	145,815	69,388	215,203
Total employment 1994	114,613	90,099	204,712
Net change in employment 1973-94	-31,202	20,711	-10,491
Total job gain 1973-94	231,999	161,866	393,885
Total job loss 1973-94	263,201	141,175	404,376

Source: IDA Employment Survey files.

[1] Includes mining, quarrying and turf production

[2] Data in this table are those collected in the IDA Employment Surveys taken on 1 January 1973 and 1 November 1994.

Industrial job losses were heavily concentrated in the 1980s. The fortunes of the indigenous sector plummeted with total employment falling from 154,400 in 1980 to 113,000 in 1988 with a slight increase to 115,615 by 1990. There was a net loss of nearly 10,000 jobs in the foreign-owned manufacturing sector from 1980 to 1988 when total employment in this sector fell to 81,666. By 1990 there had been an increase in employment to 85,573 in this sector. The aggregate employment performance of Irish industry has been achieved only through the creation of jobs on a massive scale, and in particular through reliance on the continuing inflows of foreign direct investment.

In the 1990s industrial employment levelled off in the economy. Employment in the indigenous sector fell from its 1990 level to 114,613 in 1994. In the foreign-owned sector the number employed increased by nearly 5,000 between 1990 and 1994, to a total of 90,099.

Table 12.3

Industrial Employment by Nationality of Ownership of Project, 1973-94

	1973		1994	
	Aggregate employment	Share %	Aggregate employment	Share %
UK	31,459	14.6	11,806	5.8
Germany	4,735	2.2	9,674	4.7
Other European	15,943	7.4	14,139	6.9
US	15,678	7.3	47,429	23.2
Other non-European	1,573	0.1	7,051	3.4
Total non-Irish	69,388	32.2	90,099	44.0
Irish	145,815	67.8	114,613	56.0
Total	215,203	100.0	204,712	100.0

Source: As for Table 12.2.

Structure and Composition of Industrial Employment

As Table 12.3 indicates, the period from 1973 to 1994 was one in which

American multinationals replaced their UK counterparts as the dominant group of foreign direct investors in the Irish industrial sector. These American companies were eager to take advantage not only of the financial incentives that the IDA offered them but also the unrestricted access to the large EU market that an Irish location offered. In aggregate terms foreign-owned companies accounted for 44 per cent of Ireland's industrial employment in 1994 compared with 32.2 per cent in 1973.

In addition to a shift in the share of industrial employment, output and exports accounted for by different nationalities there was also, as Table 12.4 indicates, a striking change in the sectoral composition of Irish industry. The metals and engineering sector which accounted for 36.8 per cent of total employment in 1994 replaced food as the largest contributor to Irish industrial employment. The chemicals and pharmaceuticals sector also gained ground. In contrast there was a sharp reduction in the importance of textiles, clothing and footwear, and drink and tobacco. The replacement of traditional sectors of industrial activity with modern, higher-technology sectors has been a feature of the development experience of all of the advanced industrial countries. In aggregate terms Ireland's composition of industrial activity now looks very similar to that of other small European countries. However, the aggregate figures conceal the dual nature of the Irish industrial structure. A modern sector with a high level of productivity which is for the most part foreign-owned coexists with a traditional indigenous sector characterised by low productivity that has been in decline since the 1970s.[3]

Table 12.4

Industrial Employment by Sector, 1973-94

	1973		1994	
	Aggregate employment	Share %	Aggregate employment	Share %
Metals & engineering	47,154	21.9	75,284	36.8
Food	48,127	22.4	39,361	19.2
Chemicals	10,318	4.8	17,716	8.7
Paper & printing	15,338	7.2	13,888	6.8
Clothing & footwear	28,335	13.2	11,346	5.5
Non-metallic minerals	15,797	7.3	10,023	4.9
Textiles	20,330	9.4	9,813	4.8
Wood & furniture	10,430	4.8	9,232	4.5
Drink & tobacco	11,296	5.2	5,967	2.9
Other	8,078	3.8	12,082	5.9
Total	215,203	100.0	204,712	100.0

Source: As for Table 12.2.

The overall productivity performance of the Irish industrial sector has improved dramatically in comparative perspective in recent decades.

Measured in terms of net output per head the average productivity of the Irish manufacturing sector in 1987 was 137 per cent, 121 per cent, 106 per cent, 117 per cent, and 69 per cent of that in Britain, West Germany, the Netherlands, France and the US respectively. There has however been a levelling-off in productivity growth since the late 1980s. Annual productivity growth fell from an average annual rate of 10.6 per cent in the period 1986 to 1989 to 4.9 per cent in the following three year period. The overall trend in productivity figures has been driven to a large extent by the performance of foreign-owned firms in industrial sectors such as electronics and pharmaceuticals; in the period 1989 to 1992 productivity growth was 3.8 per cent in metals and engineering and 7.4 in chemicals compared with 19 per cent and 10.5 per cent respectively between 1986 and 1989.[4]

The gulf between productivity in the indigenous and foreign-owned sectors is as striking as the sectoral differences between them. During the late 1980s the level of output per head in the foreign-owned sector was more than two and a half times that of indigenous enterprises. The performance of Ireland's foreign-owned sector has been spectacular not only in comparison to the Irish indigenous sector but even relative to advanced industrial countries in the EU. In pharmaceuticals, for example, Ireland's measured gross value added per employee in 1988 was 166,000 ECU compared with only 52,400 in West Germany and 54,300 for the EU on average.

Some economists have argued that these figures are indeed too good to be true and that the figures reflect the transfer-pricing policies of multinational companies rather than improvements in the real productive capabilities of Irish-based industry (see Chapter 9). Ireland's low rate of corporate taxation for industrial companies gives them a strong incentive to report the maximum level of their group profits in this country. This can be accomplished by recording artificially low prices on inputs brought into Ireland and high output prices on products and services exported on sales to other parent company subsidiaries from the Irish base.

Policy for the 1990s
At the beginning of the 1990s the government commissioned the first major review of industrial policy and performance since the Telesis Report. The results of this inquiry were published in 1992 in the Culliton Report. It recommended a broader approach to the formulation and evaluation of industrial policy than had been adopted in Ireland in the past. It highlighted a number of structural problems that affected the competitiveness of the industrial sector including taxation, infrastructure, education and training. Its major recommendations included the reorganisation of existing grant-giving agencies into two main agencies. It proposed that one of these agencies should address the development needs of indigenous, Irish-managed industry

and that the other should be focused on the attraction of the greatest possible level of internationally-mobile investment to Ireland. In the provision of direct-investment incentives to industry the Culliton Report proposed that state assistance be directed toward those companies that, because of their risk pattern, have difficulty obtaining finance from existing financial institutions. It also recommended that greater use be made of equity rather than non-repayable grants in the provision by development agencies of support to industry. The part of the report that was potentially most innovative was its proposal of a general shift in the focus of industrial policy toward a more selective policy that would promote the growth of industrial clusters around niches of national competitive advantage. The report did not however specify whether these clusters should be based on existing advantages or on strategically-created advantages. A proposal of the latter type would have required a more radical new approach to industrial policy than the Culliton Report seemed to suggest and the use of the food sector as an example of how these clusters might work suggests that what was envisaged was a better leveraging of existing competitive advantages.

In Employment Through Enterprise, published in May 1993, the government outlined a new approach to industrial policy based on some of the recommendations contained in the Culliton Report. In particular it proposed a plan of increased investment in roads and ports, the creation of a new division in the state training agency (FÁS) that would concentrate on training those at work, and the introduction of measures to improve the efficiency of the postal and telecommunications service. It also made a somewhat vague commitment to taxation reform. The reorganisation of industrial promotion agencies recommended in the Culliton Report was undertaken; they were restructured into two main agencies by the Industrial Development Act of 1993. One agency, Forbairt, was intended to promote indigenous industry; the other, the Industrial Development Agency, was given a mandate to attract foreign investment. With regard to the general direction of industrial policy the changes were more hesitant. In place of Culliton's industrial clusters the government opted for a more conservative approach, that of 'maximising the growth potential of our natural resources through the preparation of specific development strategies' and 'increasing the operation of competitive forces generally throughout the economy with the aim of achieving increased efficiency and reduced costs'.

3 THEORETICAL APPROACHES TO INDUSTRIAL DEVELOPMENT AND IMPLICATIONS FOR INDUSTRIAL POLICY[5]

Industrial Development in Theoretical Perspective
In the introduction an increasing awareness of the need to understand the social foundations of industrial performance even among economists who

have traditionally focused on macroeconomic aggregates was noted. This need is even more pressing for those concerned with the practical use of economic theory in the evaluation of past industrial policy and performance and with their improvement. Macroeconomic aggregates such as overall market share, export performance and productivity indicators are symptoms of the ability of a nation, region or enterprise to produce higher-quality and/or lower-cost products than its competitors. Although the evaluation of long-term trends in these indicators must form part of any economic diagnosis of industrial policy and performance they are only a beginning. That the leading macroeconomic performance indicators often send conflicting signals about Irish industrial performance is an even more compelling reason to take the analysis beneath the aggregates. Only through understanding the depth of the foundations for Ireland's industrial success can we hope to evaluate whether that success is likely to be sustained in the future and the types of industrial policies that might increase the likelihood of such an outcome.

Industrial development is the process through which productive resources are developed and utilised in an economy to generate higher-quality and/or lower-cost products than were previously available. To evaluate a country's industrial policy and performance we need a theory that is capable of analysing how that process takes place. Unfortunately, it is easier to identify a need for a theory of industrial development than to actually find one. Mainstream economists cannot yet lay claim to such a theory.

To a large extent this shortcoming reflects the focus in mainstream economics on the allocation of existing productive resources to alternative uses rather than the process through which resources are developed as well as utilised. Mainstream economists have elaborated a theory of the market economy – often called neoclassical theory – in which the perfection of capital, labour, and product markets is supposed to lead to optimal economic outcomes. For superior economic performance, nothing should inhibit the free flow of economic resources from one use to another, and any impediment to that flow is deemed a market imperfection.

Most economists recognise that in the real world markets are not perfect – that the unimpeded flow of resources from one use to another does not, even as a general rule, actually prevail. Hence, there is considerable research into the impact of 'market failures' and 'market imperfections' on economic performance. These market imperfections are regarded as phenomena in the absence of which the economy would be better off. In other words the benchmark for superior economic performance employed in the economics of imperfect markets is the theory of the market economy in which perfect markets allocate scarce resources to their optimal uses.

The last thirty years has seen the emergence of a substantial and rapidly expanding body of comparative-historical research on the foundations for industrial development in the advanced industrial countries by historians of business and technology, industrial sociologists, political scientists, business school academics and a small group of economists. The evidence synthesised by these researchers supports the proposition that the 'social organisation' of enterprises, regions and nations is integral to the process of industrial development. Social organisation refers both to the enterprises directly engaged in productive activity and to the social institutions which influence and are themselves influenced by the activities of those enterprises. An understanding of the social foundations of development in nations such as the US, Germany and other European countries, as well as in more recent developers like Japan and the Four Little Dragons – Hong Kong, Singapore, Taiwan and South Korea – suggests that the 'perfect market' benchmark is the wrong one in the study of the process of industrial development.

It is wrong because the theory of the market economy contains no theory of the development and utilisation of productive resources. The theory of the market economy posits that the free working of the market mechanism results in the superior utilisation of productive resources. But the theory of the market economy takes the productive capability of these resources and the alternative uses to which they can be allocated as given, and makes no attempt to analyse the development of superior products and processes. In the absence of this development, productivity is increased through the more complete utilisation of resources, but industrial development does not occur. It is for this reason that neoclassical growth theory has long treated much of productivity growth as an unexplained residual (see Chapter 7).

The social organisations that have been the foundation of industrial development, whether public sector or private sector, cannot be viewed as 'market imperfections'. From the perspective of industrial development, the most critical 'market imperfections' that conventional economists cite – 'imperfections' in financial markets, labour markets, and product markets – may not be imperfections in economic activity at all but rather improvements in social organisation that foster technological innovation and industrial performance.

Industrial development depends on the development and utilisation of productive resources to generate higher-quality and/or lower-cost products than had previously been available – a phenomenon that can broadly be termed 'innovation'. What emerges from the literature on the process of industrial development is the fact that the innovative process in successful industrial nations, regions and enterprises has increasingly become a collective process in which learning and strategy are integrated. (See also Chapter 7 for a discussion of this issue.)

By definition, underlying the innovative process is a learning process; if we already knew how to generate high-quality, low-cost products then the act of doing so would not require innovation. As economists we are concerned not with the process of learning in general but with economic learning – the acquisition of knowledge and skills to make and do things valued on product markets. People in business enterprises do not learn as they please. Rather the learning process in which they participate is directed and structured to allow it to produce products and services that are valued by customers. Since learning is a process of discovery the type and direction of learning that will result in the successful production of higher-quality and/or lower-cost products – that is, in innovation – cannot be known in advance; it is uncertain.

The uncertainty inherent in the innovation process means that the choices that are made about the extent, structure and direction of the learning process are vitally important to its ultimate success. Should a learning process be undertaken? Who should be included in it? Can a company sustain a prior competitive advantage by building on a learning process inherited from the past or must it fundamentally change the direction and the characteristics of the learning process? These types of choices we describe as strategic choices.

The innovative process is expensive as well as uncertain. The scale of upfront investment is high, not necessarily because of technological indivisibilities but because of the complex array of productive activities that must be planned and coordinated to develop and utilise technology. These costs must be covered all through the learning period until the investments in innovation can be translated into product market success. In part these costs comprise expenditure on physical assets but they also cover the costs of ensuring that those with specialised productive capabilities make their skills continuously available to the enterprise and are willing to integrate them to the learning process. All of this investment takes place without any assurance of a return. The learning process may fail to deliver a high-quality and/or low-cost product, another competitor may produce a better product first, or an unexpected shift in customer preferences may render the innovation unsuccessful. Accordingly it is not true that more learning is always better from an economic perspective. Investments in an innovative process must be strategically directed if they are to produce goods and services that are valued on product markets. The extent, direction and structure of the learning process that makes sense from a strategic perspective will depend to a large extent on the enterprise's existing stock of skills and knowledge, the nature of product market competition and the state of technology in the industry in which a company is competing.

Strategic choices are not simply automatic responses to the dictates of market incentives. In fact, as Schumpeter, one of the first economists of innovation, long ago observed market prices cannot serve as a guide for innovative activities because they coordinate the existing flow of economic life – what Schumpeter called 'the circular flow' – and thus direct resources into the accustomed channels of economic activity. Innovation is about usurping that flow, about breaking out of accustomed channels, and thus requires the detachment of productive resources from the circular flow.

To initiate and implement economic learning processes and to coordinate them strategically, the advanced economies have relied primarily on business enterprises that must compete for product markets to survive. The most potent source of sustained competitive advantage has been the pursuit of strategies that initiate, direct and structure a collective and cumulative learning process to generate higher-quality and/or lower-cost products.

Since there are no objective guidelines or rules for making successful strategic decisions there are likely to be disagreements among different people and groups about the merits of alternative strategies. Strategic decision makers therefore require control of productive resources – human skills and non-human assets – if they are to have the requisite autonomy to invest strategically in a learning process and to sustain it during the learning period that must occur before returns can be generated.

In an economy in which productive goods and services command a price, control of financial resources is the necessary conduit to the control of productive resources that is necessary to build and sustain an innovative process. Control over financial resources may be necessary but it is not sufficient to build and sustain an innovative process. A collective learning process is a social process and to be successful it must be based on the cooperative efforts of those who participate in that process.

If individuals are to engage in a collective learning process they must have not only the ability but also the incentives to commit their knowledge, skills and efforts to the innovation process. Since the knowledge and skills that are useful in industrial production are generally specific to the products and processes of particular enterprises, those enterprises that are successful innovators have tended to invest in the development of the skills and knowledge of their members. Individuals must also have the incentive to exert their initiative to learn as part of a collective learning process in the investing organisation. The prospects of sharing in the gains of successful innovation by the investing organisation can lead even mobile participants to forego the lure of the market and remain committed to the pursuit of organisational goals.[6]

What determines whether and, if so, how people and money are committed to an organisation? In part it depends on the business enterprise itself, on its particular history and resultant 'corporate culture'. But empirical evidence reveals that the institutional arrangements within a society also affect the innovative success of business enterprises in that society. Existing research strongly supports the hypotheses that the social institutions that affect the financial commitment to innovative strategies and the ability and incentives of individuals to participate in organisational learning processes vary markedly across advanced economies, and that these institutional arrangements exert a significant influence on the innovative capabilities of enterprises that operate within their ambit.

What is of relevance about the financial system to the study of industrial development is not so much the quantity of financial resources that flows through that system but the manner in which these resources are allocated.

That allocation depends on the incentives and abilities of those who control financial resources. The financial system defines the range of options available to those who control financial resources for the investment of their money and in particular whether they have an incentive to finance innovative investments by industrial companies. To understand when it makes sense to commit money to an innovative strategy, the success of which is uncertain, and whether to keep that money committed as the learning process unfolds, decision-makers who control financial resources must have intimate knowledge of the possibilities of the investment strategy, or entrust their money to strategic managers who have such knowledge.

The system of education and training clearly affects people's abilities to participate in a learning process within industrial enterprises. But the skills and knowledge developed in these systems is relevant to the process of development only to the extent that they are integrated into the learning process that takes place at the level of productive activity. Other institutional arrangements affect the process of development including the legal framework, the system of taxation, the property regime, the class structure and the social structure more generally.

In summary the innovative capability of an enterprise is shaped by a combination of the enterprise's own organisational history, the technological characteristics of its particular industry, and the social institutions of the national economy in which it has grown and continues to operate. Research on the evolution of the developmental capability of a nation must, therefore, analyse how organisations, technologies, and institutions interact to influence the wealth of different nations.

This perspective on the financial and organisational requirements of economic development confronts the basic assumptions of the theory of the market economy. In the theory of the market economy, the mobility of factors of production facilitates the operation of the central coordinating mechanism – the choices of individuals to reallocate the productive resources that they own to alternative uses in response to market incentives. The theory of the market economy assumes that any immobility of resources is a market imperfection. From this perspective, when market opportunities exist that offer higher rates of return, commitments of financial and human resources to particular organisations manifest market imperfections.

Yet such is the situation whenever resources are committed to an organisation that is pursuing an innovative investment strategy. The immobility of resources required for innovation occurs not because of market imperfections but because of the prospects of the success of particular organisations. The success of the innovative process depends on the immobility of money and people to alternative uses via the market, and thus the social foundations of innovation require the innovative enterprise to control market forces rather than be controlled by them. This control of market forces in turn provides a basis – although always an uncertain one – for the development and utilisation of productive resources.

Industrial Policy in Theoretical Perspective

The construction of an historically relevant theory of industrial development is not simply an academic exercise. Policy debates on investments in productive resources, restructuring of organisations, and the transformation of institutions are concerned with the economic impact of alternative proposals. In most countries, including Ireland, industrial policy debates have been substantially influenced by the prevalent 'conventional wisdom' in economic theory. In debates in Ireland and other countries, most people have tended to justify their stance on industrial policy on the basis of their perception of the extent of market imperfections in real economies.

On one side of these debates are those who believe that once the necessary institutional arrangements are in place for generating efficient resource allocation, in particular a regime of competitive markets, development will take care of itself. Private actors will increase their industrial investment and industrial growth will ensue. From this perspective governments should focus on improving the functioning of markets and provide only those goods where the government has a clear advantage relative to private actors. Other than the provision of 'public goods' governments should focus on improving market mechanisms and leave private actors to make decisions about the allocation of resources in the economy.

In contrast a number of more active policy prescriptions have been founded on the theory of 'imperfect' markets. In practice there is a wide range of policies that is justified on this basis and disagreement abounds even among people who hold this view in common about the level of government intervention that can be justified on the grounds of market failures. Many mainstream economists in Ireland, like their colleagues in other countries, accept that there are sufficiently widespread failures in 'markets' for technological development, education and training and credit for small companies to justify government intervention. O'Malley is an example of an economist who has taken the imperfect market argument much further in arguing that economies of scale and other barriers to entry allow powerful incumbents in certain product markets to resist external competitive challenges. From this point of view government assistance is necessary to assist 'second-mover' enterprises, regions and nations in their efforts to grow by helping them to overcome these structural barriers. Another common argument in policy debates is that positive 'externalities' – side-effects of economic activity that are not reflected in market prices – such as technology or training spillovers from one firm to another provide a justification for policies to promote the development of enterprises and industries that are the source of such external effects. Endogenous growth theory is based on such arguments and has recently been invoked in a number of countries as a theoretical justification for policies that promote support for education, protection of intellectual property rights, support for R&D and other policies that encourage the widespread production and transmission of ideas (see Chapter 7).

Proponents of neoclassical theory in policy debates therefore contend that deliberate intervention in the operation of the economy is only warranted to eradicate imperfections that will permit the market to operate nearer to its ideal – the perfectly competitive market economy. Recently, among Western economists, an understanding of the development experiences of Japan and the Four Little Dragons – the so-called 'East Asian miracle' – has cast doubt on the general applicability of the neoclassical ideal. A growing body of detailed research on these economies makes a strong case that the success of these countries can be attributed not to reducing market imperfections but to 'getting prices wrong' strategically and to 'governing the market', a process in which social organisation has played a central role.[7]

More generally, the evidence on the institutional and organisational foundations of the economic success of countries that industrialised at an earlier stage raises serious questions about whether, for understanding economic development in the twentieth century, the idealisation of perfect markets and the characterisation of reality as market imperfections has had any applicability at all. If conventional economic doctrine systematically ignores the social foundations of the development process, policies based upon it that attempt to foster economic development will systematically ignore them too. Indeed, in an attempt to remove 'imperfections', policies based on the theory of the market economy may undermine the very organisations and institutions that promote industrial development.

What is important to observe, however, is that although an historically relevant theory of the development of the most successful national economies can help us to understand the social foundations of that process, and to explain why it has not occurred in other countries, it is far from a 'silver bullet' when it comes to policy prescriptions. In particular it does not advocate more government intervention in the economy to build the social foundations of industrial development. Indeed in recognising the cooperative relations that underpin development it rejects as simplistic such conceptions of political action as a panacea for social and economic ills. Since it regards economic problems as deeply embedded in social and political organisation it considers that changes in industrial policy of necessity entail and require social and political support and transformation if they are to be successful. The possibilities for social and political transformation therefore drive the potential for major changes in development policy and the success of their implementation.

4 THE ORGANISATION OF MANUFACTURING

In considering the social foundations of manufacturing in Ireland this chapter focuses in particular on the organisation of productive activity by business enterprises. It does not contain a detailed analysis of the influence of the institutional framework in which those business enterprises operate due to the constraints of space. However, since the weaknesses in the structure of Irish industry are intertwined with the shortcomings in these institutional arrangements their consideration in what follows may shed light on some aspects of Ireland's institutional problems.

The Organisation of Manufacturing in Comparative Perspective

In the advanced industrial economies the basis for the improvement and sustenance of high living standards has been the strategic commitment of human and financial resources to a cumulative and collective learning process. The structure of organisation that has formed the basis for this learning process has, however, differed substantially across countries, industries and enterprises in terms of the scale of companies involved and the relations between them. Substantial differences in the extent of the learning process within enterprises, and in particular in the level of investment in shop-floor skills, are also evident.

In the late nineteenth century and early twentieth century an organisational transformation took place in American, German and Japanese industry that provided the foundation for a period of extensive and sustained technological development – a period that is described by some as the Second Industrial Revolution. In part the organisational transformation that took place was the result of technological advances in activities such as metalworking, chemistry and the electrical industry. Market expansion allowed companies to exploit these technological opportunities in a profitable manner. But the enterprises that emerged to dominate these industries subsequently became important drivers of further technological and market opportunities. These enterprises ultimately gained dominant shares of a broad range of product markets and drove the development of the economies in which they emerged.

The development experience of the US, Germany and Japan has not been a history of small-scale enterprises coordinated by the market mechanism. The invisible hand of market coordination was usurped by the visible hand of large multiunit enterprises. The sustained dominance of business enterprises that have grown to be large-scale in the development and utilisation of productive resources is an empirical feature of the development experience not just of the US, Germany and Japan, but of most of the advanced industrial economies in this century.

Some scholars have interpreted the evidence on the organisational foundations of industrial development as support for the proposition that

'Big is Better'. They have argued that economies of scale and scope allow large enterprises with diversified activities to achieve lower costs than their smaller competitors.[8] To attribute the continued success of large-scale enterprises in the advanced economies to these factors is to make a static argument about a dynamic process. It is to neglect the fact that companies who have maintained their dominant position over the long run in these economies have generally done so only by being continuously innovative. Of course an enterprise must sell enough products *ex post* to cover the high fixed costs of the investment that it incurred *ex ante* to pursue its innovative strategy. But to say that economies of scale are the source of sustained competitive success is the theoretical equivalent of putting the cart before the horse. The source of these companies' sustained competitive advantage is their ability to sustain a dominant product market position by continuously investing in upgrading the organisational and technological foundations of their innovative success.

Although the sustained dominance of organisations that grow to be large-scale is an empirical feature of the development of all of the advanced industrial economies this does not mean that small and medium-sized enterprises have been unimportant to their economic performance. In the last 25 years there has been a wave of academic literature on small-scale industrial organisations that takes this contention farther in arguing that large dominant enterprises are unnecessary for industrial success. From this perspective the organisation of manufacturing around smaller enterprises in a system of 'flexible specialisation' has emerged as a viable alternative to mass production. Flexible specialisation is defined as a strategy of permanent innovation based on flexible, multi-use equipment and skilled workers and the creation through politics of an industrial community that restricts the forms of competition to those favouring innovation. Proponents of flexible specialisation have pointed to the networks of technologically-sophisticated, highly-flexible manufacturing firms in certain regions in Italy – generally referred to as the Third Italy – as examples of their vision in action. German medium-sized enterprises – the Mittelstand – has also been invoked as an example to illustrate the potential success of this form of organisation.

There is a danger with taking the argument too far. The industrial districts of the Third Italy that have received most attention in this work are confined to a very small number of industrial sectors. Where small and medium-sized enterprises have been successful on a broader scale, for example in Germany, the importance of their linkages with their larger counterparts as customers have sometimes been ignored in discussions of flexible specialisation. Some of the most ardent proponents of flexible specialisation have recently retreated substantially from their initial enthusiasm in the wake of recent problems – 'surprise rigidities' – in the German *Mittelstand* brought on by supplier rationalisation by large companies such as Daimler Benz and Volkswagen.

Porter has also used the Third Italy as an example of the innovative momentum that 'clusters' of firms within confined geographical areas can achieve. But in emphasising the importance of competition among these firms in spurring them to greater efforts Porter ignores what political scientists and economists have emphasised – the degree of cooperation that the success of these districts has required and the foundations for this cooperation in the political structures and histories of these regions.[9] Best has outlined in detail the vital cooperative relations between firms in the provision of marketing, financial and other business services and the links between these relations and the political structure of these regions.[10] A similar point could be made about Denmark a country that in a number of important ways is similar to Ireland. Small companies comprise an important share of Danish industrial activity and cooperate extensively with each other in the supply and use of technology. The close relations between firms is to some extent the legacy of the historical strength of the Danish agricultural cooperative movement a strength that dates from the last century.

There are substantial differences across countries and regions not only in their industrial structures but also in the manner in which work itself is organised. The degree of integration of the specialised skills and knowledge of individuals in the managerial structure and on the shop floor varies substantially across companies. The organisational transformation that took place around the turn of the century in the US, Germany and Japan involved the employment by enterprises of teams of salaried line and staff personnel to plan and coordinate the production and distribution of goods and services. The most successful organisations were those that invested heavily in building up their managerial structures, by recruiting the best people, training them and retaining them to gain continuous access to their specialised skills and knowledge. As the twentieth century progressed systematic management practices spread in various forms to France, Italy and other smaller European countries such as Denmark, Sweden, Switzerland, Austria and Finland.

Despite the similarities in the structure of their managerial organisations the extent to which the learning process has been extended not just to managers but also to workers has varied substantially between the US, Germany, Japan and other countries. As the twentieth century unfolded each national system developed a distinctive dynamic of its own and these differences had an important influence on their technological trajectories, product market strategies and international product market performance. In the American case, the shop floor investment strategy was skill-destroying in its substitution of machines and materials for the skills of workers. In contrast the Germans and Japanese pursued a strategy of skill creation on the shop floor although in the manner in which they extended the learning process to the shop floor they differed substantially from each other, being shaped by different product market strategies. What is apparent in the changing success of countries on product markets is that the companies who have invested in the skills and knowledge development of their managers and workers and have pursued polices to retain them have for some time been outcompeting companies who have failed to make these investments.[11]

The Organisation of Manufacturing in Ireland

Has Irish-based industry succeeded in developing sophisticated capabilities that can serve as a source of competitive advantage on product markets today and in the future? How successful has Irish industrial policy been in promoting the commitment of people and money to cumulative and collective learning processes that could provide the foundation for high and sustainable living standards for a broad range of Irish people?

That Irish industrial policy has managed to stimulate considerable job creation in the indigenous and foreign sectors but has proven unsuccessful in generating sustainable industrial employment reflects the fact that

Table 11.5

Total State Aids[1] in the European Union

Country	Per cent of manufacturing gross value-added		
	1981-86[2]	1986-88[3]	1988-90[3]
Belgium	4.5	4.3	4.1
Denmark	1.7	1.9	2.1
France	3.6	3.8	3.5
Greece	13.9	24.3	14.6
Ireland	*12.3*	*6.4[4]*	*4.9[4]*
Italy	15.8	6.2	6.0
Luxembourg	3.5	2.3	2.6
Netherlands	4.1	3.1	3.1
Portugal	n.a.	2.2	5.3
Spain	n.a.	6.8	3.6
UK	2.9	2.6	2.0
West Germany	2.9	2.7	2.5
EU10 or EU12	5.5	4.0[5]	3.5[5]

Source: Cited in D. Hitchens and J. Birnie, *The Competitiveness of Industry in Ireland,* Avebury, Aldershot 1994.

[1] Includes tax reliefs but excludes impact of differences in tax rates. Thus, Ireland's EPTR is included but the effects of her relatively low rate of taxation of corporate profits is not.
[2] Excluding shipbuilding and steel industries.
[3] Including shipbuilding and steel industries.
[4] After 1986 EPTR in Ireland was of declining importance prior to its phasing out in 1990. It was being replaced by the 10 per cent manufacturing tax as the major fiscal incentive to manufacturing firms. The effects of the latter incentive are not included above.
[5] EU12.

industrial learning processes have not become deeply embedded in Irish industry. As noted in Section 2 the net loss in employment between 1973 and 1994 conceals enormous turmoil in the industrial sector. That the net job loss in this period was only 10,491 jobs, despite a gross jobs loss of 404,376 was a result of the creation of jobs on a massive scale. The industrial policy that has induced much of this job creation has proven to be very costly. In the period from 1981 to 1986 Ireland sustained one of the highest levels of government aid to industry among the EU countries. There was a reduction in the total resources directly allocated to the development effort in accordance with the recommendations of the Government White Paper in 1984. Between 1985 and 1989 the total industry budget (direct expenditure) fell from about IR£390 million to IR£317 million in nominal terms. Since 1989 there has, however, been a resumption in spending on industrial policy.

Irish-based industrial activity seems to be caught in a vicious circle. It neither relies on highly-sophisticated technological nor marketing capabilities nor does it provide a basis on which such sophisticated capabilities can be developed. In the indigenous sector investments to develop such capabilities have never been made on a significant scale. In the foreign-owned sector parent companies who have already invested in cumulative learning processes in their country of origin or elsewhere to build up their competitive advantage have had little incentive to invest in new learning processes in Ireland to sustain that advantage. They have preferred instead to transfer knowledge from their overseas plants for use in their Irish operations.

R&D expenditures are best suited as measures of technological activity in science-based industries although they are far from perfect indicators of the level of technological activity even in these sectors. In terms of industry-financed expenditure on R&D Ireland's relative performance has improved since the late 1960s but she continues to rank well below much of the advanced industrial world, including some of the smaller countries. In 1991 R&D in business enterprises in Ireland was 0.8 per cent of GDP compared with 2.7 per cent in Sweden, 2.5 per cent in West Germany, 2.1 per cent in the UK, 1.5 per cent in the Netherlands, and 1.3 per cent in Denmark and Norway.[12]

When a broader range of industrial activities is of interest there is a risk associated with excessive emphasis on the scientific knowledge that is generated by R&D activity. Although often treated by economists as an 'impure' form of knowledge, given its specific and particular character, technological and engineering knowledge is economically far more important than 'purer' forms of knowledge. As Nathan Rosenberg, a leading economist of technology, put it, 'relatively grubby and pedestrian forms of knowledge' have been at the heart of the process of economic development in all of the advanced industrial countries.[13] However, evidence on the nature of Irish-based industrial activity, in the indigenous and the foreign-owned sectors, also supports the proposition that Ireland has as yet failed to acquire sophisticated capabilities in marketing and in the development and utilisation of technology.

Indigenous Industry
The basis for continuous innovation has not been established on a widespread basis either in individual indigenous companies nor on the basis of linkages between them. The low level of technological sophistication in indigenous companies, officially recognised in 1961 by the government appointed Committee on Industrial Organisation (CIO), has persisted into the 1990s and if anything has deteriorated in comparative perspective. Most of the job losses sustained in the indigenous sector in the 1970s were in the traded sector in industries such as textiles, clothing, footwear, wood and furniture. These losses were partly compensated for by expansion in other sectors but most of the gains were in low-skill, non-traded activities such as construction, mechanical and electrical contracting, industrial imports and installation and metal fabrications.

Given these trends it is not surprising that the Telesis Report, published over 20 years after the CIO report, revealed that there had been little improvement in the overall technological and marketing sophistication of indigenous industry in the intervening period. Companies had still not managed to utilise or develop sophisticated capabilities in technology and marketing and remained concentrated in predominantly low-skilled, low-value-added activities. The comparative weakness of the indigenous sector became starkly apparent in the 1980s when indigenous industrial activity declined precipitously in the face of increasing competition on international product markets (see Section 2).

Even the indigenous companies that have been successful enough to grow to large-scale have not done so by utilising or developing sophisticated technological and marketing capabilities. A recent study showed that the 686 largest firms in the world (the smallest of which employs about 8,000 people) accounted for just under half of the world's technological activities, as measured by US patenting for the period 1981-86, and for about 60 per cent of patenting by all business enterprises. Not one of these firms was Irish even though companies in other small countries such as Belgium, the Netherlands and Switzerland were well represented.[14] The dominant Irish food companies, for example, are agricultural food cooperatives and meat processors that have confined themselves to low-value-added activities that require little technological sophistication. Other large Irish companies, with a few notable exceptions, have grown up in low-value-added activities often in sheltered sectors of the economy.

The predominant organisational form in Ireland is the small autonomous manufacturing company. Nearly 65 per cent of the private industrial sector in Ireland is concentrated in enterprises with less than 100 employees. This kind of industrial structure is not unusual in comparative perspective;

enterprises with less than 100 employees accounted for 80 per cent of private sector employment in Greece, 71.1 per cent in Italy, 66.3 per cent in Spain, and 63.7 per cent in Portugal. As noted above what is important to industrial development is not so much the size of enterprises as the extent to which they are organised in a way that facilitates the development of a cumulative and collective learning process. Small firms have managed to sustain such learning through cooperation with each other at the district, regional and even at the national level in parts of Italy and Spain and on a broader scale in Germany and Denmark. However, there has historically been hardly any long-term cooperation between Irish small firms in the provision of purchasing, marketing, financial services or through supply linkages.

Nor is there much evidence of cooperation within Irish enterprises in the development and utilisation of specialised skills of the type that one finds in more advanced countries who have developed cumulative and collective learning processes. Irish indigenous companies, unlike those that have become dominant in the advanced industrial countries, have, with a few notable exceptions, not invested in building and sustaining strong managerial hierarchies. Nor have these companies invested in a skill formation process for shop floor workers. The Culliton Report identified a significant 'skills gap' between Irish companies and best-practice firms in competitor countries. It observed that:

> There is a deficiency of intermediate production skills, an absence of multiskilling, both among technicians and craftspeople, and an absence of integrated financial and technical skills at the management level. These deficiencies inhibit productivity growth and competitiveness in the typical Irish industrial firm. (p.54)

A similar 'gap' is evident at the managerial level. In a recent survey the chief executives of the 1,000 largest private companies in Ireland ranked the technical and production management training needs of top managers relatively low compared with perceived deficiencies in general management, finance, marketing and industrial relations. The investigators who carried out the survey suggested that the limited emphasis on technological matters reflected a lack of experience by Irish executives of world manufacturing standards.[15] This conclusion is supported by a survey of selected measures of competitiveness published by the World Economic Forum in 1994. Ireland was ranked fifteenth among all the OECD countries in terms of overall competitiveness. She scored fifteenth in management development compared with third place for Denmark, a country that is comparable in terms of scale and other vital characteristics. In technical management Ireland did even worse in comparative perspective scoring only twenty first to Denmark's fifth place. Ireland was placed seventeenth in in-company training whereas Denmark was sixth.[16] The problem of low capabilities and the absence of ongoing knowledge creation and skill development is clearly still endemic in the indigenous sector.

The history of industrial development reveals that
of innovation has proven successful the most impor
funding is the retained earnings of the enterprises the
initial development. This feature of investment financing
across successful companies in the advanced industria
significant differences in the structures of national fin
Ireland the successful indigenous companies who ha   up large
reserves of cash have tended not to reinvest that money in upgrading the
innovative capabilities of the Irish industrial sector. To the extent that they
have reinvested it in Ireland they have tended to do so by expanding in the
low-skilled, sheltered activities in which they had already proven successful.
They had not developed the requisite skills in their managerial structures to
diversify into sectors that demanded sophisticated technological and
marketing capabilities. In the Irish indigenous sector there has not been a
major commitment of human nor financial resources to the initiation and
sustenance of a cumulative and collective industrial learning process.

Foreign-Owned Industry in Ireland
As was noted in Section 2 the organisation of the Irish industrial sector is
characterised by a dual structure. The Irish subsidiaries of large foreign
companies dominate certain industrial sectors, and in particular sectors often
associated with technologically-sophisticated industrial activities. These
subsidiaries are the drivers of most of the favourable trends in Ireland's
aggregate macroeconomic performance indicators. Sustained growth in
manufacturing output, a rise in the percentage of output exported to
international markets and high and increasing productivity are generally
associated with an increase in an economy's technological and marketing
sophistication. However, in Ireland's case this conclusion is not warranted
because most of the foreign subsidiaries have sustained their performance on
the basis of capabilities that are embedded in other economies. The
contribution that foreign-owned enterprises have made to the development of
strong technological and marketing capabilities in Ireland have thus been far
less impressive than the aggregate figures suggest.

Most of the foreign firms that located in Ireland in the 1960s came with
technically-mature, labour-intensive products such as textiles, clothing,
footwear, plastics and light engineering. The Irish subsidiaries generally
required few skills to perform their operations. They relied to a great extent
on the parent company for their technologies and were rarely regarded as an
important source of technological innovation by the parent company.
Although these companies exported a large proportion of their output they
tended to rely on the parent company for marketing expertise.

In the late 1970s and 1980s there was substantial growth in the Irish-based
electronics and chemicals sectors, and other 'high-technology' activities, as
foreign companies responded to the attractive incentives offered by the IDA

these industrial sectors. However, most of these companies, with some exceptions, have behaved like their predecessors in locating their critical business functions outside of Ireland. The rate of R&D spending in foreign-owned plants has fallen short of that in most industrialised countries and some of the NICs too. For example, R&D was estimated to represent 0.9 per cent of Irish sales in office machinery and data-processing equipment plants in 1981 compared to 1.3 per cent in electronics plants in South Korea, 6.4 per cent in Japan, and 8.1 per cent in the US. A similar difference was also apparent in pharmaceuticals, a sector which in Ireland spent 5 per cent of sales but 14 per cent in Britain and 10 per cent on average in the EU (11).[17]

Only low levels of skill are demanded of most of the Irish workforce in foreign-owned plants. Technological and marketing innovations and industrial expertise in general continues to be imported from parent companies. Although newer foreign firms in the high-technology sectors employed significantly greater numbers of technically-skilled and professional people than is typical for such firms in the newly-industrialising countries (NICs), the proportion of skilled workers in the Irish subsidiaries compared unfavourably with more developed countries where strong marketing functions and some degree of technical development are generally evident in foreign subsidiaries. Of course this does not mean that these companies carry out no training of Irish managers and workers whatsoever but most of this training is designed to improve dexterity in routine operations rather than to develop multiple, flexible skills that could serve as a basis for innovative activities. Thus even though the products produced by foreign companies in Ireland have been increasingly 'high-tech' the operations that Irish people perform for these companies continue to be predominantly low-skilled. Whether a worker spends his whole day checking the printout from a machine that makes microprocessors or the stitching on the sole of a cheap shoe it is unlikely that in either case he is developing skills or acquiring knowledge that might allow him to advance to more challenging activities. In national terms what this logic implies is that the Irish workforce is not generating the knowledge and developing the skills that could form the social foundation for a more sustainable industrial base.

The low level of skill formation and knowledge creation among employees in foreign-owned enterprises in Ireland means that these enterprises have made little direct contribution to the initiation and sustenance of a learning process that is embedded in the Irish economy. However, it is possible that the foreign sector has contributed indirectly to the development of indigenous capabilities through technology transfer and knowledge sharing more generally on the basis of supply linkages. Unfortunately, the foreign-owned sector in Ireland does not seem to have generated substantial spillovers of this type. The low level of supply linkages between domestic supplier and foreign-owned companies emphasised in the Telesis Report has persisted. In the highest growth sectors of the foreign sector linkages are particularly low. The office machinery sector, for example, sourced only 4 per cent of its industrial input needs in Ireland in the late 1980s and in the electrical and chemicals sectors the figure was less than 7 per cent.

The lack of interest exhibited by foreign-owned enterprises in building up a greenfield learning process in Ireland given that they can rely on sophisticated technological and marketing capabilities elsewhere is evident from their financial behaviour. The volume of repatriated profits, dividends and royalty payments leaving Ireland has greatly increased over the 1980s (see Chapter 9). Since they do not rely on distinctive capabilities within their Irish subsidiaries to sustain their competitive advantage these companies have tended to behave in a relatively footloose way when the competitive climate changes. In particular, when technological innovation within these companies or by their competitors renders obsolete the products and processes on which their Irish plants rely parent companies have often responded by shutting these plants down.

5 AN ASSESSMENT OF POLICY TOWARDS INDUSTRY IN IRELAND

The extent of the problems that it perceived in the indigenous sector in the late 1950s persuaded the CIO that a radical policy response was required. The recommendations of this committee would have, in its own words, 'radically changed the whole organisation character of private enterprise industry in Ireland'; 'instead of the traditional encouragement of competition among firms, cooperation on a massive scale is recommended'. It was envisaged that this cooperation would take place in purchasing, production rationalisation, training, design and export development. The actual policy response was the establishment of a number of grant schemes to help indigenous companies to finance fixed industrial investment. The more ambitious proposals promulgated by the CIO were rejected or ignored.

Although Irish industrial policy since then has entailed significant intervention by the government in the economy that intervention has not taken place at the level of productive activity. In allocating grants to indigenous companies the government did not interfere with their operations and strategies. For this approach to have been successful would have required decision-makers in indigenous companies to have understood the extent of their competitive problems and the strategies through which they could be remedied. However, as is clear from the discussion above the level of technological and marketing capabilities in indigenous companies was too low to facilitate the successful operation of the relatively hands-off policy that the government attempted to pursue.

The predominant focus in grant allocation until the mid-1980s on the financing of investments in fixed assets investment rather than in organisation and technology also seems to have been misguided given the problems facing the indigenous sector. As it became obvious that an upsurge in indigenous activity was not taking place in response to government incentives there was an increasing emphasis in Irish industrial policy on the attraction of foreign direct investors from the early 1970s. Although grants and manufacturing tax concessions continued to be made available to the indigenous sector no major new initiatives were introduced to promote it.

In response to criticisms in the Telesis Report of the government's neglect of the indigenous sector an increased share of the grant budget was allocated to indigenous companies although the more interventionist strategy of 'picking winners' promulgated by this group was rejected. The shift in the grant budget as the 1980s progressed away from incentives for fixed industrial investment towards the support of investments in R&D, training and technology acquisition reflected a growing recognition of the centrality of the generation of knowledge and the development of skills to the process of industrial development. A range of programmes was also introduced to redress deficiencies in management and marketing capability and in product development.

The Culliton Report recommended an even greater attention to these factors and advocated a number of policies to increase the level of R&D, to improve the level of industrial training, and to promote the utilisation of best-practice technology in the Irish economy. But the government once again responded in a conservative way to these proposals. It sought to redress the skills gap in Irish industry by creating a new division within the existing training agency (FÁS) to focus on the development of the skills of those at work without significant investment in the capabilities within this agency. It proposed to increase the technological capability of Irish industry through yet another refocussing of the grant allocation process towards investment in R&D, technology acquisition and training.

The Culliton Report's suggestion that the structural problems of indigenous industry be redressed through the promotion of industrial clusters was not adopted. By the middle of the 1990s the basic structure of industrial policy in Ireland established in the late 1950s remained in place. Financial incentives were provided by centralised grant-giving agencies and the government attempted as much as possible to stay out of the business of doing business.

The policy of the Irish government stands in stark contrast to that pursued in countries that have developed relatively recently such as Japan and the East Asian Tigers. In these countries governments have played an active and highly-selective role in their attempts to ensure that cumulative learning processes become deeply embedded in their national economies. Government agencies in these countries have not only promoted technology transfer from the advanced industrial countries; they have acquired the rights to this technology themselves and have then transmitted it to selected firms in the domestic economy. Teams of government researchers have undertaken industrial R&D and have diffused the results to the indigenous industrial sector. Governments in these countries have also used their control of financial resources to promote certain strategies by industrial companies and the development of particular sectors of the economy. To facilitate this level of government involvement in productive activity learning, processes were established within government bureaucracies. Substantial investments in the education and skill formation of public sector officials prepared them for their active role in industry.

There has been a recognition in these countries that to facilitate a development process sophisticated technological capabilities must be strategically created somewhere in the economy. In the early stages of the development process capabilities within government bureaucracies were strengthened to facilitate the creation of capabilities in the private sector. Ongoing development in these countries has depended on the close cooperation of business and government in a cumulative learning process. Industrial policy has been less concerned with the degree of government intervention that is appropriate than about the most efficacious means to develop the organisational basis for a sustained process of development. In Ireland, in contrast, capabilities were not created within the government or the private sector. At the heart of Irish industrial policy was the hope that given the right financial incentives such capabilities would simply emerge, a hope that reflects a lack of understanding of the complexity of the social process underlying the process of development.

The attraction of foreign direct investment has been an important part of industrial policy in a number of developing countries but there have been striking differences in the manner in which foreign investors are treated across countries. In its approach to foreign direct investors the same 'quick-fix' approach has been apparent in Irish policy as has been evident in its treatment of the indigenous sector. In Ireland the government has offered very attractive financial incentives to induce foreign investors to locate here with almost 'no strings attached'. Despite the fact that an Irish location offers investors from outside the EU unrestricted access to the European market the Irish government has not leveraged this 'carrot' to demand anything more than money and jobs from foreign investors. Foreign investors have not been required to make the type of commitments to the Irish economy that would be necessary if they were to contribute to the development of capabilities in the Irish industrial sector. As concerns have grown about the lack of linkages between foreign and indigenous companies new incentives have been made available to promote their development. There have been few attempts to make foreign investors commit to the promotion of domestic supply linkages up front, a strategy that in other countries has forced foreign investors to train local companies to provide them with inputs of the cost and quality that they require. Nor has there been a concerted attempt to gain access to the technologies that these companies develop and utilise so that they can be diffused to other sectors of the Irish economy.

The development agencies have argued that foreign investors will be less willing to locate here if they are forced to comply with restrictive standards. But without this commitment foreign investors add little to the local economy. Despite the evidence to support this perspective in Ireland and in other countries this perspective is not widely advocated in Irish policy circles. Indeed it often seems that the IDA has become caught up in the 'market' for mobile investment to such an extent that the need to ensure that foreign investors make massive profits in Ireland has overtaken the real priority of establishing capabilities in the Irish industrial sector that will allow it to compete into the 21st century.

Ireland's hands-off approach to foreign direct investment is starkly contrasted to the policies of other countries, and in particular the East Asian economies, in attracting foreign investors. Governments in the East Asian economies have refused to allow foreign investors to take advantage of investment incentives unless they use existing domestically-supplied inputs or work with local companies to produce new sources of supply. The basic rationale for the attraction of foreign investors in these countries is the access to advanced technologies that they provide. To ensure that this opportunity is fully exploited governments in these countries have set up agencies that are charged with learning about the technologies that foreign investors bring and integrating the knowledge and skills required to utilise and develop them into indigenous industry through continuous innovation in the education and training systems.

In other cases of successful development, for example in the industrial clusters that have become popular in academic and policy circles, the process of development has been facilitated less by the intervention of a strong central government than by political institutions that have supported a collective and cumulative process of learning through cooperative relations within and between firms, and between management and workers. The role of industrial policy has been to facilitate the operation of these cooperative networks by shaping the structure of the financial, educational and legal systems.

To understand the social foundations of industrial development is to recognise the importance of the interaction between policy and the organisation of capabilities in the private and the public sectors. Ireland has in the last 35 years attempted to implement a relatively hands-off industrial policy for the indigenous sector that had little chance of success given the low levels of capability in the private sector. This policy has not proven successful in promoting the initiation and sustenance of a cumulative learning process in indigenous industry. Nor has Ireland succeeded in using FDI as a basis on which to acquire and develop sophisticated capabilities and embed them in the national economy. The absence of technological capabilities in the government bureaucracy in part explains the failure to utilise and further develop technological capabilities brought to Ireland by foreign investors.

To draw insights about the social foundations of industrial development from the experience of advanced industrial economies and from the barriers to sustained development in countries like Ireland is however only the first step towards prescribing industrial policy to promote development.

6 FUTURE PROSPECTS AND CHALLENGES

Ireland needs to take that step if not under the compulsion of past failures then because of the threats that changes in the world economy present for her existing industrial policy. The possibility of sustaining an industrial policy based on foreign direct investment (FDI) seems increasingly unlikely in the future. Ireland's share of FDI has fallen significantly in the last fifteen years as competition in the market for mobile investment has become more vigorous. There has also been a change in the composition of FDI away from investment in manufacturing towards services and a decline in investment in greenfield plants in favour of acquisitions, joint ventures and other alliances with strong indigenous enterprises. These trends do not augur well for Ireland given the lack of capabilities in her indigenous sector that could form the basis for alliances with foreign partners. There has also been an increase in competition among host countries for FDI. The Eastern European countries, India and China have become increasingly important in recent years as sites for foreign-owned manufacturing plants and given their lower levels of wages have proven formidable competitors for the Irish. Early in 1995 the United Nations Conference on Trade and Development (Unctad) responded to this increasing competition by calling for international negotiations to curb incentives for FDI to be integrated with discussions on investment and trade distortions by the World Trade Organisation.

There is no easy alternative in industrial policy terms for Ireland. She cannot simply switch from a relatively hands-off industrial policy today to a more active one tomorrow. Certainly any attempt to undertake a more selective approach to industrial development is not an option whilst the skills and knowledge that such an approach would require are not embedded in the public sector. It is possible of course that such capabilities could be created through strategic investments in the development of organisational and technological capabilities among those employed in the industrial promotion agencies. The political implications of such a strategy are substantial. The East Asian economies have avoided political controversy only because industrial policies have been designed and implemented by a 'hard state' or authoritarian government.

An alternative approach would be to make these investments at the local level through the creation of public-private partnerships with considerable autonomy in the shaping of local financial and educational structures. There have been a number of tentative attempts to move towards this with the recent establishment of County Enterprise Boards. But to have any chance of success such an approach to industrial policy would require a significant overhaul of the social and political institutions in a country that has long been used to government from above by a centralised administration. Once again such a change in industrial policy could not occur overnight but would have to be integrated into a long-term strategy of social and political change.

Industrial policy, be it successful or unsuccessful, hands-off or hands-on is always deeply political because it is both rooted in the institutional framework of a society and transforms that framework through its implementation. Even in Ireland where industrial policy has been relatively hands-off it has relied on a social consensus that has allowed wage restraint, the allocation of large sums of money to the attraction of foreign investment, the payment by manufacturing corporations of taxes at a reduced rate, and other development policies. Its implementation has also transformed the social structure in Ireland in a number of important ways.

These social and political dimensions of industrial policy are not unfortunate 'imperfections' in the economy. They are central to the success of a national strategy of industrial development. If discussions of industrial policy in Ireland continue to neglect their importance in the design and implementation of industrial policy or to consider them as endogenous to economic concerns, changes in industrial policy will continue to be piecemeal, relatively ineffective and even counterproductive in attempts to raise living standards on a sustained basis.

Although both the Telesis Report and to a greater extent the Culliton Report recognised the importance of developing skills and accumulating knowledge in industrial development they neglected to consider the social and political dimensions of the changes that they proposed. The dangers of this neglect can be seen in the Culliton Report's proposals for improvements in the Irish system of skill formation. The report suggested that a high-quality and respected stream of technical and vocational education with a new curriculum and close involvement with industry should be developed along the lines of the German system of apprenticeship.

The German system of skill formation has in the post-war period depended for its success on the cooperation of unions and employers in the design and implementation of its dual system of apprenticeship training. The regulation of the system at the national and industry level is undertaken through the cooperation of union and management representatives. Local chambers of industry and commerce in which unions and management participate regulate the operation of training programmes. German enterprises have maintained a high level of commitment to worker training. They finance a large part of training expenditures and promotional and other reward structures within companies are closely integrated with the training system. Cooperation between workers and managers within the enterprise through works councils that control the organisation of work also facilitates the operation of the system.

To highlight the need for greater training in industry as the Culliton Report did is an important observation but it is only a prelude to the development of an industrial policy to redress that problem. How one develops the social foundations for the cooperation that is necessary between workers and managers, business and government, and competing enterprises if such a system is to work effectively is central to the viability of this type of policy proposal.

Given Ireland's role as a member of the EU the political prerequisites for different industrial policies are even more pertinent today than in the past. Ireland faces less autonomy in some areas of national economic policy than she has in the past but membership also opens up new possibilities to her in terms of social and political structures particularly through greater cooperation with the many other regional economies in the EU that are struggling to develop their industries. Without social and political innovation of this type it is difficult to see how a sustained process of economic development can be initiated and sustained in Ireland.

Endnotes

1 'Irish industrial sector' is used herein to refer to all Irish-based industrial activity in Ireland. When there is need to distinguish by nationality of ownership between different types of industrial activity the terms 'indigenous' and 'foreign-owned' industry will be used.

2 K. Kennedy, T. Giblin and D. McHugh, *The Economic Development of Ireland in the Twentieth Century,* Routledge, London 1988.

3 E. O'Malley, *Industry and Economic Development: The Challenge for the Latecomer,* Gill and Macmillan, Dublin 1989.

4 D. Hitchens and J. Birnie, *The Competitiveness of Industry in Ireland,* Avebury, Aldershot 1994.

5 This section draws on a more extended theoretical and empirical argument in W. Lazonick and M. O'Sullivan, 'Organisations, Finance and International Competition', *Industrial Corporate Change,* 1996 (forthcoming). I would like to thank my co-author for allowing me to use this material here.

6 See W. Lazonick, *Business Organisation and the Myth of the Market Economy,* Cambridge University Press, Cambridge 1991, for a theoretical discussion of the social foundations of industrial innovation.

7 See for example R. Wade, *Governing the Market: Economic Theory and the Role of Government in East Asian Industrialisation,* Princeton University Press, Princeton NJ 1990; The World Bank, *The East Asian Miracle,* Washington DC 1994.

8 See for example A. Chandler, *Scale and Scope: The Dynamics of Industrial Capitalism,* Cambridge University Press, Cambridge 1990.

9 M. Porter, *The Competitive Advantage of Nations,* Macmillan, London 1990.

10 M. Best, *The New Competition: Institutions of Industrial Restructuring,* Harvard University Press, Cambridge MA 1990.

11 W. Lazonick and M. O'Sullivan, 'Skill Formation in Wealthy Nations' (paper presented at History and Economics Conference, Cambridge University), 1994.

12 Report of the Science, Technology and Innovation Advisory Council, *Making Knowledge*

Work for Us: A Strategic View of Science, Technology and Innovation in Ireland, vol. 3, Government Publications, Dublin 1995.

13 N. Rosenberg, *Perspectives on Technology,* Cambridge University Press, Cambridge 1976.

14 P. Patel and K. Pavitt, 'The Innovative Performance of the World's Largest Firms: Some New Evidence, *The Economics of Innovation and Technology,* 2, 1992.

15 F. Roche and P. Tansey, 'Industrial Training in Ireland,' *Report to the Industrial Policy Review Group,* Government Publications, Dublin 1992.

16 *The World Competitiveness Report,* World Economic Forum, Geneva 1993.

17 Hitchens and Birnie, *op.cit.*

Selected Bibliography

Books/Reports

1 S. Cantillon, J. Curtis and J. FitzGerald (editors), *Economic Perspectives for the Medium Term,* Economic and Social Research Institute, Dublin 1994.
2 S. Cantillon, J. Curtis and J. FitzGerald, *Medium-Term Review: 1994-2000,* Economic and Social Research Institute, Dublin 1994.
3 P.J. Drudy and D. McAleese (editors), *Ireland and the European Community,* Cambridge University Press, Cambridge 1984.
4 A. Foley and M. Mulreany (editors), *The Single European Market and the Irish Economy,* Institute of Public Administration, Dublin 1990.
5 D.A. Gillmor, *Economic Activities in the Republic of Ireland: A Geographical Perspective,* Gill and Macmillan, Dublin 1985.
6 D. Hitchens and J. Birnie, *The Competitiveness of Industry in Ireland,* Avebury, Aldershot 1994.
7 P. Keatinge (editor), *Ireland and the Single European Act,* Pinter, London 1991.
8 K. Kennedy, T. Giblin and D. McHugh, *The Economic Development of Ireland in the Twentieth Century,* Routledge, London 1988.
9 A. Leddin and B. M. Walsh, *The Macroeconomy of Ireland* (third edition), Gill and Macmillan, Dublin 1995.
10 J.J. Lee, *Ireland 1912-1985,* Cambridge University Press, Cambridge 1990.
11 D. McAleese and A. Foley (editors), *Overseas Industry in Ireland,* Gill and Macmillan, Dublin 1991.
12 NESC (National Economic and Social Council), *Ireland and the European Community: Performance, Prospects and Strategy* (Report no. 88), Stationery Office, Dublin 1989.
13 NESC, *A Strategy for Competitiveness, Growth and Employment,* (Report no. 96), Stationery Office, Dublin 1993.
14 E. O'Malley, *Industry and Economic Development: The Challenge for the Latecomer,* Gill and Macmillan, Dublin 1989.

Journals, Monographs, etc.

1 *Administration* (quarterly journal of the Institute of Public Administration of Ireland).
2 *Central Bank of Ireland Quarterly Bulletin* and *Central Bank of Ireland Annual Report.*

3   Economic and Social Research Institute's *Broadsheet Series, General Research Series, Policy Research Series* and *Quarterly Economic Commentary.*
4   *Economic and Social Review* (quarterly journal of the social sciences published by Economic and Social Studies, Dublin).
5   European Commission and Eurostat Publications.
6   Government Publications, including *National Income and Expenditure* (annual), *Budget* (annual), Commission on Taxation Reports, and *Economic Review and Outlook* (annual).
7   International Monetary Fund, *World Economic* Outlook (annual).
8   *Irish Banking Review* (quarterly).
9   *Journal of the Statistical and Social Inquiry Society of Ireland* (annual).
10 OECD (Organisation for Economic Cooperation and Development), *Economic Outlook* (quarterly), *Economic Studies* (quarterly) and *Economic Surveys* (annual).
11 *Studies* (an Irish quarterly review).

Subject Index

Aggregate Production Function, 198-200

Agricultural Policy (see also Agriculture; Common Agricultural Policy)
education and training, 348
Farm Improvement Programme, 347-348
Farmer Retirement Scheme, 349-350
food policy, 356-358
and the General Agreement on Tariffs and Trade, 341-343
land policy, 349-350
leasing, 350
reform, 340-359
research, 348
Structural Funds, 347

Agriculture (see also Agricultural Policy; Common Agricultural Policy)
agrarian violence, 16-17
competitiveness, 340-359
composition, 330-331
and consumer concerns, 356-358
diversification, 353-354
employment, 334
and the environment, 358-359
farm income, 333-336
farm viability, 336-337
foreign trade, 332-333
and government intervention, 329, 338-359
history of, 5-7, 13, 20-21, 25, 27-28, 31, 33
importance of, 328-329
output, 331-332
structure, 20-21, 25, 333-337, 349-350

Arrow's Impossibility Theorem, 73

Balance of Payments
accommodating transactions, 94, 273
automatic adjustment mechanisms, 274-276
autonomous transactions, 94, 273
capital account, 95, 272, 275
and capital flows, 273-274
and competitiveness, 277
components, 94, 272
current account, 95, 272, 275
deficit, 95
and devaluation, 277
and efficiency, 98-99
and free trade, 98
and growth, 99, 273
policy, 276-278
position, 274-276
problem, 95-96, 276
profit repatriation, 272
trade balance, 272
UK deficit, 97

Baumol's Disease, 111

Budget Deficit
current, 163, 167

Exchequer Borrowing
    Requirement, 163, 167
General Government Deficit, 163,
    167
Public Sector Borrowing
    Requirement, 163, 167
Business Expansion Schemes, 136

Cattle Acts, 6
Central Bank of Ireland
    history of, 174-176
Central Banking (see Monetary
    Policy)
Commission on Taxation, 150-155
Common Agricultural Policy and
    Eastern Europe, 343
    export refunds, 339
    and the General Agreement on
        Tariffs and Trade, 341-343
    intervention support, 339
    and Ireland, 38, 329, 338-345
    price support, 339-340
    rationale, 338
    reform, 340-345
    variable levy, 339
Comparative Advantage, 97
Competition Act, 323-324
Competition Authority, 323-324
Competition Policy
    and efficiency, 312-313
    and the European Union, 323-324
    general equilibrium effects, 312
    and government monopoly, 317-
        319
    mechanisms, 314-324
    and natural monopoly, 314-315,
        319-320
    regulation, 119, 121, 314-315, 319-
        320
    regulatory capture, 315
    and un-competitive behaviour, 315-
        317
    and welfare, 312-313
Competitiveness
    and agriculture, 345-346
    and the balance of payments, 277
    and industry, 383-389
    and services, 309

Consumption Taxation
    and EU harmonisation, 139-140,
        148-149, 155-157, 279
    excise duties, 139-140
    reform, 139, 155-157
    value-added taxes, 131, 139, 148,
        155-157, 279
Convergence (see Growth)
Corporatism (see Trade Unions)
Culliton Report, 372, 390
Cumann na nGaedheal, 28-30
Currency
    history of, 174-175
Currency Crisis, 40-41, 184-188

Demography (see also Labour Supply)
    age structure, 231
    birth rate, 27
    death rate, 14, 27
    and emigration, 25, 27, 34, 230-233
    and labour force, 230-233
    participation rate, 231-232
    population growth, 4, 10-11, 15-16,
        19, 26, 31, 230-233
    and public expenditure, 111-112
    rate of natural increase, 230
Direct Foreign Investment
    and growth, 214, 221-222
    and industry, 214, 221-222, 365-
        367, 370-371, 387-389
Distribution (see also Equality)
    and chance, 68
    and human capital, 67-68
    intergenerational, 66
    preferences for, 67-70
    and taxation, 71
    transfers, 71
    and unemployment, 77-78, 238-
        240, 143-150

Economic and Monetary Union
    benefits, 191-194, 289-290
    convergence criteria, 190, 290
    costs, 192-193, 290
    and Ireland, 190-194, 289-291
    stages, 188-190, 290
Economic War, 31-32
Education

expenditure, 108-109, 112
and growth, 202-204, 216
Efficiency (see also Market
  Mechanism; Pareto-efficiency)
  in exchange, 51-53
  and the market mechanism, 52-53
  in production, 51-53
Efficiency Wage Theory, 76
Emigration
  composition, 217
  extent, 25, 27, 34, 216-217
  and unemployment, 238
Employment (see also Unemployment)
  agricultural, 334
  full, 74-78
  growth of, 233-234
  industrial, 365-370
  international comparison, 233-234
  labour supply, 230-233
  part-time, 234
  sectoral composition, 233, 236
  services sector, 305
  temporary, 235
Employment-Protection
  Legislation, 255-256
Environment
  and agriculture, 358-359
  and growth, 79-81
  international cooperation, 125
Equality (see also Distribution)
  and growth, 81-82
  measurement, 65-66
  Rawls' Difference Principle, 70
  utilitarianism, 69
European Central Bank, 189-190, 290-291
European Union (see also Economic
  and Monetary Union; European
  Monetary System; Maastricht
  Treaty; Single European Market)
  accession to, 37, 38
  Common Agricultural Policy, 38,
    329-345
  Community Support Framework,
    281-282, 347
  convergence, 42-44
  enlargement, 282
  and foreign trade, 38, 278-280

Maastricht, 171-174, 283
  regional policy, 280-281
  Structural Funds, 118, 280-282, 347
  and unemployment, 40
European Monetary System
  accession to, 40, 181, 285-287
  cost of adjustment, 40, 183-185,
    285-287
  currency crisis, 40-41, 287
  exchange rate mechanism, 40-41,
    285-287
  and inflation, 285-287
  and interest rates, 186, 286
  and price competitiveness, 183
Exchange Rate, 286-292
Exchange Rate Policy
  devaluation, 187, 277, 287
  and the European Monetary
    System, 40-41, 181-188, 285-
    287
  history of, 29, 181-188, 285-287
  and inflation, 285-287
  purchasing power parity, 182-183
Exchequer Borrowing Requirement,
  163, 167
Excise Duties (see Consumption
  Taxation)
Externalities, 105, 109, 300-301

Famine, 13-15
Fianna Fáil, 30, 39-40
Fiscal Illusion, 113
Fiscal Policy (see Taxation;
  Government Intervention)
  automatic stabilisers, 164
  in the classical model, 161-162
  and convergence, 171-174
  credit risk effect, 166
  crowding-out, 166
  and growth, 222
  history of, 38-40, 166-170
  and interest rates, 165-166
  in the Keynesian model, 161, 164-
    165
  measures, 163
  and the multiplier, 164-165
  and public debt, 166-171
  Ricardian Equivalence, 166

in a small open economy, 162, 165
stance, 163-164
Foreign Trade
agriculture, 332-333
commodity composition, 267
Eastern Europe, 271
and the European Union, 278-280
and foreign-owned companies, 268-269
gains from, 97-98
and the General Agreement on
Tariffs and Trade, 284
geographical diversification, 269-270
and growth, 97-98, 107-109, 219-221
history of, 3-6, 28-38
international comparison, 266-267
intra-industry, 268
manufacturing, 268-270
services, 271, 298, 302-304
of small open economy, 97-98, 111-112, 267
terms of trade, 270
and transport costs, 97, 302-304
UK share, 269-270
and unemployment, 245-246
Full Employment, 74-78

General Agreement on Tariffs and
Trade (see also World Trade
Organisation)
Uruguay Round, 284, 341-343
General Equilibrium (see Market
Mechanism; Efficiency)
General Government Deficit, 163, 167
Government Borrowing (see Public
Debt; Public Borrowing)
Government Intervention (see also
Agricultural Policy; Industrial
Policy)
and agriculture, 337-359
competition policy, 312-324
education, 108-109
health, 108
history of, 13, 28-40
and industry, 364-393
international policy coordination,
123-125
and market failure, 105, 108-109
planning and social partnership,
122-123, 225, 288-289
rationale, 104-106, 159
regulation, 104, 119-121, 314-315,
319-320
and services, 300-302, 319-320
and stabilisation, 105-106
state-owned enterprises, 121-122,
319-320
transfers, 109-110
Growth
aggregate production function, 198-200
and convergence, 43, 201-202, 212-214
dependency theory, 45
and direct foreign investment, 213,
220-221
economies of scale, 207
and emigration, 18, 218-219
and employment, 248-250
and the environment, 79-81
and equality, 81-82
and fiscal policy, 223
and foreign trade, 97-98, 107-109,
219-221
and human capital, 17-18, 203-204,
217-218
and innovation, 205-206
institutional factors, 46, 204-206,
224-225
and intergenerational equity, 88
and investment, 17, 200-202, 215-217
Marxist interpretation, 45-46
nationalist interpretation, 6, 45
new economic geography, 208-209,
223-224
new growth theory, 206-207
and rent-seeking, 206, 224-225
research and development, 205
and savings, 78-79
services, 304-305
in a small open economy, 79
Solow model, 202-205
and technology, 80, 206-208

and unemployment, 18, 41, 248-250
and welfare, 78-82

Health Care, 108
Human Capital (see also Education), 203-204, 218-219

Income Distribution
    history of, 4, 9-10, 15, 24-25, 33
    international comparison, 42
    measurement, 65-66
Income Growth
    history of, 210-215
    international comparison, 210-214
    measurement, 211
Income Taxation
    allowances, 132, 135-136
    bands, 132
    base, 132
    capital gains tax, 138
    corporate income tax, 138-139
    deductions, 136-137
    levies, 137
    Pay-As-You-Earn, 135
    Pay-Related Social Insurance, 133-134, 137
    rates, 132
    reform, 143, 151-152
    reliefs, 136
    replacement rate, 146-147, 259-260
    schedules, 135
    and unemployment, 146-147, 256-257
    welfare system integration, 145-147
Industrial Development
    and enterprise size, 380-382, 385
    and innovation, 374-377, 380-382
    international comparison, 380-382, 394
    and Ireland, 365-372, 382-392
    and learning processes, 374-377, 386-389
    and the market mechanism, 373, 378
    research and development, 384, 387
    social organisation, 373-377, 380-382

Industrial Development Authority, 220-222, 366-367
Industrial Policy
    direct foreign investment, 220-221, 365-367
    grant aid, 308, 367-368, 371, 383, 389-390
    and growth, 220-222
    history of, 364-372
    indigenous industry, 366-367
    protectionism, 30-32,
    Small Industry Programme, 366
    and taxation, 152, 365, 368
Industry
    competition from Britain, 18-19
    competitiveness, 384-389
    employment, 265-270
    foreign-owned, 365-367, 370-371, 387-389
    and government intervention, 364-393
    growth of, 43, 366, 371
    indigenous, 385-386
    output, 365, 371
Inequality (see Equality; Distribution)
Inflation
    anticipated, 91-92
    causes, 88-89
    consequences, 90-94, 99
    definition, 86-87
    and distribution, 93
    and efficiency, 90
    and the European Monetary System, 285-287
    and exchange rates, 89, 285-287
    and expectations, 91-94
    and growth, 93
    and indexation, 91
    imported, 89
    institutional factors, 92
    measurement, 87
    menu costs, 92
    and money supply, 88
    and policy, 88, 285-287, 289
    shoe-leather costs, 91
    spiral, 90
    transmission mechanism, 89
    unanticipated, 93

and uncertainty, 94
and unionisation, 288-289
Interest Rate Policy, 179-180
International Cooperation
    and distribution, 124
    and the environment, 125
    and fiscal policy, 124
    and foreign trade, 123
    and monetary policy, 124
Investment
    composition, 215-217
    and growth, 215-217

Keynesian Economics
    fiscal policy, 161-166
    and unemployment, 77

Labour Force (see Demography;
    Labour Supply)
Labour Supply
    age structure, 231
    definition, 230
    and emigration, 230-234
    growth, 230-234
    participation, 231-232
    population, 230-234
Labour Market Policy, 261
Land Tenure
    history of, 9, 16, 23-24, 349
Law of Diminishing Marginal Returns,
    201

Maastricht Treaty
    convergence criteria, 171-174
    Economic and Monetary Union,
        283
    and integration, 283
Manufacturing (see Industrial Policy;
    Industry)
Market Failure
    externalities, 105, 109, 300
    and government intervention, 105,
        111-112, 300-301
    imperfect competition, 105, 111,
        301
    information problems, 110, 301
    public goods, 109
Market Mechanism (see also
    Competition Policy; Efficiency;
    Pareto-efficiency)
    choice, 54
    efficiency, 52-53
    political freedom, 54
    preferences, 53-54
    price flexibility, 58-59
    and welfare, 59-61
Mismatch, 248-250
Monetary Approach to the Balance of
    Payments, 178
Monetary Policy (see also Central
    Banking; Interest Rate Policy;
    Exchange Rate Policy)
    credit guidelines, 176-179
    and money supply, 176-179
Monopoly
    barriers to entry, 321-322
    collusion, 316
    and competition policy, 119, 312-
        324
    costs, 310-311
    general equilibrium effects, 311
    in government, 317-319
    natural, 301, 313-315
    price discrimination, 316
    x-inefficiency, 310-312

Navigation Acts, 6-7
Neoclassical Economics, 52
New Classical Economics, 77
New Keynesian Economics, 77
Non-Traded Goods Sector (see
    Services)

Pareto-Efficiency
    definition, 51-52
    and distribution, 61-62
    limitations, 59-61
    and the market mechanism, 51-54
    and potential Pareto-improvements,
        61-63
    and value judgements, 62-63
Pay-Related Social Insurance, 133-
    134, 137
Penal Laws, 9-10
Planning and Social Partnership, 122-
    123, 225, 288-289

Political Business Cycle Theory, 114
Population (see Demography)
Potato, 7, 13-15, 25-26
Price Stability (see Inflation)
Property Taxes,
    capital acquisitions tax, 141
    reform, 152
    residential property tax, 140
Protectionism, 30-32
Public Borrowing (see also Exchequer
    Borrowing Requirement; Public
    Sector Borrowing Requirement;
    General Government Deficit)
    history of, 39-40, 166-172
    monetary financing, 117-118
    rationale, 116-117
Public Debt (see also Public
    Borrowing)
    accumulation, 38-39, 116, 166-168
    and fiscal rectitude, 39-40, 168-174
    international comparison, 173
    and the Maastricht convergence
        criteria, 171-174
    ratio to Gross National Product,
        169-173
    servicing, 110, 112, 168, 170
Public Expenditure (see also
    Government Intervention)
    capital, 107
    current, 107
    and demography, 111-112
    Downs' paradox, 113
    financing, 114-118
    and fiscal illusion, 113
    and government failure, 113-114
    institutional determinants, 112-114
    level of, 106, 113
    and the political system, 113
    and the public debt, 110, 112
    social welfare, 107, 109-110, 112
    technical determinants, 110-112
Public Goods, 109
Public Sector Borrowing Requirement,
    163, 167
Purchasing Power Parity, 180-181

Rawls' Difference Principle, 70
Real Business Cycle Theory, 77

Regulation (see Competition Policy;
    Government Intervention;
    Monopoly)
Rent-Seeking, 206, 224-225
Replacement Rate, 146-147, 259-260
Rural Development
    agritourism, 353-354
    and agriculture, 353-355
    diversification, 353
    and employment, 355
    forestry, 354
    LEADER programmes, 352-355

Second World War, 32-34
Self-Sufficiency (see Protectionism)
Services
    and competition policy, 314-324
    competitiveness, 309
    definition, 296, 299
    employment, 305
    foreign trade, 271
    government policy, 296-298, 307-
        310
    government provision, 300-302,
        319-320
    growth, 305
    international comparison, 305-306
    labour intensity, 307
    non-market, 300, 324
    output, 305-306
    sectoral composition, 305-307
    and the Single European Market,
        280, 303
    and technology, 303
    tradability, 298, 302-304
    and the traded sector, 298
    transport costs, 302-304
Single European Market
    consequences, 279-280
    and factor mobility, 280
    and fiscal harmonisation, 148-149,
        155-156, 279
    and industry, 279
    and services, 280
Solow model, 200-205
State-Owned Enterprises
    and competition policy, 313, 319-
        320

efficiency, 313
history of, 28-29
objectives, 121-122
Structural Funds, 118, 280-282, 347

Tariffs (see Protectionism)
Taxation (see also Consumption
    Taxation; Income Taxation;
    Property Taxes)
    administration, 129-131
    Commission on, 150-153
    efficiency, 115-116, 129-131, 141-
        143
    equity, 114-116, 143-145, 149-150
    and EU-harmonisation, 139-140,
        148-149, 155-156, 279
    incidence, 141-142
    and industrial policy, 152, 365, 368
    international comparison, 132-134,
        148-149, 153
    rationale, 127
    revenue, 115, 132-134
    structure, 131-141
    and unemployment, 146-147, 256-
        257
Tax Reform, 143, 153-155
TEAGASC, 348, 353
Telesis Report, 367-368, 385
Terms of Trade, 270
Textile Industry, 7-8, 13, 18
Theory of Second Best, 58, 312
Trade Unions
    and unemployment, 250-255, 288-
        289
    and wage bargaining, 122-123, 225,
        288-289
Transfer Pricing, 214, 268-269
Treaty on European Union (see
    Maastricht Treaty)

Unemployment (see also Employment)
    causes, 244-261
    discouraged workers, 75, 241
    and distribution, 77-78
    and education, 244
    and efficiency, 76
    efficiency wage theory, 76
    and emigration, 238

employment intensity of growth,
    248
employment-protection legislation,
    255-256
    extent, 237-238
    frictional, 75-76
    and the globalisation of trade, 245-
        246
    international comparison, 237-239
    involuntary, 74
    involuntary part-time workers, 240-
        241
    Keynesian, 77
    labour market policy, 261
    long-term, 242-244, 257-261
    measurement, 238-239
    mismatch, 248-250
    occupational background, 243
    payments, 258-260
    replacement rate, 146-147, 259-260
    and taxation, 146-147, 256-257
    and technological change, 246-248
    and trade unions, 250-255, 288-289
    underemployment, 75, 239-241
Utilitarianism, 69
Utility
    lifetime utility function, 63-68

Value-Added Tax (see Consumption
    Taxation)

Wagner's Law, 111
Welfare
    aggregation, 72-73
    Arrow's Impossibility Theorem, 73
    assumptions, 51
    and choice, 54
    comparison, 64
    and growth, 78-82
    individual, 63-65
    measurement, 66
    social welfare function, 72-73
    theorems, 52
Woollen Acts, 6, 7
World Trade Organisation (see also
    General Agreement on Tariffs and
    Trade), 123, 284
X-Inefficiency, 310-312